Academic Freedom on Trial

Academic Freedom
_on_ *Trial*

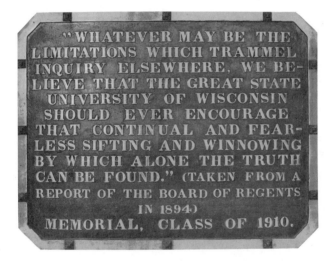

**100 YEARS OF SIFTING AND WINNOWING
AT THE UNIVERSITY OF WISCONSIN–MADISON**

Edited by W. Lee Hansen

Office of University Publications
University of Wisconsin–Madison
1998

The text of this book is composed in Janson 11/14.5.
The display heads are in Galliard bold and bold italic.

The book was designed and produced by the
Office of University Publications at the
University of Wisconsin–Madison.

ISBN 0-9658834-1-8

Library of Congress Cataloging-in-Publication Data

Academic freedom on trial: 100 years of sifting and winnowing at the
    University of Wisconsin–Madison / edited by W. Lee Hansen.
        p.   c.m.
    Papers presented at the Academic Freedom Conference, held Sept.
    16–17, 1994 in Madison.
        Includes bibliographical references and index.
        ISBN 0-9658834-1-8 (pbk.)
        1. Academic freedom—Wisconsin—Madison—History—Congresses.
    2. University of Wisconsin—Madison—History—Congresses. 3. Ely,
    Richard Thomas, 1854–1943—Congresses.   I. Hansen, W. Lee.
    II. Academic Freedom Conference (1994: Madison, Wis.)
    LC72.3W6A33   1998
    378.1'21—dc21   97-39096

Distributed by University of Wisconsin Press
Madison, Wisconsin
www.wisc.edu/wisconsinpress/

Dedication

*To the courageous defenders of academic freedom
and their commitment to the search for truth,
which is the hallmark of sifting and winnowing.*

Table of Contents

Foreword

As we approach the University of Wisconsin's 150th anniversary and, shortly thereafter, the dawn of a challenging new century, we as an institution must take stock of who we are, how we became what we are, and what we want to be. What could be a better way to begin this task than by reflecting on one of the defining events in this institution's history? I refer to the "trial" of economist Richard T. Ely who, in 1894, stood accused of fomenting labor unrest and discussing "dangerous" ideas. The outcome was the Board of Regents' exoneration of Ely, its ringing defense of academic freedom in the now-famous "sifting and winnowing" statement, and the intriguing story of the plaque containing the sifting and winnowing statement, which is mounted at the entrance to Bascom Hall. That plaque serves as a constant reminder of our obligation, as faculty members, administrators, students, alumni, and citizens of this great state, to "ever encourage that continual and fearless sifting and winnowing" in our search for truth, and to encourage that search, however difficult and controversial the task may be.

I invite you to examine the product of our September 1994 100th anniversary celebration of academic freedom on the University of Wisconsin–Madison campus. Quite naturally, this celebration centered around the sifting and winnowing statement. Faculty, students, alumni, university officials, and citizens joined in not only reviewing the origins of that statement but also reexamining its meaning in today's environment.

We hope that reading this volume will convey two important ideas. One is an increased appreciation for the State of Wisconsin's long-standing commitment to the University of Wisconsin and its search for truth. The other is the benefits that accrue to the University of Wisconsin–Madison from taking time to rethink and in some cases reinterpret the meaning of the sifting and winnowing statement. We profited enormously from the occasion. We hope you can, too, through the pages of this book.

David Ward
Chancellor

Acknowledgments

An extraordinarily large number of people—faculty, staff, students, university officials, and others—deserve our generous thanks for their enthusiastic support and participation in the 1994 Academic Freedom Conference and its attendant activities.

The authors of the conference papers and discussions responded eagerly to our invitation to take part, they stimulated their audiences with their thinking and reflections, and they participated actively in the discussion during their sessions and afterward. Their names are listed in the table of contents.

Thanks also go to the conference session leaders who set the tone for the discussion that followed. The session leaders included: Robert H. Haveman (Economics) for the papers included in part 1, James L. Baughman (Journalism) for the papers included in part 2, John Kaminski (History) and Sharon L. Dunwoody (Journalism) for the papers included in parts 3, 4, and 5.

Arthur Hove of the Provost's office deserves special thanks for his crucial help at every step of the way. He played a key role in getting this project launched, obtaining the needed financial support, and keeping the project on track through to the completion of this book.

Chancellor David Ward quickly endorsed the concept of celebrating this important event in the University's history, as did the University Committee; indeed, the chancellor and the University Committee became joint sponsors of the celebration. Much of the planning was accomplished by members of the Academic Freedom Conference Committee, appointed by the chancellor and University Committee. The committee met regularly beginning in the summer of 1993 to define the objectives of the conference, the nature of the celebration that would occur, who would participate, and the other logistics of such events. As an unanticipated byproduct, these meetings produced some lively intellectual exchanges about the meaning of academic freedom and the interpretation of the sifting and winnowing statement. The committee members included:

Alexandra Atkins, *Undergraduate Student*

E. David Cronon, *Professor of History, and then Director of the Humanities Institute*

Judith Croxdale, *Professor of Botany*

Sharon Dunwoody, *Professor of Journalism*

Joel Grossman, *Professor of Political Science and Law, and then chair of the University Committee*
Robert H. Haveman, *Professor Economics, and Chair of the Department of Economics*
Arthur Hove, *Special Assistant, Provost's Office*
John Kaminski, *Professor of History, and Director of the Center for the Study of the American Constitution*
Robert J. Lampman, *Professor Emeritus of Economics*
Ian Rosenberg, *Undergraduate Student*
Michael Stevens, *State Historian, State Historical Society*
Invaluable administrative support was provided by Patricia Elsner from the office of the Secretary of the Faculty; she was assisted by her colleagues Ruthi Duvall, Lisa Norquay, and Helen Tetzlaff. We thank David Musolf, Secretary of the Faculty, for his generous help. Additional assistance came from the staff of the Department of Economics, particularly June Bennett, Maggie Brandenburg, Katrin Johnson, Bonita Rieder, and Suzanne Vinmans. The financial accounts were ably handled by Betty Rhyner of the Provost's Office.

Thanks also go to:

The State Historical Society staff, for arranging access to the State Historical Society Auditorium: Michael Stevens; for mounting the "Untrammeled Inquiry" exhibit on Richard T. Ely, which was displayed in the lobby from August through December 1994: David Kendall, David Mandel, and Carolyn Mattern; and for making it possible to show, from the State Historical Society's Film Archive, the 1964 "Profiles in Courage" TV video on Richard T. Ely: Maxine Ducey.

The Memorial Union, for cosponsoring the Nat Hentoff lecture as a part of its Ideas and Issues Lecture Series: Rauel LaBreche and Ian Rosenberg; the Union Film Committee for arranging the Academic Freedom Film Festival during the fall 1994 semester: Holly Kaster and Ian Rosenberg.

The Department of Music, particularly John Aley and John Stevens, for selecting the music and arranging for the appearance of the Quintessential Brass Group at the Plaque Rededication ceremony; the group's members included Charles Fix, Jon Schipper, Ryan Shirt, Patrick Schulz, and Jessica Valeri.

John Rieben from the Art Department, who designed the eye-catching new Sifting and Winnowing poster that now hangs in many offices around the University.

Earl J. Schoff and his colleagues from the Buildings and Grounds Department who set up the celebration on Lincoln Terrace in front of Bascom Hall and spruced up the appearance of both Bascom Hall and Bascom Hill.

The audio and videotaping of the conference carried out by Barry Teicher from the Oral History Project of the UW–Madison Archives and William P. Tishler from the College of Letters and Science's Learning Support Service.

The UW–Madison Office of News and Public Affairs for publicizing the celebration: Susan Trebach, Liz Beyler, and Jeff Iseminger; the student newspapers for their extensive coverage: the *Daily Cardinal* and the *Badger Herald*; and the state's newspapers for their generous coverage: *Capital Times*, *Wisconsin State Journal*, and *Milwaukee Journal*.

The State Historical Society and Paul Hass, editor of the *Wisconsin Magazine of History*, as well as Theron F. Schlabach, for permission to reprint Theron Schlabach's paper.

The Board of Regents for permission to reprint Theodore Herfurth's booklet on the sifting and winnowing plaque.

The University Archives for permission to use the photos shown in the photo section of this book. The photograph of Prof. Waclaw Syzbalski on page 329 was taken by Brent Nicastro.

The University of Wisconsin–Madison's Office of University Publications for creating the invitations and programs for the conference: Albert Friedman, director, and staff including Kent Hamele, Francine Hartman, Linda Kietzer, Nancy Rinehart, and Marty Wallace.

The Office of University Publications also assisted in the editing, design, and production of this volume: Albert Friedman, director, Kent Hamele, Nancy Rinehart, and, particularly, Francine Hartman. The manuscripts were copyedited by Nancy Brower, the manuscript preparation was done by Beth Johnson, and the final book was indexed by Michael Gossman.

The University of Wisconsin Press for acting as the distributor of the volume: Allen N. Fitchen.

Finally, and most important, we acknowledge the generous financial support provided by the Anonymous Fund of the College of Letters and Science; the Evjue Foundation; and the University of Wisconsin Foundation. Funding for publication of this book was made possible by a grant from the Chancellor's Sesquicentennial Fund.

"WHATEVER MAY BE THE LIMITATIONS WHICH TRAMMEL INQUIRY ELSEWHERE, WE BELIEVE THAT THE GREAT STATE UNIVERSITY OF WISCONSIN SHOULD EVER ENCOURAGE THAT CONTINUAL AND FEARLESS SIFTING AND WINNOWING BY WHICH ALONE THE TRUTH CAN BE FOUND." (TAKEN FROM A REPORT OF THE BOARD OF REGENTS IN 1894)
MEMORIAL, CLASS OF 1910.

Introduction

W. Lee Hansen

In early 1993 I proposed that the University of Wisconsin–Madison celebrate the 100th anniversary of the Board of Regents' "sifting and winnowing" statement and its long-standing commitment to academic freedom. The Department of Economics's 100th anniversary celebration in 1992 had reminded me of Richard T. Ely's importance to the department and his role in the controversy leading to Bascom Hall's sifting and winnowing plaque, which commemorates that controversy. The anniversary conference would serve to reaffirm the overriding importance of academic freedom, highlight the university's role in helping to define the concept of academic freedom, and focus on the Ely trial as a defining event in the university's history.

The Chancellor, David Ward, and the University Committee, represented by Political Science Professor Joel Grossman, reacted enthusiastically to this proposal and offered their wholehearted support. A committee was formed (see the acknowledgments for members' names), and the program took shape (see the appendix for a copy of the program). The result was the September 1994 Academic Freedom Conference, accompanied by a ceremony rededicating the University of Wisconsin's commitment to the principles of academic freedom. These two events took place almost one hundred

W. Lee Hansen is professor of economics, University of Wisconsin–Madison.

years to the day since the Board of Regents issued its historic sifting and winnowing statement.

The quality of the conference's presentations and the attendant events clearly warranted a more lasting testimonial of our indebtedness to Ely, the Board of Regents, and the University of Wisconsin's continuing efforts to live up to the ideal of "constant and fearless sifting and winnowing, by which alone the truth shall be found." The papers and comments are gathered together in this volume, which is published as the University of Wisconsin approaches its 150th anniversary celebration.

In a world of increased academic specialization, weakened institutional citizenship, and busy professional and personal lives, it is important to remember that the benefits of academic freedom enjoyed by faculty members, and too often taken for granted, have not always prevailed in American higher education. These hard-earned benefits—freedom of inquiry, freedom of teaching, and freedom of speech and actions as citizens—are essential to the academic enterprise.

During the latter part of the nineteenth century, when the social sciences emerged as distinctive academic disciplines, a quite different situation prevailed. Increasingly, academics began speaking out on political, social, and economic issues. They quickly learned, however, to be cautious about what they said, how they said it, and where they said it. All too frequently, professors found that their college and university presidents, and very often the business members of their institutions' governing boards as well as public officials, took offense at both their public and classroom utterances. Indeed, what professors said was often found so objectionable that they were summarily dismissed from their teaching positions. In many cases, those who lost their jobs experienced considerable difficulty finding new academic appointments.

College and university professors could do little, individually or collectively, to protect themselves from the whims of their employers, who reflected the prevailing and quite conservative intellectual and social conventions of the day. As a consequence, college professors as a group witnessed a stifling of the freedom they believed necessary to carry out their tasks of acquiring and exchanging new knowledge. The flavor of the era and details of the numerous academic freedom cases are fully described in Richard Hofstadter and Walter P. Metzger's magisterial 1955 volume, *The Development of Academic Freedom in the United States*.

Among the most celebrated academic freedom cases is that of Richard T. Ely, who in 1894 stood accused by an ex-officio member of the Board of Regents of supporting labor union strikes, organizing boycotts of nonunion businesses, and teaching socialism and other "dangerous" theories. A "trial," as it came to be known (actually, it was more akin to a hearing), ensued, conducted by the board. Interestingly, in addition to proclaiming his innocence of the charges, Ely argued that if the charges were true, he should indeed be dismissed (Ely, 1938). After considering the evidence, the Board of Regents exonerated Ely, finding the charges without merit. To the board's great credit, and despite Ely's statement, the board defended Ely's right to say what he did and offered a stirring defense of academic freedom. The board's defense is captured by its easily understandable "sifting and winnowing" language. As a result, the principle of academic freedom became firmly established at the University of Wisconsin as an essential component in the university's shared governance tradition.

Because of the regents' firm stand on academic freedom, Ely remained on the Wisconsin faculty. Soon, however, he began to retreat from many of his more controversial views, in considerable part because his own ideas began to change; it also seems clear that he was heavily influenced by his close brush with possible dismissal. Still, he continued to be a strong champion of academic freedom, helping to bring other outstanding professors to Wisconsin, several of whom had also experienced dismissal at other universities for their controversial views.

Ely had several notable students at Johns Hopkins University. Frederick Jackson Turner became an eminent professor of history at Wisconsin, and Woodrow Wilson went from being the president of Princeton University to the 28th president of the United States. The University of Wisconsin economist John R. Commons was one of Ely's most illustrious students at Johns Hopkins. He suffered much more serious consequences for expressing himself prior to joining the Wisconsin faculty. Commons's views on economics did not go over well at Indiana University, where, in 1895, he was not retained. He then moved to Syracuse University where he was awarded a chair in economics. Again, Commons spoke out on economic issues. Once again, his views were found objectionable, and as a result, the funding for his chair was abruptly withdrawn. Disheartened, Commons left academe for the next five years, continuing his research under private auspices. In 1904, through the efforts of his former professor, Ely, he received and accepted an invitation to join the Wisconsin faculty. All of this is described in Commons's 1934 autobiography, *Myself.*

Another prominent victim of dismissal was sociologist Edward A. Ross, who was brought to Wisconsin in 1905, again with Ely's help. While a professor at Stanford University, Ross, who was another one of Ely's Johns Hopkins students, spoke out on a variety of controversial issues. In so doing, he offended Mrs. Leland Stanford, Sr., whose late husband had been the principal benefactor of Stanford University. As a consequence, Ross was forced to resign.

As a result of these and similar assaults on academic freedom during the 1890s, professors began searching for ways to ensure their freedom to speak out on controversial issues. Initially, the newly emerging professional academic associations, such as the American Economic Association and the American Political Science Association, took the lead in trying to thwart efforts to dismiss their members who had made what others regarded as offensive and dangerous statements. While some progress was made, academic professional associations proved to be ill–equipped to counter the strong pressures exerted by college presidents and their governing boards on the academic freedom of members of their own disciplines.

A much broader systemwide approach became necessary to protect academic freedom. The big breakthrough came in 1915 when faculty members from eight major universities convened to discuss the creation of a national organization of professors that would exist for the explicit purpose of protecting faculty from unwarranted dismissal for their views on controversial topics. Several Wisconsin faculty members participated in this historic organizing meeting.

Out of this meeting and a long record of infringements of academic freedom emerged the American Association of University Professors (AAUP). It took upon itself the task of defining academic freedom, elaborating its purposes, and establishing procedures for determining in cases of dismissal or discipline whether issues of academic freedom were involved. It argued that academic freedom is essential in promoting inquiry and advancing knowledge, providing general instruction to students, and developing experts for the various branches of public service. Without the protections of academic freedom, it feared continued attacks on faculty members, a decline in the reputation and influence of universities and colleges, and difficulty in attracting to the profession people of high ability and strong personality.

This new organization formally launched itself later that year, with Philosopher John Dewey of Columbia University, the nation's most preeminent thinker and public philosopher, serving as its first president. In the very next year AAUP established its committee structure, utilizing letters to designate each committee. It began with Committee A on Academic Freedom and continued alphabetically through Committee P on Pensions and Insurance for University Teachers; later, it added other committees, culminating with Committee Z on the Economic Status of the Profession.

Wisconsin faculty members lent strong support to this exciting new organization. Many joined the AAUP immediately, and a number of them quickly assumed prominent positions in the organization. By 1916 more than a dozen of Wisconsin's most illustrious professors served in various capacities at the national level. Ely headed up Committee A on Academic Freedom, Commons served on the Executive Committee and as vice president in 1917, and Ross served on the AAUP's governing Academic Council.

In subsequent decades, Wisconsin faculty members continued to play an important role in the AAUP. Mark Ingraham, mathematics professor, and later Dean of the College of Letters and Sciences, served as AAUP's national president from 1938 to 1940. Under his guidance, AAUP developed its famous and still basic 1940 Statement of Principles on Academic Freedom and Tenure. The statement begins:

> The purpose of this statement is to promote public understanding and support of academic freedom and tenure and agreement upon the procedures to assure them in colleges and universities. Institutions of higher education are conducted for the common good and not to further the interest of either the individual teacher or the institutions as a whole. The common good depends upon the free search for truth and its free expression.

It goes on to elaborate:

> Teachers are entitled to full freedom in research and in the publication of the results, subject to the adequate performance of their other academic duties.

> (From *AAUP Policy Documents and Reports.*)

Faculty and institutions throughout the nation view this statement as underpinning the concept of academic freedom and tenure. Most colleges and universities abide by it. In addition, almost 150 professional academic associations endorse this statement. Ingraham maintained a lifelong interest in the AAUP and later became concerned about faculty retirement issues, publishing several books on the subject of the adequacy of faculty retirement benefits.

English Professor Helen C. White continued this tradition, serving as AAUP's national president from 1956 to 1958. During her tenure the AAUP established the concept of "academic due process" in its Statement on Procedural Standards in Faculty Dismissal Procedures. The flavor of that statement is captured by its introductory paragraph:

> Any approach toward settling the difficulties which have beset dismissal proceedings on many American campuses must look beyond procedure into setting and cause. A dismissal proceeding is a symptom of failure; no amount of use of removal process will help strengthen higher education as much as will the cultivation of conditions in which dismissal rarely if ever is needed.

It goes on to say:

> This statement deals with procedural standards. Those recommended are not intended to establish a norm . . . but are presented rather as a guide to be used according to the nature and traditions of particular institutions in giving effect to both faculty tenure rights and the obligations of faculty members of the academic community.
>
> (From *AAUP Policy Documents and Reports*.)

As both a prominent UW–Madison faculty member and AAUP President, White spoke at the ceremony celebrating the reinstallation of the sifting and winnowing plaque after a suspected student prank led to its removal from the front of Bascom Hall in late 1957; the plaque was found several months later in a remote campus area. At that time the Regents reaffirmed their faith in freedom of inquiry: "The search for truth is the central duty of the University but truth will not be found if the scholar is not free, it will not be understood if the student is not free, it will not be used if the citizen is not free. At a time when both truth and freedom are under attack The University of Wisconsin must seek the one and defend the other. It must employ with utmost energy the power of truth and freedom for the benefit of mankind. The University will ever be dedicated to the truth and to the freedom that gives it life."

Political Science Professor David Fellman continued Wisconsin's involvement in the AAUP, serving as its president from 1964 to 1966, chairing Committee A on Academic Freedom and Tenure for many years, and serving in a variety of other capacities. As a prominent member of the faculty, he took the lead in the early 1960s in codifying the various laws and regulations of the University of Wisconsin. Fellman, with assistance from Ingraham and Robert Taylor (journalism professor and then vice president of UW–Madison) drafted the Board of Regents important 1964 statement on academic freedom, cited below.

Still another faculty member, Peter O. Steiner (economics), who left Wisconsin in 1968 and later became Dean of the University of Michigan's College of Arts and Sciences, served as AAUP's national president from 1976 to 1978. He, too, served on Committee A on Academic Freedom and also headed up Committee Z on the Economic Status of the Profession. Many other faculty members over the years participated actively in AAUP affairs at the national, state, and campus levels.

The UW–Madison Chapter of the AAUP is now dormant, and faculty interest in AAUP has diminished. Interestingly, membership in this important national organization serves less to ensure the academic freedom rights of Wisconsin faculty members than to protect faculty members at other institutions where academic freedom safeguards remain weak or in some cases are nonexistent. Maintaining strong campus support for academic freedom is essential in ensuring that the "continual and fearless sifting and winnowing by which along the truth can be found" continues to flourish here and throughout academe.

The University of Wisconsin's long-standing commitment to academic freedom is now embodied in state statutes, faculty legislation, and the spirit of free inquiry that has long characterized this institution. The most explicit statement describing the purposes of academic freedom appears in the University of Wisconsin–Madison's regularly updated *Faculty Policies and Procedures*. Central to this discussion of academic freedom and tenure is the Board of Regents resolution, mentioned above, approved in early 1964 when the Laws and Regulations of the University were recodified:

> In adopting this codification of the rules and regulations of the University of Wisconsin relating to tenure, the Regents reaffirm their historic commitment to security of professorial tenure and to the academic freedom it is designed to protect. These rules and regulations are promulgated in the conviction that in serving a free society the scholar must himself be free. Only thus can he

seek the truth, develop wisdom and contribute to society those expressions of the intellect that ennoble mankind. The security of the scholar protects him not only against those who would enslave the mind but also against anxieties which divert him from his role as scholar and teacher. The concept of intellectual freedom is based upon confidence in man's capacity for growth in comprehending the universe and on faith in unshackled intelligence. The University is not partisan to any party or ideology, but it is devoted to the discovery of truth and to understanding the world in which we live. The Regents take this opportunity to rededicate themselves to maintaining in this University those conditions which are indispensable to the flowering of the human mind. (Chapter 8: Faculty Rights and Responsibilities, Section 8.01 A)

In essence, academic freedom is designed to promote intellectual inquiry by scholars and teachers without being fearful for the consequences of their activities. This kind of intellectual freedom is essential to the acquisition and exchange of knowledge. To ensure their freedom to pursue these activities, faculty members are afforded protection against arbitrary dismissal by those who might find their views offensive or threatening. In addition, faculty members are afforded the freedoms accorded to all citizens to speak out on political subjects and other issues of concern to them (Van Alstyne, 1993).

Academic freedom is not a one-way street. Both state statutes (Wisconsin Administrative Code, October 1994) and University of Wisconsin–Madison documents (Faculty Policies and Procedures, December 1995) spell out the rights and responsibilities of faculty members. The latter document offers more detail than the former, and the statement authored by David Fellman in the mid-1960s, its language now more compressed, states the continuing case for academic freedom.

Academic freedom would be meaningless without tenure. Academic freedom and tenure are closely intertwined and mutually reinforcing. The concept of tenure has its limitations, sometimes being viewed as protecting incompetent professors and at other times inhibiting the infusion of new blood into colleges and universities. Tenure's more important and overriding virtue is the protection it provides tenured professors to explore new ideas, augment existing knowledge, and communicate this knowledge to students and society without fear of retribution.

Tenure protects professors from capricious termination or dismissal due to expressions that may offend. It insulates faculty members from being victimized, as was the case with Ely, Commons, Ross, and many other college professors across the nation. Faculty members holding tenure appointment cannot be terminated except under particular circumstances. Termination can occur only for cause, for reasons of financial emergency, or through resignation or retirement.

Procedural rules have been established to determine what constitutes "adequate cause" for discipline or "just cause" for dismissal. For the former, the language in University of Wisconsin–Madison, *Faculty Policies and Procedures* (1995) reads (section 9.02): "No faculty member shall be subject to discipline except for adequate cause, based upon a determination that the faculty member has violated a University rule or policy or has engaged in conduct which adversely affects the faculty member's performance of his/her obligation to the University but which is not serious enough to warrant dismissal." For the latter, the language reads (section 9.03): "No faculty member shall be subject to dismissal except for just cause based on a determination that the faculty member's conduct directly and substantially affects adversely the ability to carry out satisfactorily his/her responsibilities to the University." A detailed set of procedures is in place to ensure that academic due process is followed, with a faculty committee empowered to conduct whatever fact-finding hearings are appropriate (section 9.04 and following sections). Essentially similar information is contained in the Wisconsin Administrative Code (1994).

Nothing prohibits the layoff and termination of tenured faculty members because of a financial emergency confronting the university, as might occur as a result of a sudden and substantial decline in revenues. Again, *Faculty Policies and Procedures* details the procedures to be followed, both to ensure that a legitimate financial emergency exists and that such an emergency is not used to terminate particular individuals who may be viewed with disfavor (Chapter 10).

By now, academic freedom and academic tenure are firmly established throughout higher education. Attacks on the concept of academic tenure have mounted in recent years for various reasons. Many people do not understand its close link to academic freedom. Others believe tenure provides unwarranted job security to ineffective faculty members. Still others object because tenure makes it more difficult for governing boards and university presidents to move quickly in reshaping their institutions to meet what some people view as the demands of a new era.

Concerns such as these about academic tenure are being met in innovative ways by the University of Wisconsin System and elsewhere in higher education. New programs are being put into place designed to enhance the performance of faculty members and at the same time reduce tenure–generated concerns about incompetence and intellectual stagnation. Of particular note are the recently established programs at the University of Wisconsin–Madison for periodically reviewing the performance of tenured professors, mentoring new faculty, increasing the emphasis on improving undergraduate instruction, and measuring what competencies students acquire in their experience here. These programs will surely help invigorate both teaching and learning and in the process strengthen the meaning of tenure. Combined with the continued freedom to explore new and often controversial ideas, we can look forward to a new era of advancing knowledge and stimulating learning.

The success of these efforts depends critically on fending off often unwarranted attacks on academic freedom and tenure. While the freedom of private sector organizations to fire and downsize their work forces may be essential to meet the competitive demands of increasingly global markets, the production and dissemination of knowledge can flourish only by taking a longer-run perspective. Professors and students alike must have the freedom to develop and explore new ideas and their implications. The production of new ideas occurs not by magic but only as a result of sustained effort. Because the benefits of new ideas can have such long-term effects, we must make sure that the popular zeal for short-term cost savings and efficiency gains does not undermine the hard-earned and increasingly valuable benefits provided by academic freedom and its corollary, tenure.

Issues of academic freedom will continue to crop up from time to time at a vibrant institution such as this one. Historically, threats to academic freedom have been for the most part external in origin, as noted in the discussion of the origins of the AAUP. But in recent years perplexing questions have been voiced about whether "hate speech codes" adopted by universities themselves threaten the intellectual freedom essential to a university's mission. These codes, written and approved by faculty bodies, and subsequently approved by governing boards, such as our Board of Regents, are designed to shield students in protected groups (defined in terms of race, ethnicity, and gender) from objectionable or harassing language that might impede their ability to learn and benefit from their educational opportunities. The existence of these codes raises, for both faculty and students, important questions of academic freedom and free speech that are still being debated and litigated. Indeed, one session of the conference directly addressed the issue of speech codes, focusing in considerable part on UW–Madison's speech code, which was subsequently declared unconstitutional. The UW–Madison faculty speech code still remains in force and has not yet been contested in the courts. Efforts are now underway to reconsider the merits of the faculty speech code.

Another threat to academic freedom emerged at the University of Wisconsin–Madison as this volume was being readied for publication. The University of Wisconsin–Madison was in the midst of negotiating a contract with Reebok, the well-known athletic equipment and apparel manufacturer, which would provide free athletic equipment to the Department of Athletics. A group of faculty members objected to one clause of the contract between the university and Reebok, called the "No Disparagement by University Clause" (6.2). That clause reads:

> During and for a reasonable time after the Term, [the] University will not issue any official statement that disparages Reebok, [the] University's association with Reebok, Reebok's products, or the advertising agency or others connected with Reebok. Additionally, [the] University will promptly take all reasonable steps necessary to address any remark by any University employee, agent or representative, including a Coach, that disparages Reebok, [the] University's association with Reebok, Reebok's products, or the advertising agency or others connected with Reebok. Nothing herein is intended to abridge anyone's First Amendment rights.

The final sentence was added only after early criticism of the clause. Criticism continued to simmer. After final campus and Regent approval, a number of faculty and staff members mounted still stronger objections. They claimed that this "no disparagement" clause compromised the constitutional free speech rights and academic freedom of faculty and staff, including coaches and other athletic department employees. As a result of these objections, the entire clause was subsequently deleted from the final version of the signed contract. While the full story of this episode will have to be told in another place, it illustrates the disparate nature of the threats to academic freedom and the vigilance required to protect academic freedom. More particularly, it reveals a continuing tension in the academic-business relationship, a topic touched on briefly in the A. W. Coats's paper in this volume.

He refers to the threat to professional ethics posed by outside business interests. In this case, the potential threat to professional ethics came from the
forging of a business relationship that, while financially advantageous to the
university, was believed by many to pose a threat to academic freedom.

Clearly, the hard-won principle of academic freedom cannot be taken
for granted. It must be guarded continuously and zealously if we—university
faculty, administrators, staff, and students, as well as the State of Wisconsin
and its citizens—are to benefit from our shared commitment to the "constant and fearless sifting and winnowing by which alone the truth shall be
found."

• • • • • •

What follows is a brief review of the contents of this volume.

Part 1, "Ely, the Ely Trial, and Academic Freedom," lays the groundwork for the volume by highlighting the emergence of academic freedom at
the University of Wisconsin. It begins with John G. Buenker's description of
the intellectual climate surrounding the Ely trial and the Progressive Era
that was taking shape in Wisconsin at that time. This is followed by Theron
F. Schlabach's detailed description of Ely, the unfolding of the accusations
against Ely, his trial and exoneration by the Board of Regents, and the
board's issuance of the sifting and winnowing statement. (Interestingly, the
conference began with a replaying of the 1964 *Profiles in Courage* television
series on Ely and academic freedom, which in typical television style presented Ely as a far more laudatory figure than the record would indicate.)
Another view of the trial is offered by Theodore Herfurth, who also discusses the subsequent controversy over the mounting of the sifting and winnowing plaque at the front entrance to Bascom Hall. To summarize that
interesting episode, the Class of 1910 decided to present, as its traditional
graduation gift to the university, a bronze plaque containing the sifting and
winnowing statement. The Board of Regents declined the gift, and the
plaque found its way to the basement of Bascom Hall where it gathered
dust. Only after intense pressure by students and considerable controversy
was the plaque formally accepted by the board and finally affixed to the
front of Bascom Hall in June 1915. Art Hove offers a lively description of
the plaque's theft in late 1957 and the early 1958 rededication ceremony
when the plaque, after being found, was restored (this time bolted down

firmly) to its rightful place at the front entrance to Bascom Hall.

Benjamin G. Rader broadens the focus by placing Ely, ever the reformer, in the context of late nineteenth-century and early twentieth-century intellectual history. Ely continued to believe in nurturing the responsibilities of civic humanism at a time when advancing knowledge through research was becoming the mark of professionalism, and it was this that led to his troubles. Another facet of Ely's professional life is taken up by coauthors Robert J. Lampman and David B. Johnson who explore the strange professional relationship that prevailed between Ely and his former student and by now famous colleague, John R. Commons. This section concludes with the paper by A. W. Coats, which describes the active role of economists and the economics profession in dealing with academic freedom issues involving their colleagues and traces the gradual erosion of that interest and support as the protections of academic freedom became institutionalized under AAUP.

Part 2 focuses on an important contemporary issue in academic freedom, namely an attempt at "Clarifying the Issues: Free Speech, Hate Speech Codes, and Academic Freedom." Three papers, the first by a political scientist and the other two by UW–Madison Law School faculty members, consider the appropriateness of the limitations on speech imposed by hate speech codes. These codes are designed to restrict certain kinds of speech, and exist at many colleges and universities, including the University of Wisconsin–Madison. Donald A. Downs, Jr., questions the constitutionality and effectiveness of these codes in promoting what he calls the *vita activa* role of the university. Linda S. Greene focuses on whether the benefits of eliminating the adverse effects of hate speech may warrant some curtailment of our free speech liberties. Ted Finman discusses the evolution and effects of the University of Wisconsin's speech code and his changing views on the issue. The reactors, none of them lawyers, offer a wide range of perspectives. Undergraduate student Rebecca Schaefer takes strong exception to speech codes, arguing that freedom to discuss and confront all issues is essential to promoting tolerant and critical thinking among students. English Professor Cyrena Pondrom "deconstructs" speech codes by examining the assumptions underlying the positions people take on these codes. Alumnus and former state legislator Mordecai Lee explores the links between hate speech codes, free speech, and academic freedom, largely from a legislator's point of view. Editorial page editor Thomas A. Still questions the appropriateness of speech codes on First Amendment grounds. The final paper is by the well-known author and commentator, Nat Hentoff, who voices his strong disapproval of any curtailment of free speech and preaches the importance of due process for both faculty and students.

The papers in Part 3 attempt to reinterpret the meaning of sifting and winnowing. The first, by Oncology Professor Waclaw Szyablski, praises the extent of academic freedom at the University of Wisconsin–Madison, describing its importance to him as a scholar and as an immigrant who grew up in pre–World War II Poland. Undergraduate student Raymond J. Kotwicki views academic freedom from a student perspective, urging that greater effort be made by the university to engage students in intellectual debate. The final paper by History Professor E. David Cronon draws on his recently published third volume of the history of the University of Wisconsin (Cronon and Jenkins, 1994) to indicate this institution's less than perfect record in protecting academic freedom, notwithstanding the noble sentiments expressed in the sifting and winnowing statement.

Part 4 describes how academic freedom is being challenged in new and often difficult ways as universities operate within an ever more complex, interdependent world. Political Science Professor Joel B. Grossman offers a forward-looking discussion of the threats and limits to academic freedom coming both from outside and inside the academy. Administrator Joseph J. Corry examines the implications for academic freedom of society's call for greater accountability by colleges and universities, and for demonstrations of what students are learning through outcome assessment. Zoology Professor Robert Auerbach turns to a quite different issue, namely, the limitations imposed on the freedom of investigators to pursue their research interests because of difficulties in securing the funds they need to push forward their research programs. Associate Graduate School Dean Janet L. Greger explores the difficult issues in academic freedom resulting from academic-business partnerships where proprietary and academic interests often conflict when it comes to reporting and disseminating the results of jointly financed research projects.

The two papers in Part 5 offer a reappraisal of the meaning of the sifting and winnowing concept. Letters and Science Dean Phillip R. Certain comments as an "insider" in sketching a picture of the changing character of American higher education, the new demands that will be made on it, and the implications for continuing the sifting and winnowing tradition at the University of Wisconsin. Former State of Wisconsin public official and alumna Mary Lou Munts reflects on the many papers, touching in particular at the long and close link between the sifting and winnowing tradition and the "Wisconsin Idea," which called for bringing newly created knowledge to the people of the state and nation, under the motto: "The boundaries of the campus are the boundaries of the state."

This celebration of academic freedom called for more than academic papers can provide, namely, reflection and ceremony. Accordingly, conference participants, state officials, university administrators, faculty and staff, and students gathered in front of historic Bascom Hall on a beautiful fall afternoon to rededicate a continuing commitment by the University of Wisconsin and the State of Wisconsin to the sifting and winnowing process and to the maintenance of academic freedom. Part 6 presents the comments made by University of Wisconsin–Madison Chancellor David Ward, Wisconsin's Secretary of Administration James Klauser (representing Governor Tommy Thompson), Regent President Michael W. Grebe, University of Wisconsin System President Katharine Lyall, and University Committee Chair William S. Reznikoff.

Their comments are followed by Regent Phyllis M. Krutsch's statement at the October 1994 meeting of the Board of Regents and the Resolution she introduced reaffirming the regents' commitment to academic freedom.

The final section of the book offers a collection of photographs, picturing many key figures mentioned in the book as well as several photos pertaining to the sifting and winnowing plaque.

References

American Association of University Professors. *Bulletin of the AAUP*, annual volumes beginning in 1915 (renamed *ACADEME: Bulletin of the AAUP*, in the 1970s).

American Association of University Professors. *AAUP Policy Documents and Reports*. Washington, D.C.: AAUP, 1995 edition.

Commons, John R. *Myself*. New York: Macmillan, 1934.

Cronon, E. David and John W. Jenkins. *The University of Wisconsin: A History, 1925–1945— Politics, Depression, and War*, Volume 3. Madison: University of Wisconsin Press, 1994.

Ely, Richard T. *Ground Under Our Feet: An Autobiography*. New York: Macmillan, 1938.

Hofstadter, Richard and Walter P. Metzger. *The Development of Academic Freedom in the United States*. New York: Columbia University Press, 1955.

University of Wisconsin–Madison. *Faculty Policies and Procedures*, 1996 edition. Office of Secretary of the Faculty.

Van Alstyne, William W., editor. *Freedom and Tenure in the Academy*. Durham, N.C.: Duke University Press, 1993.

Wisconsin Administrative Code. *Rules of Board of Regents of the University of Wisconsin System.* October 1994.

Ely, the Ely Trial, and Academic Freedom

Sifting and Winnowing: The Historical Context

JOHN D. BUENKER

The two decades that framed the 1894 academic freedom hearing of Richard T. Ely and the installation of the "sifting and winnowing" plaque at the main entrance to Bascom Hall were the most momentous in the history of both the university and the state. Transformed by a dynamic series of interacting socioeconomic and demographic processes, Wisconsin emerged as a modern, urban, industrial, multiethnic society. Responding to myriad demands from a variety of constituencies, and advised by social scientists and public servants, politicians crafted a social-service state, administered by apolitical, expert commissions. Their achievement helped earn Wisconsin a national reputation as a "laboratory of democracy," a model whose various programs and institutions were frequently emulated. The Madison campus experienced unprecedented growth, evolving from a liberal arts college to a university, with a full complement of graduate and professional programs and a mounting emphasis on research and publication. Its daring experiments in extension work, "practical" research, and government service earned it such sobriquets as "the campus whose boundaries were those of the state" and as "the university that runs a state." Unique cooperation among private sector institutions, state government, and university faculty was the foundation for what became known as the "Wisconsin Idea." Within this highly charged environment, academic freedom became a political football, one that won an apparent hard-fought victory by 1915.

Wisconsin's metamorphosis began in the 1880s, with a three-pronged socioeconomic transformation. The first prong consisted of "the industrial revolution in dairying," the transfer of dairy processing from "the domesticity of the farm to the impersonal environment of the factory." Together, the Dairymen's Association, the burgeoning College of Agriculture, and various agencies of state government pushed farmers to embrace the stringent discipline and intellectual rigor of dairy husbandry, inventing the "Wisconsin Idea in Dairying" and facilitating the state's coronation as "America's Dairyland."[1]

John D. Buenker is professor of history, University of Wisconsin–Parkside, and is writing a history of the Progressive Movement in Wisconsin for the State Historical Society's Wisconsin History Series.

The second prong was the sustained effort by industrialists in the northern two-thirds of the state to develop a "post-lumbering economy." Lumbermen, railroad executives, local businessmen, and the College of Agriculture ambitiously promoted agricultural settlement, while an increasing number of professionals, intellectuals, and public servants championed reforestation and resource conservation. The majority of northern businessmen and politicians labored to establish a manufacturing base that utilized cheaper grains of wood, especially in paper and pulp production. Facilitated by the fortuitous development of electrochemical processes that made papermaking from wood pulp far cheaper than its manufacture from rags or straw, the industry proliferated throughout the Fox River Valley in the 1880s, spreading to the Wisconsin and Chippewa regions by the turn of the century.[2]

The third prong was the remarkable change in the nature and scope of manufacturing in the already highly industrialized southeast between 1889 and 1915. Wisconsin experienced the "neotechnic revolution," fostered by the transmission of electricity, the internal combustion engine, and the mass production of high grade steel by the open hearth process. In less than two decades, this metamorphosis firmly established the technological base on which rested mass production, horizontally and vertically integrated corporations, nationwide distribution systems, advertising, scientific management, and all the other hallmarks of modern industrial capitalism. By 1915, Wisconsin ranked ninth among the various states in value added by manufacturing, and tenth in product value, causing the authors of the *Blue Book* to boast that it "leads all of the states west of Ohio in value of manufactures in proportion to population."[3]

As the New Industrialism transformed the state's economy, it fostered a New Urbanism that involved the relocation of a substantial portion of the population from town and village to city, the explosive spatial and demographic growth of its leading municipalities, and the evolution of the industrial or radial city. Between 1880 and 1914, Wisconsin's urban population increased nearly twice as rapidly as that of the state as a whole and a little more than four times as fast as that of rural territory. By 1920, one Wisconsinite in four lived in Milwaukee, Racine, or Kenosha, which were integral parts of the burgeoning Great Lakes steel and machinery belt. Scarcely less remarkable was the spatial expansion of Wisconsin's major cities, made possible by the electric trolley and improvements in construction technology. Wisconsin cities were reconfigured by interactive centripetal and centrifugal forces that produced both suburban sprawl and central core congestion, sorted out land use, segregated people by a complex formula of socioeconomic, ethnocultural, and personal factors, and accelerated the inherent mobility and instability of urban life. Escalating demands for myriad municipal services led to bitter struggles over how, by whom, where, and in what order these services would be delivered, as well as how they would be financed. The 1890s were characterized by scores of municipal reform movements, differing widely in composition, motivation, program, and effectiveness.[4]

Significantly complicating both the New Industrialism and the New Urbanism was the substantial influx of immigrants from southern and eastern Europe. In 1890, Wisconsin boasted an immigrant population that was half German, one-fifth British or Canadian, and one-fifth Swedish, Norwegian, or Danish. During the next three decades, the proportion of foreign-born Wisconsinites from those countries declined by 38 percent, while the percentage of those from southeastern Europe jumped from 4 to 33 percent. Most newcomers settled in the urban, industrial southeast corner; the vast majority settled in cities, even in the New North counties that were their secondary target of settlement. Overwhelmingly peasant in origin, and generally bereft of capital, education, or job skills, most new arrivals became unskilled or semiskilled laborers, settling near factory districts. This group was disproportionately represented among those who suffered industrial accidents, experienced unemployment, low wages, and long hours, occupied substandard housing, contracted debilitating diseases, and felt the results from any number of other "social problems." Mostly Catholics, Orthodox Christians, or Jews, they constituted a critical mass for tipping the balance toward "personal liberty" on such issues as prohibition, while their increasing presence and social debasement provided powerful ammunition for those who advocated nativism, anti-Catholicism, or anti-Semitism as constructive responses to bewildering change.[5]

Dislocated and disoriented by rapid, massive change, large numbers of Wisconsinites scrambled to "organize or perish," assiduously practicing the "New Interventionism," in both the private, voluntary sector and the public, political arena. Each organization framed its legislative demands as specific proposals, designed to remedy concrete problems or inequities. The cycle of coalition building, compromise, and consensus that characterized the legislative process all but guaranteed a hodgepodge of piecemeal reforms that resembled a series of tire patches or Band-Aids. While reformers never completely succeeded in making order out of chaos, they did produce the most coherent and comprehensive policy ever achieved in a single state, an accomplishment that was largely the result of the interactive efforts of four groups of "systematizers," each of whom contributed to the "Wisconsin Idea."[6]

The first was a remarkable collection of University of Wisconsin professors and administrators, including President Charles R. Van Hise, Richard T. Ely, John R. Commons, Edward A. Ross, and Frederick Jackson Turner. Trained primarily in the biological and social sciences, and educated largely in the Germanic tradition, they concurred with Ely that modern people "form more truly than ever before a social and industrial organism, whose numberless parts are in an infinite variety of manner interdependent. Infinite interrelations! Infinite interdependencies!"[7]

The second organizing force was a group of dedicated and innovative civil servants, headed by Legislative Reference Library Director Charles McCarthy. A Ph.D. historian who was also an adjunct lecturer in political science, McCarthy's concept of "social dynamics" involved "the development of the efficiency of the individual and the safeguarding of his opportunity, the jealous guarding of the governmental machinery from the invasion of the corrupting force and might of concentrated wealth, the shackling of monopoly, and the regulating of contract conditions by special administrative agencies of the people." The Bureau of Labor and Industrial Statistics also evolved into an effective advocate for a wide range of labor and welfare measures, including child labor, housing regulation, and health and safety legislation.[8]

The third group of systematizers consisted of Robert La Follette, Francis McGovern, and their cohorts of progressive Republican politicians. Collectively, they evolved the concept of an activist state government, providing a wide variety of social services, at the direction of a strong governor, leading a greatly expanded executive branch, consisting primarily of quasi-independent, expert commissions. La Follette and McGovern aimed to transfer the fulcrum of state government from a legislature distributing limited benefits on the basis of clout, and a judiciary that stymied government activism, to an executive branch performing the interactive tasks of administration, regulation and planning. They formulated a comprehensive policy agenda and state budget, intervened in legislative elections, established a civil service bureaucracy, and developed strict cost accounting procedures. La Follette and McGovern vested as much authority as possible in expert commissions, whose members were selected by the governor, and which operated under general policy guidelines mandated by the General Assembly. They also attempted to restructure and reorient the electoral process, to make loyalty to the chief executive's programs and leadership the principal criteria for reelection. By backing the open primary, the Australian ballot, nonpartisan local elections, and civil service, they could throw support to, and receive votes from, "fair-minded" democrats and socialists.

Finally, systematization received a significant boost from "radical" social democrats and Society of Equity leaders, who shared a vision of an ultimate "cooperative commonwealth." Their votes were crucial to the adoption of socioeconomic legislation; some of their innovations served as models for progressive republican legislation. Their legislative and electoral successes pushed progressive republicans farther and faster to the left, while the latter freely admitted that "the way to beat the Socialists is to beat them to it."[9]

It was the dynamic interaction among systematizing intellectuals, civil servants, politicians, and "radicals," and the various organized interest groups proffering agendas of piecemeal reform, that ultimately produced the Wisconsin Idea and the service state. The Idea's most ambitious formulation, that of McCarthy in 1912, suffered greatly from lack of organization, analysis, and integration. A careful, considered reading reveals much that seems paradoxical or contradictory, and that fails to address the mixture of change and continuity between La Follette and McGovern. Even so, it is possible to discern several important themes and variations.

Most fundamental was a "commonwealth" conception of society, in which there was a definable "public interest" that transcended particularistic concerns, and that would be achieved by enlightened cooperation between the public sector and elements of the private sector. To accomplish that goal, the state must foster the "new individualism," generate and invest the required social capital, build the necessary infrastructure, establish and monitor the operational guidelines, guarantee equitable distribution of the benefits, provide for the welfare of the "worthy poor," and protect the public interest. The university should supply the necessary theoretical knowledge and technological expertise. Together, the government and the university should provide the social investment for a variety of endeavors, whose immediate and obvious beneficiaries were private citizens and organizations, but which ultimately would enhance the general prosperity, security and quality of life. Cooperatively, government, higher education, and private groups should generate an environment conducive to the realization of individual potential, and to the pursuit of all goals deemed legitimate.[10]

Equally crucial was the conviction that the state should function through the systematic application of professional expertise, under policy guidelines established by the elected representatives of an educated, enlightened citizenry. The only effective way to protect "the public interest" and "the new individualism" in a modern, urban, industrial setting was to replace "miscellaneous law" with "scientifically derived rules and regulations," made by trained workers using "tests, measurements and close observation." To achieve this goal, the entire public educational system had to be made "democratic" and "practical," i.e., combining the theoretical and the academic with the vocational/technical, in a synthesis that would equip graduates for work, life, and citizenship.[11]

Even more ambitious was the transfer of authority from the legislative and judicial branches to a greatly articulated executive. Harshly critical of "judge-made" law, and of the judicial overthrow of labor and welfare legislation, progressives favored the election and recall of judges, the supremacy of statutes over precedents, the teaching of "sociological jurisprudence" in law schools, and the use of experts in drafting legislation that would be immune from judicial negation. To reform the legislature, McCarthy insisted upon lobbyist regulation, legislative reference and bill drafting, and the standardization of procedures. He proposed that the legislature limit itself to the enactment of broad policy guidelines, leaving the details to commissions charged with the law's enforcement. Such commissions were to be nonpartisan, appointed for long, staggered terms, have expert staff, and earn relatively large salaries. On the one hand, systematizers put their faith in constant publicity, cost accounting, civil service, and the professional integrity of apolitical experts. On the other, they insisted that sufficient popular control was guaranteed by the fact that "executive officers and those who legislate and form policies" had to submit themselves to frequent elections.[12]

To ensure popular control over appointive commissions, progressives endeavored to design an electoral system that would give the individual voter maximum leverage over nominations, elections, and legislation (insulated from the machinations of corporate lobbyists and professional politicians) and that required candidates to deal with "the real issues." Such a system was to be made operational by the open primary, the Australian ballot, corrupt-practices legislation, lobbyist regulation, and the initiative, referendum and recall. Beyond that, democratic control over government agency rested only with what McCarthy called a "half-dozen, concrete, vital elements—the accountant, the statistician, the actuary, the chemist, red blood and a big stick."[13]

Typically regarding themselves as indispensable champions of reform, and as "tribunes of the people," progressive republican governors built personalized organizations. La Follette resolutely constructed his own personal party machine, ruthlessly purging those who refused to swear fealty to his leadership and legislative agenda. In the 1904 elections, La Follette and his followers ostracized the Stalwarts, and left them for dead. Courting a substantially different constituency, and espousing a more working-class reform agenda, McGovern crafted his own personal/ideological organization, and leavened the greatly expanded executive branch with his appointees, alienating both La Follette supporters and Stalwarts. Although seeking nonrepublican votes, both at the polling booth and on the legislative floor, La Follette and McGovern remained staunchly partisan in their endorsements and appointments. Internecine warfare between La Follette and McGovern distorted the 1912 election, decimated McGovern's 1913 legislative program, and facilitated the victory of Stalwart Emanuel Philipp as governor in 1914.

Attempting to institutionalize their reformist electoral coalition, progressive republicans and social democrats sought to transform the existing system of ethnocultural, partisan politics into a new issue-oriented, candidate-centered brand. Progressive republicans consistently appealed to independents, democrats, and socialists on the grounds of ideology and personality, counting on them to provide the political support increasingly withheld by disaffected conservatives and moderates. Progressive appeals to cross party lines and vote split tickets, along with their advocacy of nonpartisan local elections and open primaries, significantly undermined ethnocultural, partisan politics, inaugurating a tradition of independent voting that escalated over the years.[14]

Although the pressure for reform was virtually continuous between 1895 and 1915, there were two undisputed high water marks. During the first period, from 1903 through 1905, La Follette engineered the enactment of his legislative program. The adoption of the direct primary, civil service, a lobbyist registration law, and an electoral corrupt-practices act significantly revamped the political system. The taxation of railroads on the actual value of their property, the proposal of an income tax amendment to the state constitution, and the establishment of a permanent state tax commission all responded to the growing demand for tax equity. The creation of a railroad commission to oversee rates and service marked the beginning of a growing trend toward the regulation of business. In the first election in which reformist rhetoric and the candidates' "character" were the focus of the campaign, progressives won a smashing victory in 1904, ensuring their supremacy for the next decade.[15]

The second high water mark was reached by the first McGovern administration in 1911. Together, progressive politicians and intellectuals conceived a "leftward strategy," a strong appeal to urban, working class voters, including organized labor and social democrats, on a platform of conserving Wisconsin's natural and human resources. Directed by McGovern, and advised by Commons and McCarthy, the 1911 legislature compiled an unsurpassed record, including workmen's compensation, tightened child labor laws, strengthened protective legislation for working women, and minimum health and safety standards for industrial establishments. It created the nation's first comprehensive Industrial Commission, giving it jurisdiction over all labor and welfare legislation, and facilitated cooperative agricultural marketing, establishment of schools of agricultural and domestic economy, a commission to reform rural education, continuation schools in the state's industrial cities, a State Board of Industrial Education to oversee them, and the use of public school buildings as "social centers." It established a state Conservation Commission, a Board of Forestry, a Water Power Act, state aid for highway construction and a Highway Commission. It enacted the first successful state income tax, while ratifying the Sixteenth and Seventeenth Amendments to the U.S. Constitution, increased municipal authority over street railway systems, submitted a constitutional amendment providing for municipal home rule, inaugurated a state life insurance fund, provided for nonpartisan municipal elections, and proposed a woman suffrage constitutional amendment. It enacted work release programs for prisoners, adopted the "second choice" provision for primary elections, and submitted constitutional amendments for initiative, referendum, and recall. As a capstone, the 1911 legislature created the Board of Public Affairs, empowering it to conduct a wide range of investigations into the operation of state government.[16]

At its zenith in 1911, Wisconsin came closer than any of its sister states to the realization of the "central vision" that illuminated a "transatlantic community of discourse" between European social democrats and American progressives: a *via media* between state socialism and laissez-faire liberalism.[17] However, that achievement proved to be highly transitory. As La Follette's presidential aspirations were frustrated by Theodore Roosevelt in 1912, McGovern cannily endorsed T.R., a stratagem that prevented the emergence of a Wisconsin Progressive Party, but that shattered what was left of the La Follette-McGovern collaboration. La Follette exacted his revenge by trashing McGovern's legislative program in 1913, and by stymieing his bid for election to the U.S. Senate the following year. During the 1914 republican primary and general election, the fragile progressive coalition came completely unglued, allowing Philipp to gain nomination and election. A master organizer, fund-raiser, and propagandist, Philipp effectively stigmatized the Wisconsin Idea and the Social Service State with three cardinal sins: fiscal extravagance, socialist-leaning radicalism, and undemocratic elitism. He concentrated his fire on the three pillars of the systematized state: McCarthy's "progressive bill factory," the "University state," and the "elite" commissions. Although Philipp's three-term regime dismantled little of the service state and established a *modus vivendi* with McCarthy, Van Hise, and other progressives, his election clearly marked the end of the Progressive Era in Wisconsin.[18]

Increasingly vital to the economy and polity of an emerging urban, industrial state, the University of Wisconsin experienced remarkable growth and articulation during the Progressive Era, establishing itself as one of the nation's foremost public institutions. In 1891, the campus served less than 1,000 students, nearly 70 percent of whom were in Letters and Science. By 1915, the student population had more than quintupled to 5,128, of whom 43 percent were in the schools of agriculture, engineering, law, or medicine. Over that same period, the faculty increased from 35 to nearly 700, while the annual budget ballooned from under three hundred thousand dollars to just over three million. During the presidencies of Thomas C. Chamberlain (1887–92) and Charles Kendall Adams (1892–1900), the law and engineering schools attained separate buildings, the College of Agriculture constructed several edifices, a gymnasium and an armory were built, and the joint library–State Historical Society structure was completed. During Charles R. Van Hise's tenure (1903–18), the area of the campus's landed property doubled, and three million dollars worth of new buildings were constructed. Under those three administrations, departmental structure and curriculum were revised on several occasions, mainly to reflect the growing importance of preprofessional programs. The increasing emphasis on professionalism, specialization, research, and public service was mirrored in the rapid expansion of the College of Agriculture, the revival of extension work, the establishment of the graduate school and the summer session, and by the participation of numerous faculty in service to state government. McCarthy insisted that the social science departments concentrate on the preparation of enlightened public servants, while Ely pronounced them a "West Point" for citizenship and civic life. Ely, Turner, Commons, Ross, Van Hise, McCarthy, and a handful of other UW faculty achieved national reputations outside the academic cloister, while many of their colleagues enjoyed celebrity within those confines.[19]

Van Hise's national reputation as a progressive thinker was assured by publication of *The Conservation of Natural Resources* (1910) and *Concentration and Control: A Solution of the Trust Problem in the United States* (1912). Although he stressed the importance and benefit of "practical" research, Van Hise added that "the practical man of all practical men is he who, with his face toward the truth, follows wherever it may lead, with no thought but to get deeper insights into the order of the universe in which he lives." Defining the "search for truth and freedom in teaching truth" as "the spirit that the university must not yield," Van Hise insisted that "science and applied science should be taught in the university alongside the traditional subjects and with equal privileges," that people "must continue their education throughout life," and that the university must be "willing to undertake any line of educational work for which it is the best suited instrument." The university must "forever retain in this commonwealth the essentials of democracy" by making it possible for every qualified boy and girl "to obtain an education, broad and complete, fitted to the demands of the present time. . ." and must make its contributions of people and ideas to "government by experts." While denying that such a course meant that the university was "in politics," Van Hise boldly asserted that if "it was meant that the University is attempting to lead in the advancement of the people; if it was meant that problems which relate to water powers, to forests, to marketing, to the public utilities, to labor are legitimate fields of university inquiry and teaching, then the university is in politics."[20]

Led by several prominent social scientists, the UW emerged as a leading seat of progressive thought. Van Hise's books became virtual bibles, as did McCarthy's *Wisconsin Idea*. Ely was celebrated as a founder of both the "New Economics" and the American Economic Association, which regarded "the

State as an educational and ethical agency whose positive aid is an indispensable condition of human progress." Ely's blending of Christian socialism and social science reoriented the study of political economy, and inspired two generations of economists, even after the master grew more conservative. His erstwhile protégé, Commons, eventually surpassed his master in the "struggle against laissez-faire," pioneered institutional economics and labor history, and directed the writing of monumental studies on industrial society and labor history. Ross, another Ely protégé, provided much of the intellectual underpinning for factory safety, child labor, maximum working hours, and minimum wage legislation, as well as eugenics and immigration restriction. Turner's emphasis on the historical importance of geography and environmental factors, and on the evolutionary nature of socioeconomic development and democratic institutions, reinforced the reformist temper of the times.[21]

Especially instrumental in the evolution of the service state and the Wisconsin Idea was the development of the College of Agriculture. Beginning with a base of four students in 1893, its enrollment soared to over one thousand during the next two decades. Under the leadership of deans William A. Henry and Harry L. Russell, the college established the fields of agricultural science as legitimate academic disciplines, and achieved an acceptable balance between broad scientific courses and specialized ones. The Experiment Station struggled to compromise between pure and applied science. Its discoveries in livestock breeding and feeding, milk fat testing, cheese curing, and tuberculosis control won over many who doubted the school's utility. Its innovations in agricultural education, engineering, economics, journalism, and rural sociology achieved national recognition, while its outreach activities enriched every region of Wisconsin.[22]

More problematic was the emergence of the Extension Division. Its prototypes—the Short Course and the farmers' institutes—were established in 1888, in response to pressure from farm organizations. Although Extension work flagged somewhat in the 1890s, interest was renewed by La Follette's first message to the legislature, in which he contended that the "State will not have discharged its duty to the University, nor the University fulfilled its mission to the people until adequate means have been furnished to every young man and woman in the state to acquire an education at home in every department of learning." The staff of the Free Library Commission, led by McCarthy, Frank A. Hutchins, and Henry E. Legler, importuned Van Hise to resuscitate the Extension Department. After ignoring the subject for some time, Van Hise proclaimed, in November 1905, that it "seems to me that a state university should not be above meeting the needs of the people, however elementary the instruction necessary to accomplish this." During his twenty-year tenure as director, Louis E. Reber built Extension into a powerful organization that combined Van Hise's service ideal with the social reformist aspirations of McCarthy, Hutchins, and Legler. Anxious to establish a separate identity, Reber demanded a special staff, set up a network of administrators and teachers, utilized itinerant instructors, and produced a specific textbook for each correspondence course. While the Department of Instruction by Lectures functioned primarily as a speakers' bureau, the Department of Debating and Public Discussion sought to generate intelligent and active interest and enthusiasm, among a wide spectrum of Wisconsinites, for a variety of social and political issues. The Department of General Information and Welfare proposed "to act as a medium between the great federal and state departments, national societies and state universities, on the one hand, and the people of the state, on the other, in the dissemination of results of investigation and research."[23]

Much dearer to Van Hise's heart was the idea that University faculty should be of direct service to state government. In his inaugural address, Van Hise praised the practice of Germany and Austria in utilizing scholars in government service, and predicted the growth of similar practice in Wisconsin. By coincidence or design, La Follette had already begun "to appoint experts from the university whenever possible upon the important boards of the state." The role of Commons in drafting legislation and serving on the industrial and other commissions was both crucial and extraordinary. Ely claimed that La Follette regarded him as his primary teacher in political economy, but there is little corroborating evidence. Van Hise not only encouraged faculty service at every opportunity, but served on several commissions himself. Economists Thomas S. Adams and Balthazar H. Meyer were members of the tax and railroad commissions, while Birge, Reber, and others also made occasional contributions.

In *The Wisconsin Idea*, McCarthy identified forty-six UW faculty members and administrators who served on state commissions, but the majority of these were limited to proffering advice on the technical aspects of agriculture, engineering, or forestry. Few UW people had any real say in policy formulation. Commons later insisted that he "was never called in except by Progressives, and only when they wanted me." Even Van Hise, by 1913, challenged claims that he presided over "a university that rules a state," insisting that UW professors "carefully refrain from offering advice or assistance except as they are called upon to do so." As the reaction against progressivism set in after 1912, it became increasingly apparent that UW involvement in governance and politics was a double-edged sword that could be turned against both progressive politicians and the campus.[24]

Although the UW emerged as a first-rate academic institution, its national celebrity resulted primarily from government service, extension, and agricultural outreach. When the prestigious Mosely Education Commission ranked it second only to Michigan among state universities, one of its members placed Wisconsin first, because it was "the wholesome product of a commonwealth of three millions of people; sane, democratic, industrial and progressive; with ideals and unafraid of ideas." It "responds to every need of humanity; it knits together the professions and labor; it makes the fine arts and the anvil one." Progressive journalist Lincoln Steffens exulted that the "democratization of knowledge is in sight at the University of the People of the State of Wisconsin." Theodore Roosevelt asserted that "in no other state in the union has any university done the same work for the community that has been done in Wisconsin by the University of Wisconsin." The author of *Great American Universities* gushed that "the campus has an area of about 56,000 square miles" and that, with university leadership, "Wisconsin has become the recognized leader in progressive and practical legislation, the New Zealand of the United States." Universities and civic groups in Georgia, Texas, Arkansas, Ohio, Pennsylvania, and North Carolina sent delegations to Madison to study extension, faculty service, and the operation of the Legislative Reference Library.[25]

As real as its accomplishments were, the university establishment could not resist the temptation to embellish by operating its own propaganda machine, headed by the University Press *Bulletin*, and its own legislative lobby, both of which often exaggerated accomplishments and papered over conflicts and controversies. These efforts guaranteed the campus an influential constituency that supported its escalating requests for state funding, often because university spokesmen promised particular interest groups financial or other material "payoffs." When some of these promises inevitably proved to be overblown, the resulting disillusionment turned supporters into detractors. Relations between the university and the legislature were frequently antagonistic, even when progressive republicans were in power. The primary battleground was usually the university budget, as the rapidly growing campus not only requested ever larger appropriations, but also virtual autonomy over expenditures and priorities. Increasingly, it justified its requests with the "confident belief that every dollar will be returned many fold to the state, even if the material point of view above be considered." The legislature, predictably, demanded greater and more detailed "accountability," the larger the appropriation. In 1897, 1906, and 1913, the legislature launched full-scale investigations of university operations, to gain greater control over spending and governance. While its partisans usually succeeded in mitigating the most drastic of these recommendations, the long-term trend toward greater legislative involvement in university operations was firmly established by 1914.[26]

More important to the essence of higher education were the continuing challenges to academic freedom after 1894. The conflict came to a head, between 1909 and 1915, in a series of incidents that revolved around the freedom of scholars and teachers to advocate restrictions on the rights of private property and profit-making. Such activities increasingly aroused the ire of the state's businessmen, conservative and moderate politicians, and like-minded members of the Board of Regents, who regarded adherence to the tenets of private enterprise capitalism as the sine qua non of political correctness. The conflict first erupted when muckraking journalist Richard Lloyd Jones, writing in *Colliers*, charged that a few powerful regents, exercised by faculty activism in public utilities regulation and resource conservation, were exerting pressure in academic matters. Specifically, Jones accused certain regents of trying to coerce the economics department, and of plotting to depose Van Hise. Despite the president's efforts to disassociate the university from Jones's charges, progressive newspapers gave them greater currency, even attributing Turner's acceptance of a position at Harvard as a protest against regent interference in academic freedom. Much of the discussion involved the legitimacy of faculty research into current socioeconomic issues, such as the control of water power and forests, and the right of faculty members to teach what some regents regarded as "socialism." The discussion resulted in a consensus, in which the regents pledged to respect "the customary methods of educational administration by the faculty," but insisted that the board's recent actions were "within the legal and technical rights of the regents." The faculty, for its part, conceded the regents' good will and honorable intentions.[27]

This shaky compromise was immediately challenged when Ross defended the right of anarchist Emma Goldman to speak in Madison, and gave her a guided tour of the campus. While chiding Ross's judgment, both the regents and the Board of Visitors generally exonerated him, and the UW faculty, from advocating either anarchism or socialism. When Ross invited progressive educator Parker Sercombe to address his class a few days later, the regents unanimously adopted a resolution of censure against the prominent sociologist. Privately, Van Hise informed Ross that some of the regents had been seeking for a pretext on which to dismiss him, ever since the publication of his *Sin and Society* in 1907. The state's newspapers quickly chose up sides, with conservative journals accusing the university of preaching anarchism and radicalism, and progressive papers attributing Ross's problems to the efforts of water-power monopolists and their Stalwart allies. The situation was exacerbated when geology professor Eugene A. Gilmore, in a report to the Conservation Commission, recommended that the state take back all water power that private holders had failed to develop.[28]

During a visit to Madison, Lincoln Steffens expressed his concerns over the state of academic freedom on the campus to the editor of *La Follette's Weekly*, suggesting that wider circulation of the regents' 1894 declaration of academic freedom might aid the cause. Expanding on Steffens's sentiment, editor Fred MacKenzie remarked to the editor of the *Cardinal* that the graduating class of 1910 might make a plaque containing the regents' pledge its customary parting gift to the campus. When the class's memorial committee seized upon the plan, and petitioned for permission to hang the plaque on Bascom Hall, the regents rejected the proposal, charging that the students had been duped by "radicals." In his commencement address, Van Hise ignored the specific controversy, but warned about the dangers inherent in political control of public universities, in demanding purely material benefits from higher education, and in efforts to curtail academic freedom. The president of the class reiterated the students' intention to donate the plaque, "in order that their class might leave a memorial that was really worth while," cautioning that the board's refusal might occasion adverse criticism.[29]

As part of their leftward strategy, progressive republicans incorporated the regents' 1894 statement into their 1910 platform verbatim, associating themselves with the protection of academic freedom, and implying that the regents and the Stalwarts were numbered among its enemies. After Mc-

Govern had used his appointive authority to achieve a progressive majority on the board, the regents finally agreed, in April 1912, to accept the plaque, but refused to display it on the Bascom Hall facade. Three years later, the class of 1910 renewed its request for installation of the plaque. Persuaded by its conservative minority, the regents agreed to grant the request, only if the alumni explicitly retracted its earlier statements accusing the board of violations of academic freedom. The political atmosphere was even more tense because Philipp, who now occupied the governor's chair, began appointing more business-oriented regents. Eventually, the regents and the alumni group agreed to a compromise, in which both sides acknowledged previous misunderstandings and misstatements, ending the five-year controversy with considerably more whimper than bang. Van Hise proclaimed that, from 1894 onward, "no responsible party or no responsible authority has ever succeeded in restricting freedom of research and teaching within these walls," while progressive democratic leader Joseph E. Davies wrote to Ross, rejoicing that academic freedom had been "cemented into the very foundations of the University" and that "never again will the questions be raised." Even as they held forth, the outbreak of World War I was spawning conditions that would result in new challenges to academic freedom.[30]

It was more than coincidence that the crisis over academic freedom that began with the Ely trial in 1894 achieved a symbolic consummation in 1915. Still largely a rural, agrarian society in the year of the trial, Wisconsin was emerging as a modern, urban, industrial state by 1915. A polity notorious for its domination by railroad, lumber, and other business interests in the early 1890s, the Badger State was widely hailed and emulated as a progressive model and a laboratory for democracy by 1915. For two decades, the course of political progressivism had been increasingly intertwined with the growth of the university, and with the involvement of its faculty in practical research, public service, and community outreach. The connection was perhaps the most widely celebrated tenet of the Wisconsin Idea. However, the events of those two decades, and especially those of 1909 through 1915, revealed an inherent tension between the maintenance of academic freedom and the participation of scholars in public and political affairs. The more "relevant" the academic world became, the more it raised the hackles of the rich and powerful, and the less tolerant the general public became of retreats behind the walls of the cloister. Identifying itself closely with a partisan political movement all but guaranteed that the institution, its prerogatives,

l its ideals would suffer, when the winds of political change inevitably
ersed direction. The arena of democratic politics proved to be something
; than the ideal environment for the "continual and fearless sifting and
inowing by which alone the truth can be found."

Notes

ric E. Lampard, *The Rise of the Dairy Industry in Wisconsin* (Madison: State Historical
Society of Wisconsin, 1962).

Ioward R. Kleuter and James J. Lorence, *Woodlot and Ballot Box: Marathon County in the
Twentieth Century* (Wausau: Marathon County Historical Society, 1977), 37–68; Charles
N. Glaab and Lawrence Larsen, *Factories in the Valley, Neenah-Menasha, 1870–1915* (Madison: State Historical Society of Wisconsin, 1969), 48–77; Maurice Lloyd Branch, "The
Paper Industry in the Lake States Region, 1834–1947" (Ph.D. dissertation, University of
Wisconsin, 1954).

Wisconsin Blue Book, 1915, 34.

J.S. Bureau of the Census, *Fourteenth Census, 1920*, vol. 3, *Population: Composition and
Characteristics of the Population by States*, 1131.

bid., 1118, 1121, 1135–39.

amuel P. Hays, *The Response to Industrialism, 1885–1914* (Chicago: University of Chicago
Press, 1957), 48–70; John Whiteclay Chambers, *The Tyranny of Change: America in the
Progressive Era, 1900–1917* (New York: St. Martin's, 1980), David P. Thelen, *The New Citizenship: Origins of Progressivism in Wisconsin, 1885–1900* (Columbia: University of Missouri Press, 1971), 290–312.

ichard T. Ely, *An Introduction to Political Economy* (New York: Chautaqua Press, 1889),
6–29; Benjamin G. Rader, *The Academic Mind and Reform: The Influence of Richard T. Ely
n American Life* (Lexington: University Press of Kentucky, 1966), 50.

harles McCarthy, *The Wisconsin Idea* (New York: Macmillan, 1912), 15–18.

IcCarthy, *Wisconsin Idea*, 294–300; Robert S. Maxwell, *La Follette and the Rise of Progressivism in Wisconsin* (Madison: State Historical Society of Wisconsin, 1956), 59, 100, 125,
53–57; Herbert F. Margulies, *The Decline of the Progressive Movement in Wisconsin,
1890–1920* (Madison: State Historical Society of Wisconsin, 1968), 124–63.

McCarthy, *Wisconsin Idea*, 1–18, 273–306; John D. Buenker, "Wisconsin as Maverick,
Model, and Microcosm," in James H. Madison, *Heartland: Comparative Histories of the
Midwestern States* (Bloomington: Indiana University Press, 1988), 59–85.

McCarthy, *Wisconsin Idea*, 124–58, 172–93, 233–72.

Ibid., 172–272.

Ibid., 88–123, 190–93.

Roger E. Wyman, "Voting Behavior in the Progressive Era: Wisconsin as a Test Case"
Ph.D. dissertation, University of Wisconsin, 1970), demonstrates the rise of the "new
politics" of class, ideology and personality, but also argues effectively that it never completely displaced the "old" ethnocultural, partisan politics during the Progressive Era.

Robert M. La Follette, *La Follette's Autobiography: A Personal Narrative of Political Experience* (Madison: University of Wisconsin Press, 1960), 98–137; Maxwell, *La Follette and Rise
f Progressivism*, 10–127; Margulies, *Decline of Progressive Movement*, 51–82.

16. Maxwell, *La Follette and Rise of Progressivism*, 153–72; McCarthy, *Wisconsin Idea*, 273–86.

17. James T. Kloppenberg, *Uncertain Victory: Social Democracy and Progressivism in European and American Thought, 1870–1920* (New York: Oxford University Press, 1986), 349–94.

18. Margulies, *Decline of the Progressive Movement*, 51–82; Maxwell, *La Follette and Rise of Progressivism*, 173–94.

19. Merle Curti and Vernon Carstensen, *The University of Wisconsin: A History, 1848–1925*, 2 vols., (Madison: University of Wisconsin Press, 1949), vol. 1, 501–658, 711–39; vol. 2, 3–122.

20. Charles R. Van Hise, "Inaugural Address," The Jubilee of the University of Wisconsin (Madison: University of Wisconsin Press, 1905), 123–25; "An Address by Charles R. Van Hise, May 23, 1913," in Curti and Carstensen, *University of Wisconsin*, vol. 2, 611–24.

21. Curti and Carstensen, *University of Wisconsin*, vol. 2, 19–27, 87–111; Rader, *Academic Mind and Reform*, 28–105; Richard T. Ely, *Ground Under Our Feet: An Autobiography* (New York: Macmillan, 1938), 121–63; Lafayette G. Harter, *John R. Commons: His Assault on Laissez-Faire* (Corvallis: Oregon State University Press, 1962), 69–130; John R. Commons, *Myself: The Autobiography of John R. Common* (Madison: University of Wisconsin Press, 1964), 95–165; Julius Weinberg, *Edward Alsworth Ross and the Sociology of Progressivism* (Madison: State Historical Society of Wisconsin, 1972), 56–176; Edward A. Ross, *Seventy Years of It: An Autobiography* (New York: Appleton, 1936).

22. Wilbur H. Glover, *Farm and College: The College of Agriculture of the University of Wisconsin: A History* (Madison: University of Wisconsin Press, 1962), 89–148, 269–339; Lampard, *Rise of the Dairy Industry*, 244–93; Curti and Carstensen, *University of Wisconsin*, vol. 2, 374–424.

23. Curti and Carstensen, *University of Wisconsin*, vol. 1, 711–39; vol. 2, 549–94.

24. Van Hise, "Inaugural Address," 120–26; Curti and Carstensen, *University of Wisconsin*, vol. 2, 87–107; La Follette, *La Follette's Autobiography*, 13–15; Ely, *Ground Under Our Feet*, 216; Commons, *Myself*, 110; McCarthy, *Wisconsin Idea*, 304–6.

25. Curti and Carstensen, *University of Wisconsin*, vol. 2, 107–11, 588–91.

26. Ibid., vol. 2, 159–90, 267–94.

27. Richard Lloyd Jones, "Among La Follette's People," *Colliers*, July 17, 1909, 9; Curti and Carstensen, *University of Wisconsin*, vol. 2, 57–62.

28. Curti and Carstensen, University of Wisconsin, vol. 2, 63–68; Weinberg, *Edward Alsworth Ross*, 143–47; Ross, *Seventy Years*, 101–9.

29. Lincoln Steffens, "Sending a State to College," American Magazine 67 (February, 1909): 349–64; Curti and Carstensen, *University of Wisconsin*, vol. 2, 68–70. See also Theodore Herfurth, *Sifting and Winnowing: A Chapter in the History of Academic Freedom*, (Madison: University of Wisconsin Board of Regents, 1949).

30. Curti and Carstensen, *University of Wisconsin*, vol. 2, 70–72; Ross, *Seventy Years*, 104.

An Aristocrat on Trial:
The Case of Richard T. Ely

THERON F. SCHLABACH

As the world now stands, we hold it to be the solemn duty of all writers, preachers, and professors, who are engaged in the work of reform, to refrain from denunciations of the existing society and social arrangements." Thus wrote the editors of *The Nation*, Edwin L. Godkin and Horace White, in June of 1894, a year of economic depression, unemployment, and the violent Pullman railway strike and boycott. Godkin and White's solution to the prevailing social ills was to reassert the principles of laissez-faire. "The common practice among Christian and other socialists and utopians of abusing . . . the existing constitutions of society as an engine of fraud and oppression," they continued, "has undoubtedly done much to produce the 'militant anarchist' and give a sort of moral justification to his attacks on life and property."[1]

The editors did not reveal to just which socialists and utopians they were referring, but when Oliver E. Wells read the editorial he was able to apply its charges more specifically. Wells was Wisconsin's state superintendent of education, an ex-officio member of the University of Wisconsin's Board of Regents, and, according to one observer, "as pugnacious as an Irishman at a fair."[2] In a letter to the editors Wells asserted that "the teaching and practice of the University of Wisconsin" supported the *Nation*'s statement—especially the teaching and practice of the German-educated director of Wisconsin's School of Economics, Politics, and History, Richard T. Ely.[3]

Ely, charged Wells, justified strikes and practiced boycotts. A year or so earlier, when printers had struck against two Madison printing firms, Ely had entertained in his home a union organizer from out of town and had constantly consulted with him. At one firm where Ely was having some printing done, he had demanded that the management sign a contract with the union and had withdrawn his printing when the firm did not comply.

Theron F. Schlabach is professor of history at Elizabethtown College, Pennsylvania. This paper is reprinted by permission of the author and the editor of the Wisconsin Magazine of History. *This article appeared under the same name in Volume 47 (Winter 1963–64), pp. 146–59.*

Furthermore, Wells alleged, Ely had told a proprietor of the firm that it was better to employ "a dirty, dissipated, unmarried, unreliable, and unskilled" union man than "an industrious, skillful, trustworthy, non-union man who is head of a family"; the skilled family man could join the union, and if he had scruples against that, he was merely a "crank." In effect, Ely had said to citizens and taxpayers, "Stand and deliver, or down goes your business," and to the laboring men, "Join the union or starve with your families."[4]

Such was Ely the "socialist," Wells continued. Ely the professor taught the same principles and incorporated them in his scholarly writings, but he adroitly masked them "by glittering generalities and mystical and metaphysical statements" to prevent troubles ensuing to himself. The university, Wells contended, was promoting Ely's books, which had great appeal because even the uneducated could easily understand them; because they pandered to prohibitionists; and because they appealed to "the religious, the moral, and the unfortunate," by their ostentatious sympathy for all who were in distress. "Only the careful student will discover their utopian, impracticable and pernicious doctrines."[5]

Godkin and White were receptive to Wells's indictment of Ely. Eight years earlier an unsigned book review in the *Nation* had accused Ely of a bias and bitterness against wealthy classes which only "the ravings of an Anarchist or the dreams of a Socialist" could parallel, and had concluded that Ely seems to be seriously out of place in a university chair." Two years later, in 1888, the *Nation* had again complained that "in season and out of season" Ely had been pleading for state and municipal socialism. Embracing the "socialism of the chair, not that of the streets," Ely was putting forward worthless suggestions to revolutionize the existing system. So in 1894 the editors were quite happy to print Wells's condemnatory letter. Not only did they publicize it in the *Nation*, but also in their newspaper, the *New York Evening Post*, in which they had recently accused economics professors who had learned anti-laissez-faire doctrines in Germany of returning and "transplanting a pestilent crop of social fallacies."[6]

In the *Nation* Godkin and White followed Wells's letter with their own editorial rebuke to the "ethical professor." "Nobody can say surely" that Ely was "heading directly for the camp of the socialist and the anarchist," they admitted, for Ely was too clever to let his writings reveal that. But they accused him of being far too suspicious of millionaires as the source of industrial poverty, when he should have considered the extravagance, the improvidence, and the dissipation of workingmen themselves. Instead of seeing "insidious capitalist deviltry," Ely should have appreciated the good works of industrialists, particularly those of George Pullman, the railway car manufacturer, whose system of company-owned housing for workers Ely had denounced as enmeshing labor in the capitalists' net of control. Quoting no less a champion of laissez-faire than Professor William Graham Summer of Yale, the editors denounced all would-be "world movers and renovators," with their "doctrine of making the world over again."[7]

That Ely had a vision of a world made over was a fair charge, for he found "inspiration" in the faith that America was "entering on the dawn of a more glorious civilization than the world has yet seen." But he believed that the new order should come by long and patient scientific study, rather than by the natural impulse to use direct means.[8] Ely's writings in the years preceding 1894 certainly implied no covert belief in anarchy, as Godkin and White had suggested, nor any kind of revolutionary or complete socialism. Ever the champion of law, order, authority, and tradition, Ely entertained a reform philosophy which drew heavily on the past for its ideals and which contained deeply conservative strains.

At times Ely described his philosophy as the Golden Mean, the path "between the too little; namely rigid, obstructive, and revolutionary conservatism—that conservatism which refuses to recognize defects in the existing social order, and resists obstinately all reform and progress—and the too much; namely reckless radicalism, which in reaching out for improvement, risks" the constructive work of many ages.[9] Insofar as the Golden Mean suggested looking at the extremes and merely splitting the difference between them, however, it was too negative and passive adequately to describe Ely's entire social philosophy. A better description of the positive strains in his thought was his other favorite label, Progressive Conservatism. "*Progressive Conservatism*," Ely wrote in 1890, was "a conservatism which recognizes . . . that in its thousands of years of history and struggle humanity has accumulated treasures of all kinds;" a conservatism "which is determined to cling to them tenaciously; but a conservatism which . . . recognizes the fact that much remains for humanity yet to achieve" and therefore resists the "brute-like" objection to change which in the end would lead to violence.[10]

Central in Ely's philosophy was his Christianity. As a staunch proponent of the social gospel, he blamed social institutions for men's sins and looked forward to nothing less than the establishment of a kingdom of righteousness on earth. But he continually looked backward as well to past Christian tradition for its inspiration, revelation, accumulated wisdom, and specific social values. A convert to Episcopalism whose rearing had been puritanical, he condemned the traditional vices of intemperance, "bad habits," idleness, and pauperism, elevating the virtues of thrift industry, self-control, and stewardship, as well as charity, patience, and long-suffering.[11] He vigorously denounced anarchy by terming it an old-fashioned social disease "with an old-fashioned name . . . namely sin, and that fundamental sin, *rebellion*."[12] Even as he looked forward to a better social order, Ely's model was strongly reminiscent of a preindustrial society in which some men lived by the craftsman's skills and others ruled by divine right. The model for the masses was "not the self-made man—that is the self-made millionaire," Ely wrote, "but the contented and reasonably prosperous artisan or mechanic, gradually getting ahead in the world, enjoying life, developing all his powers and living worthily with his family."[13] And the way to meet the challenge of the disruptive anarchists was for political scientists to reassert the divine origins of the authority of the state.[14]

A second basic strain in Ely's philosophy was an organic view of the state and society. "The great thinkers in economics and politics in all ages," he wrote, had seen society as "not a mere aggregation of individuals, but a living, growing organism," operating under laws different from the laws of individual action. His ideal was a Christian state, where men submitted to the authority and sovereignty of God, recognized the state as God's instrument and therefore something sacred, and lived harmoniously in a social organism held together by righteous laws, a sense of stewardship among the upper classes, obedience by the lower classes, and a consciousness of duty and mutual obligation among all. It was a state led by a natural aristocracy, a "true aristocracy . . . serving the entire people with all their gifts, natural and acquired." The masses, unequal to solving the problems of industrialism by themselves, he declared, would "willingly follow culture and wealth, provided culture and wealth are wise and virtuous and show sincere devotion to their interests."[15]

Ely vigorously opposed any suggestion of allowing the working classes themselves to bring about industrial reform through class conflict. Socialists who advocated class struggle, he wrote in 1891, failed to see the need to "compel submission, and introduce a kind of subordination into the industrial ranks of society." He strongly supported labor unions, but his chief defense of them was that they were conservative organizations. "The labor leaders . . . are always holding back and restraining the rank and file," and union constitutions were instruments to strain the hot tempers and impetuosity of union members. "Workmen are so frequently ignorant, low in tastes, immoral" and "rude and coarse," Ely wrote, and so seldom "thoroughly competent and honest." The rich seemed to feel their ethical obligations more strongly than did workingmen, who did not even appreciate efforts and self-sacrifice made in labor's behalf. "Put aside bitterness and contention," Ely counseled workmen during the labor strife of 1893 and 1894. "Cultivate peace, patience, and long-suffering." Pursue your purposes, but pursue them with "charity" and "friendly relations."[16]

If the "mobocracy" was not fit to lead society, according to Ely, neither was the "plutocracy." He admitted that a society organized around monopolies and run by plutocrats might have made for steady work, no strikes, and even high wages; but he did not believe that it would have been a healthy society. Already the ethic of the entrepreneur had too much invaded political and social thought, making public office an article of merchandise and the dollar the only measure of a man. Yet Ely stoutly defended the institution of private property, rightly understood, and advocated private entrepreneurship in fields of economic activity that were not naturally monopolistic.[17]

The reformer's task, Ely maintained, was not to destroy private property but only to modify it by measures such as the inheritance tax so that it might better serve society. When many reformers were advocating that a government acquiring the property of a monopolist should pay the monopolist only the cost of duplicating the property, Ely advocated paying the full market value, so strong was his respect for the individual's property rights. Private property had definite social usefulness as an incentive to thrift and industry, he believed, and private entrepreneurship had made men responsible, cautious, and yet prudently bold. Competition between entrepreneurs had led bold and daring men of individualistic bent to make admirable exertions which redounded to the benefit of all. And so Ely had no wish to destroy private capitalism, particularly in agriculture, commerce, and much of manufacturing where it had not led to monopoly.[18] He only wished to put it on a higher ethical plane and to circumscribe it within its own proper sphere. That sphere, however, was strictly limited to economic leadership and services and did not include ideological leadership in society. Ideological leadership was to be the task of men of culture, as well as of wealth. "We must remember that the universities contain the flower of the land," Ely wrote in 1894, in reference to professors such as himself.[19]

A third strain in Ely's social thought, which operated within the limits set by his Christianity and his organic view of society, was a kind of pragmatism that came into play whenever Ely moved from the more theoretical realm to the advocacy of concrete measures. It was this pragmatism, this willingness to consider the consequences of change and to accept what he considered beneficial, that helped open him to the frequent charge of being a socialist. He was a persistent student of socialism, and although he usually claimed to regard it only with the "perfect impartiality" of an "unbiased searcher after truth," in 1889 he told a group of Boston churchmen that "Christian socialism—if you will take it in my conservative sense—is what I think we need." Socialism, he declared in 1892, harbored much truth, and had a mission to make its truths a part of American consciousness. It served to expose the evils of the American industrial situation and to place high ideals of humanitarianism, brotherhood, and service before the people. Although he considered the proletarian socialism of the Socialist Labor Party, with its theory of class conflict, a social disease only somewhat less serious than anarchy, he was willing to cooperate with "the extreme right of socialism."[20]

Ely's reluctance to go any further with the socialists lay in his belief that their system had certain potentially fatal weaknesses. In a system where government would provide all goods and services, people would direct all dissatisfaction with those goods and services against the government, and possibly revolt. Since most men had not progressed to the point of being willing to exert their best efforts solely for the general welfare, socialism did not provide adequate motivation for many of the most talented leaders in society. A socialistic state, being too egalitarian, might not provide adequate material support to learning, the arts, and the cultivation of the finer graces of life by the few, which were necessary for a full flowering of civilization. A socialistic order would face the technical problems of equating supply and demand, of bringing centralized control to agriculture, of coping with population growth, and of actually providing the promised level of material production. And finally, socialism aroused too much opposition from private interests. "Wise social reform will always seek the line of least resistance," Ely wrote in 1891. "Before committing ourselves to any extreme doctrines it is well to ask, What can be done without radical change?"[21]

Nevertheless, Ely believed that socialism, being a theory of monopoly, "roughly speaking" held good insofar as the reformer was facing the problem of monopoly;[22] and he saw a sharp distinction between nonmonopolistic and monopolistic industries. Consequently, while defending private enterprise in large economic spheres, Ely's favorite reform was the municipalization of electric companies, gasworks, waterworks, and street railways. He also favored the nationalization of telegraph and telephone companies, railroads, canals, and forest and mineral lands, and supported a roster of other reforms, many of them requiring more active government—the inheritance tax, factory regulation for women and children, civil service reforms, better court treatment of labor organizations, slum clearance and the creation of urban parks to benefit city populations morally as well as materially, savings banks to help the masses cultivate the habit of thrift, restriction of immigration, and tax relief for the lower classes. His reform program, he believed, went far enough along with the radicals to capture what was good in their programs and, therefore, to dissipate their strength and prevent their excesses. But as for a complete program of socialization, he wrote pragmatically, he feared that "judged by the social consequences it is likely to produce," this "untried remedy involving uncertainties and dangers of its own" would not pass the test.[23] Such pragmatism was a conservative strain in Ely's thought, for it put the burden of proof on the advocates of change; but it was progressively conservative, because it was willing to listen to evidences of proof. It was in the spirit of his Progressive Conservatism that Ely wrote his book, *Socialism and Social Reform*, published early in 1894. No doubt, Ely wrote in his preface, those "whose one test of conservatism, or radicalism, is the attitude one takes with respect to accumulated wealth" might charge him with radicalism. "A writer's whole nature may be that of a conservative; he may love the old ways; he may to some extent draw his social ideals from a past which he considers, with respect to feeling about wealth, saner than the present age, and yet, because he would, by social action, endeavor to change certain tendencies, and to conserve the treasures of the past which he feels threatened by new and startling forces, he is still a radical in the eyes of those men whose one and sole test is money."[24]

With Oliver Wells's public attack in June 1894, Ely's words became ironically prophetic.

Although Ely's father's reaction to the attack was to advise his son to "fret not thyself because of evildoers" and to "commit thy way unto the Lord," Ely was genuinely alarmed by Wells's letter and immediately consulted a number of his friends asking their advice as to whether or not to sue for libel, to seek a vindication before the university regents, or both. Their counsels indicated a wealth of sympathy and support, but were rather uncertain. At first his friends favored some sort of decisive confrontation with Wells. But on second thought they began to see dangers in creating a public furor. Breese J. Stevens, a Madison attorney and regent of the university, advised silence and no lawsuit—at least for a time. Frederick Jackson Turner, professor of history under Ely, and William Scott, Ely's associate professor of economics, agreed that it would not be wise to drag Ely's writings too much before the public during the agitation over the railway strikes. Scott feared that a hearing before the regents might result in an unfavorable minority report, and perhaps even in an unfavorable majority report.[25]

Ely's friends advised him to lean heavily on the advice of the president of the university, Charles Kendall Adams. In an address in June, Adams had expounded economic views somewhat at variance with Ely's, which the editors of the *Nation* had interpreted as a deliberate repudiation of Ely's philosophy. But Adams wrote privately that while he and Ely had arrived at somewhat different conclusions, he was sure that their "fundamental ethical concepts" were similar. At any rate, Ely was entitled to be understood and Adams was sure that Ely's writings could stand the test of searching public scrutiny in a trial. As a personal friend, but not officially as president and ex officio regent, Adams advised Ely that if he felt perfectly sure of his ground, he might do well to ask for an investigation by the regents.[26]

The regents, however, decided the matter before Ely and his friends had chosen a course of action. At a regents' meeting on July 31, 1894, the regents' president, William Bartlett, proposed that, since one of their number had made the attack, the board should appoint a committee to study the matter carefully. Stevens objected on the ground that "the times were too much disturbed to permit of a careful investigation." But the board sustained its president, and Bartlett appointed Herbert Chynoweth, a Madison attorney, John Johnston, a Milwaukee banker, and Harvey Dale, an Oshkosh physician to conduct the inquiry.[27]

Ely had reason to believe that Johnston might be sympathetic, for in the preceding months the two men had been in friendly correspondence. Johnston was something of a man of letters, having earned a master's degree in his native Scotland and written several scholarly encyclopedia articles. In

May he had assured Ely that a "teacher who can teach only what is accepted by everybody, will be confined to a very narrow line of tuition," and that he hoped that "the University of Wisconsin will always hold fast to the apostolic injunction to 'prove all things and hold fast to that which is good.'" Ely, in turn, had assured Johnston that he would never teach in a dogmatic fashion, because he believed in freedom and independence of thought for both himself and his students. And, he added, his students were liberal and progressive leaders in many communities, "but at the same time conservative men in the true sense of the word."[28]

Ely had little cause for such confidence in Chynoweth and Dale. Scott reported that he suspected Chynoweth to be unsympathetic and that Dale had actually expressed himself unfavorably. A number of Ely's friends quickly began working to change the opinions of the investigators, as well as those of the general public. Jerome Raymond, a sociologist at the University of Chicago who knew Dale slightly, wrote to him in Ely's favor and induced a friend, who he believed could be even more influential, to do the same. He also worked to get favorable material printed in Chicago papers, which smaller Wisconsin papers often copied. In Cincinnati, Philip Ayres, secretary of a Cincinnati charitable organization and a former student of Ely, induced his city's papers to print several articles in Ely's favor. Another former student, a free-lance newspaper writer, Edward Ingle, used his influence on newspapers in the Baltimore area. And when the *Chicago Evening Post* published an editorial absolving Ely of charges of socialism and expressing confidence that the regents would judge him fairly, Scott requested that the newspaper send a copy to each of the university regents.[29]

Ely had a valuable friend on the editorial staff of the *Wisconsin State Journal* in the person of Amos P. Wilder. Although a rather conservative owner-editor, Hod Taylor, prevented Wilder from making Ely's cause the editorial campaign that he would have liked, Wilder found ways to put Ely's case before the Madison public. On several occasions he published Ely's views and denials of Wells's charges and on other occasions printed statements which probably originated in his own office, attributing their source to "a friend of Dr. Ely" or to "sentiment on the curbstone." He published a long interview with David Kinley, one of Ely's students who had become professor of economics at the University of Illinois. Kinley contended at length that while study in Germany had perhaps influenced Ely excessively, he certainly was not a socialist.[30]

It was Kinley, vacationing in Madison, who did the most to prepare Ely's defense. First he offered Wells the opportunity to withdraw the charges. When Wells refused, Kinley set about to substantiate Ely's firm denials that he had done anything to aid the printers' strike, had withdrawn his printing in order to coerce the company to unionize, or had stated that a shiftless union man was better than a respectable nonunion man. He also kept Ely, who was vacationing in the East, informed with encouraging letters—which Ely no doubt needed, for the attack had come soon after the death of Ely's nine-month-old child, and while Mrs. Ely was ill. Ely himself maintained an overt public silence, although his denials of the charges reached the public through the discreet publishing efforts of Wilder and of Lyman Abbott, editor of the *Outlook*. Finally, however, taking an opportunity that his position as a Chautauqua lecturer provided, Ely prepared a forthright public statement which the Reverend John Vincent, chancellor of the Chautauqua lecture system, read in the Chautauqua, New York, amphitheater on August 14, six days before the regents' hearing. Thus Ely defended himself before a vast audience from many parts of the nation, and by arrangement of his friends got wide press coverage for his statement; but he avoided turning his case into the journalistic fight which he and his friends believed their opponents wanted.[31]

Ely's statement specified each of Wells's charges and categorically denied every one "in each and every particular." "The man who makes these charges against me," he declared, "is well known to his neighbors as a politician of the meaner sort, who, too small to appreciate the most important trust ever committed to him, betrayed it in his insensate love of notoriety." The statement went on to assure the Chautauqua audience that Ely was neither an anarchist nor a socialist, and that although he favored labor unions, he had only limited faith in them. While he had not changed his fundamental beliefs, he had become increasingly conservative over the years. Nor had President Adams rebuked him, Ely asserted; Adams would speak out for him when the proper time came. This, indeed, was what Adams, who was staying in the background, had privately promised Ely. Ely was attempting to reap the full benefit of Adams's covert support, while following Kinley's advice of not in any way forcing Adams openly to take sides.[32]

Meanwhile, Chynoweth, Dale, and Johnston met and set the date of their hearing for August 20. They requested that Wells appear and present whatever evidence he could to support his charges concerning Ely's conduct in the printers' strike, and they instructed Ely to come bringing whatever lecture notes he could produce from classes he had taught at Wisconsin. Chynoweth, the chairman, announced that the committee would concern itself only with Ely's activities in the strike and with his teachings in the university: it would not probe into his personal beliefs nor consider his books. A *Wisconsin State Journal* editorial protested that this limitation was fair neither to the public, who wanted a complete, unrestricted investigation, nor to Ely, who should have been allowed to introduce any of his writings that he wished to use in his defense. But Kinley thought that the scope of the investigation was just right, inasmuch as it provided "a clear, definite series of charges to meet."[33]

Kinley was beginning to feel elated about Ely's prospects for complete vindication. "I feel today that the sky is clearing rapidly for you in the local situation," he assured Ely on August 10. He believed that the investigating committee was feeling the drift of sentiment and would not dare to show any hostility toward Ely if, indeed, it had any. And from conversation with the man of whom Ely allegedly had made his demands in favor of the union, Wheeler A. Tracy of the printing firm of Tracy & Gibbs, Kinley became more and more convinced that Ely and his friends had Wells "in a nice little hole of his own digging." Wilder did what he could to help clear the sky by publicizing some of the facts that Kinley dredged up, and when Ely, after returning to Madison, became ill three days before the hearing date, Wilder used even that fact to maximum advantage. Although Ely had fairly recovered, Wilder, in his last issue before the hearing, stressed the fact of Ely's illness and had "a friend of Dr. Ely" declare that the regents ought to finish the whole investigation in twenty-four hours and be done with the excruciating, irresponsible attack on the university's most prestigious professor.[34]

The evening of the hearing arrived and Ely appeared with his counsel, Burr W. Jones, Madison attorney, politician in Wells's own Democratic party, and teacher in the university's law school. About 200 observers attended. Wells, however, did not appear. Shortly before the time of the hearing he sent a messenger to the committee with a letter stating that he had been called out of town on business, and that the committee did not need his presence until they had decided to change their procedure to include Ely's books as evidence. He argued that the committee's policy excluded the only evidence that he could produce in his own behalf, while Ely, being allowed to present anything he wished as lecture material, had a free hand. To support his position, Wells attempted to show, by quoting from Ely's books, that Ely had made strong statements in favor of socialism, but only weak refutations against it. After considering Wells's objections and conferring with Ely and Jones, the committee adjourned the hearing until the following evening.[35]

The next day the committee again requested Wells to be present, informing him that they had only meant to follow the regents' resolution which had initiated the investigation. This resolution, noting that Wells had charged that "Ely's teachings in the University" were socialistic, utopian, and pernicious, had authorized an investigation of " the charges made, the effect of Dr. Ely's teachings upon the students, and the whole matter connected therewith." The committee informed Wells that it understood the resolution to exclude Ely's books, especially since Wells had not specified any books in his charges. But they assured him that they would listen to any of his suggestions if he would attend.[36]

That evening Wells did attend with his counsel, Madison attorney George Bird, and the protagonists spent much of the evening arguing whether or not Wells might introduce the books as evidence. The committee insisted that it did not intend to scrutinize all of Ely's voluminous writings, since the regents could not hold themselves responsible for the writings of about 200 faculty members—Johnston arguing that position most emphatically, while Chynoweth supported it and Dale remained virtually silent. Bird, trying to distract the hearing from charges surrounding the printers' strike, argued that the charges against Ely's books were the only ones of any consequence, but Jones insisted upon examining the strike charges in order to vindicate Ely's personal character. In an argument over just who should bear the burden of proof, Wells suggested that Ely answer the charges so that the committee would have specific issues to discuss. Chynoweth, in turn, suggested that Wells file formal charges against Ely. Finally they agreed to accept the original letter to the *Nation*'s editors as a statement of charges, and Jones read a statement for Ely, once more categorically denying each specific charge. This drew applause from the audience, leading Bird to protest and Chynoweth to promise to prevent further demonstrations. After more arguments, the committee decided that Wells might prepare excerpts from Ely's writings to produce as evidence at a later time, and proceeded to consider the specific charges surrounding the strike.[37]

The record of the strike was particularly disappointing for Wells. His key witness, Tracy, testified that Ely had not threatened to withdraw his own printing from the firm if it expelled the union, but that he had said that the executive board of the Christian Social Union, of which Ely was secretary, might require that he withdraw the Union's printing. Ely had eventually stopped patronizing Tracy's firm, but under cross-examination by Jones, Tracy admitted that he and Ely had disagreed over the payment of a bill. Tracy indicated that the statements concerning a dirty, profligate union man versus a lean, trustworthy nonunion man had been his own words, put to Ely in the form of a question. Ely had replied that the trustworthy man could join the union, and Tracy himself had replied that the man might be a crank with scruples against union membership. The most that the prosecution could establish was that Ely had admitted that unions at times had to resort to unlawful boycotts to win their goals and that was one of the"bad things" about them. The testimony of Thomas Reynolds, a striking printer who was supposed to know that Ely had counseled and entertained J. F. Klunk, the out-of-town union organizer, was even more disappointing. Reynolds could produce only hearsay evidence, and had mysteriously changed his mind about information that Wells and Bird were sure he had held a month earlier. At that juncture the committee adjourned the hearing until two evenings later, when Wells presumably would produce allegedly damaging extracts from Ely's writings.[38]

The next day, however, Kinley made public the fact that he had a letter from Klunk indicating that Ely had neither entertained Klunk in his home nor advised him in regard to the strike. Klunk did believe that he had interviewed Ely once, but Ely's friends asserted that he had mistaken another man for Ely.

Wells decided not to attend another hearing. He complained that he had attended one hearing against the advice of his friends, and the demonstrations by the audience had prevented a fair trial. Once again he attempted to show by a lengthy letter to the committee that excerpts from Ely's writings showed a prosocialistic influence. And while he admitted that certain specific accusations concerning Ely's role in the strike had been false, he asserted that it was still true that Ely had encouraged the strike and had tried to coerce Tracy. Nor was Ely's statement that union boycotts were "bad things" enough to appease Wells.[39]

With Wells absent and the observers nearly all friends of Ely, the final hearing was virtually a pro-Ely demonstration. Edward F. Riley, secretary to the Board of Regents, read Wells's latest letter. Then Stevens read a number of communications which Adams had sent, and which, along with Wells's letter, the committee accepted as evidence. These included a review of Ely's book *Socialism and Social Reform*, in which Adams asserted that Ely had been thoroughly scientific, had written not "a paragraph or a sentence that can be interpreted as an encouragement of lawlessness or disorder," and had led the reader away from, not toward, socialism; a statement from E. Benjamin Andrews, president of Brown University, asserting that while Ely's teachings led to enlarged government action, they were not socialistic and did not advocate lawlessness; a statement from U.S. Labor Commissioner Carroll Wright, stating that it was too strong even to label Ely a Christian Socialist, and that Ely's students were men of "conservative judgement"; and similar letters from Albert Shaw, editor of *Review of Reviews*, and Albion W. Small, professor of sociology at the University of Chicago. Ely, Kinley, Turner, and Professor Henry H. Swain, an Ely student and teacher at Yankton University in South Dakota, testified in Ely's behalf concerning the harmlessness and the positive value of his teaching. Jones read some extracts from Ely's writings to illustrate Ely's "reverence for law, government, and the rights of private property," and submitted a number of reviews of Ely's books. Although Jones had earlier stated that Ely did not wish to see the investigation closed as long as undecided accusations remained, the investigating committee, clearly disgusted with Wells's performance, closed the hearing and terminated the investigation.[40]

Throughout the entire trial Ely did not raise the issue of academic freedom, but took a safer line of defense. He even admitted that if the attacks on his character had been true, they would have shown him "to be unworthy the honor of being a professor in a great university." Yet before the trial he had declared privately that "if I am slaughtered, others in different Universities will perish, and what will become of freedom of speech, I do not know." He encouraged Wilder to argue for academic freedom in his newspaper, because if the university "should yield to popular clamor and discharge me for my views, it would be an injury to the University from which it would not soon recover. . . . Freedom is the glory of a State University and intolerance is its shame."[41]

His friends also saw the implications for academic freedom. Wilder had his "friend of Dr. Ely" compare the trial to "the Salem witchcraft iniquity," and predict that the community, like Cotton Mather, would soon "rub our eyes in self-contempt." Turner declared that "surely the University must be a place where a man can seek the truth, and present both sides in a scientific way," and Abbott assured Ely that the *Outlook* would always support liberty of teaching in the nation's universities. At the final hearing President Andrews's communication advised the regents that if they deposed Ely it would be "a great blow at freedom of university teaching in general and at the development of political economy in particular." And Kinley, before the trial, publicly predicted "a vindication of the principle of free speech and the harmlessness of truth," declaring that "even if it were true that Dr. Ely's views were far in advance of those commonly accepted, it would be a serious matter to curtail freedom of opinion."[42]

Other commentators, however, were not all agreed that the regents ought to allow opinions that were too far advanced. Even the editors of liberal religious journals who gave Ely general support qualified their defense. The fact that Ely differed with his accuser on social questions was not enough to prove him "politically heretical," wrote the editor of the *Evangelist*, and only if "the State authorities are defied openly, as well as theoretically," was there "peril in any man's hypothesis or theory." But if Ely's views were "radically erroneous and inconsistent with loyal citizenship," he was an unsafe teacher of youth. George Gates, president of Iowa College, writing an editorial for the *Kingdom*, strongly defended Ely's "liberty to prophesy," arguing that truth was always dangerous, but dangerous only to firmly entrenched wrongs, never to righteousness. But he asserted that the liberty to prophesy did not mean that a man had "a right to say and teach anything he pleases," for society had to walk a narrow path between censorship and "fatal license of speech."[43]

The editor of a secular newspaper, the Springfield, Massachusetts, *Republican*, struck much the same note when he warned of the seriousness of the state's branding any doctrine a heresy, but maintained that certain conditions might justify retirement of a professor for economic heresy. The editor of the Milwaukee *Wisconsin* was less equivocal. While calling for a fair trial, he declared that if the regents found that Ely was teaching heresies, they would have to remove him. The state could not "maintain a propaganda directed against the political and social principles embodied in the constitution." The Milwaukee *Journal* editor agreed. "Our free institutions are too valuable to be imperilled by such teachings as are attributed to Dr. Ely," he wrote.[44]

John Olin, a professor in the University's College of Law, had rather different ideas for protecting free institutions. Olin had fought his own bout with the regents, who had fired him in 1887 for his prohibitionism, his legal counsel to people with claims against the University, and possibly his unpopularity among the state's Republicans, and then reinstated him in 1893. After the trial he wrote to Regent George Noyes of Milwaukee asserting that the committee should do more than exonerate Ely; in order to repair the University's damaged reputation they should declare the freedom of Wisconsin professors to speak out on "living questions." He believed that Johnston and Chynoweth would be willing.[45]

Encouraged, no doubt, by Olin's suggestion and by the sentiment that the trial had created in the university community, the committee turned a trial in which academic freedom had scarcely been mentioned into an occasion for a bold assertion of the right of free inquiry and expression. Noting that over two million people of vastly divergent views shared the support of the University, the committee in their final report to the regents asserted that they "could not for a moment think of recommending the dismissal or even the criticism of a teacher even if some of his opinions should, in some quarters, be regarded as visionary." A professor could not cut his curriculum to a small body of facts that everyone accepted as true. Because they could not "for a moment believe that knowledge has reached its final goal, or that the present condition of society is perfect," they welcomed from teachers discussion which might lead to the extension of knowledge and the removal of existing evils. "It is of the utmost importance that the investigator should be absolutely free to follow the indications of truth wherever they may lead," they declared. Then, in a climactic piece of rhetoric from President Adams's pen, they added: "Whatever may be the limitations which trammel inquiry elsewhere, we believe the great State University of Wisconsin should ever encourage that continual and fearless sifting and winnowing by which alone the truth can be found."[46]

Despite the fine rhetoric, Ely and his friends had based their defense not on the sanctity of academic freedom but on denials of specific charges and on assertions of Ely's essential conservatism. It had been the expediential course to follow, and it had worked, aided by Wells's ineptness. Wells had not only made the mistake of typing his attack to completely unprovable charges concerning Ely's personal conduct, but had also alienated the regents by including the university in his attack. He had, moreover, brought embarrassment to this entire community by making his attack through Eastern papers and, in general, had confirmed his local reputation for being a contentious, irresponsible politician. Ely's triumph was complete. Not only did he win technical acquittal, but also his friends arranged a great reception for him as an expression of their support, and he saw his opponent humiliated.

"We are pleased to say that the result is a complete vindication of Dr. Ely and the teachings and the practices of our University," the regents concluded in their final report, then added an extra rebuke to Wells by resolving that they disapproved of his failure to bring his criticisms first to the president or the regents of the university. This was Wells's second public rebuke. Several weeks earlier Democratic party members, meeting in a state convention, had greeted his name with hisses and boos. In 1890 another convention had raised Wells, whose highest previous office had been superintendent of Waupaca County Schools, from the principalship of Appleton's public schools to candidacy for the office of state superintendent. The 1894 convention nominated another man for his place. And finally the *Nation's* editors hastened to disassociate themselves from Wells. Godkin and White declared that the apparently unjust charges concerning Ely's personal conduct were matters solely between him and Wells, and professed that they were very pleased to see Ely vindicated. But, they added, Ely's economic teachings were still a proper subject for public discussion.[47]

During the crisis, Walter Hines Page, editor of the *Forum*, asked Ely to spell out his economic creed as a sequel to the trial. Ely's statement, "Fundamental Beliefs in My Social Philosophy," once more systematically set forth the tenets of his Progressive Conservatism. While reasserting the value of studying socialism, and declaring that socialism was a force which had stimulated consciences and beneficially transformed men's lives, Ely asserted that it was "radically different" from his own thought, and gave a summary of his reasons for rejecting it. He emphasized the limitations of trade unionism, denounced the violence surrounding the recent railway strikes as "barbarism and not civilization," and, in an obvious reference to the government's use of militia in those strikes, declared that a discussion of abstract rights could not interfere with determined action. Once more he upheld his ideas of government ownership of monopolistic industries, but declared that not everyone who had a scheme of achieving that goal had the mental capacity nor the moral qualifications to lead the country through a change that would require "the best brains and the ripest experience." Did a party have wild ideas in regard to money and public finance? Ely asked in the midst of a strong campaign by the Populists. "If so, we may conclude that adherence to older parties is preferable to support of a party deficient in leadership." He emphasized strongly that his own scheme of socialization did not include the unremunerated confiscation of any private property, and ended his article on the note that the doctrine of the essential equality of men was the source of much misfortune and misdirected social effort. To treat the "feebler members of the community" as equal to the superior merely caused them to suffer; and to treat the superior members as equal to the inferior robbed them of their feeling of responsibility toward their brethren.[48]

"I say then that I am a conservative rather than a radical . . . an aristocrat rather than a democrat," he concluded. " I have in mind . . . not an aristocracy born for the enjoyment of special privilege, but an aristocracy which lives for the fulfillment of special service."[49] In Ely's view, men of culture and refinement were the naturally superior aristocrats who should lead society, and men who lead by reason of their entrepreneurial abilities were to be relegated to second place and even subjected to social controls, through government ownership and regulation, and through toleration of the trade-union movement. It was his misfortune that his sophisticated kind of conservatism differed from the more popular brand current in the 1890s, and that the difference led to his public embarrassment.

Notes

1. "The Moral of Carnot's Assassination," *Nation* 58 (June 1894): 480.
2. *Manitowoc Pilot, Wisconsin State Journal*, July 21, 1894.
3. Oliver E. Wells to the editor, *Nation* 59 (July 1894): 27.
4. Ibid.
5. Ibid.
6. "Dr. Ely and the Labor Movement," *Nation* 43:293–94 (October 7, 1886), ascribed in Ely's autobiography, *Ground Under Our Feet* (New York, 1938) 178–79, to Simon Newcomb; "Ely's American Municipal Taxation," in *Nation* 47:359–60 (November 1, 1888); *New York Evening Post*, July 14, 1894; "Our Socialists of the Chair," *New York Evening Post: Semi-Weekly*, June 11, 1894.
7. "An Ethical Professor Rebuked," *Nation* 59:41–42 (July 19, 1894).
8. Richard T. Ely, "A Programme for Labor Reform," *The Century Illustrated Monthly Magazine* 39 n.s. 17:940 (April, 1890); Ely, "The Unemployed," *Harper's Weekly* 37:845 (September 2, 1893).
9. Richard T. Ely, *Socialism, An Examination of Its Nature, Its Strength and Its Weakness, with Suggestions for Social Reform* (New York) and Boston, 1894), 255 (hereafter cited by its cover title, *Socialism and Social Reform*).
10. "Peabody Lecture," manuscript in Ely's handwriting, dated February 11, 13, 1890, in the Richard T. Ely Papers, Manuscripts Library of the State Historical Society of Wisconsin.

11. See the following articles by Richard T. Ely: "A Programme for Labor Reform," 940, 951: "The Inheritance of Property," *North American Review* 153:66 (July, 1891); "Suggestions on Social Topics: Making Men Good by Statute," *Christian Advocate* 66:321 (May 14, 1891); "Social Observations in Germany," *Congregationalists* 77:222 (July 14, 1892); "Natural Monopolies and the Workingman," *North American Review* 158:303 (March, 1894); and his book *Socialism and Social Reform* 236, 307.

12. Richard T. Ely, "Anarchy," *Harper's Weekly* 37:1226 (December 23, 1893).

13. Ely, "A Programme for Labor Reform," 951.

14. Ely, "Anarchy," 1226; Richard T. Ely, "Suggestions on Social Topics: The State," *Christian Advocate* 66:386 (June 11, 1891).

15. Ely, *Socialism and Social Reform*, 3–4; Richard T. Ely, "Objections to Socialism," *Harper's Weekly* 38:58 (January 20, 1894); Ely, "A Programme for Labor Reform," 951.

16. See the following articles by Richard T. Ely: "Valid Objections Against Socialism," *Independent* 43:7 (May 28, 1891); "Suggestions on Social Topics: Labor Organizations," *Christian Advocate* 66:602 (September 10, 1891); "Other Favorable Aspects of Socialism," *Independent* 43:14 (May 7, 1891); "Suggestions for Social Topics: The Widening and Deepening of Ethical Obligation," *Christian Advocate* 66:538 (August 13, 1891); "Natural Monopolies and the Workingman," 303.

17. Richard T. Ely, "Socialism and the General Welfare," *Independent* 43:13 (April 23, 1891): Ely, "A Programme for Labor Reform," 938; Ely, *Socialism and Social Reform*, 197.

18. Ely, *Socialism and Social Reform*, 307–10, 198; Ely, "Natural Monopolies and the Workingman," 302; Richard T. Ely, "Underestimate by Socialists of the Benefits of Competition," *Independent* 43:7 (June 4, 1891); Ely, "Objections to Socialism," *Harper's Weekly* 38:31 (January 13, 1894).

19. Ely, "Objections to Socialism" (January 13, 1894), 31.

20. Ely, *Socialism and Social Reform*, 113, 169–170, vi, 256; Richard T. Ely, "Socialism, Its Nature, Its Strength, and Its Weakness," in *The Independent*, 43:8–9 (March 26, 1891); Richard T. Ely, *The Needs of the City: An Address Delivered Before the Boston Conference of the Evangelical Alliance*, December 4, 1889 (printed as a pamphlet), 6; Richard T. Ely, "Suggestions on Social Topics: Are We Going Too Fast?," *Christian Advocate* 67:206 (March 31, 1892); Ely, "A Programme for Labor Reform," 951; Richard T. Ely, "The Elements of Socialism, *Independent* 43:5 (February 19, 1891).

21. Richard T. Ely, "Objections to Socialism," *Harper's Weekly* 38:15 (January 6, 1894); Ely, "Objections to Socialism" (January 13, 1894), 31; Ely, "Objections to Socialism" (January 20, 1894), 58; Ely, *Socialism and Social Reform*, 188–248; Ely, "The Inheritance of Property," 54.

22. Ely, *Socialism and Social Reform*, 262.

23. Ely, "A Programme for Labor Reform," 938–951; Ely, "Suggestions on Social Topics: Are We Going Too Fast?," 206; Ely, "Valid Objections to Socialism," 11; Ely, "Underestimate by Socialists of the Benefits of Competition," 7.

24. Ely, *Socialism and Social Reform*, viii.

25. Ezra Ely to Richard T. Ely, August 2, 1894; Charles Kendall Adams to Ely, July 23, 1894; Amos P. Wilder to Ely, July 19, 1894; Lyman Abbott to Ely, July 19, 1894; Albert Shaw to Ely, July 19, 1894; Charles Gregory to Ely, July 19, 1894; William Scott to Ely, July 21, 1894; all in the Ely Papers.

26. "An Ethical Professor Rebuked," 42; Adams to Ely, July 23, 1894 in the Ely Papers.

27. Records of the University of Wisconsin Regents. Vol D, 293, in the University of Wisconsin Archives.

28. Merle Curti and Vernon Carstensen, *The University of Wisconsin: A History, 1848–1925* (2 vols., Madison, 1949), 1:513; Johnston to Ely, January 19, May 3, 1894, in the Ely Papers; excerpt of letter, Ely to Johnston (June, 1894, from internal evidence), in Papers, Board of Regents Meeting, in the University of Wisconsin Archives.

29. Scott to Ely, August 3, 1894, in the Ely Papers; *Wisconsin State Journal*, August 6, 1894; Raymond to Ely, August 9, 10, 13, 1894; Raymond to Dale, August 13, 1894 (copy); Ayres to Ely, August 15, 1894; Ingle to Ely (internal evidence suggests *ca.* August 15, 1894); Scott to Ely, August 8, 1894; all in the Ely Papers.

30. Wilder to Ely, July 19, 1894, in the Ely Papers; *Wisconsin State Journal*, July 31, August 20, 1894; ibid., August 3, 1894.

31. Ely, *Ground Under Our Feet*, 225; Kinley to Ely, August 2, 7, 10, 11, 1894, in the Ely Papers; *Outlook* 50:127–28 (July 28, 1894); "Prof. Richard T. Ely Makes a Personal Statement," *Chautauqua Assembly Herald*, August 15, 1894; Raymond to Ely, August 10, 1894; Ely to Albert Shaw, August 8, 1894; Ingle to Ely (internal evidence suggests *ca.* August 15, 1894); all in the Ely Papers.

32. "Prof. Richard T. Ely Makes a Personal Statement": Adams to Ely, August 2, 1894; Kinley to Ely, August 7, 1894, in the Ely Papers.

33. Edward F. Riley to Ely, August 9, 1894; copy of resolution requesting Ely and Wells to appear, in the Ely Papers; *Wisconsin State Journal*, August 10, 11, 1894; Kinley to Ely, August 10, 1894, in the Ely Papers.

34. Kinley to Ely, August 10, 11, 1894, in the Ely Papers; *Wisconsin State Journal*, August 16, 20, 1894.

35. *Wisconsin State Journal*, August 21, 1894; "Proceedings before Committee appointed by the Board of Regents to investigate and report concerning the charges made against Dr. Richard T. Ely contained in a communication written by State Superintendent Oliver E. Wells, Dated July 5th, 1894, and published in the *Nation* of New York, in its issue of July 12, 1894" (hereafter cited as "Proceedings Before the Investigating Committee"), document in the Papers, Board of Regents Meetings, University of Wisconsin Archives, p.1; Wells to Chynoweth, Dale, and Johnson, August 20, 1894, reprinted in the pamphlet, *The Ely Investigation: Communications of Superintendent Wells to the Investigating Committee*, 1–6.

36. Chynoweth, Dale, and Johnston to Wells, August 20, 1894, in Papers, Board of Regents Meetings; Records of the University of Wisconsin Regents, Vol. D, University of Wisconsin Archives.

37. "Proceedings Before the Investigating Committee," 1–38.

38. Ibid., 38–73.

39. *Wisconsin State Journal*, August 22, 1894; J. F. Klunk to Kinley, August 17, 1894, in the Ely Papers; *The Ely Investigation*, 6–10.

40. August 24, 1894; miscellaneous documents, manuscripts, and clippings among.the Papers, Board of Regents Meetings, University of Wisconsin Archives.

41. Untitled and undated manuscript addressed to Chynoweth, Dale, and Johnston, from internal evidence appearing to have been read at the August 20 hearing by either Ely or Jones, in Papers, Board of Regents Meetings; Ely to Shaw, August 8, 1894; Ely to Wilder, July 22, 1894, in the Ely Papers.

42. *Wisconsin State Journal*, August 20, 1894; Turner to Ely, August 4, 1894; Abbott to Ely, July 19, 1894, in the Ely Papers; Andres, quoted in *Wisconsin State Journal*, August 24, 1894, and August 3, 1894.

43. *Evangelist*, August 16, 1894; George Gates, *Kingdom*, August 24, 1894.

44. *Wisconsin State Journal*, August 7, 1894; Milwaukee *Wisconsin*, quoted in ibid., August 3, 1894; *The Milwaukee Journal*, quoted in ibid., August 10, 1894.

45. Curti and Carstensen, *The University of Wisconsin*, 1:457–58. 524.

46. Report by Chynoweth, Dale, and Johnston to the Board of Regents, September 18, 1894, in Papers, Board of Regents Meetings. For the authorship of the "sifting and winnowing" statement, see Theodore Herfurth, *Sifting and Winnowing: A Chapter in the History of Academic Freedom at the University of Wisconsin* (Madison, 1949), 12–13.

47. Report by Chynoweth, Johnston, and Dale to the Board of Regents, September 18, 1894, in Papers, Board of Regents Meetings; Reports of the University of Wisconsin Regents, Vol. D, 295; "Wells Displaced," unidentified newspaper clipping in Vol. 9 of Ely's personal scrapbooks, in the Ely Papers; *Wisconsin State Journal*, August 21, 1894; *Nation* 59:151 (August 30, 1894).

48. Page to Ely, August 20, 1894, in the Ely Papers; Richard T. Ely, "Fundamental Beliefs in My Social Philosophy," *Forum* 18:173–183 (October 1894).

49. Ibid., 183.

Sifting and Winnowing: A Chapter in the History of Academic Freedom at the University of Wisconsin

THEODORE HERFURTH

Dedication

Genevieve Gorst Herfurth, my wife, was a gracious member of the class of 1910. Her lamented demise occurred on December 26, 1943.

She had pride in the traditions of her class and recounted with fine pleasure her experiences as a member of it. In conversation she often referred to the class memorial tablet and quoted from it—particularly the words "that continual and fearless sifting and winnowing by which alone the truth can be found." Her references to the intriguing words gave original impulse to my desire to identify their author and, later, the incentive to examine and record available facts and legends relating to the tablet itself, the reasons underlying its initial rejection by the Regents, the cause of the five-year deferment of its authorized dedication, and, finally, its antecedent history.

To her revered memory this study is dedicated.

Theodore Herfurth

The Author

The author of this booklet, Mr. Theodore Herfurth, is one of the University of Wisconsin's most loyal friends. His interest in the University and concern for the welfare of its students span several generations of Wisconsin men and women.

He entered the University with the Class of 1894, and upon leaving it, became associated with his father in the conduct of an insurance business established many years before. Mr. Herfurth later became the chief executive of Theodore Herfurth, Inc., and serves in that capacity today.

In 1928 he established for senior men at the University of Wisconsin "The Theodore Herfurth Award for Initiative and Efficiency," and in 1943 a similar award for women; both evidence of his concern for the recognition and advancement of competency and achievement among Wisconsin students.

He also created a series of comparatively similar awards at Madison public high schools.

In addition to this effective aid in the University's scholarship program, Mr. Herfurth has made a sound contribution to his Alma Mater by writing this document concerning one of Wisconsin's historic events.

L. E. LUBERG
Assistant to the President, University of Wisconsin

Theodore Herfurth entered the University of Wisconsin–Madison as a member of the class of 1894. This paper was published as a booklet under the same title in 1948. It is reprinted here by permission of the Board of Regents of the University of Wisconsin System.

July 31, 1948

Preface

Bascom Hall is the citadel of power of the University of Wisconsin. In this building the Regents of the University officially convene. Theirs is the prerogative and the responsibility to establish, to defend, and to reserve the spiritual, the ethical, and the cultural values which comprise the essence of a great University. Securely riveted to the wall in the loggia, immediately to the left of the main entrance, is a tablet cast in enduring bronze In picturesque language the tablet heralds to the world that the University of Wisconsin is permanently dedicated to the principle of academic freedom. By reason of its location the plaque extends a greeting and flings a pertinent challenge to university officials and to the multitudes who enter Bascom Hall by its main portal. The tablet proclaims:

WHATEVER MAY BE THE LIMITATIONS WHICH TRAMMEL INQUIRY ELSEWHERE, WE BELIEVE THAT THE GREAT STATE UNIVERSITY OF WISCONSIN SHOULD EVER ENCOURAGE THAT CONTINUAL AND FEARLESS SIFTING AND WINNOWING BY WHICH ALONE THE TRUTH CAN BE FOUND.

Whence came this noble sentiment, and why? Upon whose excellent mind was the thought first mirrored, and whose facile pen etched it out in words so colorful and expressive? Perhaps the words "sifting and winnowing," thoughtfully penned by their author, hark back to that earlier day when he, himself, as a farm boy, may have been required to turn the crank of a winnowing machine, then very generally used by farmers, which separated chaff and refuse from good grain. That early experience and simple lesson may have prepared his mind for a master stroke of his pen in later years in framing a great declaration. At whose behest was this permanent declaration of academic freedom cast in bronze? By whose dictum, under what circumstances, and when was it erected in so prominent a place? To answer these and related questions is the object of this study

To all who have assisted in this reconstruction of the past, I express sincere appreciation.

Theodore Herfurth
Madison, Wisconsin
Spring, 1948

I

This story of the struggle for academic freedom at the University of Wisconsin begins with a political revolution in the year 1890. In the preceding year the Republican legislature, under Governor William D. Hoard, had passed the Bennett Law which brought all parochial schools under the control of the State Superintendent of Public Instruction. Despite the protests of those favoring complete independence for parochial schools the Republicans chose to support the Bennett Law in the election of 1890. The first plank of the party platform disclaimed any design "to interfere in any manner with such schools, either as to their terms, government, or branches to be taught therein," and argued that since the law was "wise and humane in all its essential purposes" it should not be repealed.

Opposedly, the last plank of the Democratic platform contended that the law represented needless interference with parental rights and liberty of conscience, and denounced the regulation as "unnecessary, unwise, unconstitutional, un-American and undemocratic." The Democrats demanded repeal.

In the campaign that followed, debate centered principally on the Bennett Law. Republicans plastered all parts of the state with placards bearing a picture of the little red school house and a legend urging support of the law. Their campaign failed. Except for the single term of Governor Taylor (1874–1876), the Republican party had dominated in Wisconsin since 1856. In 1890 the Republican control was broken. George W. Peck of Milwaukee, author of widely known stories about *Peck's Bad Boy*, became Democratic governor for two consecutive terms. Under Democratic auspices the legislature promptly repealed the Bennett Law.

The Democratic victory also elevated Oliver E. Wells, an obscure teacher from Appleton, to the office of State Superintendent of Public Instruction. He assumed his position July 1, 1892. By virtue of this office, Wells automatically became an *ex-officio* member of the Board of Regents of the University of Wisconsin. Within a few years he achieved notoriety by becoming the antagonist and violent public accuser of Professor Richard T. Ely, liberal director of the School of Economics, Political Science and History at the University.

Professor Ely had come to Wisconsin as one of America's most distinguished political economists. He had taken his doctorate at Heidelberg in 1879, and after 1881 had been a member of the faculty of the Johns Hopkins

University, then the foremost graduate institution in the United States. According to Professor Edward A. Ross, who had taken work with Ely at Hopkins, his courses were by far the most pervasive and influential offered in the social sciences. Long before he had moved to Madison, Ely had freed himself from orthodox free-trade economics and had pioneered with a realistic, inductive approach to the subject. Since his economics aimed at promoting the welfare of human beings, Ely's attentions turned frequently to the concerns of the workaday world. He had a special interest in organized labor, an interest which involved him in dispute with Oliver E. Wells shortly after his removal to Madison.

Labor relations had been untroubled in Wisconsin's capital city prior to Ely's arrival. Then in the winter of 1892–93 a union organizer named Klunk, of Kansas City, came to town to organize the printers of the Democrat Printing Company. In January the printers struck, just as the company began fulfillment of its contract for state printing, which in that year amounted to more than $25,000. The company imported strike breakers and housed them in upper rooms of the Democrat building. There were numerous fights, clubbings, a stabbing in a North Pinckney Street saloon, and other disorders between strikers and strike breakers. A lockout followed the failure of the strike.

Within seven weeks there was another unsuccessful strike, this time at the shop of Tracy-Gibbs Printing Company. Five weeks before the strike Professor Ely called on W. A. Tracy to urge him to unionize his shop. At the time Ely was secretary and member of the executive committee of the Christian Social Union, an organization which sought to apply Christian principles and pressures to the solution of social problems. The printing of the organization's periodical was in Ely's hands, and it was his expressed desire to have this work done in a union shop. When he spoke to Tracy about the desirability of unionizing his shop he coupled the request with a veiled hint that unless the shop were organized the officers of the Christian Social Union might require him to withdraw the printing from Tracy-Gibbs. Ely spoke to Tracy five weeks before the strike, during the strike, and again after the strike, always in the same vein. His suggestions were adroitly discreet: in personal capacity he never threatened a boycott. However, Tracy thought he could divine the professor's intent.

While talking with Tracy about the strike, Superintendent Wells heard of Ely's urgings in the matter. Wells also interviewed strikers at the Democrat company, from whom he gained the impression that Ely had not only fomented their strike, but had also conferred with, advised, and entertained Klunk, the organizer. His suspicions aroused, Wells then read Ely's new book, *Socialism: An Examination of Its Strength and Its Weakness*, with *Suggestions for Social Reform*. Wells' hasty conclusion was that the book was a piece of rank socialistic propaganda.

Convinced that Ely was an economic heretic, Wells resolved to move against him. Several times he complained to President Charles Kendall Adams and the Regents about Ely's diabolical practices and teachings. They were not interested. Disappointed by his inability to get official action, Wells decided to make public charges against Ely, charges which would force the Regents to take cognizance and settle the question for all time.

On July 5, 1894, Wells prepared a scathing, excoriating and denunciatory letter which *The Nation* published under the heading, "The College Anarchist." It read as follows:

TO THE EDITOR OF THE NATION:

Sir: Your statement in the last *Nation*, to the effect that there is a sort of moral justification for attacks upon life and property based upon a theory which comes from the colleges, libraries, and lecture rooms, and latterly from the churches, is supported by the teaching and the practice of the University of Wisconsin.

Professor Ely, director of the School of Economics, believes in strikes and boycotts, justifying and encouraging the one while practicing the other. Somewhat more than a year ago a strike occurred in the office of the Democrat Printing Company, the state printers. An agitator or walking delegate came from Kansas City to counsel and assist the strikers. He was entertained at Professor Ely's house and was in constant consultation with him. A little later a strike occurred in another printing office in this city, in which Professor Ely was also an abettor and counselor. He also demanded of the proprietors that their office should be made into a union office, threatening to take his printing away if they did not comply. (They were publishing a paper for him as secretary of some organization or association.) Upon the refusal of his repeated demands, Professor Ely withdrew his printing, informing them that he had always been in the habit of dealing with union offices. In conversation with one of the proprietors he asserted that where a skilled workman was needed a dirty, dissipated, unmarried, unreliable, and unskilled man should be employed in preference to an industrious, skillful, trustworthy, non-union man who is the head of a family. He also stated that the latter would have no ground of complaint, as he could easily remove the objections to him by joining the union, and that conscientious scruples against joining the union would prove the individual to be a crank.

Such is Ely the citizen and business man—an individual who can say to citizens and taxpayers, "Stand and deliver, or down goes your business," and to the laboring men, "Join the union or starve with your families." Professor Ely, director of the School of Economics, differs from Ely, the socialist, only in the adroit and covert method of his advocacy. A careful reading of his books will discover essentially the same principles, but masked by glittering generalities and mystical and metaphysical statements, susceptible of various interpretations according as a too liberal interpretation might seem for the time likely to work discomfort or loss to the writer. His books are having a considerable sale, being recommended and advertised by the University and pushed by publisher and dealers. Except where studiously indefinite and ambiguous, they have the merit of such simplicity of statements as makes them easily read by the uneducated. They abound in sanctimonious and pious cant, pander to the prohibitionist, and ostentatiously sympathize with all who are in distress. So manifest an appeal to the religious, the moral, and the unfortunate, with promise of help to all insures at the outset a large public. Only the careful student will discover their utopian, impracticable and pernicious doctrines, but their general acceptance would furnish a seeming moral justification of attack on life and property such as this country has already become too familiar with.[1]

Within a few days the Wells letter had been reprinted in the New York *Post*, and from there many other newspapers reprinted the story with varying comments. Wells had proceeded effectively. He had precipitated so highly embarrassing a situation that the Regents[2] could not afford to ignore it. A prompt hearing of the case became imperative.

The board appointed a committee to investigate the charges. Members of the committee were H. W. Chynoweth of Madison, chairman, Dr. H. B. Dale of Oshkosh, and John Johnston of Milwaukee. The committee decided that the Wells letter should constitute the complaint, and that the scope of the hearing should be limited to the charges that Ely had encouraged and fomented strikes in Madison, that he had practiced boycotts against nonunion shops, and that he had taught socialism and other vicious theories to students at the University. The committee decided against a complete investigation of Ely's books, lectures and professional papers.

Since Ely was in New York on a lecture engagement when the crisis developed, the defense of his interests was voluntarily taken over by his friends. David Kinley, a former Ely student who later became president of the University of Illinois, and Frederick Jackson Turner, the noted historian, busied themselves in his behalf. They collected evidence, and engaged one of Madison's most skilled and scholarly attorneys, Burr W. Jones, to represent the economist before the Regents' committee.[3]

Both Wells and Ely were summoned to the first hearing, scheduled for the evening of August 10, 1894 in the senior classroom of the Law Building. Many students, faculty members and prominent townspeople were present, as were Ely and his attorney. Wells did not appear. Instead he sent a letter, explaining and justifying his absence, and protesting against the limited scope of the trial; he was particularly anxious to investigate all of Ely's professional writings.[4]

In an effort to lure Wells to the next session, the committee wrote a letter assuring him a full and impartial hearing, and urging him to appear on the evening of August 21. This time he came, reinforced by a distinguished local attorney, Colonel George W. Bird. The latter operated at a disadvantage, for he had been called into the case so suddenly that he had no time to interview witnesses or make other necessary preparations. Ely's attorney suffered under no similar handicap. The accused also enjoyed the advantage of a large and sympathetic audience. As points were scored by Ely, the audience registered approval with noisy applause, much to the discomfiture of Wells and his attorney, who threatened to withdraw if demonstrations of favoritism continued.

One of the first to testify before the committee was Thomas Reynolds, a striker at the Democrat office. Presumably he could offer proof that Ely had been involved in that dispute. Colonel Bird tried to compel Reynolds to admit that he had said that Ely had conferred with and counseled the organizer, Klunk. Reynolds declared that if he had ever thought that Ely was involved, he had been mistaken; that if he had said that Ely was implicated it was because someone had unreliably told him so; and that he, personally, had no such knowledge. Unable to get worthwhile testimony from Reynolds, Bird found it impossible to prove that Ely had encouraged a strike.

When W. A. Tracy, the printer, was called to the stand he testified that, although on three separate occasions Ely had urged him to unionize his shop, he had not coupled it with a threat that he personally might assume responsibility for taking the Christian Social Union's printing to another establishment. In fact, even though Tracy's shop remained unorganized, Ely had left the printing with Tracy. In view of this it was impossible to prove that Ely had practiced a boycott.

Had Ely indoctrinated students with socialist ideas? Wells demanded that all of the professor's pamphlets, books, lectures and professional papers be investigated as pertinent to this question. Chairman Chynoweth laughingly rejected this suggestion as involving too stupendous and irrelevant a task. Wells and Bird, who assumed such an exploration was implicit in the promise of a full and impartial hearing, were tremendously dissatisfied with the chairman's ruling. With Wells in full retreat the hearings were adjourned until the evening of August 23.[5]

Once again Wells failed to appear, and once again he submitted a lengthy letter expressing dissatisfaction with the narrow scope of the trial. Despite the fact that his letter repeated many charges previously made, it contained one important admission: "It is proper to state that I am unable to establish the correctness of the information upon which I made the statement in my letter of July 5th to *The Nation*, that the walking delegate from Kansas City was entertained at Professor Ely's house and was in constant consultation with him, or that Professor Ely's connection with the strike in the Democrat Printing Company's office was as there stated." However, he insisted that since Ely had urged unionization on the firm of Tracy-Gibbs company, he had, "whether intentionally or not . . . aided and abetted this strike."

After the Wells communication had been read at the third session, formal trial procedure was abandoned at the suggestion of Ely's attorney. The meeting was then thrown open to the search for truth, wherever found. At this juncture David Kinley presented a letter he had received from Klunk, the organizer. Klunk reported that while at Madison he had had a long conference with one he had assumed to be Ely at the professor's seminar room in the old Fuller Opera House, now the Parkway Theatre. Klunk made a point of describing the physical appearance of his conferee; the description obviously did not fit Ely. It did fit a student in Ely's seminar, H. H. Powers, so the supposition was that Powers, and not Ely, had conferred with the labor organizer. At that time both Ely and Powers wore short full beards. This superficial similarity might have led to error in identification. The Klunk letter made a profound impression on those present at the hearing; its effect was an alibi for Ely.

This was followed by a reading of many letters, highly commendatory of Ely, over the signatures of prominent American economists, historians and educators. E. Benjamin Andrews, president of Brown University, wrote that Ely was America's most influential teacher of political economy. "For your novel university to depose him," declared Andrews, "would be a great blow at freedom of university teaching in general and at the development of political economy in particular." Carroll D. Wright, United States Commissioner of

Labor, offered the opinion that Ely had given workingmen catholic views of their relations to industry and society. "His influence upon workingmen has been the influence of the pulpit," Wright averred. Dr. Albert Shaw, writer and editor, observed that Ely's teachings and writings, considered in their totality, encouraged reverence for government, law and order. President Charles Kendall Adams of Wisconsin who had undertaken an analysis of Ely's *Socialism* for the committee, reported that "From the beginning of the book there is not a paragraph or a sentence that can be interpreted as an encouragement of lawlessness or disorder." Granting that parts of the book, taken out of context, might suggest a sympathy for socialism, Adams insisted that "I am utterly unable to see how any careful reader can read the whole of the book without commending the fairness of its spirit and the general elevation of its tone and without conceding that the reasoning of the author leads away from socialism rather than towards it." When the reading of testimonials had been finished the dramatic trial of Richard T. Ely was brought to a close.[6]

It was evident that Wells had lost his case, and that Regents Chynoweth, Dale and Johnston would submit a report exonerating Ely. Another matter was less evident. During the course of the trial little had been said about the question of academic freedom. Would the Regents be content with clearing the accused, or would they use the occasion to publicize some larger statement favorable to academic freedom?

On September 18, 1894, the trial committee submitted its final report to the board. The report, unanimously adopted, exonerated Ely, and heralded the board's devotion to academic freedom:

> As Regents of a university with over a hundred instructors supported by nearly two millions of people who hold a vast diversity of views regarding the great questions which at present agitate the human mind, we could not for a moment think of recommending the dismissal or even the criticism of a teacher even if some of his opinions should, in some quarters, be regarded as visionary. Such a course would be equivalent to saying that no professor should teach anything which is not accepted by everybody as true. This would cut our curriculum down to very small proportions. We cannot for a moment believe that knowledge has reached its final goal, or that the present condition of society is perfect. We must therefore welcome from our teachers such discussions as shall suggest the means and prepare the way by which knowledge may be extended, present evils be removed and others prevented. We feel that we would be unworthy of the position we hold if we did not believe in progress in all departments of knowledge. In all lines of academic investigation it is of the utmost importance that the investigator should be absolutely

free to follow the indications of truth wherever they may lead. Whatever may be the limitations which trammel inquiry elsewhere we believe the great state University of Wisconsin should ever encourage that continual and fearless sifting and winnowing by which alone the truth can be found.[7]

The outcome of the Ely trial, and especially the proclamation of academic freedom, were given wide publicity by the press. Years later Richard T. Ely could pridefully refer to the Regents' report as "that famous pronunciamento of academic freedom which has been a beacon light in higher education in this country, not only for Wisconsin, but for all similar institutions, from that day to this. Their declaration on behalf of academic freedom . . . has become to be regarded as part of the Wisconsin Magna Charta. . . ."[8]

II

This entire study had its inception in a desire to identify the author of the "sifting and winnowing" motto for which the University of Wisconsin has become famous. When inquiries on this point were first addressed to friends at the University, two candidates for the honor of authorship were prominently mentioned. Attention was called to the declaration of the elder La Follette that "This declaration of freedom was framed by Herbert W. Chynoweth, then a member of the board. . . ."[9]

Contradicting this, however, was the assertion of J. F. A. Pyre, historian of the University: "The sentences were written by President Adams, though they have sometimes been ascribed to the chairman of the committee which reported them to the Board of Regents."[10] The association between Professor Pyre and President Adams had been quite intimate, so that Pyre might well have had direct evidence on the authorship of the well-known words. Unfortunately, neither Pyre nor La Follette bolstered his nomination with supporting testimony.

Of the major participants in the Ely trial, Ely was the sole survivor when this study was undertaken in 1942. Inquiry disclosed that at that time Ely was in his 89th year, was living in semi-retirement near New York City, and was in declining health. It was not known whether Ely could or would bear evidence as to the authorship of the words on the tablet. Of all living men it seemed patent that he, the defendant in the trial of 1894, should have such first-hand knowledge. He had had the friendship, the aid, and presumably also the confidence of President Adams in 1894. His testimony, if obtainable, was vital to the purposes of this study.

At the request of the author, three of Ely's close acquaintances successively consented to solicit a statement from Ely. The three letters were written at varying intervals because of Ely's failure to make seasonably reply to the first two inquiries. However, he did make prompt answer to the letter addressed to him by W. S. Kies, a prominent New York alumnus who was closely associated with Ely for a number of years and was one of the trustees of Ely's Foundation.

The text of the letter appears below.

About the same time Professor E. E. Witte also received an answer from Ely, offering the same emphatic information. It is evident that the quest was initiated seasonably. Ely died in the following year.

The Alfred T. Rogers mentioned in the Ely letter was the son-in-law of H. W. Chynoweth, chairman of the hearing committee.

In view of this evidence each reader may decide for himself whether or not, in the spirit of the motto, the truth has been found.

June 8, 1942

Mr. W. S. Kies,
Graybar Building,
New York, N.Y.

Dear Kies:

In reply to your inquiry of June 3, the words were undoubtedly written by C. K. Adams. Adams told me so, himself, and the internal evidence bears this out. It was a style natural to Adams and not to Chynoweth.

I have only pleasant recollections of Chynoweth and only praise for his conduct of the trial but he did not and could not have written those words. La Follette was mistaken and naturally so, because Chynoweth, as Chairman, signed the whole report although he did not write it all.

I have had a number of inquiries from various people in Madison, recently, on this same point, including a letter from Alfred T. Rogers and Professor Witte. I wonder what the origin of all these inquiries could be.

I am feeling quite well, again and spent a part of this morning weeding our corn which is about knee high.

With best regards,
Faithfully yours,
Richard T. Ely

III

Even though the declaration of 1894 had put the University on record as favoring academic freedom, the principle and the practice were not guaranteed simply by a declaration. In 1910, and again in 1915, bitter battles were fought over the principle; in these struggles the Regents and the Class of 1910 were the chief combatants.

Political considerations were important in 1910. The dominant Republican party in Wisconsin was split into two factions: the Stalwarts and the Progressives. The Progressives, led by Robert M. La Follette, were also known to their opponents as Liberals, Radicals, Socialists and La Folletteites. Stalwarts were awarded the uncomplimentary titles of Standpatters, Reactionaries, Monopolists and Tories; of these labels, that of Tory seemed most invidious. During the campaign these names were freely applied, adding to the intensity of feeling. When the ballots were counted, the Progressive action emerged victorious.

Divisions within the Republican party were reflected in the University. Undergraduates, and especially the members of the Class of 1910, seem to have been overwhelmingly and ardently pro–La Follette. During the election year the Regents sensed that a "radical" element controlled class politics, while classmen felt that Stalwart sentiment predominated among the Regents. There is little doubt that political partisanship affected the contests between classmen and Regents.

All Regents[11] on the board in January, 1910, either had been appointed or reappointed by Governor James O. Davidson, a leader of the Stalwarts after his split with La Follette in 1906. While no completely reliable check can be made now, available evidence suggests that of the fifteen members of the 1910 board, ten were Stalwarts and five Progressives. That partisanship was not unknown was amply testified to by the resignation of W. D. Hoard in 1911. In a letter of resignation, addressed to Governor Francis E. McGovern, Hoard wrote:

> I hereby tender my resignation from the Board of University Regents to take effect at once. Failing health and an unwillingness to longer remain as a member of a body that has lately been reconstructed upon the basis and for the main purpose of political partisanship for the La Follette faction in politics are my chief reasons for resigning. I do not believe that a great state school like our University can be wisely, honestly or efficiently administered from so narrow a standpoint.[12]

This was the response of a Stalwart who disapproved the liberal reconstruction of the board after 1910.

Prior to 1910 the liberal press lost no opportunity to heckle and criticize the Regents. In 1908 the Milwaukee *Journal* reported that "There is considerable talk that reactionary members of the Board of Regents believe that teachings in some departments of the University are too liberal and that they propose to limit it even if they have to interfere with the pedagogical management. . . . " John R. Commons, Richard T. Ely and Edward A. Ross were the professors reported to be most eligible for the lash. The *Journal* alleged that President Van Hise, who was known to be close to La Follette, was having difficulties with the board. At the beginning of his regime Van Hise had laid great stress upon research as a basis for academic advancement. In a direct attack on this position the Regents were said to have adopted a promotion policy in which teaching counted as heavily as research. "Some claim," said the *Journal*, "that research work has resulted in the class of discussion to which a majority of the Regents object."[13]

Professor E. A. Gilmore of the law faculty was reputed to have courted Regent displeasure with his researches on the right of the state to control its water powers. Gilmore, who subsequently became vice-governor of the Philippines and later president of the University of Iowa, had prepared a brief favorable to state control, at the request of a legislative committee. Among the Regents were two who were interested in private exploitation of water power, and reportedly these gentlemen had censured the law professor for jeopardizing their interests. The alleged Gilmore censure was widely discussed and did little to promote good feeling between students and faculty on the one hand and Regents on the other.

Conflicts within the University were sharpened by other episodes of the years 1909 and 1910. The first of these involved Lincoln Steffens, the muckraking journalist who had set out to expose La Follette. However, after conferences with La Follette, he not only experienced complete conversion, but became a militant advocate of La Follette's entire political philosophy. In February, 1909, Steffens published in the *American Magazine* an article captioned, "Sending a State to College." The article was highly complimentary to the University of Wisconsin, and to President Van Hise and his extension program in particular. However, in a paragraph on academic freedom, Steffens hurled a shaft at the Regents. "The conclusion I drew from talks with both sides," wrote Steffens, "both the Tory Regents and the 'radical' instructors, was that while there are no 'Socialists' on the faculty, there are several men who are more radical than they dare to teach. They do 'the best they can'; they 'suggest' the truth, but as one of them put it, 'we have to smear it a little.'[14] Steffens' comments were not appreciated by the Regents.

Less than a year after Steffens had cast doubt on the board's devotion to academic freedom, an incident involving Emma Goldman, the anarchist, and Edward A. Ross, professor of sociology, seemed to lend confirmation to the doubt. Emma Goldman visited Madison between January 25 and 27, 1910. During this time she met with the student Socialist Club at the Y.M.C.A., and delivered an evening lecture downtown. For each appearance she had a goodly audience, which included many university students and members of the faculty. Professor Ross was accused of displaying undue friendship for the lecturer: he was charged with announcing her evening address to his classes, and of escorting her around the university campus. Much of the state press was furious at Ross, at the University, and at Emma Goldman.

The cries of the rabid were not completely justified. As a local newspaper reported, "Those who attended the lecture . . . for the purpose of seeing bombs thrown or listening to inflammable utterances, were doomed to disappointment. The proceedings were entirely orderly and good-mannered to the last degree."[15] As for Ross' part in the incident, he tells his own story best:

> . . . About this time Emma Goldman came to town to lecture on Anarchism and on my way to class I learned of infuriated patriots tearing down her posters. This struck me as not quite sportsmanlike and, since the topic of the day was Tolerance, I characterized such manifestations as anti-social and un-American, thereby calling attention to the Goldman lecture.
>
> I did not attend it, but the next morning Miss Goldman called on me at my office, and I took her over the campus pointing out its beauties. Promptly the newspapers shrieked that I was an anarchist; and then certain financiers and capitalists on the Board of Regents (clever team-work!) solemnly shook their heads and gave it out to the newspapers as their pondered opinion that I was not fit to remain at Wisconsin. This was sheer pose, for President Van Hise told me my real offense was publishing *Sin and Society*, and that for more than two years certain Regents had been looking for a pretext to oust me.[16]

On January 31, four days after Emma Goldman's departure, Parker Sercombe of Chicago lectured in the classroom of Professor Ross, without prior approval of university authorities. For some time Sercombe had sought an invitation to address Ross' large sociology class; finally Ross permitted him to come to Madison to talk on "Education in a Democracy." Ross said Sercombe's educational theories were "not without merit," but this was lost sight of when word leaked out that Sercombe was an advocate of free love. Ross recalls:

> Promptly Chicago sources supplied the Wisconsin capitalistic newspapers with certain half-baked proposals of his regarding marriage, which had not come to my attention, and their readers were told. "This is the sort of man Professor Ross allows to address his class. Your sons and daughters at the University of Wisconsin run the risk of being corrupted."[17]

Matters were made worse when Sercombe used his acceptance at the University to advertise himself as a lecturer. Again the press yielded to violent outbursts and the Regents were furious at the unwarranted assumption of academic privilege by Ross.

When the board met on March 2, 1910, the greater part of their deliberations was taken up with the Goldman and Sercombe incidents. As a result of the discussions a resolution of censure was unanimously adopted by the board. The resolution declared:

> WHEREAS, it has come to the knowledge of the Board of Regents that Professor E. A. Ross of the department of sociology in our University has invited to lecture in the University and under its auspices, persons whose record and expressed views are subversive of good morals, therefore be it
> RESOLVED, by this Board of Regents that we strongly disapprove of such action, and that the President of the University is requested to inform Professor Ross of the censure of the board and their unanimous disapproval of his indiscretions.[18]

Without the support of courageous President Van Hise, Ross probably would have been ousted. When called upon to make a formal report on the Goldman and Sercombe incidents, Van Hise strongly opposed any summary action, and warned that the faculty would rise in defense of Ross if necessary. Said Van Hise:

> . . . it has been suggested that Professor Ross be removed from his professorship in the University. I do not know whether or not this suggestion is to be seriously considered; but it is clear to me that such an action would be wholly indefensible. In the first place it would be an injustice; for the mistakes which Professor Ross has made are not sufficiently grave to have more weight than

years of service as a teacher highly appreciated by his students, including many of the higher grade; second the removal of a professor on the grounds considered would damage the University most seriously in the eyes of the academic world. The effects of such a drastic action as the removal of a professor holding a continuing appointment for so inadequate a cause would not be overcome for years.[19]

Ross was in China when his fate was decided. At Vancouver and Shanghai he had received cables from Van Hise warning him to expect the worst. He was worried, for he foresaw a return to American with no academic chair waiting for him. Two weeks after his arrival in China he attended a missionary service in Peking, where Luther's "A Mighty Fortress Is Our God" was sung:

As we sang I recalled *his* daring and compared what *he* faced with what *I* faced. Luther's fighting spirit rose in me, I worried no more but from then on gave my whole attention to studying the Chinese. In April a cable from the staunch Van Hise notified me that the motion to oust me failed. Playing for time he had been able to gather protests from so many liberals out in the state that some of the hostile Regents lost their nerve and an adverse majority was converted into a minority.[20]

How were these episodes viewed by the members of the Class of 1910? Did they see in the 1910 occurrences a resurgence of the unenlightened bigotry which in 1894 had placed in jeopardy the tenure of Richard T. Ely? The class leaders thought this was the case. Soon they would set in motion a project designed either to make unavoidable an official rededication of the University to the principle of academic freedom laid down in 1894, or, if that should fail, to expose the Regents to the peril of widespread public criticism.

IV

For at least two decades Wisconsin graduating classes had left memorials, usually gravestones bearing class numerals, to be placed in the woodlot behind Main Hall. The presentation and acceptance of the memorial had become a traditional feature of Class Day exercises prior to 1910. As events proved, the presentation of the 1910 memorial was of special significance in the history of the University.

While the Goldman and Sercombe episodes were still under discussion the Class of 1910 was busy with class politics. One candidate for the presidency, James S. Thompson, campaigned on a platform which called for the popular selection of the class memorial and guarantee of its dedication at graduation time.[21] Despite the fact that Thompson lost the election to Francis Ryan Duffy on March 18, 1910, his voice was heard when the memorial committee considered the selection of a gift.[22] Thompson urged that no gravestone mark the resting place of the Class of 1910; instead he recommended that the class memorialize itself through the 1894 academic-freedom proclamation, the statement to be cast in bronze and erected in a prominent place on the campus.

This novel suggestion did not originate with Thompson. It came from Lincoln Steffens. While preparing his article on the University, Steffens had discovered the 1894 statement, and had expressed regret that it had never been adequately publicized and preserved. To Fred MacKenzie, managing editor of *La Follette's Magazine*, he suggested the use of the class memorial to rededicate the Regents to the 1894 principle. Through MacKenzie the suggestion was transmitted to James S. Thompson, and through Thompson to the memorial committee. "I can still recall very definitely that Fred called me out from luncheon one day at the Phi Kappa Psi house to propose this idea," said Thompson. "He cautioned me against revealing too much of the source of the subject for fear that political discussion or argument might hamper the execution. He and I agreed that the idea was fundamentally excellent and that political implications ought not to be permitted to interfere with its successful adoption by the class. Fred was always enthusiastically gleeful in observing the success of our efforts."[23]

Even though the majority of the classmen had not the slightest hint that Lincoln Steffens had conceived their memorial, the suggestion seemed so reasonable that it was quickly agreed upon. Hugo Hering, chairman of the memorial committee, recalls the homely manufacture of the much-publicized plaque:

> I personally prepared the pattern of the Tablet for casting. It was purely a hand-made job, in which I used a three-ply wood veneer panel as a background. I bought white metal letters, such as used by Pattern Makers, and fastened these letters to the veneer back. Each letter had prongs on the reverse side, and after being properly aligned, was hammered down into the wood. I carted the pattern to the Madison Brass Foundry, and Henry Vogts made the casting, at a cost of $25.00.[24]

With the plaque ready for dedication, class officers approached the Regents on the matter of its acceptance and erection. The members of the board were cool and evasive. Some asserted that as individuals they could not grant approval; that the question must be decided by the entire board at a formal meeting; that there would be no formal meeting prior to graduation day, at which time it would be too late. Others objected that the classmen had bypassed President Van Hise in bringing the question before the board directly; others that the approach had been too oblique, through the board's secretary and executive committee. There was also an opinion that it would be inadvisable to extend to each graduating class the privilege of prescribing the character and placement of its memorial gift. Like Laocoön, high priest of Apollo at Troy, the Regents feared the Greeks even though bearing gifts.[25]

Baffled and disappointed, but determined to wring eventual victory from present defeat, the classmen conducted the traditional Class Day exercises on June 20, 1910. Despite the withholding of Regent approval, class orator Carl F. Naffz of Madison presented the tablet to the University. Genial and popular Professor William A. Scott of the School of Commerce accepted the plaque and made the response. His response must have been made in purely personal capacity, however, for the record shows that Scott's acceptance was authorized neither by the Regents nor the faculty. The response seems to have been Scott's valorous gesture of friendship towards the class and its project.

If the classmen hoped that Scott's gesture would effect a transfer of the gift to the University, their hope died quickly. On June 22, two days after the exercises, the following entry was made in the records of the Board of Regents:

> A request from the President of the senior class to place a memorial tablet in one of several locations named was presented and was referred on motion of Regent Thwaits, with second by Regent Keller, to President Van Hise with instructions to notify the class why the request could not be granted.

While the record gave no hint of the explanation which Van Hise was to offer, newspaper reports summarized the ostensible reason. A local paper said the Regents were opposed to "making a 'graveyard' out of the university grounds," and they hesitated to "establish a precedent which would lead to the mutilation of the buildings. . . ."[26] Regent Magnus Swenson was quoted as saying, "You know, they allowed that to occur some years ago until the campus began looking like a graveyard and then they dug up all the old memorials and put them back in the woods. People pass by and say, 'Well, who's buried there?'"[27]

On the day that the governing board decided against accepting and erecting the memorial, President Van Hise, in his commencement address, spoke on the dangers to state universities from political control, from the demand for returns measurable in dollars and cents, and from restrictions on freedom of teaching. This did not imply that Van Hise was championing the memorial crusade. As one Regent recalled, Van Hise "showed considerable feeling at the want of courtesy on the part of the students in not having in any way consulted him about this tablet, and appeared to be against its acceptance by the Regents."[28]

After commencement a report was circulated that the class planned to buy a piece of property four feet square, on State Street, on which to erect the memorial.[29] Nothing came of this enterprise. Meantime the classmen carried their case to the newspapers. The item most cordially resented by the Regents was an interview given out by class president Francis R. Duffy. Duffy announced that President Van Hise's conservation work had "met with opposition from some interests in the state which do not have the public welfare as their basis." He recalled that Professor Gilmore had been rebuked by the water-power interests and declared that "At about the same time another member of the faculty was instructed not to carry on certain research work in connection with the early history of Wisconsin." These incidents inspired the Class of 1910 to select their special memorial, for the class believed "the search for truth should not be interfered with, in a great university. . . ." Events of 1910 also raised the question of how long Wisconsin could retain its place as the leading state university, and as a university of the people, "if the Regents will not allow members of the faculty to express their honest convictions on problems that are of interest to all the people, or at least object to their doing so." Duffy promised that Regent rejection of the memorial tablet would be widely publicized in newspaper and magazine articles during the next few months, and named Lincoln Steffens as a likely commentator.[30]

The stir created by the classmen was heard in high political councils in the fall of 1910. On September 28, a Progressive-dominated Republican platform convention met at Madison. Whether as a gesture of partisanship towards the Class of 1910, or of reproach to the Regents, or merely as a remarkable coincidence, one plank of the Republican platform pledged the party to the defense of the 1894 view of academic freedom.

Not until 1912 was the memorial question reconsidered by the Regents.

The minutes of the Board meeting of April 25, 1912, record that:

> The matter of the memorial tablet of the Class of 1910 was brought up for consideration. On motion of Regent Mahoney, second by Regent Seaman, the tablet was accepted, Regent Jones voting "No."

Significantly, nothing was said about the erection of the plaque. If unerected, the purpose of the class would be thwarted.

Meantime, what had become of the tablet? Soon after its original rejection it had been carried, by parties unknown, to the dingy basement of the Administration Building. There it accumulated dust and cobwebs for five years, until rescued by the 1910 alumni in the spring of 1915.

V

At the time of the plaque's rejection classmen suspected that the defacement of buildings and grounds had little to do with the board's adverse decision, though this was the announced basis of the action. In 1942 ex-Regent C. P. Cary, who had participated in the 1910 decision, was asked whether the Regents were primarily interested in discouraging graduating classes from thinking that whatever memorials they might tender would necessarily be accepted and erected by the board. "It is quite possible that such was the minor purpose in the minds of some Regents," replied Cary, "but that was not the chief reason for the rejection."

As seen by Cary, how did the board view the 1910 situation? Were the Regents distressed by the attentions paid Emma Goldman, and did they assume that a considerable number of students had radical inclinations? "Yes, beyond question," said Cary. "The dominating element in the Class of 1910 might have presented such a plaque if there had been no Emma Goldman visit to Madison, but it is highly improbable." The Regents also knew there were some radicals among the students and faculty, but "like the humorist who thought a reasonable number of fleas were good for a dog, the Regents did not bother about it. In fact, most of them were pleased to have it so; they did not desire a dead sameness of views."

Did the Regents believe that the Class of 1910 was under the influence of some radical political element which made acceptance of the tablet undesirable? "There was a suspicion that such might be the case," said Cary. "The student radicals may have been stimulated to activity by politicians, at least encouraged by the general political upheaval. In fact I think they were."

Did the Regents assume that in tendering the plaque the class was aiming an unmerited thrust at the board, one which implied that the Regents were ultra-conservative industrialists and politicians opposed to academic freedom? "To this question my answer is *yes*," replied Cary. "No single Regent was opposed to the working or sentiment of the plaque—except the gratuitous fling in the opening sentence at other institutions that might be cramped in their instruction—but they were opposed to being slapped in the face without occasion for it." Cary recalled that "It was the entire situation and spirit of it all that was resented. The spirit as the Regents interpreted it was something like this: There, dern ye, take that dose and swallow it. You don't dare refuse it even if it gags you, and it probably will."

What induced the board to accept the tablet, but not erect it, in 1912? Cary's recollection was that "The representatives of the class of 1910 came back in 1912 to the Regents in a chastened spirit; admitted mistakes on their part, as I recall it. Politics had settled down in the meantime. As before stated, the board unanimously approved, in the abstract, the principle of freedom in the university classrooms."[31]

The Class of 1910 looked upon Granville D. Jones as the Regent who most strongly opposed the acceptance and erection of the tablet. As Francis R. Duffy informed a Regent in 1915, "Regent Jones of Wausau has been the backbone of the opposition and has really constituted practically the only opposition to the acceptance of this memorial. You are aware that Mr. Jones has been closely identified with the water-power interests in his section of the state. In fact, he told me himself."[32] A man strong in opinion and forthright in expression, Jones never wearied of resisting affronts to the Regents, and never abandoned the opinion that the memorial tablet was intended as an affront. Hiding behind the plaque he saw the figures of Lincoln Steffens, Fred MacKenzie of *La Follette's Magazine*, and Richard Lloyd Jones, Progressive editor of the Wisconsin *State Journal*. "I know that the inspiration of this memorial tablet was vile," Jones told his fellow board members. "I believe the class was duped and made use of for the purpose of discrediting the Regents."[33] To class president Duffy he wrote, "I have always considered that the attempt of a lot of malicious and vicious pups to use your class as a 'cat's paw' for their own selfish purposes was monstrous."[34]

According to Jones, the students had never known the truth about the Ross and Gilmore incidents. "They were incited by mischievous persons and with the enthusiasm and loyalty of youth, reached the conclusion that the Regents of the University, or at least some of them, were endeavoring to interfere with academic freedom and the search for truth. . . ." Jones assured the misinformed that there was "no Regent action that school year which interfered or attempted to interfere in any way with reasonable academic freedom." When the memorial was rejected he "anticipated there would be a good deal of magazine and newspaper discussion of the matter, in which Mr. Lincoln Steffens of evil memory would participate."[35]

Regent Jones had no special regard for the noble phrases of the memorial tablet. "So far as the words on your tablet are concerned," he wrote to Duffy, "they are only objectionable in connection with the time and manner of their application."[36] To his brethren on the board he confided, "The sentiment on this tablet, though somewhat dogmatic, is harmless and inoffensive. So, for that matter, is the multiplication table and all the axioms. This, however, does not justify inscribing them on monuments and posing them on the university buildings and grounds. The purpose of this tablet was to wantonly insult the then Regents."[37]

Had the class intended to insult the Regents? According to one classman who should have known, "The motive was simply to commit the University to a policy of academic freedom which seemed to have been infringed by the Goldman and other incidents."[38] Never did the Regents win any admission that insults were intended.

In view of the testimony offered by the Regents themselves, it is evident that the 1910 board did not reject the plaque primarily because it threatened to deface university buildings. They rejected it because they despised Lincoln Steffens, who fathered the project. They rejected it because they saw in it an attempt of Wisconsin Progressives and student radicals to embarrass a Stalwart board. They rejected it because they could not agree that the board's behavior in the Ross episode constituted a violation of academic freedom.

VI

By the spring of 1915 the stage was set for the final act in the drama of the memorial plaque. There were new faces, and a new balance of power, in the Board of Regents.[39] Whereas the 1910 board had numbered ten Stalwarts and five Progressives, the 1915 body was made up of nine Progressives and six Stalwarts. The ascendancy of the liberal element was an omen favoring peace between the board and the Class of 1910. Early antagonisms had lost much of their sharpness, so that even the Stalwarts, except for G. D. Jones, were prepared to look with favor on the memorial tablet.

The approaching class reunion inspired a new sense of urgency among the class leaders in 1915. Francis R. Duffy still retained the presidency; he, together with Milton J. Blair, attendance chairman, and William J. Meuer, general reunion chairman, organized the homecoming. It was agreed that Regent approval of the dedication and erection of the memorial would constitute the greatest inducement in luring classmen back to Madison. In pursuing this end, Blair in Chicago, and Duffy and Meuer in Wisconsin, worked independently of one another, and so much to cross purposes as to place in jeopardy the success of their project.

So far as Blair knew, the Regents had been "tough" and had not changed their attitudes in five years. Assuming that a frontal attack on the enemy was most likely to yield results, he assailed the legislature and the Regents in the pages of the *New Republic*. He charged that the legislature was trying to impose on the university faculty "a particular brand of economic teaching which will receive a certificate of orthodoxy." He reviewed the Ely and Ross incidents, and railed against the original rejection of the class memorial:

> The bronze tablet with its troublesome inscription lies in the dust of a university building basement. This memorial epitomizes the thing for which the University is now fighting. The Class of 1910 is making a determined effort to have its memorial placed on the campus at its Quinquennial Reunion this spring. The granting or withholding of consent may indicate whether the University will continue to be a great educational institution or will become merely the dispenser of a particular brand of certified orthodoxy.[40]

At about the same time, printed placards appeared in all Madison street cars. The legend on the placards was as follows:

> Whatever may be the limitations which trammel inquiry elsewhere, we believe that the great state UNIVERSITY of WISCONSIN should ever encourage that continual and fearless sifting and winnowing by which alone the TRUTH can be found.

> This is the legend on a handsome bronze tablet—the Memorial of the Class of 1910. The Regents have never granted this tablet a place on the campus. If they will finally consent we will dedicate our Memorial at Wisconsin's greatest Reunion.

> 1910 COMING BACK—500 STRONG![41]

Following the Blair article and the placards by only four days came an editorial by Richard Lloyd Jones in the Wisconsin *State Journal*. Jones complained that "while the tombstones of other classes have found permanent place to make our campus ridiculous, the class tablet of 1910 with its heroic challenge secreted away in some darkened cellar, and the Regents have not yet found a place for it in the light of day." Returning classmen would ask the board embarrassing questions about the tablet. "Why has it been set up against a cellar wall? What is there in this declaration that can embarrass the University in the light of day? . . . Let the Regents answer."[42]

Meantime, Francis R. and William J. Meuer had pursued a course quite different from that initiated by Milton J. Blair. Believing that time and change of personnel had already softened Regent opposition, they assumed that through friendly conference and conciliation, harmony could be restored and the desired object attained. With the assistance of President Van Hise they had approached some Regents directly, and had written friendly letters to others.

Their work had proceeded with fair effectiveness until Blair's letter appeared in the *New Republic*. When Meuer conferred with Van Hise on May 28, the president was indignant. He felt that the classmen had not been dealing in good faith, and warned that if further attacks were made on the Regents the memorial crusade would be lost. Meuer wrote to Blair:

> Briefly, we had our point won so far as putting up the tablet was concerned, but the article your wrote in the *New Republic* has upset everything. President Van Hise told me yesterday that he considered it the most infamous and insidious representation of facts that could have been issued. That it comes as a distinct blow to the University at this time, that if the Regents had any backbone or manhood about them, they would never grant the request now.[43]

Both Meuer and Duffy begged Blair to refrain from giving further offense.

The chief peace-making efforts had to be directed at Regent G. D. Jones, who clung to his opinion that the plaque had been inspired by "malicious and vicious pups," such as Lincoln Steffens. "I believe the same forces were back of that movement that are now pressing the consideration of this matter by the Regents," Jones declared. "I believe the class was duped and made use of for the purpose of discrediting the Regents."[44] This was stoutly denied by Duffy, who told Regent Hammond, "there is nothing in the memorial which is an effort to slip something over on the Regents, Mr. Jones' opinion notwithstanding."[45]

By way of placating Jones, and at the same time making the class position clear, William Meuer wrote a lengthy letter to him. Pertinent passages are quoted:

> I am sure the class does not want to have trouble, and I'm equally sure that the Regents do not want trouble. I am also confident that Mr. Blair did not mean to stir up any animosity and that it was merely in his enthusiasm to get five hundred people back for the reunion that he has been guilty of any possible indiscretions. I am sending you a copy of the street car sign and Mr. Jones is sending you some of the circulars. This lays before you everything that has happened and it seems like good evidence to the effect that we merely want a big crowd back and that we do want to put our memorial up. However, we want to put it up only for the sake of the tablet itself and want it divorced absolutely from all previous history. My hope is that we merely find a place for it quietly, in some satisfactory location—satisfactory to all concerned, and then stage a dignified dedication which will commemorate the words for what they are and not for the unfortunate circumstances they have been connected with. Such a procedure will not embarrass your board and it will, at the same time, satisfy the class which is justly indignant at the long five-year delay it has endured.
>
> Certainly, the University has no more staunch friend than I and I am very much afraid that a refusal will cause a tremendous upheaval which the University, at this crisis cannot afford to endure . . . As man to man, I ask you then for the good of our University and all concerned, that you work with us in finding a place to put the tablet. I sincerely hope you will agree with me that this is the best way out.[46]

Regent Jones replied immediately, but the tenor of his reply betrayed his misgivings:

> I am very glad to get your letter of May 27th. I am entirely agreeable to the arrangement you suggest. I have exerted my best efforts for many years to avoid involving the University in controversy. I have submitted to much gross personal misrepresentation to avoid this. . . .
>
> The truth is the Regents have at no time, so far as I am aware, opposed in any way academic freedom within the University. The hue and cry raised in February and March, 1910, was chiefly the work of politicians, in which, unfortunately, some self-styled friends of the University joined. Much was said that was imprudent. Much was said that was wholly false and vicious. There is some blame on some university officials. I honestly believe none of this attached to the Regents . . . I am confident your class does not want to besmirch the Regents of 1910, though I have no doubt certain mistaken enthusiasts are inclined to do so. I think that once and for all there should be

an honest, temperate statement made that will be just to the Regents and university authorities of 1910, so that as a historical incident the erecting of this monument on a suitable place on the university grounds shall be free from sinister effect.[47]

To class president Duffy, Jones also wrote, "I believe a manly statement from your class of the facts, which would completely exonerate the Regents of 1909–10 from the false charges that were then, and to some extent are now circulated against them, would be honorable and beneficial to our University."[48] He did not want the tablet to be a memorial to the Regents' behavior in the Ross incident.

In order to satisfy Jones' demand for a statement absolving the board of blame, two letters were addressed to the board. The first, prepared by William J. Meuer, said:

The Board of Regents in delaying the matter of accepting the class memorial and later delaying in the designation of a site, acted in good faith on their part and . . . the trouble has been due to misunderstandings and to an unfortunate trend of events which beclouded the true motives of the class in adopting the memorial.[49]

The second statement, submitted by Meuer and Milton J. Blair, declared:

We wish to state that there was no ulterior motive in the choice of this memorial. Our sole desire was to put into enduring bronze the splendid idea for that academic freedom which has made the University of Wisconsin one of the world's greatest institutions of learning. We deplore the fact that any political significance was attached to this memorial. We assure you that it was not conceived with any such consequence in view. Our motives were sincere and were inspired only by the great love and respect which we have for our Alma Mater.[50]

The board rejected both statements as unsatisfactory. Regent Jones came forward with the opinion that the class declaration "substantially includes an assertion that the Regents discussed, and sought to interfere with academic freedom. This is untrue and should certainly be eliminated."[51]

By way of eliminating untruth, Jones and A. P. Nelson, then president of the board, prepared a "satisfactory" statement which the classmen were expected to sign. The Regent version read as follows:

To the Regents of the University of Wisconsin and to the Public:

The Class of 1910 of the University of Wisconsin presented a bronze tablet to the University at the Commencement of 1910 as the class memorial. There was at the time considerable untrue and unfortunate newspaper comment relating to this tablet, which has recently been revived.

Upon careful investigation we find that the events in the University during the school year 1909–10, and especially during the winter and spring of that year, were greatly misrepresented at that time, and that there was, in fact, no action of the Regents of the University which unduly interfered with or sought to interfere with reasonable academic freedom in the University, or that was in any way prejudicial to what we believe are its best interests.

We have made this investigation as representatives of the University of Wisconsin Class of 1910, and for the purpose of fairly ascertaining the facts and clearing this entire matter from misstatements and injustice. We hope this true statement will prevent further misunderstandings in this matter.[52]

Milton J. Blair was one of the class officers whose signature was required. Upon reading the Nelson and Jones statement, Blair exploded:

In regard to that part of the statement which reads "and there was, in fact, no action of the Regents which unduly interfered with or sought to interfere with reasonable academic freedom in the University," I wish to say that such a statement is a misleading sophism. . . .

Neither can I subscribe myself to any doctrine of "reasonable academic freedom." This phrase imputes that there should be only a limited academic freedom, and that the majority on the Board of Regents should prescribe this limit. To me this is not freedom. A man is either free or his is not free. If he is reasonably free he is under restraint. Convicts are reasonably free on parole, political appointees are reasonably free as long as they do not incur the displeasure of the person appointing them, children are reasonably free as long as they do not exceed parental authority. Perhaps the "reasonable academic freedom" to which the Board of Regents asks us to subscribe ourselves is the political sort of reasonable freedom, perhaps it is only the paternal sort. In either case, I do not wish, nor do I think the Class of 1910 wishes, to propose a freedom for the University of Wisconsin which is only conditional.

I cannot agree to the statement "that there was no action in any way prejudicial to what we believe are its best interests." I found that the conflict of authority between the Board of Visitors and the Board of Regents, created a set of conditions which were prejudicial to what I believe are the best interests of the University of Wisconsin. I found that there was a sentiment and an attempted action which were prejudicial. I found that there had been an antagonism to President Van Hise, Professor Ross, Professor Gilmore and Professor Turner which was prejudicial to the best interests of the University, as I see these interests. To cover all of this antagonism and to say that there was no prejudicial action merely because prejudicial attempts did not crystallize into formal action is a grave misrepresentation, which it would be neither honorable nor just for us to subscribe to.

In regard to the last paragraph I wish to say that I wish the entire matter might be cleared from misstatements and misrepresentations, but to "hope that this true statement will prevent further misunderstandings in the matter" is merely to delude ourselves and the public because I do not consider it a true statement and I cannot in honesty to myself and our class, subscribe my name to it.[53]

For a time it appeared that Blair's strong stand would wreck the hopes for peace. However, Van Hise, as mediator, saved the negotiations. In collaboration with William J. Meuer he worked out a compromise statement acceptable to all parties. From the Jones and Nelson form a few words and phrases were deleted, and a few added; afterwards, on his own account, Meuer "doctored it up" a little more. The expurgated version was altogether harmless and devoid of objectionable confessions. It acknowledged no victor, conceded no defeat. It was a draw.

On June 15, 1915, Van Hise went before the board to read the compromise letter:

> *To the Regents of the University of Wisconsin and to the Public:*
> The Class of 1910 of the University of Wisconsin presented a bronze tablet to the University at the Commencement of 1910 as a Class memorial.
>
> There has been considerable discussion relating to the tablet and a number of statements have been made which are untrue and unfortunate.
>
> Upon careful investigation we find that the events in the University during the school year 1909–10 were, in several instances, misrepresented at the time, and that, in fact, no action was taken by the Board of Regents which interfered with academic freedom in the University.
>
> We have made this investigation as representatives of the University of Wisconsin Class of 1910, and for the purpose of fairly ascertaining the facts and clearing this matter from misstatements and injustice. We hope this statement will prevent further misunderstanding in the matter.

> (Signed)   (Signed)
> F. Ryan Duffy   Wm. J. Meuer
> President U.W. Class of 1910   General Reunion Chairman
> Chairman Attendance Committee   Reunion Secretary

Van Hise followed the reading with a verbal report; he announced that the tablet had already been placed on University Hall. Appropriately, it was G. D. Jones, bulwark of the opposition, who moved that the president's report and the class letter be accepted.[54]

On the same day President Van Hise addressed the happy classmen who assembled to witness the dedication of the plaque. Said Van Hise:

> The principles of academic freedom have never found expression in language so beautiful, words so impressive, phrases so inspiring. It was twenty-one years ago that these words were incorporated in a report of the Board of Regents exonerating a professor (Dr. Richard T. Ely) From the charge of "socialism" that was brought against him. This professor had incurred the displeasure of some who regarded socialism as so dangerous that they wanted no mention of this great social fact made in the University. This report back in 1894 marks one of the great landmarks in the history of the University. And from that day to this, no responsible party or no responsible authority has ever succeeded in restricting freedom of research and teaching within these walls. There are no "sacred cows" at Wisconsin. There is no such thing as "standardized" teaching in any subject. Professors and instructors present faithfully the various sides of each problem. Their duty is to train the students to independent thinking. They are in no sense propagandists for any class or interest. A university to be worthy of its name must be progressive—not progressive in the partisan sense, but in the dictionary sense. I would not care to have anything to do with a university that was not progressive.[55]

Joseph E. Davies, a rising Democrat from Milwaukee, had been invited to make the principal address on this occasion. Even though he was unable to appear he sent a message which Francis R. Duffy read to the assemblage. Said Davies:

> The Class of 1910 has rendered a great service to the University of Wisconsin, and to those ideals in education and government, which the University of Wisconsin has come to stand for in so splendid a way, throughout the world. The principle which is enunciated in bronze upon the tablet . . . is the expression of the spirit which has made the University of Wisconsin great in fame and great in the service which it has rendered . . . that principle has become settled, and cemented into the very foundations of the University, and into the relation of the state toward academic freedom. . . . Never again will the question be raised. The issue has been settled and determined. The dedication, in my judgment, of your memorial tablet signalizes the permanent redemption of the great principle, which is vital to our great University, and to the enduring interests of the citizens of the commonwealth.[56]

After a century of service to the people of Wisconsin, the University may be justifiably proud of its tradition of academic freedom.

In its innermost significance, the memorial tablet stands as a sentinel, guarding, interpreting and proclaiming the ever-buoyant and progressive spirit of the University of Wisconsin in its unceasing struggle upward for more light and its untrammeled search for truth wherever found.

When time and the elements shall have effaced every resistive letter on the historic bronze tablet, its imperishable spirit shall still ring clear and true.

How appropriate today, in rekindling the torch of freedom set ablaze by the sturdy pioneers of 1894, to say with them:

WHATEVER MAY BE THE LIMITATIONS WHICH TRAMMEL INQUIRY ELSEWHERE, WE BELIEVE THAT THE GREAT STATE UNIVERSITY OF WISCONSIN SHOULD EVER ENCOURAGE THAT CONTINUAL AND FEARLESS SIFTING AND WINNOWING BY WHICH ALONE THE TRUTH CAN BE FOUND.

Notes

1. *The Nation*, 59 (July 12, 1894), 27.

2. In 1894 the Board of Regents comprised the following:
   State Superintendent of Public Instruction, ex-officio: O. E. Wells
   President of the University, ex-officio: C. K. Adams
   John Johnston, H. W. Chynoweth, N. D. Fratt, B. J. Stevens, Charles Keith,
   George H. Noyes, George Heller, H. B. Dale, William P. Bartlett, Orlando E. Clark,
   D. I. Plumer, John W. Bashford

3. Richard T. Ely, *Ground Under Our Feet* (New York, 1938), 218–233 describes Ely's reactions to his trial for economic heresy.

4. Madison *Democrat*, August 21, 1894. Newspaper coverage of the trial was complete, and remarkably accurate. A full stenographic transcript was taken during the hearings. One copy of this transcript is filed with the manuscript papers of the University Board of Regents, for August, 1894. Other copies are available in the Ely Collection, located in the Manuscript Division of the Wisconsin Historical Society.

5. Madison *Democrat*, August 22, 1894.

6. Complete texts of the letters and reports from which the above extracts were taken, were published in the Madison *Democrat*, August 24, 1894.

7. *Ibid.*, September 19, 1894

8. Ely, *Ground Under Our Feet*, 232.

9. Robert M. La Follette, *La Follette's Autobiography* (Madison, 1913), 29.

10. James F. A. Pyre, *Wisconsin* (New York, 1920). 293.

11. At this time the Board of Regents comprised the following:
    State Superintendent of Public Instruction, ex-officio: Charles P. Cary
    President of the University, ex-officio: Charles R. Van Hise
    Magnus Swenson, W. D. Hoard, Pliny Norcross, Lucien S. Hanks, Enos L. Jones,
    Frederick C. Thwaits, James S. Trottman, D. P. Lamoreux, Edward Evans,
    Mrs. Florence G. Buckstaff, Gustave Keller, Granville D. Jones, A. P. Nelson

12. Milwaukee *Sentinel*, April 1, 1911.

13. Milwaukee *Journal*, November 30, 1908. In this period Fred MacKenzie, U. W. 1906, a La Follette Progressive, was Madison correspondent for the Milwaukee *Journal*.

14. Lincoln Steffens, "Sending a State to College." *American Magazine*, 67 (February, 1909), 362.

15. Madison *Democrat*, January 27, 1910.

16. Edward A. Ross, *Seventy Years of It* (New York, 1936), 289–290

17. *Ibid.*, 289.

18. Madison *Democrat*, March 3, 1910.

19. Records of the Board of Regents, March 2, 1910.

20. Ross, *Seventy Years of It*, 290.

21. Shortly after his graduation from the University of Wisconsin, Thompson accepted a position with McGraw-Hill Book Company. He has had no other employer. After a long term as vice-president he was elected and still serves as president of McGraw-Hill.

22. After graduating from the University of Wisconsin, Duffy practiced law at Fond du Lac. In November, 1932, he was elected to the United States Senate as a Democrat. On June 26, 1939, he was confirmed as United States District Judge for the Eastern District of Wisconsin, with offices at Milwaukee. This position he continues to hold.

23. Thompson to Milton J. Blair, April 14, 1944. (In author's possession.) That Steffens fathered the project is confirmed by Hugo Hering, chairman of the 1910 memorial committee, in a letter to the author, April 26, 1944; and by Milton J. Blair, in response to the author's questionnaire, in 1942.

24. Hering to the author, April 26, 1944. That the tablet was the work of an amateur is attested by the uneven lines of the finished product.

25. M. E. McCaffrey, then secretary of the Board of Regents, informed the author that within the governing board suspicion was rife; that underneath the ostensibly ingenuous tender of the memorial plaque was an insidious, clandestine purpose to stigmatize or "smear" the Regents.

26. Madison *Democrat*, June 23, 1910.

27. Milwaukee *Journal*, June 28, 1910.

28. Granville D. Jones to the Regents, May 25, 1915. Van Hise's position was further defined by Jones in a letter to Francis R. Duffy, June 9, 1915. Copies of these letters, and all correspondence hereafter cited, now in the author's possession, will be placed in the Manuscript Division of the Wisconsin Historical Society in the near future.

29. Milwaukee *Sentinel*, June 28, 1910; Milwaukee *Journal*, June 28, 1910.

30. Fond du Lac *Daily Commonwealth*, June 30, 1910.

31. The above quotations are excerpts taken from Cary's written answers to a questionnaire prepared by the author in 1942.

32. Duffy to Regent Theodore Hammond, May 26, 1915.

33. Jones to the Regents, May 25, 1915.

34. Jones to Duffy, May 13, 1915.

35. Jones to Duffy, June 9, 1915. According to the late M. E. McCaffrey, for many years secretary to the Board of Regents, the 1910 board customarily referred to Lincoln Steffens as "Stinkin' Leffens."

36. Jones to Duffy, May 13, 1915.

37. Jones to the Regents, May 25, 1915.

38. The quotation is taken from Milton J. Blair's answer to a questionnaire prepared by the author in 1942.

39. At this time the Board of Regents comprised the following:
    State Superintendent of Public Instruction, ex-officio: Chas. P. Cary
    President of the University, ex-officio: Charles R. Van Hise
    Gilbert E. Seaman, Mrs. Florence G. Buckstaff, A.J. Horlick, F.W.A. Notz, Edward M. McMahon, Theodore M. Hammond, James F. Trottman, Miss Elizabeth A. Waters, D.O. Mahony, Granville D. Jones, Orlando E. Clark, Ben F. Faast, A.P. Nelson

40. Blair's letter was printed in the *New Republic*, 3 (May 15, 1915), 44. Before retiring, Milton J. Blair spent twenty-five years in the advertising business, the last fifteen as vice-president of the great J. Walter Thompson Company. He served with the War Advertising Council, and for the last two years has devoted himself to the writing of a book. He now resides in New York.

41. The placards were printed at a cost of $5.50; advertising space cost $22.50 for one month. One of the original placards is in the author's possession.

42. Wisconsin *State Journal*, May 19, 1915.

43. Meuer to Blair, May 29, 1915. William J. Meuer is a business man; at present he is the proprietor of the Meuer Photoart House in Madison.

44. Jones to the Regents, May 25, 1915.

45. Duffy to Hammond, May 26, 1915.

46. Meuer to Jones, May 27, 1915. At the time of these negotiations the tension between the University and the state administration was considerable. In 1914 the Board of Public Affairs sponsored the Allen Survey, which proved to be highly critical of the University. Furthermore, Governor Phillip was known to be unfriendly towards Van Hise and the University. This explains the "crisis" to which Meuer referred in writing to Jones.

47. Jones to Meuer, May 28, 1915.

48. Jones to Duffy, June 9, 1915.

49. Meuer to the Regents, June 1, 1915.

50. Meuer and Blair to the Executive Committee of the Regents, no date.

51. Jones to Duffy, June 9, 1915.

52. Copy furnished by William Meuer.

53. Milton J. Blair to William Meuer, June 4, 1915.

54. Records of the Board of Regents, June 15, 1915. President Van Hise and State Architect Arthur Peabody decided that the plaque should be placed in the loggia of University Hall where it would have the advantage of "being exposed to the public at all times, at the same timebeing protected from the weather by the portico."

55. Wisconsin *State Journal*, June 16, 1915. Note that Van Hise did not say that no responsible authority had ever attempted to restrict freedom of research and teaching; he said no responsible party had ever succeeded in restricting research and teaching."

56. Wisconsin *State Journal*, June 14, 1915.

Now You See It, Now You Don't: The Plaque Disappears

ARTHUR HOVE

O n the afternoon of October 29, 1956, Professor Henry Hill did one of those classic double takes. Now you see it, now you don't. Hill had taken Professor Gordon Greenwood, a visitor from Australia, to the summit of Bascom Hill to see one of the University of Wisconsin's treasured icons, but the artifact was not in its accustomed place. The "sifting and winnowing" plaque, which had been affixed to the front of Bascom Hall since 1915, was gone. As Hill explained it:

> We had just been visiting with [College of Letters and Science] Dean [Mark] Ingraham, and we walked back to Bascom Hall. As we looked towards the Capital, I pointed at the statue of Abraham Lincoln, and said, "One of our proudest possessions is a plaque, which I'd like you to see." Then we looked at the plaque, but it wasn't there. I thought it was only being cleaned, but when we stepped into [presidential assistant] Leroy Luberg's office, we discovered it was missing.[1]

No one, apparently, saw the plaque disappear. Some, like Professor Hill, thought it had been removed for cleaning in anticipation of a visit by representatives from *Holiday* magazine, who were scheduled to be on campus to photograph the plaque in conjunction with a story on the university. It took nearly twenty-four hours to discover this was not the case.[2]

The assumption that it had been taken away to be cleaned was not unreasonable. Two years earlier, the *Daily Cardinal* had reported that "pranksters desecrated the 'winnowing and sifting' plaque with red paint," and it had indeed been removed by maintenance men for cleaning.[3]

Once the news of the plaque's unauthorized removal became more widely known, rumors about its possible whereabouts began to surface. The *Cardinal* reported that it had received a phone call "early Wednesday [October 31] morning, with a tip that the university's famous 'sifting and winnowing' plaque is somewhere in Lake Wingra."[4]

Obviously, if it were in the lake, it would have gone rapidly to the bottom. Supervisor of Buildings and Grounds A. F. Ahearn had described the

---

Arthur Hove is special assistant to the provost at the University of Wisconsin–Madison.

plaque as a 42-by–36-inch bronze tablet weighing approximately 300 pounds. Ahearn's description makes it difficult to conceive of how the plaque could have been removed in broad daylight without someone having noticed. But it was gone, and police were searching the immediate campus area as well as making inquiries along Langdon Street.[5]

On November 5, University President E. B. Fred issued a public statement calling for "those who removed the . . . plaque to let us know, as soon as possible, where it is, so that it can be returned to its place of honor on Bascom Hall."[6]

Not all were enthusiastic about the plaque's immediate return. Verne P. Kaub, president of the American Council of Christian Laymen in Madison, contended that: "The plaque should have been removed from its place of honor many years ago, but this should have been done by the Regents or some other university authority in open confession that the process of sifting and winnowing wherever the truth might be found was abandoned long ago."[7]

At the December 8 meeting of the regents, President Fred noted that offers of financial assistance in creating a new plaque had been forthcoming from many quarters. The regents responded by adopting a resolution that created a Freedom Plaque Fund, which "should be used not alone for the recasting of this symbol of our ideals but also for the perpetuation of the principles for which it stands."[8]

Echoes of the announced fund-raising drive had hardly stopped reverberating when the missing plaque was retrieved, the day after the regents' meeting. University police, responding to an anonymous telephone call, found the plaque in a woods near Willow Drive on the west end of the campus.[9] The recovery, while met with relief, also presented some problems. The projected fund drive, which was going forward under a committee headed by Professor Scott Cutlip, was left at a standstill. The project was suspended, even though as Cutlip noted, besides replacement of the plaque, "the fund had several other worthwhile objectives." The committee proposed a rededication ceremony and agreed to the "return of the several hundred dollars already generously given to the Freedom Plaque Fund by the Class of 1955, the Rothschild Post of the American Legion, the members of the Board of Visitors, and several individuals."[10]

The rededication ceremony was set for February 15, 1957.[11] The program, which included a roster of distinguished speakers, would begin in the Union Theater and then adjourn to Bascom Hill. The ceremony there would be highlighted by the placement in the wall of a copper chest filled with relevant printed material.[12] This would then be sealed over by the reinstallation of the original plaque.

Dean Mark Ingraham presided over the ceremony in the Union Theater.[13] Principal speakers included Wisconsin Governor Vernon Thomson and Judge F. Ryan Duffy, U.S. Court of Appeals, President of the Class of 1910. The featured speaker was UW English Professor Helen C. White, who at the time served as president of the American Association of University Professors.

Speaking on "The Wisconsin Tradition of Academic Freedom," Professor White noted that:

> "I know of no readier way to disarm ourselves than to try to hide from disturbing knowledge, and, conversely, I know of no surer way to steady our nerves and find the courage we need than to take arms against a sea of rumors and alarms and, by understanding, end them.
>
> "The fact is that truth in any age is hard to find, and wisdom more difficult of compass than the world's wealth. In the free give-and-take of the University students get a vision of what a life-long undertaking the pursuit of both is. Indeed, I think that that is the most valuable thing we give them on this campus. For there is only one thing more important than the preservation of freedom, and that is its use."[14]

The ceremony at Bascom Hall was highlighted by President Fred inserting the final bolt into the plaque, firmly and permanently setting it in place. Fred, who was entering the thirteenth year of his presidency, had been recognized at the theater ceremonies by Dean Ingraham, who had singled him out as someone "who has always recognized that the safest way to deal with ideas is to give them freedom."[15]

The proceedings closed, as do so many university events, with the playing and singing of "Varsity."

Notes

1. *Daily Cardinal*, October 31, 1956.
2. See Officers' Report—Case No. 12637, Albert D. Hamann, Director, Protection and Security: October 30, 31, and November 1, 6, 17, and 18, 1956. The magazine article was: "*The Mighty Big Ten*" by Paul Engle *Holiday*, 21, March, 1957, pp. 62–71 ff.
3. *Daily Cardinal*, November 1, 1954.
4. *Daily Cardinal*, November 1, 1956.
5. See Hamman report.

6. News Release, University of Wisconsin News Service, November 5, 1956.

7. Letter to the *Wisconsin State Journal*, November 16, 1956.

8. Regent Resolution, December 8, 1956; *Wisconsin State Journal*, December 9, 1956. Plans for the establishment of such a fund had been discussed at the President's Administrative Council meeting in November and previous to the December regents' meeting. See "Minutes" November 27, 1956, Item VI, and December 4, 1956, Item I.

9. *Daily Cardinal*, December 11, 1956; Wisconsin Alumnus, January 1957, p. 2.

10. News Release, University of Wisconsin News Service, December 10, 1956. There was some reaction to the Legion's presence in the list of contributors, a seeming reflection of the free speech and loyalty issues raised on the national level by the actions of Wisconsin Senator Joseph McCarthy. The *Racine Journal-Times* had earlier editorialized (November 17, 1956) that "The American Legion in Wisconsin, particularly in recent years, has showed itself to be a ruthless opponent of the very principle of freedom stated on that plaque. The Wisconsin Department of the Legion has made false and unfounded charges against the University, held this great institution up to public censure and ridicule and done all in the Legion's power to suppress and interfere with free inquiry. . . . It would be better that the University have no new plaque at all, or that it write the words of the old plaque on a brick wall in chalk, than to accept those donations. Surely there is in the state some other more appropriate source of funds to replace those words in bronze, even if it is necessary to solicit the pennies of school children."

11. "Memo to President Fred" from Scott M. Cutlip. See also, letter from Cutlip to James S. Thompson, January 17, 1957; *Daily Cardinal*, January 22, 1957, February 4, 1957, February 13, 1957, February 15, 1957; and *Wisconsin State Journal*, February 15, 1957.

12. The chest contained "copies of the Regent resolutions of 1894 and 1956, a copy of the history of the plaque by the late Theodore Herfurth, a 1910 class roster, a copy of the Curti-Carstensen history of the University, and clippings telling of the plaque's loss and return last fall." Letter to the Class of 1910 from Scott M. Cutlip, January 28, 1957.

13. University Archives: "Freedom Plaque Rededication Program, Bascom Hall, February 15, 1957." See also, accounts carried in the following: *Wisconsin State Journal*, February 16, 1957; *Daily Cardinal*, February 19, 1957; and *Wisconsin Alumnus*, March 1957. The University A Cappella Choir under the direction of J. Russell Paxton provided musical selections at the Union Theater, and the University of Wisconsin Band led by Professor Raymond F. Dvorak played at the Bascom Hall installation. The proceedings were broadcast over WHA and the State Radio Network.

14. University Archives: main address by Prof. Helen C. White, chairman of the University of Wisconsin English department and president of the American Association of University Professors at ceremonies rededicating the Freedom Plaque, Bascom Hall, University of Wisconsin, Feb. 15, 1957, pp. 3–4.

15. *Wisconsin State Journal*, February 16, 1957.

"That Little Pill": Richard T. Ely and the Emerging Parameters of Professional Propriety

Benjamin G. Rader

J Franklin Jameson, who was later to become a distinguished historian and .director of the Library of Congress, kept a revealing diary of his experiences as a student at the Johns Hopkins University during the 1880s. In it, he had no reluctance about assessing the merits of his fellow students nor his teachers. By and large, he judged them harshly. Among his victims was Richard T. Ely, a fledgling instructor in political economy.

Jameson recorded that Ely was obsessed with the contrasts between the English laissez-faire economics and the German historical school. For instance, as noted in an 1882 entry: "Was late to Dr. Ely's paper, but didn't miss much, for what I heard was the same as he said over and over again in his lectures of last year. He fought his man of straw, the *a priori* economist over again, and demolished him as usual." Ely did not welcome comments or queries in class that challenged his views; at times, he even lost his temper, according to Jameson. Jameson finally gave up efforts to engage Ely in a dialogue, because, as he scribbled in his diary, he did not want to "rile" the "little pill."[1]

Jameson was not alone in characterizing Ely as a little pill, though he was alone, as far as I know, in using these exact words. While Ely obtained important academic positions, trained or helped train a brilliant group of students, and exercised a large influence on American thinking about public issues, controversy swirled about him throughout his life. Contentiousness extended both to his personal relationships and to his stand on public questions. Personally, he had major quarrels with (among others), Simon Newcomb, Herbert Baxter Adams, Thomas C. Chamberlain, and John R. Commons. Publicly, he was a key warrior in heated controversies regarding the proper role of the state in the economy and the purpose and nature of the American Economic Association. That he was the protagonist in the cele-

---

Benjamin Rader is professor of history at the University of Nebraska-Lincoln. He is the author of the 1966 Ely biography, The Academic Mind and Reform: The Influence of Richard T. Ely in American Life.

brated academic freedom case at the University of Wisconsin in 1894 should not therefore occasion surprise. It fit into a larger career pattern.

This paper focuses on why Ely was "a little pill." Why was it Ely rather than someone else who was brought to trial for alleged economic heresies? Such a quest will also illuminate, I hope, related issues regarding the intellectual history of late nineteenth-century America.

A psychologist might begin an analysis of Ely's personality by noting his size. As Jameson's exclamation indicated, Ely was short; he stood at only five feet and five inches tall. Perhaps he had a "Napoleonic complex." But as I am unequipped by training or temperament to engage in such an inquiry, and as I am conscious of the need to be politically correct on the issue of verticality, I will leave such speculation to others. My inquiry will lead in more conventional directions.

I begin with Ely's background. Ely, like many of the other early social scientists, was the product of New England culture, or what David Hackett Fischer has called "Massachusetts folkways."[2] Unable to have a religious conversion experience and therefore become a minister, he found an alternate vocation in academe; more specifically he discovered his equivalent to a religious calling in the developing academic discipline of economics. He entered academe when the modern university was beginning to take shape. It was a time when intellectuals had not yet forsaken their commitment to civic humanism. Neither had the new universities. They at first sought simultaneously to nurture the nation's civic life and advance knowledge through research.[3]

Ely took the responsibilities of civic humanism seriously, indeed, in the view of many of his contemporaries, too seriously. While his fellow social scientists mostly limited their efforts to training students so they could become more useful members of the community, or encouraged noncontroversial "genteel" reforms such as civil service, Ely openly confronted the burning issue of his day. That issue was class warfare. Not only did he examine the plight of workingmen sympathetically, but, speaking in the tone of a friendly member of a superior class, openly endorsed the present and potential beneficence of labor unions. In similarly supportive ways he analyzed socialism as an alternative to capitalism. At the same time, he condemned the callousness of the owning classes. Invariably, he clothed his "message" in what our late twentieth-century secular perspective would label a pervasive, almost suffocatingly self-righteous religiosity.

In doing so Ely stepped outside emerging, but as yet not carefully drawn, parameters of professional propriety. Implicitly, these parameters began to exclude actions that antagonized groups who could endanger the status of the professorate. Thus criticism of captains of industry or the advocacy of socialism had to be kept inside the classroom or muted in the arcane language of the discipline. Moreover, professionalization increasingly required a secular pose. Even in his own day, Ely's espousal of reforms on behalf of the promotion of "Christian brotherhood" seemed incongruent with a naturalistic world-view and the objectivity encouraged by academic professionalization.

In 1894, the year of his fateful "trial," Ely half-consciously recognized his painful situation: he either retreated inside the emerging parameters of professional propriety or continued to preach his message. At the least, had he remained unrelenting in his advocacy, he would have found himself ostracized from the mainstream of his chosen vocation. He might even have found himself without a job.

Richard T. Ely as a Minister of Reform

It would be an accurate description to say that Richard T. Ely was "born a reformer." Reared on a ninety-acre farm in upstate New York, he came from a family of reform Protestants. Richard himself had been named for a Puritan ancestor who had fled the Mother Country during the Restoration of the 1660s for New England. Several Elys had been ministers; only poverty prevented Richard's father, Ezra Stiles Ely, from becoming a preacher. His father, a devout Presbyterian, who was, according to his son, well read, gloomy, and introspective, held his family to austere standards.

Much to the distress of his father, young Richard was unable to have a conversion experience. "I should feel much more at ease and settled about you," his father wrote in 1876 when Richard was twenty-two, "were I satisfied that you had given yourself . . . to the service of Christ and His church. I never shall feel satisfied with anything else."[4] But Richard could never quite accept the harsh Calvinism of his father. Unable to embrace evangelical Protestantism or become a minister, he sought an alternate career. He became, in Robert Crunden's apt phrase, a "Minister of Reform."[5]

He groped toward a vocation that would both provide the personal recognition that he so desperately craved and allow him to lead a purposeful life. First at Dartmouth and then at Columbia he studied philosophy; upon graduation from Columbia he won a scholarship to continue philosophic study in Germany. In Germany, through some newly made American friends, he discovered political economy. At once, it seems, he became an enthusiastic convert to the German version of the discipline—both in terms of method and in terms of ultimate goals. "You learn here, and only here, how to do independent, real scientific work," he wrote home.[6]

"Convert" is the proper metaphor to apply to Ely's adherence to the German historical school. As taught by his mentor, Karl Knies at Heidelberg, the "New Economics" (Ely's term for the American version of the German historical school) was not merely an analysis of how the economy presently worked but also insisted that research and conclusions should be guided by moral imperatives, that is, by *"what ought to be."* In bringing the New Economics to an American audience, Ely visualized himself as a missionary, both to his students and to the public. Religious rhetoric suffused everything he said and wrote. He embarked upon a kind of holy war against the adherents of classicism.

As Jameson indicated, Ely's enthusiasm for the new economics knew few bounds. Like typical converts to a new faith, he bridled at any criticism, even implicitly, of his stance. Only three years after taking an appointment as an untenured instructor at Johns Hopkins University in 1881, he presented a blistering attack on classicism and a glowing endorsement of the New Economics to the Johns Hopkins History and Political Science seminary and published a version of it in the *Johns Hopkins University Studies.*[7]

Without exaggeration, the American Economic Association, which Ely organized two years later in 1885, might be described as his new-found church. Its purpose was to propagate the new economic faith. In Ely's view, as Simon Newcomb correctly concluded, the new association was "intended to be sort of a Church requiring for admission to its full communion a renunciation of ancient errors, and an adhesion to the supposed new creed."[8] He wanted it to exclude nonbelievers. It should, he wrote to a fellow economist, combat "the [William Graham] Sumner, [Simon] Newcomb crowd," two of the leading professorial proponents of classical economics.[9]

Ely prepared for the association a creed, to which all prospective members should cleave. Members of the association should accept the belief that "the doctrine of *laissez-faire* is unsafe in politics and unsound in morals," the creed said. The dogmatism entailed in such a requirement went too far for most of Ely's fellow economists, though they did agree upon a compromise with Ely. The new platform of the association regarded the state "as an agency whose positive assistance is one of the indispensable conditions of human progress."[10]

These two instances—his attack on classicism and his conception of the American Economic Association—provide striking evidence of support for the contention that Ely conceived of himself as a minister of reform. That he was trained as a political economist and was employed by a university was almost incidental to his larger purpose in life—his commitment to the work of transforming American society into his conception of a Christian brotherhood.

The Emergence of the Modern University and the Culture of Civic Humanism

Yet Ely's activities and pronouncements were not as far removed from the parameters of professional propriety as they may appear at first glance. It would be a serious mistake to project backward the modern university world in which we inhabit to that of the 1880s and 1890s. There are many striking similarities: the formation of professional associations, the emphasis upon research, the production of clones of ourselves, and the prevalence of academic entrepreneurship. But there is one particularly arresting difference as well. The pioneering universities, such as Johns Hopkins, Columbia, Chicago, and Wisconsin, took seriously their commitment to a tradition of civic humanism.

A larger civic culture in which intellectuals played conspicuous roles existed long before the arrival of the late nineteenth-century university and its professional culture. Although modified by historical circumstances, the vision of a civic culture extended at least as far back as medieval Florence. Its contents included a belief in the preeminence of the public good, that individual interests ought to be subordinated to a greater good, the good of the larger community. Fantasies of a new Christian Sparta, as students of American republicanism have shown, flooded the imaginations of the eighteenth-century founders of the United States. Only widespread self-sacrifice, the practice of public virtues, and the absence of corruption could ensure the survival of nations that had no monarchies, they believed.[11]

An active civic life on the part of the wealthy, the powerful, and the learned, those who in the eighteenth century could still be described as a "natural aristocracy," was essential to the cultivation and maintenance of public virtue. Their orientation tended to be local rather than national. Professors and teachers, as members of this natural aristocracy, were far less concerned about building scholarly reputations than in cultivating the mind and improving the moral tenor of their communities. Those active in promoting the civic culture built public libraries, formed philosophical and historical societies, and participated in benevolent societies. In the revolutionary era, Benjamin Franklin was a model civic humanist. After having made his fortune, Franklin dedicated his life to doing good.

In the nineteenth century, the nation's intellectual leadership, particularly those with a New England background, continued to promote a civic culture. They took seriously their responsibilities of promoting civic humanism. Commitments to civic humanism furnished the driving force behind the American Social Science Association (ASSA, 1865–85), which represented a national version of civic culture. The ASSA's membership included ministers, doctors, lawyers, writers, artists, and teachers rather than professionally trained social scientists. Many of the members served as volunteers in humanitarian activities or were public officials. Normally conceptualizing the community in organic rather than contractual terms, they were not interested in simply analyzing what existed, but in the solution of community problems.

As members of an elite, class consciousness informed the humanitarianism of these amateur social scientists. With study and conscientious application of their talents, they were confident that they could ultimately determine what was best for the community. Their recommendations were moderate. They urged more benevolence on the part of the wealthy, civil service reform, the practice of more self-restraint on the part of the less fortunate, and the election to public office of "the best men." Politically they tended to be liberal republicans or, in the words of Richard Hofstadter, "genteel reformers."[12]

As Thomas Bender has shown, the tradition of a civic culture initially exercised a strong influence on the pioneering universities of the late nineteenth century. The leaders of these universities at first conceived of their institutions mainly in terms of the cultivation of civic humanism rather than in terms of research or professional training. One of the first acts of Daniel Coit Gilman, who had been prominent in the ASSA and was the president of Johns Hopkins University, was to establish a series of public lectures in Baltimore. The lectures were to demonstrate "the methods and principles on which we rely." Huge numbers of journalists, social reformers, and political figures passed through the famed Hopkins historical, political, and economics seminars.[13]

The main purpose of their training was not the acquisition of expertise nor preparation for a future career in academe. The Johns Hopkins catalog was explicit on this point: the seminars offered "advanced instruction, not professional" training to those who intended to become civic leaders. The professors understood that their work entailed social engagement, that such work was a significant extension of their scholarly enterprises. Columbia University's Faculty of Political Science, established in 1881, made similar assumptions. It was designed to educate men in "mental culture" so they could take up careers in the civil service or as "public journalists" and more generally assume the "duties of public life."[14]

As conceived by Richard Ely, the American Economic Association also represented a national version of civic culture rather than the emerging professional culture. As Ely explained in a letter to Gilman, he visualized the association as part of a larger effort to form "an influential movement which will help in the diffusion of sound, Christian political economy."[15] He invited ministers, public officials, and even a small contingent of businessmen to attend the founding meeting of the association. Under Ely's tutelage, the association organized branch societies in at least eight cities; apparently clergymen were the main group behind each of these local societies.

Ely was active in local civic cultures in both Baltimore and Madison. During his first year at Johns Hopkins he gave a series of public lectures on civil service, which incidentally failed dismally, drawing the smallest audience of any speaker in the series. Early in his career, he also led student devotional meetings of the Young Men's Christian Association and prepared a bill for the students' "House of Commons." He served on special tax commissions for both Baltimore (1885) and the state of Maryland (1886), though, significantly, he refused to sign the majority report of the Maryland Commission and wrote a 108-page report of his own.

Upon moving to Madison, Ely quickly joined a local circle of business, professional, and educational leaders who were interested in promoting the community's civic life. During his first year in Madison he became a member and vice president of the Madison Civil Service Reform Association and formed the Historical and Political Science Association with himself as president and Charles N. Gregory, a prominent Madison attorney, as secretary.

The association brought important townspeople (including Lucius Fairchild, former governor and Civil War general) and university people together to discuss current social problems and "to create a close relationship between the graduate departments of the university and the practical outside world."[16] He joined and took an active role as a vestryman in the Grace Episcopal Church. He even helped to found the Four Lakes Kindergarten Association in Madison and served as its president for several years.

On the defensive during his ordeal in 1894, Ely tried to explain his philosophic stance in terms of promoting civic culture. "As far as my general philosophy is concerned, I am a conservative rather than a radical, and in the strictest sense of the term an aristocrat rather than a democrat." As if to acknowledge that such a statement hardly squared with much of his writings or his activities, he added, "When I use the word 'aristocrat,' I have in mind of course not a legal aristocracy, but a natural aristocracy."[17] Here, Ely used the very words—"natural aristocracy"—that the founding fathers of the republic liked to accord to themselves. He was also trying to assert his credentials as a bona fide member of respectable civic culture circles.

In the meantime, however, Ely's professorial colleagues were retreating from the tradition of civic humanism and creating a culture of their own, a "professional culture." By 1894 Ely found himself dangerously close to not having a home within either the older civic or the emerging professional cultures. For his rhetoric and his activities associated with late nineteenth-century class conflict threatened to isolate him from both cultures. Indeed, even "the little pill's" job was in jeopardy.

The Emerging Parameters of Professional Propriety

The development of a professional culture of intellectuals accompanied the creation of the modern university. Even earlier, the traditional association between society and the intellect, which was central to the civic culture, had weakened. The genteel class no longer commanded the prestige nor the political authority that it had once enjoyed. Moreover, the complexities accompanying the industrial revolution eroded the authority of amateur social scientists.

The fast-growing universities and their faculties seized upon professionalism and specialization as a way of carving out for themselves a bounded and protected space within American society. Unlike civic culture, their professional culture turned inward, away from the community. It emphasized research, relentless specialization, and the employment of an arcane discourse that the general public, indeed even fellow academics outside the discipline, had difficulty comprehending. Success in the professional culture ultimately depended on the establishment of a national reputation for work within the confines of the discipline rather than achievements in local communities. Professionalization encouraged the concentration of the most serious thought within academic, disciplinary communities. Inevitably the result was the impoverishment of public culture.

The academy's professional culture erected four major boundaries or parameters, each of which helped to define the profession and added to its security if not its power within American society. First, the professional economist, historian, or other academic had to be a member in good standing in one or more national association of one's peers. The establishment of limits of inquiry, or what Thomas Kuhn has called paradigms, represented a second parameter of professional culture.[18] The third parameter entailed the determination of what audience the intellectuals intended to reach; in the end they chose an academic rather than a broadly public audience. Finally, each profession created its specific forms of discourse.

Let us briefly consider each parameter of professional propriety in turn.

At the same time that President Daniel Coit Gilman of Johns Hopkins was urging his professors to be active in the civic culture of Baltimore, he was also encouraging the formation of what was to become an opposing professional culture. One example was his support of the formation of national disciplinary associations. Johns Hopkins provided the leadership in forming the Modern Language Association in 1883, the American Historical Association in 1884, the American Economic Association in 1885, the American Political Science Association in 1903, and the American Sociological Association in 1905. Each of the associations held annual conventions, published a scholarly journal, and established procedures for evaluating the research of its members. The professional associations became an important agency for aspiring academics to show their wares and thereby establish their identities in the national professional culture of their discipline rather than in a local civic culture.

Likewise, the drawing of disciplinary boundaries was an important strategy in the promotion of a professional culture. Because of the potential relevance of political economy to the controversial issues of the day, the economists in particular wrestled mightily with defining their subject matter. In the end (that is, by the end of the century) the overwhelming majority of academic economists had worked out a middle ground. They rejected all ideologies; both strident defenses of laissez-faire and socialism were placed off-limits. The consideration or construction of holistic or global alternatives to the existing economic system was no longer considered proper subjects for professional economists.

Instead, the professionals advocated a kind of piecemeal empiricism that represented no direct threat to the existing distribution of power. Claiming to possess greater objectivity, detachment, and expertise than amateur economists, the professionals approached each issue separately and historically. Their specialized and more detailed knowledge, they insisted, gave them a unique capacity to monitor continuously the complexities of rapidly changing economic conditions.

Nothing distinguished the professional academics from the civic humanists more than audiences they intended for their work. Mainly, the academics spoke to one another rather than to the general public. Economists who wrote for popular periodicals or newspapers, or who spoke to general audiences, were increasingly charged with being popularizers or with being unprofessional. In other words, such men or women stepped beyond the parameters of professional propriety.

On the other hand, economists could offer their expertise to private and governmental agencies and to political leaders. The proper role of the economist, E. R. A. Seligman concluded in the 1890s, was as an "adviser to the leaders," "not of propagandist to the masses."[19] It was entirely proper for economists to propose technical solutions to legislative committees, to serve on special investigatory commissions, and to advise public office holders, but it was improper for them to engage in public advocacy. So while this service ideal provided for a link between the university and a significant sector of the public, it did not include the general public.

Finally, the professional culture created its own mode of discourse. In part, the new language, which might entail the use of the vernacular in unfamiliar ways, was necessary in order to convey the complexities or nuances of the subject matter. But at the same time, the new language helped to separate the professionals from the amateurs. Mastering the new language increasingly required not only four years as an undergraduate but advanced training in a graduate or professional school. The substitution of Latinate words and phrases for Anglo-Saxonisms, in particular, seemed to add to professional profundity and surround each discipline with a special, almost mysterious aura.

Furthermore, professional discourse turned in a decidedly secular direction. No longer was it proper for academics to use patently religious terms or to appeal overtly to religious principles. Indeed, professionals frequently disguised their moral commitments behind a secular guise of objectivity and devised a discourse with implicit moral meanings unfamiliar to the untutored.

As a minister of reform and an activist in the fading civic culture of his day, Richard T. Ely collided with each of these professional boundaries. At the outset, Ely never conceived of the American Economic Association as simply or exclusively an organization to enhance the professionalization of the discipline. When fellow economists began to move the association in a professional direction, he resisted. He not only opposed dropping the association's platform, or "confession of faith," as Arthur T. Hadley had called it, but he angrily resigned as secretary in 1892 when the association's leadership opposed his selection of Chautauqua for the 1892 convention.[20] Associating the American Economic Association with Chautauqua struck his professorial colleagues as being unprofessional.

Ely's involvement with Chautauqua potentially violated both the religious-secular boundary and the prohibition against addressing popular audiences. (Chautauqua had been founded as a training institution for Methodist Sunday School teachers and continued to have a strong religious flavor). On the other hand, Ely patently ignored the emerging professional strictures; each summer he taught courses to students of all ages, various backgrounds, and both sexes at the Chautauqua Summer School. Many of his students were ministers or ministerial candidates. His lectures treated the great social movements of the day. His *Introduction to Political Economy*, which was to become, in revised form, the most popular economics textbook in the country, was originally written for the Chautauqua's extensions division, the Scientific and Literary Circle, and printed by the Methodist concern, Hunt & Eaton.

To leaders in the developing profession—such as E. R. A. Seligman of Jewish origin, and Frank Taussig and Arthur Hadley, both from urban families without strong religious convictions—Ely's publicly pronounced religiosity was something of an embarrassment, both personally and in terms of their aspirations for economics as a discipline. General Francis A. Walker, the longtime president of the American Economic Association, joked that Chautauqua was "the first intellectual camp meeting in the country."[21] Ely's numerous articles in religious periodicals, his frequent speeches to religious groups, and his publication of *Social Aspects of Christianity* (1889), though presented in an age in which academe was far less ostentatiously secular than it is today, weakened his standing among fellow professional economists.

While Ely's engagement in what historians would later label the "social gospel movement" provided a basis for the emerging profession of economics to define more precisely the audience it wished to reach and the proper means of discourse, it was his persistence in giving attention to class conflict that aroused the most opposition among his colleagues. To many of the economists of the laissez-faire tradition, class conflict simply did not exist or was irrelevant to the subject of economics. For example, Simon Newcomb, one of Ely's protagonists, did not include a single chapter on the subject in his economics textbook.

A distinguishing characteristic of the younger, heavily German-trained historical economists, however, was the importance that they attached to the effects of the industrial revolution on labor. The attention given by classical economics to the processes of production ignored the equally important issue of its effects on workers. "The paramount question of political economy to-day is the question of distribution," wrote E. R. A. Seligman in 1886. Economists should try to determine what kinds of reforms might bridge "the chasm between the 'haves' and the 'have nots'" and lessen "the tension of industrial existence, to render the life of the largest social class indeed worth living."[22] Yet, the imperatives of professionalization led nearly all of them, including Seligman, to approach the labor-capital conflict with excruciating obliqueness.

There was one major exception. And he was Jameson's little pill, Richard T. Ely.

It is difficult today to recapture the public anxiety aroused over what one character in a novel described as the "irrepressible conflict" of his generation. In 1877 railroad workers across the nation had thrown down their tools, seized local depots, and refused to let the trains move. Before the country's first nationwide strike had been suppressed, more than one hundred people lay dead. During the 1880s there were nearly 500 strikes a year, and in the next decade the figure mounted to more than a 1,000, engaging as many as 700,000 workingmen. The Haymarket Affair, the rising popularity of Henry George, and the publication of Edward Bellamy's *Looking Backward* in 1888 all aroused deep-seated fears. With the horrible memories of the Civil War still lingering in their memories, terrified observers warned of a labor revolution.

Ely not only refused to sidestep the inflammatory issue of class conflict, he placed it at the very center of his concerns. His publications in the 1880s and early 1890s reflect the importance that he attributed to class conflict. Apart from numerous articles in periodicals, he published *French and German Socialism* in 1883, *The Labor Movement in America* in 1886, and *Socialism: An Examination of Its Nature, Its Strength and Its Weakness, with Suggestions for Social Reform* in 1894. The last two books in particular aroused a furor both inside and outside the walls of academe.

Not only did Ely address the most controversial issue of his day, but he expressed manifest sympathy for labor, labor organizations, and many aspects of socialism. Ely accepted labor organizations as a permanent feature of industrial society. He not only defended unions as necessary in the "unequal conflict" between labor and capital, Ely championed them as agencies of civic culture. He noted, for example, that the Knights of Labor promoted temperance and Christian ideals.

His books were frankly aimed at the working class and employers rather than fellow economists. "If your demands are right," Ely told the workers, "if they are reasonable, then you will win and hold your gain. The world will listen even to socialism, if properly presented."[23] At the same time he admonished employers to treat their workers fairly and open their minds to the possibilities of a more Christian social order.

Ely addressed workers directly. When the Baltimore streetcar employees held a rally for a twelve-hour day law in 1886, Ely caused something of a sensation by siding with their cause. He wrote them an open letter of sympathy that appeared on the front page of the Baltimore *Sun*. Rather than as a spokesman of the emerging professional culture, he wrote in terms of the older civic culture, even more specifically as a minister of reform. "I do not hesitate to condemn in severe terms the treatment street-car employees have received from their employers. In future years it will inevitably be described as a blot on our much-vaunted nineteenth-century civilization, that in all large American cities men worked from fourteen to nineteen hours a day in the sight of the public, and that the moral sense of the community was not sufficiently elevated to revolt against this barbarity."[24] In 1887, he became the first academic economist to address a national labor union convention, the American Federation of Labor meeting in Baltimore.

Conclusion

The upshot was that Ely persistently stepped over the boundaries of propriety imposed by an emerging professional culture. His own sense of what he should do was guided both by an adherence to the values of a traditional civic culture and his abiding New England conscience. His career prior to 1894 suggests the possibility of a career quite distinctive from that mandated by the professional culture. But that path was not taken. His 1894 trial, among other considerations, ignited a retreat by himself and others from involvement in, and promotion of, a civic culture. There remains to this day a giant chasm between the way academics write and talk about issues and the way that ordinary lay persons think and write about them. While the academics draw upon the general culture around them, they continue to orient themselves almost exclusively by the requirements of their professional culture.

Notes

1. Quoted in Benjamin G. Rader, *The Academic Mind and Reform: The Influence of Richard T. Ely in American Life* (Lexington: University of Kentucky Press, 1966), 29, 30.

2. David Hackett Fischer, *Albion's Seed: Four British Folkways in America* (New York: Oxford University Press, 1989).

3. Several books address aspects of this theme. Apart from my book, *The Academic Mind*, see especially Mary O. Furner, *Advocacy and Objectivity: A Crisis in the Professionalization of American Social Science, 1865–1905* (Lexington: University of Kentucky Press, 1975); James T. Kloppenberg, *Uncertain Victory: Social Democracy and Progressivism in European and American Thought, 1870–1920* (New York: Oxford University Press, 1986); and Thomas Bender, *Intellect and Public Life: Essays on the Social History of Academic Intellectuals in the United States* (Baltimore: Johns Hopkins University Press, 1993). See also Hamilton Cravens, "History of the Social Sciences," *Osiris* 1 (1985): 183–207.

4. Rader, *The Academic Mind*, 5–6.

5. Robert M. Crunden, *Ministers of Reform: The Progressives' Achievement in American Civilization, 1889–1920* (New York: Basic Books, 1982).

6. Rader, *The Academic Mind*, 13.

7. Ely, "The Past and the Present of Political Economy," in *Johns Hopkins University Studies in Historical and Political Science*, vol. 2, 1884.

8. Rader, *The Academic Mind*, 36.

9. Ibid.

10. Ibid.

11. For the historiography of republicanism, see Daniel T. Rodgers, "Republicanism: The Career of a Concept," *Journal of American History* 79 (June 1992): 11–38.

12. Richard Hofstadter, *The American Political Tradition and the Men Who Made It* (New York: Knopf, 1948).

13. Bender, *Intellect and Public Life*, 42.

14. Ibid., 130.

15. Rader, *The Academic Mind*, 36.

16. Ibid., 116.

17. Ibid., 151.

18. Thomas Kuhn, *The Structure of Scientific Revolutions* (Chicago: University of Chicago Press, 1962).

19. Bender, *Intellect and Public Life*, 32.

20. Rader, *The Academic Mind*, 117.

21. Ibid., 119.

22. Furner, *Advocacy & Objectivity*, 98–99.

23. Quoted in ibid., 85.

24. Rader, *The Academic Mind*, 24.

The First Economist at Wisconsin, 1892–1925

ROBERT J. LAMPMAN AND DAVID B. JOHNSON

> The regents of the University of Wisconsin removed in my particular case all
> upper age limits for retirement. They gave the LLD degree to me, while still
> in active service, a thing never done before, and they made me an honorary
> (lifetime) professor of economics . . .[1]

Thus wrote Richard T. Ely about his retirement in 1925. Of course,
great changes had occurred during his thirty-three years at Madison.[2]
Enrollment of students had grown from 1,000 to 8,000, and the Madison
faculty had expanded from 50 to 200. The Department of Economics began
with only Ely and William A. Scott, who came with Ely from Johns Hopkins, but by 1925 it numbered 36 faculty members. (This number includes
some teachers of business subjects along with some agricultural economists
and some sociologists.)

Economics had grown faster than most fields in those years, especially in
the number of Ph.D.'s granted, with 80 alumni holding that degree by 1925.
Most of their dissertations were supervised by Ely or John R. Commons, and
many addressed public policy on "Wisconsin Idea" topics. In 1909 President
Charles W. Eliot of Harvard said that Wisconsin was the best state university
in part because of the faculty's help to state and local governments. Departmental connections with state government peaked in 1911, the year before
the Progressives lost power to the Republican Stalwarts.

As of 1992, only seventy-three tenure-track economics faculty members
had served ten years or more at the UW–Madison. Fifteen of these were
hired during Ely's time at Wisconsin. In addition to Ely and Scott, this
group included Balthazar Meyer (who joined the faculty in 1898), Thomas
Sewell Adams (1902), Henry C. Taylor (1902), John R. Commons (1904),
Edward A. Ross (1906), Ralph H. Hess (1908), Henry R. Trumbower
(1912), William H. Kiekhofer (1913), Benjamin H. Hibbard (1914), Harry
Jerome (1915), Selig Perlman (1917), Don D. Lescohier (1918), and Martin
G. Glaeser (1919). Scott, Adams, Commons, and Ross were trained at Johns

Robert J. Lampman are David B. Johnson are professors emeriti of economics at the
University of Wisconsin–Madison. Lampman is editor of the 1993 book, Economists at
Wisconsin, 1892–1992.

Hopkins, and Glaeser took his Ph.D. at Harvard, while all the others on this list were Wisconsin Ph.D.'s. Other longtime faculty members who were not Ph.D.'s but who taught key commerce courses during Ely's time included Stephen W. Gilman (1905), Fayette H. Elwell (1913), and Edward H. Gardner (1914).

Around the time of Ely's departure Wisconsin offered 37 economics courses at both the undergraduate and graduate levels. Of these, 21 were in the applied fields of agricultural economics, finance, labor, and public utilities. The catalog also listed 13 courses in accounting and business administration and 10 courses in sociology. Compared to other universities of similar size, the Wisconsin department had a larger than average number of faculty and greater student enrollment. The faculty was then a largely Wisconsin-trained staff. It offered a wider range of courses, particularly in the applied fields, than did many others. It had relatively intertwined relationships with commerce, agricultural economics, and sociology.

To what extent and in what ways had Richard T. Ely changed the university during his 33 years on the faculty? And, conversely, how had Ely been changed by his experiences at Madison? Some light can be shed on these interesting and broad questions by answering three related, but more limited, questions about Ely's career as the first economist at Wisconsin. What kind of economics did Ely bring to Madison and how did he modify it over time? Why did he start out with a "school" and end up with a "department"? And, why did he have a longtime quarrel with his star colleague, John R. Commons?

What kind of economics?

Ely first encountered the subject of economics in Germany after he was introduced to, but didn't like, courses in philosophy. The economics he learned was about the history of national economies and government efforts to solve economic problems. In particular, he learned about Germany's schemes to catch up to England and other leaders of the industrial revolution. German economists thought not only in historical terms, but tended to range freely in seeking applications for problem-solving from such disciplines as political science, sociology, law, and statistics. Economics, some of his teachers believed, would function best as part of a unified social science.

When Ely came back to the United States, his first job, starting in 1881, was as the only economist in the Department of History and Moral

Sciences at the new Johns Hopkins University, founded in 1876. But he found that many of the leading economists at other American universities did not go along with the "new economics," which Ely, and a good number of his American cohort, had learned in Germany. The "old economics," based on English teachings, held that economics should draw not on history but on logic. Starting from a model of a timeless, unchanging, and no-growth economy, the student could deduce a set of analytical propositions about how markets work and might conclude that government intervention would seldom solve economic problems. The slogan "the best government is the least government" was repeated often in economics texts, and "government failure" was more to be feared than "market failure."[3] Ely portrayed the "old economics" as a highly specialized and narrowly defined subject, the study of which discouraged activists who wanted to do something to solve problems.

Ely was present at the creation of the American Economic Association, which was formed in 1886. He believed that noneconomists, particularly historians and theologians, should be invited to join the organization. He also believed that AEA members should record their votes on alternative remedies for national problems. He was overruled on both these beliefs by the 1888 amendments to the AEA constitution. He devoted much of his time to the AEA, first as secretary and later as the sixth president in 1900. A. W. Coats stated in 1968 that "Ely probably exerted a greater influence upon American economics during its vital formative period than any other individual."[4]

Ely found a following among some economists and some noneconomists for his views on the need for a strong, positive role for government in promoting economic growth and political democracy. He found support for his ethical teachings in two movements of his time, namely, the religious reform of the "social gospel" and the political reform movement of "progressivism."[5] Kloppenberg stated that Ely was at the peak of his national popularity when he arrived at Madison.[6] However, Ely had already been marked for vigorous opposition by some of the leaders of the "old economics" school, notably, Simon Newcomb at Hopkins and James L. Laughlin at Chicago.[7] Moreover, each of his two movements had opposition from within and neither one was to be very loyal to Ely.

Ely wrote a pioneering book about the labor movement in America in 1886[8] and another about socialism and social reform in 1894.[9] In the latter book, and in subsequent writings, Ely qualified his views on labor unions and socialism, stating that he didn't want unions to strike nor socialists to revolt. He was a "social democrat" and a "Christian socialist" and an "elitist progressive" or an "aristocratic populist."[10] Some writers identify him as a seeker for a viable middleway, or as an early advocate of a general welfare state.[11]

Before he was tried for heresy in 1894, he was backing away from advocacy, having been convinced it was not a proper role for a professor. Some of his political enemies may have thought him a populist charlatan of the Wizard of Oz type. He had seen the light that analysis of what might result from alternative policies was more highly regarded in academic circles than prescribing what ought to be done. He was still guided by his mission to "set the world right," but as Rader put it, ". . . he began a noticeable withdrawal from his peculiar role in the reform movements of the late 19th century."[12]

However, even in his more scholarly middle years, Ely carried out his favorite role as pioneer. During his long career, he introduced instruction and research in agricultural economics, railroads and other forms of transportation, public utilities, urban and regional planning, parks, museums, and women's role in the economy. He became more conservative over time, but late in life he pushed measures for public ownership or control of such natural resources as land, minerals, forests, and water.[13]

The answer to the question of what kind of economics Ely brought to Madison and how he modified it over time begins with the observation that he believed that industrialization caused many problems that only a strong government could solve. Hence, he sought a middle-of-the-road stance between the market economy and the centrally directed economy. He spoke for Christian socialism, social democracy, collective bargaining, regulation of business, consumerism, environmentalism, and what is now called welfare-statism.

Why did Ely start out with a "school" and end up with a "department"?

Ely justified the formation of the School of Economics, Political Science, and History in terms of a "civil service academy" parallel to the military academies. He might have seen it as similar to the program of the new or history-based economics he was familiar with in German universities. Or he may have been impressed by the several multidisciplined schools recently started at some American universities, such as Michigan, Columbia, Yale, and Cornell. (The London School of Economics and Political Science was similar to the school at Wisconsin, but did not start until 1895.)

Note that economics topped the masthead of Ely's school in 1892. Does that indicate that he thought his own discipline had more to offer than either of the other two? The three departments had separate identities and each was apparently free to leave the school. Ely was the chair of the economics department and the director of the school. Each of the chairs of political science and history reported to him, and as director he reported, as would a dean, to the president of the university. Students could enroll in the school and major in one of the departments. Economics was a popular major and attracted graduate students as well as undergraduates. The economics staff had risen from two members to five members by 1902.

On occasion Ely talked as though he wanted to enlarge his school to encompass all social sciences, including philosophy, psychology, and law. But he was to confront contraction instead. The rationale for combining disciplines is that social change always turns up new problems that are likely to yield to a team of social engineers with varied skills. A problem-oriented school may be able to hire specialized employees to deal with clients of differing needs, e.g., some employees may be researchers and some may be extension workers who translate or apply research findings. In any case, Ely protected all reductions and to the end carried the flag for multidisciplinarianism.

The College of Letters and Science did not exist until 1899. In 1900 political science was taken out of Ely's school to become a department in the college, and in that same year, in contradictory fashion, two new schools were created, one for history and one for commerce. The latter had been a part of the economics department inside the School of Economics and History. From these actions it would appear that political science, history, and commerce did not share Ely's enthusiasm for multidisciplinary organization. Each wanted its own show!

Then in 1903, president Charles R. Van Hise, in his first year in office, moved to strengthen the College of Letters and Science by wiping out the schools of commerce, history, and economics and forming a newly named Department of Political Economy. History resumed its status as a department. The new political economy department contained economics, and as subdivisions or "courses," commerce and sociology.

In this shake-up Ely was demoted from being director of a school to chair of a department. He held that position until 1911, but never held an administrative post in the university after that, except as director of the Institute for Research in Land Economics and Public Utilities from 1920 to 1925. His successors as chairmen were Thomas K. Urdahl in 1911 and William H. Kiekhofer in 1916. The latter was chairman when Ely retired in 1925.

In 1909, Henry C. Taylor, over Ely's objection, established a separate Department of Agricultural Economics in the College of Agriculture. In 1918, the Department of Political Economy changed its name to Department of Economics, but continued to think of itself as leader of a mythical "division of economics" with four parts, namely, general economics, agricultural economics, commercial economics, and social economics. This "division" also recognized some faculty members in Extension and operated as a social group with regular interchanges of information and sponsorship of cooperative ventures. The several parts of the division had faculty members with joint appointments; they also cross-listed courses and had overlapping requirements for degrees. For one example, Ely himself in his later years at Wisconsin worked with agricultural economists and also with "commercial economists" interested in urban land economics.

Ely also believed in and organized multidisciplinary professional societies that were specialized to deal with a particular type of problem, e.g., the American Association for Labor Legislation in 1906, and the American Association for Agricultural Legislation in 1918. In 1920 he set up a multidisciplinary staff in the newly created Institute for Research in Land Economics and Public Utilities.

Two years after Ely retired in 1925, the subdepartment of commerce moved to separate departmental status (although it had a director and was called a school) within the College of Letters and Science. Sociology followed suit, becoming a department in 1929. Commerce attained independence from the College of Letters and Science and first claimed its own dean in 1944.

In a manner reminiscent of the 1918 division, economics, as late as 1941, recognized the Department of Agricultural Economics and the School of Commerce as "associated departments." These several groups had joint meetings that were social in nature but also were venues for clearance of new courses and new appointments. In one case, the Department of Economics reported to the dean of Letters and Science that it could not appoint a new faculty member—Milton Friedman—to teach certain courses because those courses were claimed by School of Commerce professors.[14]

The cooperative relationships among economics, agricultural economics, and commerce (now business administration) gradually yielded to harsh separatism in the period of explosive growth in the size of the university in the 1950s and 1960s. The new pattern is reinforced by the fact that agricultural economics hires mostly faculty members with agricultural Ph.D.'s and the School of Business hires mostly those with business degrees.

Multidisciplinary organizations are still to be found at Wisconsin. Perhaps the examples closest to Ely's school are professional schools like the School of Business (graduate and undergraduate degrees) and the Industrial Relations Research Institute (graduate degrees only), and the La Follette Institute of Public Affairs (graduate degrees only). Also, there are institutes or centers that do not offer degrees. Moreover, there are nondepartmental programs that do not offer degrees, such as area studies programs or the women's studies program.

The answer to why Ely started out with a school and ended up with a department is based in the concept of what an academic department is. The departmental organization reflects a shift from the "schoolmaster," who could teach any subject, to the researcher-professor who teaches in a specialized field. A corollary of this concept is that specialists want to associate with and be judged by others of the same specialty. Hence, a school or collection of scholars from different specialties is difficult to hold together. The exception seems to be the professional school, wherein the scholar defends the profession rather than the discipline.

Why did Ely have a longtime quarrel with his star colleague, John R. Commons?[15]

The reputation of the Wisconsin economics faculty in the early twentieth century was based on the research and publications of its members in several fields of inquiry. The field of labor history was most prominent in this period. At almost the same time, Wisconsin economists, along with other members of the university, became noted for their activism in public administration and legislative affairs, inspired by what came to be called the "Wisconsin Idea." They participated in the formulation of public policy in protective labor legislation, regulation of railroads and public utilities, income taxation, and several forms of social insurance. These activities were not inconsistent with, and indeed were an integral part of, the construct laid forth by Richard T. Ely in his definition of the "new economics."

It was Ely who produced the first book on labor history, *The Labor Movement in America*.[16] It was Ely who brought John R. Commons to Wisconsin in 1904. It was Ely who raised the funds that year for a labor history project, which, in 1910 and 1911, produced the ten-volume *Documentary History of American Industrial Society*.[17] And it was Ely who became embittered by his experience with Commons between 1904 and 1910 and turned away from labor history to other interests. (It should be mentioned that Ely also had stormy encounters and tribulations with others at the university, including presidents and deans.)

Ely reassessed his approach to scholarly work in the year of his 1894 "trial" before a committee of the university regents, and he resolved to adopt a more "scientific" approach.[18] In 1893 he had published an elementary text, *Outlines of Economics*.[19] In 1900 he published *Monopolies and Trusts*[20] and in 1903 he brought out *Studies in the Evolution of an Industrial Society*,[21] a book that Rader says Ely thought would make "an enduring contribution to the science of economics."[22] Although Rader observes that neither book did much to further Ely's reputation as an economic theorist, they were both evidence of his commitment to more rigorous economic research.

In view of his announced determination to write more and better economics, it is surprising that Ely, in fact, published very little between 1904 and 1914. But it is less surprising when we examine Ely's long-running quarrel with John R. Commons and Commons's students.

Harold L. Miller has written a revealing account of the 1904–14 period.[23] Ely and Commons probably misunderstood one another's objectives at the time of the latter's appointment in Wisconsin. Although both expected to systematize scholarship in the field of labor history, it may be that only Ely anticipated that the research would contribute to the revision of his 1886 book, *The Labor Movement in America*. Ely's planning for a history of industrial democracy in the United States began in 1902 or 1903. By March 1904, he had obtained $24,000—enough to launch the American Bureau of Industrial Research (ABIR) and to convince President Van Hise and the regents of the University of Wisconsin to appoint John R. Commons to a professorship so that he, along with Ely, could be a codirector of the project. The fund paid Commons two-thirds of his salary for three years while the university paid the other third. Obligated to teach during one semester each year, the remainder of his time was to be devoted to the labor history project.

Although Ely was in administrative charge of the project, the original agreement between Ely and Commons called for a division of the research work between the two men. Commons had responsibility for the colonial period and the post–Civil War years while Ely was to cover the forty years preceding the Civil War. The original agreement also assigned Ely the first $1,000 of annual royalties from ABIR publications for a period of ten years. Ely and V. Everit Macy, perhaps the principal financial contributor, had envisioned the final result—to be completed within five years—as being an interpretive history of American industrial society in one or more volumes. In 1905, not long after the project had started, Commons, having discovered rich sources of documents on the subject, proposed that they first publish a documentary history. This change from the scheme originally specified in the agreement was accepted by Ely. The ultimate result was the publication of the ten-volume *Documentary History of American Industrial Society* in 1910 and 1911. This effort used up essentially all of the original funds. Commons's coeditors on the documentary history included Helen L. Sumner and John B. Andrews (both graduate students) and a faculty colleague in the history department, Ulrich B. Phillips, who undertook the task of document collection and interpretation in the South. Also Eugene A. Gilmore, a professor of law, managed the conspiracy case materials. Commons's famous essay on the shoemakers (not a document) appears in volume 3.

It is not hard to see how the misunderstanding about the ABIR objectives could develop into open disagreement. Sometime early in the project, Ely contracted with Helen Sumner to revise his 1886 book, *The Labor Movement in America*. This revision, he declared, was part of the work he had originally envisioned when the ABIR was created. But Commons complained in 1909 that in employing Helen Sumner "who had been his student and had worked closely with him, it was [Ely's] design to appropriate the results of [Commons's] original work."[24] Ely's counterproposal was to publish the revised edition of the 1886 book as "under the auspices of ABIR," with the title page indicating that it had been revised by John R. Commons and Helen L. Sumner. Both Commons and Sumner rejected the suggestion, according to Ely, and so he relieved Sumner of her contractual obligation.[25] Ely's later efforts to revise the 1886 book will be described later.

A second misunderstanding involved both Ely's and Commons's commitments to the work of the project. Ely complained that although ABIR was paying two-thirds of Commons's annual salary during his first three years at Wisconsin, Commons had spent a substantial portion of his time in the service of the state government and other employers. These activities are perhaps most succinctly described by quoting two paragraphs from Lafayette Harter's biography of Commons.

> Soon after he arrived in Wisconsin he drafted the Civil Service Law of 1905 for Governor La Follette. Shortly afterwards, in 1906, he participated in the National Civic Federation study of some thirty-five municipally and privately owned gas, electric light and power, and street railroad companies in the United States and England. As part of the study, he made a five-month trip to the British Isles. After his return he undertook the supervision of the labor portion of the Pittsburgh Survey, which was financed by the Russell Sage Foundation. This study was made by a number of investigators and some social workers who later published the magazine *Survey*. Commons' part of this survey of social conditions in Pittsburgh included a study of the problems of the wage earners. To aid him in his share of the work he took along several of his students.
>
> His experiences in these two studies, the one on public utilities and the second on working conditions, provided him with background for drafting two important Wisconsin laws. In 1907 he drafted the Public Utility Act, which became the model for many others throughout the nation. His observance during the Pittsburgh Survey of the need for improving safety conditions and compensating injured workers contributed to the study he made preparatory to drafting the (1911) law creating Wisconsin's Industrial Commission . . .[26]

In a later report (probably to Van Hise concerning their disputes) Ely commented that he had "urged him [Commons] not to undertake the investigation of public utilities, feeling that it was unwise," and that he had tried to discourage the five-month trip to the British Isles, which Commons later admitted had been a mistake.[27]

Commons's frequent absences were the basis of two other charges by Ely. First, in 1909 he thought that the ABIR project was being delayed unnecessarily and that it would become necessary (and difficult) to request additional funds to finish it. The shift in focus to collection of documents had not only lengthened the program but had put off what Ely considered the final objective, an interpretive history of industrial democracy. Second, Ely thought that Commons's periodic reports gave him (Ely) no credit for what he considered to be his own substantial scholarly contributions. In 1909, commenting on Commons's report of activity for the previous five years, he suggested that instead of saying "I submit the *Documentary History*," Commons should say "we submit, etc." and instead of "I have been able to index, etc." he should say "it has been possible to index." Ely recounts his many trips and his extensive correspondence to gather documentary materials, and then says: "Apart from the library work, I am confident that I have put in as much time in collecting material as Professor Commons, and I should not be surprised if I have put in even more time than Professor Commons. I have also secured very noteworthy results . . ."[28] The late Louis Kaplan, for many years director of University Libraries, supported Ely's claim that the materials in the collections made possible by ABIR were major additions to Wisconsin libraries.[29]

One of Ely's chief complaints against Commons was his failure to submit orderly accounts of his ABIR expenditures. Commons did not keep careful books. He failed to submit vouchers or receipts for specific expenditures and apparently expected reimbursement for totals of whatever he believed he had spent. This was not satisfactory for Ely, who had the responsibility for keeping the books and reporting on ABIR's fiscal affairs to the contributors. Because he believed that he had a special responsibility for managing expenditures, Ely engaged in a continuing battle with Commons throughout the period of the research to get him to submit satisfactory supporting records.[30]

Commons also directed complaints against Ely. In 1906 Ely and Commons and others formed the American Association for Labor Legislation. Ely became its first president and Commons its secretary. Later Commons complained that this work was a diversion from his principal activities and that he had undertaken it under urgent pressure from Ely.[31] Commons also complained that Ely unfairly sought royalties from the *Documentary History* series.[32]

From what has been recounted above it appears that the period between 1904 and 1910, when the first part of the *Documentary History* was published, was a time of frustration for Ely. He had been unable to revise his 1886 book on the American labor movement and had thus far been thwarted in his initial effort to produce a more comprehensive history of industrial democracy. And presumably his collecting of documents and ABIR project administrative duties, together with his department chairmanship and teaching, had left him little time to do his own writing.

Miller has described the mounting conflicts between the two men. Two confrontations with Commons in 1909 led to mediation by President Charles R. Van Hise. As a result of the president's first mediation effort it was agreed that, in addition to the *Documentary History*, there would be two more books: one by Ely, a revision of *The Labor Movement in America*, and the other by Commons, a treatment of the policy, organization, history, and philosophy of the trade union movement. The latter book was to be known as *The History of Labor in the United States*.

Shortly thereafter came the death of Carroll D. Wright, who headed the Carnegie Institution's labor history project. Commons was offered an opportunity to combine Wright's work with his proposed *History of Labor*. (This is discussed in Commons's autobiography.[33]) Another dispute arose out of Commons's proposals of how to fund this newly combined work. As a result, President Van Hise worked out a second compromise between Ely and Commons, also in 1909, that included, in addition to the two previously agreed-upon projected publications, a resurrection of Ely's 1904 vision: a book to be titled *A History of American Industrial Democracy*. It was not clear whether Ely or Commons was to be the leading author. And sometimes the word "society" was substituted for "democracy" in the title. In any event, neither Ely's revision of *The Labor Movement in America* nor *A History of American Industrial Democracy* (or "Society") was ever published.

At this point the Ely-Commons story takes a dramatic turn. It appears that the Carnegie money was to go directly to Commons without going through Ely or the ABIR. Commons drew up a plan, which, Ely said in a report to President Van Hise, ". . . completely eliminates me, and instead of a work by Ely and Commons in accordance with the original contract widely advertised to the world, we are promised a work by Commons and Sumner."[34] From this point on, Commons would raise and manage his own research funds without Ely's help.

Commons proceeded, with Carnegie Institution's money, with the assistance of current and former graduate students, and with many interruptions and diversions, to organize the writing of what turned out to be the first two volumes of *The History of Labor in the United States*, finally published in 1918.[35]

Although Ely was sharply critical of Commons for failing to devote sufficient time to the ABIR project, Commons probably took satisfaction in his overall scholarly productivity during that period. Between 1904 and 1914 Commons edited the following works: *Trade Unionism and Labor Problems* (1905); the *Documentary History* in ten volumes (1910 and 1911); and *Labor and Administration* (1913). He also published *Races and Immigrants* (1907) and several additional journal articles not included in the edited volumes noted above. Additionally, he served a two-year term as a full-time member of the Wisconsin Industrial Commission, 1911–13.

On his part, Ely made an arrangement with William H. Price, an instructor in the department between 1906 and 1909, to revise *The Labor Movement in America*. According to Miller, Price had health problems and gave up the work in 1912. By this time Ely had lost much of his interest in the endeavor and was devoting his energies to a substantial work of a different nature: *Property and Contract in Their Relations to the Distribution of Wealth*,[36] which was published in two volumes in 1914. Later Ely engaged Selig Perlman to do the work that Price's bad health prevented him from doing. Perlman presented Ely a draft of his proposed revision. Ely was not satisfied with it and thereupon abandoned the revision. It appears that the draft became Perlman's 1922 publication, *The History of Trade Unionism*, which his son Mark called "perhaps (his) best book."[37]

This cursory account of some of the occurrences in the Department of Political Economy in the decade after 1904 reveals a tone of animus, bitterness, and frustration beneath the surface of what seemed to be triumphal achievements. Although the atmosphere in the department, as evidenced by the Ely-Commons contretemps, seems not to have reduced Commons's research output, it did seem to have a negative effect upon Ely. After publishing two substantial books in 1900 and 1903, he appeared poised in 1904 to produce more of the results of what he called "scientific" investigation. Instead, his association with Commons and ABIR seems to have launched him into a rancorous period marked by scholarly unproductiveness. For approximately a decade (up to 1914) he published no new book. He did, however, make substantial contributions to building the Wisconsin collections of labor history materials.

There are several answers to why Ely had a longtime quarrel with Commons. Ely's answer: A collection of documents is not a history! Common's rejoinder: He tried to steal my stuff! A neutral observer: Neither senior partner wanted to write a labor history book.

We can summarize our discussion of Ely's service at Wisconsin as follows. The type of economics he brought to Madison was historical, empirical, problem-oriented, middle-way welfare statism. He started out with a "school" and ended up with a "department" in part because of a strong national trend toward free-standing, narrowly specialized departments. And the quarrel with his star colleague, John R. Commons, was at base caused by Commons's refusal, starting in 1904, to follow Ely's priorities for use of research time and money. Despite his quarrels with Commons, Ely's career has left a legacy that is felt one hundred years later.

Notes

1. Richard T. Ely *Ground Under Our Feet* (New York: Macmillan, 1938) p. 233.

2. In this introductory section we rely heavily on Merle Curti and Vernon Carstensen, *The University of Wisconsin: A History, 1848 to 1925* (Madison: University of Wisconsin Press, 1949); John P. Henderson, a chapter in *Breaking the Academic Mold: Economics and Higher Learning in the 19th Century*, ed. William J. Barber (Middletown: Wesleyan University Press, 1988); and Robert J. Lampman, *Economists at Wisconsin, 1892–1992* (Madison: Regents of the University of Wisconsin System, 1993).

3. Edwin E. Witte in a letter to LaFayette Harter, then a graduate student at Stanford University, writing a Ph.D. thesis on John R. Commons, 1960, Witte Papers, Wisconsin State Historical Society. Witte told Harter he believed that antigovernment bias was not strong among American economists before 1900.

4. A. W. Coats, "Richard T. Ely" in *International Encyclopedia of the Social Sciences*, ed. David C. Sills (New York: Macmillan and the Free Press, 1968), pp. 33–35.

5. Benjamin G. Rader, *The Academic Mind and Reform: The Influence of Richard T. Ely in American Life* (Lexington: University of Kentucky Press, 1966), p. 131; J. Davis Hoeveler, Jr., "The University and the Social Gospel: The Intellectual Origins of the Wisconsin Idea," *Wisconsin Magazine of History* 59 (summer 1976): 282–89.

6. James T. Kloppenberg, *Uncertain Victory: Social Democracy and Progressivism in European and American Thought, 1870–1920* (Oxford: University Oxford Press, 1986), p. 209.

7. A. W. Coats, "The Political Economy Club: A Neglected Episode in American Economic Thought," *American Economic Review* 51 (June 1961): 624–37.

8. Richard T. Ely, *The American Labor Movement* (New York: Thomas Y. Crowell, 1886).

9. Richard T. Ely, *Socialism and Social Reform* (New York: Thomas Y. Crowell, 1894).

10. Theron F. Schlabach, "An Aristocrat on Trial: The Case of Richard T. Ely," *Wisconsin Magazine of History*, (winter 1963–64): 146.

11. Sidney Fine, *Laissez Faire and the General Welfare State: A Study of Conflict in American Thought, 1865–1901* (Ann Arbor: University of Michigan Press, 1956).

12. Rader, *Academic Mind and Reform*, p. 131.

13. Richard T. Ely and George S. Wehrwein, *Land Economics* (New York: Macmillan, 1940).

14. Lampman, *Economists at Wisconsin*, pp. 118–21.

15. For this section, we have drawn heavily on Rader, *Academic Mind and Reform*, and Harold L. Miller, "The American Bureau of Industrial Research and the Origins of the 'Wisconsin School' of Labor History," *Labor History* 25, no. 2 (spring 1984): 165–88.

16. Ely, *American Labor Movement*.

17. John R. Commons et al., eds., *Documentary History of American Industrial Society* (Cleveland: A. H. Clark Co., 1910–11).

18. Rader, *Academic Mind and Reform*, pp. 154–56.

19. Richard T. Ely, *Outlines of Economics* (New York: Hunt & Eaton, 1893).

20. Richard T. Ely, *Monopolies and Trusts* (New York: Macmillan, 1900).

21. Richard T. Ely, *Studies in the Evolution of an Industrial Society* (New York: Macmillan, 1903). Also, with the help of students and colleagues Thomas S. Adams, Max O. Lorenz, and Allyn A. Young, he revised his *Outlines of Economics*, publishing a second edition in

1908. This book (revised several more times) was a leading economic text of its time and could be considered the Samuelson of the first three decades of this century.

22. Rader, *Academic Mind and Reform*, p. 159.

23. Miller, "The ABIR."

24. As cited by Miller, "The ABIR," p. 180.

25. "Statement of Richard T. Ely in regard to the report of John R. Commons, 1904–1909, and also in relation to the accompanying papers entitled 'Accounts and Supplements.'" Reel 182, *Ely Papers*, 1909, Wisconsin State Historical Society.

26. Lafayette G. Harter, Jr., *John R. Commons: His Assault on Laissez-faire* (Corvallis: Oregon State University Press, 1962), p. 72.

27. "Statement of Richard T. Ely," in *Ely Papers*, Reel 182, Wisconsin State Historical Society.

28. Ibid.

29. Louis Kaplan, *College and Research Libraries* 18 (March 1957): 141.

30. "Statement of Richard T. Ely," in *Ely Papers*, Reel 182, Wisconsin State Historical Society.

31. Ibid.

32. Miller has given an account of the royalty dispute, "The ABIR," pp. 173, 181–84.

33. John R. Commons, *Myself* (New York: Macmillan, 1934), pp. 137–38.

34. "Statement of Richard T. Ely," in *Ely Papers*, Reel 182, Wisconsin State Historical Society. The presidential papers of Charles R. Van Hise at the University of Wisconsin Memorial Library archives are incomplete with respect to this story. In the file of correspondence from 1909 (Box 10, folder 171) there is a card dated June 8, 1925, bearing this message: "Materials on Ely-Commons dispute destroyed at the request of Professor C—" The message was handwritten without a signature.

35. In addition to Commons, the authors of volumes 1 and 2 were David J. Saposs, Helen J. Sumner, E. B. Mittelman, H. E. Hoagland, John R. Andrews, and Selig Perlman. There was also an introduction by Henry W. Farnam. Volume 3 of that series (by Elizabeth Brandeis and Don Lescohier), and volume 4 (by Selig Perlman and Philip Taft), were published by Macmillan in 1935. The introduction to volume 3 states that "the cost of the enterprise, extending over six years, was covered by generous contributions made by the late Professor Henry W. Farnum to Professor Commons in 1928 and by unstinted aid from the research funds of the University of Wisconsin." It appears that Commons had nothing to do with these two volumes after 1918.

36. Richard T. Ely, *Property and Contract and Their Relations to the Distribution of Wealth*, 2 vols. (New York: Macmillan, 1914).

37. This quote appears in an article by Leon Fink: "A Memoir of Selig Perlman and His Life at the University of Wisconsin: Based on an Interview of Mark Perlman conducted and edited by Leon Fink," *Labor History* 32, no. 4 (fall 1991): 500–525. Selig Perlman's book was published by Macmillan. In this same interview, Mark Perlman reports that Ely attempted to deny Selig Perlman's promotion in 1918.

Economists, the Economics Profession, and Academic Freedom in the United States

A. W. Coats

T he raison d'être of this occasion probably seems self-evident to most members of this audience, and I do not question the presumption that Ely's trial was an important landmark in the emergence of the economics profession in the United States. Nevertheless, in adopting the long-term perspective necessary for writing this paper, it is not iconoclastic to claim that the professionalization of economics, the social sciences, and indeed the professoriate within the United States would have proceeded at much the same pace and with much the same outcome if Richard T. Ely had never been born. In other words, had he not existed, it would not have been necessary to invent him!

This is not to deny that in 1894 Ely was the most widely known—some contemporaries would have said the most notorious—economist in America; or to deny that economists were then in the vanguard in the battle for academic freedom. Ely's position as a founder and the first secretary of the American Economic Association (AEA), from 1885 to 1892, was of crucial practical as well as symbolic significance. And although he had temporarily exiled himself from the association during his early years in Madison, his former status and continuing public prominence ensured that Oliver Wells's attack would be viewed as a serious threat by other leading members of the emerging economics profession, including those who disliked Ely's ideas and disapproved of his energetic self-aggrandizement.

From this safe distance it is tempting to dismiss Wells's campaign as a damp squib. Although he enlisted the help of an influential magazine, the New York-based *Nation*, in his cause, thereby guaranteeing national publicity, Wells was neither a formidable nor a well-prepared antagonist. Moreover, the support Ely received from the university's president and from some of the regents meant that his position was exceptionally favorable compared with that of most professorial victims of academic freedom cases.

A. W. Coats is professor emeritus of economic and social history at Nottingham University, U.K., and has written extensively about the history and development of the economics profession.

Nevertheless, at the time the trial was very serious, and it directly contributed to the effective mobilization of a sizeable band of concerned social scientists. This was a major new development in the professionalization process in America. And yet, in a sense, Ely's trial did not center on the question of academic freedom. In flatly denying all of Wells's charges, Ely missed a golden opportunity to make the case for the fearless and unrestricted sifting and winnowing of truth, even declaring publicly that if the accusations against him were true, they would "unquestionably unfit me to occupy a responsible position as an instructor of youth in a great university." His forthright repudiation of radicalism and subsequent adoption of a more cautiously conservative pattern of behavior was entirely compatible with, and doubtless a direct influence on, the prevailing trend in American economics. As Mary O. Furner pointedly observed in her excellent study, *Advocacy and Objectivity*, in the contest between advocacy and objectivity, Ely chose security (p. 184; cf.p. 157).

The interrelated issues of freedom of expression, security of tenure, and professional status for American economists and social scientists evolved gradually from the 1880s through the early decades of this century. The cases of Henry Carter Adams at Cornell and Michigan, Ely at Wisconsin, Edward W. Bemis at Chicago, Elisha B. Andrews at Brown, John R. Commons at Indiana and Syracuse, and Edward A. Ross at Stanford, have been fully explored by Walter P. Metzger, Mary Furner, and other scholars, and need not be reexamined here. As Furner has stated, these cases "grew out of unresolved ambiguities in the academic power structure and domestic disagreements over contemporary American political issues" such as the tariff, labor unions, strikes, municipal monopolies, the railroads, the trusts, free silver, etc. (Furner, pp. 206, 143). The rising generation of social science professionals had to work out their collective response by a process of trial and error. As E. R. A. Seligman, the leading economist defender of academic freedom in the pre–World War I period, complained in 1897 to the trustees of Brown University: "To say that the University teacher should express no opinion on controverted questions unless that opinion is shared by the Powers that be is to strike a death blow to all intellectual progress" (Furner, p. 221). The immediate consequences would be eastern professors preaching gold and western scholars swearing by silver; northerners being hired to teach free trade and southerners to support the tariff—and this would eventually mean the end of economic science.

But what, if anything, could the economists do to counter this threat? In her account of the Madison affair, Furner tends to undervalue the support Ely received from his fellow economists, saying:

> the profession made no united effort to help Ely. No meeting of the AEA was called; no association position was taken. Nothing indicates that the Executive Council ever met or that there was any official correspondence regarding the danger to Ely, though the matter dragged on for a month before the Board of Regents issued a statement clearing him. (P. 154)

Strictly speaking, this is correct; but it fails to acknowledge the relevant context. Collectively, the economists were ill prepared for this challenge, even had they had the time to mobilize their resources. The AEA's Executive Council was not scheduled to meet until the annual conference in December, and Ely's fate was settled well before then. When the first full-blown academic freedom case involving an economist occurred a year later at the University of Chicago, the victim, Edward Bemis, was not of sufficient scientific or professional prominence to inspire the personal support Ely received, support to which he doubtless considered himself fully entitled. Even during the Andrews and Ross affairs, the association as such took no official position, though in the latter instance it came very close to doing so. In 1894, the union of economists had been neither prepared, strong, nor unified enough to do more to help Ely. Moreover, as Furner observes, the Wisconsin regents' eloquent defense of the abstract principle of academic freedom fell short of establishing guidelines for behavior in concrete situations. However, the experience gained from the series of academic freedom cases was more important than any other single factor in setting the pattern for relations between social scientists and society (Furner, p. 163).

Furner describes how, during the next decade or so, a recognizable consensus about professional behavior and standards evolved, under the influence of a dominant

> small, highly professionalized elite which determined a model for younger, less self-conscious academics to follow . . . out of all the [academic freedom and tenure] cases there emerged a rudimentary discipline which identified the degree and type of advocacy that was entitled to collective security. Within the limits where agreement could be reached on goals and tactics, the economists had exchanged the capricious discipline provided by powerful external opponents for the more steady influence of national professional control. . . .

The academic freedom cases cut two ways. They established more autonomy than professional social scientists had enjoyed before. They also demonstrated the negative results of partisanship. For better or worse, these troubles taught many academics to conserve their image, and preserve their institutions, to prepare to defend themselves but avoid the necessity, to exert influence quietly as experts rather than noisily as partisans. (Pp. 257–58)

The growth of professional self-consciousness among economists and other social scientists may not have been in fact as comprehensive and uniform as Furner suggests. The number of well-documented "cases" is insufficient to serve as a basis of confident generalizations about the professionalization process; and at one point Furner concedes that a somewhat different picture might be revealed were we able to study the academic rank and file. "If scholarly opinion in colleges and universities had been polled in 1897," Furner observes, "as many social scientists as not would probably still have thought of their own position as political sinecures where advocacy that conformed to local expectations was properly expected" (p. 228; cf.p. 308). This is surely an overly optimistic conjecture, given the variety of factors affecting any individual's academic security—such as the personal characteristics and attitudes of trustees, regents, university presidents, and potential faculty victims. It was easy to dispose of an unwanted professor, given the prevalence of annual contracts and the absence of formal guarantees of security of tenure, the kind of security that subsequently became a major goal of the American Association of University Professors (AAUP).

At the height of the Andrews controversy, in 1897, two leading conservative economists, E. R. A. Seligman of Columbia, and Frank W. Taussig of Harvard, urged their AEA colleagues to "act corporately" on Andrews's behalf. Others hesitated, arguing that an official statement would merely stiffen the trustees' resolve. AEA Secretary Charles Hull, of Cornell, was prepared to make a total commitment on the victim's behalf, but he doubted that the association's officers had the right to speak for the entire membership, and he feared that too forceful a stance would simply split the membership. Some economists believed that Andrews's predicament "was mainly a question of freedom of teaching, not a special concern of economists" (Furner, p. 218), for research and policy advising were considered to have higher priority. So, in the end, following Hull's proposal, thirty-three leading social scientists signed a petition to the Brown Trustees arguing that the university should take no action that could be construed as limiting the freedom of speech in the teaching body of our universities. . . . We believe that no questions should enter except as to capacity, faithfulness, and general efficiency in the performance of appointed duty. . . . To undertake inquiry as to the soundness of opinions expressed on any question, or set of questions, must inevitably limit freedom of expression, tend to destroy intellectual independence, and to diminish public respect for the conclusions of all investigations. (Furner, p. 218)

Twenty more social scientists signed petitions later, or indicated they would have signed, had the request arrived before they left for the summer, so that in the end, "Almost all the prominent first-generation professionals supported the protest" (Furner, p. 219). There were a few holdouts; but when all the signatures of university presidents, economists, and alumni were combined they amounted to a pile of documents one foot high, which was presented to the Brown Corporation. The next day the trustees asked Andrews to withdraw his resignation, and he did so. It was clearly a victory for academic freedom. However, a year later Andrews left Brown for the University of Nebraska, a more liberal institution.

Summing up the experience until 1897, Furner comments:

Professionalization had not progressed so far . . . that a principled defense of the economist's right of advocacy had become an aspect of professional identity. Yet the leading professionals had tentatively established a policy of defending established scholars under certain conditions: when the subject at issue was clearly a conventional concern of economics; when the controversial doctrines fell into an area where the accuracy of calculation and reasoning— one test of objectivity—could be easily demonstrated; where there was no violation of ethical procedure, excessive popularization, or indoctrination; and where the support of influential scholars and citizens somewhere, if not in the immediate area, located the controversial teaching within the range of permissible dissent. (P. 228)

Three years after the resolution of the Andrews case, the community of economists faced a new challenge, Edward Ross's dismissal from Leland Stanford Junior University. A former secretary of the AEA, Ross had incurred the wrath of Stanford's sole trustee, Mrs. Jane Stanford, because of his outspoken advocacy of free silver during the Bryan presidential election campaign, his opposition to the use of "coolie" immigrant labor in California, and his prediction that all natural monopolies, including railroads, would eventually pass into public ownership. Needless to say, the wife of the deceased railroad magnate did not find these views congenial.

Ross's outspokenness, his confident self-publicizing, and his occasionally inflammatory remarks, ensured that his dismissal would attract even more attention nationally than any previous case involving a social scientist, especially when several of his Stanford colleagues resigned in protest. This was a direct challenge to the university authorities' power. Inevitably there was a call for action in December 1900 when the economists assembled for their annual meeting in Detroit. (Oddly enough, Ely was president then.) After Ross had shown Seligman all the relevant documents, thereby convincing him that his (Ross's) attitude had been "completely scientific," various options were considered, including the conduct of an official investigation and the issue of an official AEA report. However, once again, as in 1897, there were various reservations, including the concern that the Detroit conferees lacked the authority to speak for the entire AEA membership, and the fact that an official AEA report would necessarily be issued under Ely's signature, thereby possibly diminishing its impact in some quarters. So instead of official action, a three-man semi-official committee of conservative economists, headed by Seligman, was appointed. They eventually issued the fifteen-page *Report on the Dismissal of Professor Ross from Leland Stanford Junior University* (1901). A proposal to publish all the relevant documents in the case was rejected, and, as Furner comments:

> In the end Seligman established the professional procedure—a spare, terse report addressed directly to the profession which summarized events at Stanford, described the committee's activities [including their unsuccessful effort to obtain the cooperation of the Stanford authorities], and presented textual evidence that Ross had been fired for his opinions. (P. 246)

In due course, sixteen hundred copies of the report were distributed to social scientists, university presidents, and others. Support for this document was "almost universal . . . among leading professional social scientists," although some critics (including AEA Secretary Hull, who would sign it only in his official capacity) were still concerned that it would be interpreted as an official AEA statement—and rightly so.

From this distant and comfortable perspective it is tempting to decry the AEA members' response to the Ross crisis as a half-hearted compromise. There were, admittedly, substantial individual efforts to help those Stanford faculty members who resigned in protest or were dismissed after Ross's departure; but a proposal to boycott Stanford elicited little support. Damage to Stanford was serious, but not lasting, and some members of the older generation believed that some of their juniors were too eager to fill the vacant slots, willing to sacrifice their academic principles to their career interests. Even Seligman thought the salvation of Ross's career was an important contribution to academic freedom, as though that concept incorporated a virtual guarantee of employment (Furner, pp. 250, 251).

From this time on, security of tenure and freedom of academic expression were inextricably linked, and Furner claims that universities became more circumspect in dealing with economists because of their "willingness to act collectively, on occasion, in their colleagues' defense" (p. 256). Radicalism went out of favor; acceptance of the status quo prevailed, at least among the majority of economists; and a more relativistic concept of truth probably helped to discourage confrontational responses to contemporary problems. The growth of academic specialization coupled with a more professional attitude encouraged caution, self-scrutiny, care with sources and methods, and a generally heightened rationality. Objectivity was more highly valued, while ideological considerations were generally unacknowledged (Furner, pp. 322–23). The subdivision of the social sciences was accompanied by an increasing reluctance to confront big controversial questions. "The academic professional having retreated to the security of technical expertise, left to journalists and propagandists the original mission, the comprehensive assessment of industrial society, that had fostered the professionalization of social science" (Furner, p. 324).

The academic freedom cases considered earlier prepared the ground for the founding of the AAUP, in 1915, a landmark event to which leading economists and social scientists made a disproportionate contribution. But before examining that episode, it is worth digressing to mention the case of Willard Fisher, an economist at Wesleyan University, in 1913, for the economists' unprecedented response reveals their continuing uncertainty as to the most appropriate manner of handling such matters. The central issue was religion, not economics, and this recalls an earlier era, when religious heresy was the most common issue in academic freedom cases, and when most professors and members of university and college boards of trustees were clergymen. Fisher, a religious man who had been on the Wesleyan faculty for twenty years, was asked to resign following his public statements on religious observances, which included a proposal to close the churches temporarily as an experiment, on the grounds that "if there were no churches open for a time many good religious people would be constrained to turn to more religious duties [than church attendance], of kindly service and the like" (*American Economic Review, Papers and Proceedings* [to be abbreviated as *AER P&P*] 1913, p. 255. When President Shanklin demanded his resignation, Fisher complied meekly; but surprisingly, two months later the *AER* devoted four pages to the Fisher-Shanklin correspondence.[1] Once again, the economists organized an investigation headed by Seligman, and although it proved abortive it contributed directly to the economists' decision to participate in a Joint Committee on Academic Freedom and Academic Tenure composed of members of the AEA, the American Political Science Association (APSA), and the American Sociological Society (ASS). The AEA's resolution, at its December 1913 meeting, recommended that

> a committee of three be reconstituted to examine and report on the present situation in American educational institutions as to the liberty of thought, freedom of speech, and security of tenure for teachers of economics, and that this committee be authorized to cooperate with any other committees which may be constituted by other societies. (*AER P&P* 4 [1914]: 196–67.

This committee was obviously part of a wider movement that had been gathering momentum for some time. (See Metzger, 1955 and 1973; also Wilson, 1980.)

Twelve months later a nine-man committee, under Seligman's chairmanship, with equal representation from the AEA, APSA, and ASS, presented its eight-page *Preliminary Report on Academic Freedom and Tenure* to the participating organizations. The report was preliminary, Seligman explained, because the subject was "bristling with complexities," and the next year an "extended" report (without the qualifying word "preliminary") was presented by an "expanded" committee to the AAUP at a meeting in Washington, in January 1916, and to the AEA. (The *Preliminary Report* had been published in the *AER*, but the extended version was not.) This expanded committee was the immediate precursor of the AAUP's Committee A on Academic Freedom and Academic Tenure, which is still active.[2]

The inauguration of the AAUP marks a decisive turning point in the history of the American economists' collective involvement in the cause of academic freedom. Although economists played an integral part in the emergence and early development of the AAUP, they did so as individuals, not as AEA representatives. The Andrews and Ross cases had demonstrated the economists' reluctance to undertake official AEA investigations, even when leading figures were involved, and after 1915 there are few references to academic freedom, either in the AEA's archives or in its publications. This changed in the 1940's, as will be described later. Correspondence found in the association's files gives an indication of at least some economists' attitudes to the problem.

Writing to Secretary Young, Henry Carter Adams, a cofounder and early president of the AEA, himself the victim of an arbitrary dismissal, observed:

> In this whole matter of university freedom I am in favor of anything that will allay the interest which the American Association [sic] evinces in such matters. Nine times out of ten, it is the fault of the man rather than of the institution. (AEA Archives, April 26, 1915)

In his reply, Young expressed "cordial agreement. . . . I believe that what abuse of academic freedom there is comes largely from professors rather than from administrative officers" (AEA Archives Young to Adams, May 5, 1915). It is impossible to know whether these views were representative of economists' opinions in 1915. But they may help to explain the AEA's effective withdrawal from academic freedom issues until World War II.[3] Young was undoubtedly aware that the AAUP was being flooded with requests for assistance, and he also appreciated the difficulties encountered by those who undertook investigations of particular cases. Even so, his position is surprising, given his subsequent prominence as chairman of AAUP committees. He was certainly no crusader, and his apparently unsympathetic attitude to the victims may help to explain his endorsement of the Special Committee's *Report on Academic Freedom in Wartime*, which advocated stringent restrictions on the liberty of expression during the national emergency. (Cf. *AAUP Bulletin*, Vol. 4.)

Whatever the reasons, the growth of professional self-consciousness among American social scientists during the first three decades of this century was entirely in accord with the concurrent dramatic changes in American higher education. In his powerful study, *Universities and the Capitalist State: Corporate Liberalism and the Reconstruction of American Higher Education, 1894–1928*, Clyde Barrow identifies three broadly parallel processes: the rising prominence of corporate capitalists on university governing boards; the modernizing of institutional structures in higher education; and the academic development of a professional intellectual type—the research-oriented specialist/expert scientist/scholar.[4] It need hardly be emphasized that Ely was an exemplar in this third category.

This is not the place to examine in detail the impact of the managerial revolution on the more responsive members of the professoriate. The central feature, Barrow claims, was:

> the introduction of corporate managerial techniques into higher education that have a real impact on the kinds of activities and scholarship that are rewarded. . . . . The ideology clearly originated within a corporate elite that has successfully forged a long-term coalition with other political, bureaucratic and administrative officials who remain its chief proponents. (Barrow, p. 253)

In this situation, conflict between the business and academic communities was inevitable, but it was limited, because they needed and learned to live with each other.

> To achieve political legitimacy in a democratic society . . . business has found that it must continually accommodate the demands of independent scholarship and the concerns of a wider public . . . [and consequently] a pre-existing pattern of institutional checks and balances has never been eliminated by proponents of the corporate ideal. These include tenure, peer review, consultative faculty senates, and the nomination of new faculty. The subordinate role of such checks rarely makes [them] useful for offensive strategies within the university, but they do set up defensive barriers which protect certain free space and prevent it from being eliminated altogether. (Barrow, p. 254)

Barrow's study examines in detail the centralizing and standardizing influence of such bodies as the Carnegie Foundation for the Advancement of Teaching, the National Research Council (founded in 1916), and the General Education Board chartered by John D. Rockefeller. Inspired by the concern for national security during World War I, and the long-term quest for social efficiency, the influence of these organizations was pervasive, even if indirect. As Barrow acknowledges:

> Individual scholars might have no interest in this [corporate] agenda and might not share its motivations and values. Yet they could easily lend themselves to its purposes, while maintaining the subjective illusion of professional autonomy. Most scholars were not even aware that a national research agenda existed, except to the extent that professional interest led them to respond to indirect signals, such as what proposals were being funded, the kind of research being published, and the areas of inquiry that seemed to most inter-

est professional scientific elites. A process of selection, professional advancement, and self-selection could therefore build, reinforce, and perpetuate the
content of an ideological apparatus, even while scholars maintained their subjective illusions of autonomy. The ideological character of national science did
not reside in the subjective intentions of any particular scholar but in the
institutional structure which directed that authority. (Barrow, p. 151)

How does academic freedom fit into this scenario? First, it is essential to
recognize that Americans conceived of this concept in pragmatic rather than
idealistic terms, such as: security of tenure; professorial control over hiring,
promotion, and firing; and the claim that what laymen regarded as special
privileges were in fact essential preconditions of the advancement of knowledge. As Walter Metzger observed: "Academic freedom was the end: due
process, tenure, and the establishment of professional competence were the
means" (Hofstadter and Metzger, 1955, p. 481). The emphasis on scholarly
and scientific standards was an integral part of the effort to achieve respectability and autonomy, and thereby strengthen the position of the academic establishment. Second, it is clear that the founders and leaders of the AAUP were,
like the leaders of the principal national scholarly societies, the professoriate's
elite—what Metzger has called "the aristocrats of academic labor" (ibid, p.
477). As noted earlier, the AEA played no official part in the AAUP's activities,
and the economists expressed no official misgivings about the stringent and
unprecedented restrictions on academic freedom advocated by Young's AAUP
committee on wartime conditions. Ely and John R. Commons were among
those economists whose patriotic zeal led them to advocate the dismissal of any
professor unwise enough to oppose, criticize, or in other ways undermine the
nation's war effort.[5] Their crude emotional patriotism and anti-German sentiment were wholly at odds with the spirit of scholarship.

Whatever impact the war had on academic freedom, the episode generated a greatly increased demand for economists as experts and advisers,
especially in the public domain.[6] During the 1920s, a growing number of
academic economists performed services for the business community, and
these opportunities provided flattering, sometimes intellectually stimulating,
and often lucrative experiences. Yet there were also certain risks, for example
when the client misinterpreted or misused the economist's knowledge. As
Wesley Mitchell reported at the end of the decade:

A cautious scientific enquirer is sometimes gravely disturbed by the confi-

dence with which a businessman will ask his opinion on some delicate problem and still more disturbed by the practical man's disregard of the limitations
and conditions with which he feels it necessary to hedge his answers about.
The time was when such folk as economists complained about the neglect of
their findings by men of affairs. Now they are frequently called upon to advise
about matters about which their knowledge is slight. They do not always
decline the over-flattering invitations with the firmness which befits a scientific conscience. (Wesley C. Mitchell, to the New York Bureau of Personnel
Administration, 1929. Quoted in Dorfman, vol. 4, p. 210. For another expression of concern about the business-academic relationship, expressed by a leading economist, see Frank A. Fetter, "Economists and the Public," *AER* 15
[March 1925]: 13–26.)

A potentially more serious problem in the academic-business relationship was the threat to professional ethics when scholars or scientists were, or
seemed to be, influenced by motives other than scientific conscience and the
desire for the respect of their fellow experts. In the AEA's *Report of the Committee on Academic Freedom and Academic Tenure*, 1915 (which was published
in the *AER*), it was firmly stated that the proper discharge of the professional academic's function "requires (among other things) that the university
teacher shall be exempt from any pecuniary motive or inducement to hold,
or to express, any conclusion which is not the genuine and uncolored product of his own study or that of his fellow specialists." There should not be
even a suspicion that the scholars' utterances are shaped or restricted by
inexpert and possibly not wholly disinterested persons outside their ranks.
Indeed, if the universities are to contribute to the solution of future economic and social problems,

> it is the first essential that the scholars who carry on the work of universities
> shall not be in a position of dependence upon the favor or any social class or
> group, that the disinterestedness and impartiality of their inquiries and their
> conclusions shall be, so far as is humanly possible, beyond the reach of suspi-
> cion. (*AER P&P* [March 1916]: 234, 237)

Surely there is a hint, at the end of this passage, that in practice, perfect
impartiality and objectivity may not be attainable in this imperfect world.

Fifteen years later, the influential report of May 1930 on *Academic Obligations, A Report on the Public Utility Propaganda* by the AAUP's Subcommittee
of the Committee on University Ethics, under Seligman's chairmanship,
stated as a matter of principle that:

No university professor who receives a fee or other compensation from any person or association interested in public discussion or testimony respecting a particular question of public importance should take part in such discussion, or furnish such testimony, without making it public the fact that he receives a compensation therefor, and the name of the person or association paying him said compensation. (*AAUP Bulletin* 17 [February 1931]: 140. See also the report on *Propaganda by Public Corporations* prepared by the AAUP's Committee on University Ethics in *AAUP Bulletin* 16 [May 1930]: 349–68.)

Needless to say, this austere requirement has not always been met in subsequent times.

This report is of special interest today because in 1926, Ely's Institute for Research in Land Economics and Public Utilities, based at Northwestern University, had been attacked as "a cunning propaganda institute in disguise." E. O. Jorgensen, a representative of the Manufacturers' and Merchants' Federal Tax League, a single-tax organization, protested that the institute

has laid down its conclusions in advance of its investigations . . . [and] has, before any of its facts have been gathered, condemned certain far-reaching measures which an increasing number of scholars believe to be beneficial to the people, and approved other far-reaching measures which many scholars also believe to be detrimental to the people [thereby completely disregarding the principles of fairness and impartiality]. (Jorgensen to E. W. Kemmerer, president of the AEA, July 31, 1926. In AEA Archives. Jorgensen enclosed a copy of his book, *False Education in Our Colleges and Universities*.)

As expected, Kemmerer did not accede to Jorgensen's demand for a "prompt and rigid" investigation of the case by the AEA. After a meeting of the Executive Committee, Kemmerer informed Jorgensen "that such an investigation would be outside the functions of this organization." Young's statement in a letter to Secretary F. Deibler (December 11, 1926, AEA Archives) probably accurately reflects the Executive Committee's attitude: "This is not only because it is not the business of the Association to make such investigations, but also because the proposal is an insult to Professor Ely and his associates. It comes from a prejudiced source."

Nevertheless, criticism of Ely's institute persisted, and as Benjamin Rader showed in his important biography of Ely, there was a direct connection between Ely's work on behalf of the National Electric Light Association (NELA) and the Federal Trade Commission's (FTC) investigations of utility companies' propaganda, which in turn prompted the AAUP's inquiry and report referred to earlier. As is typical with matters of this kind, the story is complex. During the twenties Ely had changed his mind about public ownership of natural monopolies, turning against public ownership, and in 1926 he assured the managing director of the NELA that the institute's new research results would please him. That same year he "became a member of the Committee on Co-operation with Educational Institutions of the NELA which directed a campaign for writing favorable utility textbooks and the teaching of utility economics in colleges" (Rader 1966, p. 225). When Martin Glaeser, Ely's former student and colleague at the University of Wisconsin, testified to the FTC about payments the institute had received from the NELA, the information "received nationwide coverage by the Hearst newspapers and drew angry protects from public power advocates" (ibid., p. 226). Needless to say, as Rader comments, "Ely answered the charges with self-righteous indignation," blaming "sensational writers" for twisting and distorting the facts in an effort to discredit scientific research (ibid.). Nevertheless, it seems clear from the FTC's investigation that Ely's behavior had inevitably compromised the integrity both of his own and related research results and investigations. And it is significant that Glaeser had apparently refused to leave Wisconsin for Northwestern, with Ely in 1925, because his research work might then come under undue influences from the utility companies.[7]

In its report on public utility propaganda, the AAUP's committee emphasized the direct connection between academic freedom and scientific and scholarly integrity. It was crucial that the public should have

> some source of information and expert advice in which it may place full confidence . . . It is indeed because of this professional function that the insistence upon academic freedom is ultimately justified. And while it may not always be true that he who pays the piper calls the tune there is no doubt that a profession which is to deserve and keep public confidence must be scrupulous in avoiding not only relationships which subtly endanger its impartiality but also those which are liable to occasion distrust.

> In other words, what is needed is not simply that the academic instructor should be absolutely honest, but that everybody else should esteem him to be not only honest and intelligent but also mindful of his professional responsibilities.[8] (*AAUP Bulletin* 14 [May 1930]: 359)

As is well known, the greatest threat to academic freedom in the United States came in the aftermath of World War II, during the Cold War and the "great fear" of the so-called McCarthy period (Cf. Caute, 1978.). There were in fact precedents for this shameful episode in the severe repression of critics of American participation in World War I, particularly those suspected of pro-German sentiments, and in the anticommunist (Bolshevik) purges of the postwar "red scare." These were essentially transitory periods, though they undeniably left their marks—for example, the fact that twenty-one states and the District of Columbia had, by 1936, followed the World War I practice of requiring teachers to sign loyalty oaths.

During the interwar years there were numerous cases of arbitrary or unfair dismissals of university and college faculty members, some of which are described in detail in the pages of the *AAUP Bulletin*. But generally speaking, there was little the association could do to protect or obtain reparations for the victims, especially the untenured nonelite, most of whom were on one-year contracts.[9] Censuring delinquent institutions, and publishing their names, probably had some beneficial effects on those institutions wishing to raise their academic status and reputation, but unfortunately there is no reliable way of gauging the results of the AAUP's efforts to disseminate acceptable standards of academic employment, or "due process" procedures for handling disputes between university authorities and their academic staff. Within the AEA, academic freedom seems not to have been a major issue or concern during the interwar years, although there was considerable debate about such related matters as professional standards and competence (including minimum qualifications for economists), the need for a code of ethics, and the AEA's general responsibilities toward the profession and the public. Most of these issues continued to be discussed in the post–World War II period.[10]

In 1939 there was apparently no widespread anticommunist sentiment in the United States, but once the Nazi-Soviet pact was signed, hostility to communists and supposed fellow travelers rapidly gained momentum.[11] The first large-scale purge of academic communists occurred in 1941, at the City College of New York. This precedent-setting process was initiated by the Rapp-Condert Committee of the New York State legislature, a body that was the direct precursor and model for Patrick McCarran's Senate Internal Security Committee, Joseph R. McCarthy's Senate Judiciary Committee, and the House Committee on Un-American Activities. These bodies became notorious for their harsh and often unscrupulous methods of identifying, investigating, and interrogating "subversives," both academic and nonacademic, especially reputed members or associates of the Communist Party or supposedly communist "front" organizations.

How did the AAUP respond to this crisis? In 1947 its Committee A on Academic Freedom and Academic Tenure boldly asserted that, since membership of the Communist Party was not illegal, such membership could not, ipso facto, constitute sufficient warrant for dismissing a university or college teacher. But this declaration carried no weight in the current climate of opinion. Later, during the peak of the anticommunist campaign in the early 1950s the AAUP proved completely ineffectual, partly owing to a disastrous failure of internal leadership and management. As Ellen Schrecker comments, perhaps the AAUP

> had always been a paper tiger. Or perhaps the anti-communist hysteria of the period was so powerful that no organization, not even one that claimed to protect the status and ideals of the academic profession, could prevent the academy from collaborating with McCarthyism. (Schrecker 1986, p. 336)

This collaboration took various forms: the universities' treatment of faculty members who took the Fifth Amendment when confronting Congressional committees; the insistence on "complete disclosure" of a witness's or defendants' personal history and associations; and the imposition of stringent loyalty or non-disloyalty oaths, most notoriously in the case of the University of California at Berkeley, in 1950. The fact that the AAUP did not publish its promised and much-deferred report on that institution until 1956 dramatically illustrates its procrastination.[12] The impact of the repeated assaults on higher education was especially disastrous in the 1950s. According to Schrecker, even contemporary observers

> noted the political reticence that blanketed the nation's colleges and universities. Marxism and its practitioners were marginalized, if not completely banished from the academy. Open criticism of the political status quo disappeared. . . . [and] college students became a silent generation whose most adventurous spirits sought cultural instead of political outlets for their discontents. (Schrecker 1986, p. 339)

A systematic study titled *The Academic Mind*, published by Paul Lazarsfeld and W. Thielens, Jr., in 1955, concluded that many teachers played safe:

"pruning their syllabi and avoiding controversial topics" (Schrecker 1986, pp. 309–10. Cf. Lazersfeld and Thielens). Moreover, as Schrecker comments in her 1983 article, "Academic Freedom":

> Because of the virtual consensus about the undesirability of communist professors, few academics, or anyone else for that matter, realized the extent to which faculty committees infringed upon the unfriendly witnesses' civil liberties.[13] (P. 35)

In commenting on assessing the impact of external threats to academic freedom, from whatever source, Schrecker observes that "there is no way to measure the books that were not written, the courses that were not taught, and the research that was not undertaken." (Schrecker 1986, p. 339). Yet it is surely significant that much of the research produced in the social sciences during the 1950s centered on "safe" topics, such as consensus history, modernization theory, structural functionalism, the new criticism, and, I would add, the "new" economic history toward the end of the decade. As Schrecker suggests:

> mainstream scholars celebrated the status quo, and the end of ideology dominated intellectual discourse. To what extent these developments were a response to the political repression of the day is something that demands further study. (Ibid.)

Clearly the AEA could no longer rely on the AAUP, and, faced with mounting contemporary pressures, the organized economists adopted a more positive stance against encroachments on academic freedom than ever before or since. This policy change seems to have occurred in the mid 1940s, for in 1941 the Executive Committee refused to endorse the American Historical Association's protest at the effort by the National Association of Manufacturers to censor textbooks.[14] Five years later, Secretary Bell, of the AEA, rejected a plea for intervention when Major Glenn McConagha of the U.S. Air Force pointed out that the *Chicago Tribune* and other newspapers had publicized so-called "perversive" passages from the economics textbook he was using in his course. Bell, never an activist, turned to President Joseph Davis for advice, saying that even if the AEA chose to act as a body it could not do so quickly enough, but suggested that some of the past presidents might be consulted.[15] No immediate action was taken, but a year later, as attacks on supposedly left-wing textbooks mounted, the association decided to publish a textbook resolution, declaring that:

> university and college teachers must have the free and untrammeled right to select for use in their teaching and research such textbooks as they, *and no others*, believe will promote the purposes which their courses are intended by their teachers to serve. (*AER P&P* [1948]: 533. Italics supplied.)

This statement was circulated to 770 colleges and universities, to department heads and to regents or chairmen of boards of trustees on behalf of the AEA's members—an unusually explicit official move.

As it transpired, the response was very limited. Some universities objected to the phrase "and no others," and President Joseph Schumpeter expressed misgivings when he was asked to sign the resolution, which was circulated during his incumbency. However, he was apparently appeased when Secretary Bell explained that in doing so he would be "merely performing an Association function and not intervening on his own" (Bell to Seymour E. Harris, 12 April 1948, AEA Archives). Bell, also a conservative economist, sympathized with Schumpeter, fearing that the response to the textbook resolution might prove "embarrassing"; and both were concerned that a "crusading spirit" might be displayed by the group of ex-presidents who were appointed to a new committee

> for the purpose of making public the position of the Association concerning academic freedom; to refer appropriate cases to the AAUP; and to give their own judgment on specific grievances referred to the Association. (Secretary's Report, *AER P&P* [1948]: 533; Bell to Schumpeter, 20 Feb. 1948, 19 Mar 1948; Schumpeter to Bell, 22 Mar 1948: "God grant them the gift of discretion." This incident illustrates the occasional influence of personalities on AEA affairs. Schumpeter's predecessor was Paul Douglas, formerly a Professor at the University of Chicago but, in 1948, a member of the U.S. Senate.

In 1948 the AEA followed up the textbook resolution by establishing its first committee explicitly concerned with the academic freedom problem. It was defined as a stand-by, not an active committee, to be prepared "to receive any grievance reports or complaints of violations of academic freedom." But this passive role proved to be totally inadequate. The response was so limited that in 1952 the Executive Committee considered expanding the Committee's brief: "to keep informed of developments, preserve a file of cases, and take the initiative in suggesting action in the interests of protecting the profession against attacks."[16] In 1953 the Past Presidents' Academic Freedom Committee was discharged and replaced by an Ad Hoc Committee on the Freedom of Teaching, Research and Publications in Economics. This body acknowledged that the AEA had taken a much less "strong and independent line" than such related organizations as the American Historical Association, the APSA [cf p. 115], and the American Psychological Association.[17]

Nevertheless, the committee advised against publicizing "a declaration of principles of academic freedom for economists," since these principles were the same as for other scholars. Also, they rejected the idea that the AEA "should undertake and report upon specific cases involving infringement on the academic freedom of economists" since the AAUP was more experienced and better equipped to undertake this task. As Chairman Clair Wilcox of the Ad Hoc Committee on Freedom of Teaching, Research and Publications wrote to President Kuznets, "the type of problem involved in the present-day drive against so-called subversives in our educational institutions concerns the academic community as a whole rather than particular disciplines, and that there is no distinctive sphere of activity for our Association as such in these controversies." If each discipline tried to act independently the results would be chaotic. (Quoted in *AER P&P* [1955]: 682) Although the AAUP's central office was "virtually paralyzed," the remedy was to reinvigorate that body, not to take over its functions. (*AER P&P* [1954]: 734, 735, 736.) In retrospect this may appear as an excuse for taking the easy way out, given that the association had received petitions "from various institutions in the country concerning the status of the profession," and the Executive Committee had promised to give "serious consideration" to the possibility of further action by the association (ibid., p. 695).

The next step in this exceedingly slow and cautious process was the formation of a new ad hoc (subsequently, a standing) Committee on the Status of the Profession (Chairman Clair Wilcox) "with its scope of activity limited, for the time being, to the preparation of reports." However, in view of "the general situation concerning academic freedom and of the developments of the past year" it was also suggested that "members of the Association be afforded an opportunity to discuss crucial problems of academic freedom and civil liberties at annual meetings," presumably because such discussions had hitherto been deemed out of order (*AER P&P* [1955]: 650–51).

Later that same year the association published its substantial eight-page

Report of the Exploratory Committee on the Status of the Profession, the first to consider the cases of particular economists. Of these, the predicament of Horace B. Davis of the University of Kansas City was quickly dismissed on the grounds of the association's inability to intervene. Davis had been discharged

> because of his unwillingness to co-operate with the university authorities and not because of his political views or his reliance upon the Fifth Amendment. In his own words, he was fired 'for refusing to answer, not the Congressional Committee but the Board of Trustees.' In the judgment of this Committee, it is altogether reasonable and proper for a university, through its appropriate officers or agencies, to insist that those who constitute its faculty shall deal with it frankly and make available to it all facts and circumstances that may bear upon their status in the academic community. (*AER P&P* [1955]: 678)

The intelligent and effective safeguarding of "the intellectual freedom we all cherish," the report added, imposed reciprocal requirements, "and not merely a one-sided obligation to protect the staff member under attack." The AAUP had had no success in dealing with the case; but the outcome of Davis's "legal test of the University's action" would be of interest to economists even though there was no adequate ground for special concern on the association's part. (Ibid. The report was signed by I. L. Sharfman and Ben W. Lewis).

This case is a clear example of academic collaboration with the anticommunist witch hunters in Washington. It also illustrates how concern with the collective interest of the academic profession overrode any sense of responsibility toward individual victims.

To judge by the Exploratory Committee's report, the case concerning Paul M. Sweezy, which was still in progress, was of much greater interest to *AER* readers. This was not only because of Sweezy's distinguished reputation but also because he had asked the editor of the *Review* to publish a brief factual note, stating that

> Paul M. Sweezy, formerly of the Harvard Economics Department, has been sentenced to jail in New Hampshire for refusing to answer questions, in a state investigation of subversion, regarding a lecture on the subject of socialism which he delivered in a course at the University of New Hampshire. (*AER P&P* [1955]: 678)

The editor of the *AER*, Bernard F. Haley, voiced certain reservations about Sweezy's request, arguing that the proposed dissemination of factual information was not as simple as Sweezy supposed. For example, he asked

> Do I take the responsibility for publishing every item of this sort involving an economist, in the form written by the complainant, describing from his point of view threats or actions that have the effect in his judgment of impairing his academic freedom or civil liberties? If so, do I attach to these items as published in an editorial note disclaiming all responsibility for their factual accuracy? Do I stand ready to provide space also for replies and comments of others who cite different facts or place a different interpretation upon the facts from that given by the complainant? Or do I, as does some other agency of the Association, first conduct some sort of investigation of the accuracy of the facts cited in the complaint? If so, what facilities does the Association have for conducting such factual investigations? And is it not pertinent to point out that the Association would be assuming the responsibilities of the American Association of University Professors? (*AER P&P* [1955]: 680)

The Exploratory Committee printed a lengthy summary of the Sweezy case based on an article by Sweezy's coeditor of the *Monthly Review*, Les Huberman (Ibid., p. 679), thereby achieving the publicity Sweezy desired. For the longer term it approved a Sweezy-Haley compromise solution whereby "statements of facts verified by the standing committee concerning alleged infringements upon academic freedom or civil liberties" were published quarterly in the *Review*, and these statements would be combined to produce an annual survey in the yearly volumes of the Association's *Papers and Proceedings*. These surveys

> would provide a potential basis for co-operation between the AAUP and the American Economic Association. The standing committee might well serve in an advisory capacity to AAUP investigating committees in such matters as involve the special competence of economists, and it might also exercise leadership in obtaining, when likely to prove helpful, the formal support of the Executive Committee for crucial AAUP actions. (*AER P&P* [1955]: 683–84)

At this point the AEA appeared to be moving toward a more active policy, but at the March 1955 Executive Committee meeting there was another step backward, because "no definite agreement could be reached concerning the functions of the AEA with respect to cases involving academic freedom or civil liberties." Again the remedy suggested called for more reports and "recommendations as occasions arise for the performance of further [unspecified] functions." There was a need for a committee with a title more specific than

"Status of the Profession," and in 1956 a new body was established, called the Committee on Academic Freedom and Civil Liberties.[18] The chairman, Fritz Machlup, was one of the profession's most active and distinguished defenders of academic freedom,[19] and there is no mistaking the relish with which his committee's first report announced Paul Sweezy's victory in the U.S. Supreme Court earlier that year. In a strongly worded judgment, Chief Justice Warren, with the support of Justices Black, Douglas, and Brennan, overturned the Supreme Court of New Hampshire's decision supporting Sweezy's conviction for contempt of court. Justice Frankfurter held that the civil liberties of an individual must not be "encroached upon on the basis of so meager a counter-vailing interest of the State as may be argumentatively found in the remote, shadowy threat to the security of New Hampshire." Chief Justice Warren added: "We do not conceive of circumstances wherein a state interest would justify infringement of rights in this field."[20]

In their opinion powerfully upholding "freedom in the community of American universities," both justices commented specifically on the social sciences. In these disciplines, according to Warren, restraints on intellectual freedom are especially harmful, because

> few, if any, principles are accepted as absolutes. Scholarship cannot flourish in an atmosphere of suspicion and distrust. Teachers and students must always remain free 'to inquire, to study and to evaluate, to gain new maturity and understanding; otherwise our civilization will stagnate and die. (*AER P&P* [1958]: 652)

Justice Frankfurter fully endorsed this view of "the pursuit of understanding in the groping endeavors of what are called the social sciences." The problems dealt with in fields including anthropology, economics, law, psychology, and sociology

> are merely departmentalized dealing, by way of manageable division of analysis, with interpenetrating aspects of holistic perplexities. . . . inquiries into these problems, speculations about them, stimulation in others of reflections upon them, must be left as unfettered as possible. Political power must abstain from intrusion into this activity of freedom, pursued in the interest of wise government and the people's well-being, except for reasons that are exigent and obviously compelling. (Ibid.)

Concluding with a brief assertion of "the dependence of a free society on free universities" he warned against government intervention, which, whatever the motive, "inevitably tends to check the ardor and fearlessness of scholars, qualities at once as fragile and so indispensable for fruitful academic labor" (Ibid., pp. 652–53).

While welcoming Sweezy's vindication, Machlup's committee also reconsidered the case of Horace B. Davis because of the principle involved: "the conflict between the scholar's 'freedom of silence' on questions of political beliefs and associations, and the controversial doctrine of his 'obligation to candor.'" Davis was dismissed despite "impressive testimony that he had not abused his position, and that his integrity was manifested in discussions with his colleagues." The committee then directly confronted a serious flaw in the academics' response, namely, the faculty's

> failure to respect the individual's moral right to remain silent . . . [which represents a failure] to live up to the highest standards of academic freedom. It is difficult to expect university administrations and trustees to be more broad-minded than their faculties, though, of course, this is exactly what the "ideal" university government ought to be. Perhaps the rigid adherence to principle on the part of some who are willing to be martyrs will gradually educate educators in the more subtle implications of academic freedom. (Ibid., p. 653)

In this outspoken passage, the committee emphasized the responsibility of faculty members in matters of academic freedom in a stronger voice than any of its predecessors had used.

The Machlup committee's main concern in 1959 was the "disclaimer affidavit" required of all recipients of loans and fellowships under the National Defense Act, and this too provided an occasion for an outspoken defense of academic freedom. "It is distressing," the report declared,

> that so many politicians, administrators of colleges and universities, and even some academic scholars lack the perception and historical knowledge to understand why oath requirements and non-disloyalty oaths in particular, are offensive to supporters of academic freedom.

To those "who believe that such a requirement cannot do much harm and . . . wonder at the fuss being made," the report offered the following response:

> They do not understand that it is demoralizing for a student to derive pecuniary advantages from affirming that he does not hold subversive beliefs; that it is inconsistent with the impartial search for truth to be by oath 'committed' in favor of or in opposition to particular positions; that an institution of

higher learning ought to refuse the admission of students who have 'forsworn' any beliefs or attitudes, even if the teachers themselves have come to reject these beliefs or attitudes; that an oath should never be taken lightly and that the requirement to sign a series of affidavits over the years cannot help reducing the respect for affirmations under oath; that loyalty to the principles of American government can never be shown by taking a loyalty oath, or a non-disloyalty oath, but only be rejecting the imposition of loyalty oaths. (*AER P&P* [1960]: 713–14)

This passage has been quoted at length because of its quality and force, and because it is so characteristic of Machlup's beliefs, as expressed in his 1955 article, "On Some Misconceptions Concerning Academic Freedom." (*AAUP Bulletin 14* [Winter 1955]: 753–84). The report, cosigned by Bowen and Francis Boddy, concluded, on an optimistic note, stating that

the Association of American Universities has resolved to work for the repeal of the objectionable provision and the President of the United States [Dwight D. Eisenhower] has spoken out against the requirement. We may now hope that an enlightened majority of the Congress will eventually remove the disclaimer-oath requirement from the law. (Ibid., p. 714)

Machlup's three-year stint as chairman of the Committee on Academic Freedom and Civil Liberties constitutes a peak in the AEA's propagation of the cause. By comparison, all the previous and subsequent AEA pronouncements on the subject seem lacking in eloquence, conviction, and determination to confront the enemy. One can only speculate as to what might have occurred had Machlup's views and courage been more widely shared in the economics profession.

During the next two years, under the chairmanship of Machlup's successor, Francis Boddy, the AEA's Committee on Academic Freedom and Civil Liberties presented no new reports of violations of academic freedom to the Executive Committee. Nor is there any evidence of closer collaboration with the AAUP. Whether this reflected the changing conditions of the times, rather than a change in the committee's leadership or activities, it is impossible to say, but the wave of anticommunist repression had undoubtedly been receding for some years. A cynic might suggest that by the early 1960s, many, perhaps most, of the supposed "subversives" had either been driven out of the academic community or had found safe havens in more tolerant colleges and universities. (Cases of both types are well represented in Schrecker's study.)

In 1962 the Committee on Academic Freedom and Civil Liberties reported that the AEA had never endorsed the AAUP's 1940 statement of principles of academic freedom and tenure, and proceeded to do so, with the caveat that "certain provisions regarding academic tenure as outlined in the statement of principles seemed not to be relevant to the question of academic freedom" (*AER P&P* [1963]: 690). The reasons for this curious reservation are unclear, yet it is significant in its effort to decouple two elements that had for so long seemed to be indissolubly linked. Using the economists' own habitual mode of reasoning, one must perhaps infer that the ever-buoyant market for their services, both within and outside academia, had made strict tenure conditions seem less necessary, and possibly more obstructive to mobility, than in earlier times. As always, to the faithful, the market would provide!

In the following years the problem of academic freedom, in whatever form, seems to have dropped off the AEA's agenda. Academic Freedom and Civil Liberties disappeared from the AEA's list of committees, and there was no formal discussion of the reasons for its demise.

Yet the saga is not yet quite complete, for during the 1970s, as the result of pressures from certain members, the association set up a Committee on Political Discrimination (in 1974) to investigate and report on certain specific cases, in the manner traditionally associated with the AAUP. However by 1978 progress was so slow that a merger with the AAUP's work was proposed. Nevertheless the committee survived, and in 1982 produced a report on a case of political discrimination at San Diego State University, one of the two cases for which it had started its work. But the report remained confidential, and the AEA's members were not informed of the outcome.[21]

Political discrimination was evidently still a matter of current concern, for there were periodic requests that the AEA should offer resolutions and letters of support for beleaguered economists abroad, for example in Chile, Argentina, and Poland. This is, of course, evidence of the association's increasing cosmopolitanism. In this period, as in the 1960s, the AEA was repeatedly bombarded with proposals designed to expand its functions and, in particular, to abandon its traditional nonpartisanship. But these temptations were consistently resisted.

This long story raises the question of whether any single discipline could, working alone, make a significant impact on the issue of academic freedom. The AEA's record reveals repeated hesitations, uncertainties about the most effective and appropriate course of action, and changes of direction. No doubt this reflects its leadership and organizational structure in the ever-changing annual presidency; the continually changing composition of the Executive Committee; and the influence of the secretary (or secretary treasurer), the one permanent official. In the AEA's case, the long career of Secretary James Washington Bell, who served from 1936 to 1961, helps to explain in part the association's inertia, for he was conservative in his political, economic, and social views, and usually hostile to innovations, especially those likely to involve an expansion of his official responsibilities. As custodian of the organization's principles and traditions he could usually raise significant objections to any potentially radical change; and while periodic pressures from groups of members could not be entirely resisted, the individuals involved had to be both determined and, above all, persistent if they were to sustain new departures. Then, again, external as well as internal conditions were changing, and with the academic freedom problem in particular the AAUP was present in the background, as a kind of last resort for those dissatisfied with the AEA's response to external challenges.

References

American Economic Association Archives, Northwestern University. Evanston, Illinois.

American Economic Review, Papers and Proceedings (Abbreviated in the text as *AER P&P*.)

Barrow, Clyde. *Universities and the Capitalist State: Corporate Liberalism and the Reconstruction of American Higher Education, 1894–1928* Madison: University of Wisconsin Press, 1990.

Bloland, Harland G., and Sue M. Bloland. *American Learned Societies in Transition: The Impact of Dissent and Recession.* A Report Prepared for the Carnegie Commission on Higher Education. New York: McGraw Hill, 1974.

Buckley, William F., Jr. *God and Man at Yale: The Superstitions of Academic Freedom.* Washington, D.C.: Regnery Gateway, 1986. Originally published in 1951.

Bulletin of the American Association of University Professors (AAUP).

Caute, David. *The Great Fear: The Anti Communist Drive Under Truman and Eisenhower.* New York: Simon and Schuster, 1978.

Church, R. L. "Economists as Experts: The Rise of an Academic Profession in the United States, 1870–1920," in *The University in Society*, edited by Laurence Stone. Vol. 2, *Europe, Scotland and the United States from the Sixteenth to the Twentieth Century.* Princeton N.J.: Princeton University Press, 1974.

Coats, A. W. "The American Economic Association and the Economics Profession," *Journal of Economic Literature* December 1985. Reprinted in *On the Sociology and Professionalization of Economics, British and American Economic Essays.* Vol. 2. Edited by A. W. Coats. London: Routledge, 1992, 433–73.

Davis, Bertram H. "Academic Freedom, Academic Neutrality, and the Social System." In *The Concept of Academic Freedom*, edited by Edmund L. Pincoffs. Austin: University of Texas Press, 1972.

Dorfman, Joseph. *The Economic Mind in American Civilization*. Vol. 4, 1918–33. New York: Viking Press, 1959.

Ely, Richard T. *Ground Under Our Feet*. New York: Macmillan, 1938.

Fetter, Frank A. "Economists and the Public." *American Economic Review* 15 (March 1925): 13–26.

Fisk, Milton. "Academic Freedom in Class Society." In *The Concept of Academic Freedom*, edited by Edmund L. Pincoffs. Austin: University of Texas Press, 1972.

Fisk, Milton. "Comments on Hardy, Jones, and Bertram Davis." In *The Concept of Academic Freedom*, edited by Edmund L. Pincoffs. Austin: University of Texas Press, 1972.

Furner, Mary O. *Advocacy and Objectivity: A Crisis in the Professionalization of American Social Science, 1865–1905*. Lexington: University of Kentucky Press, 1975.

Gruber, Carol S. *Mars and Minerva: World War I and the Uses of Higher Learning in America*. Baton Rouge: Louisiana State University Press, 1975.

Huer, Jon. *Tenure for Socrates: A Study in the Betrayal of the American Professor*. New York: Bergin and Garvey, 1991.

Hofstadter, Richard, and Walter P. Metzger. *The Development of Academic Freedom in the United States*. New York: Columbia University Press, 1955.

Innis, Nancy K. "Lessons from the Controversy over the Loyalty Oath at the University of California." *Minerva* 30 (1992): 337–65.

Jones, Hardy E. "Academic Freedom as a Moral Right." In *The Concept of Academic Freedom*, edited by Edmund L. Pincoffs. Austin: University of Texas Press, 1972.

Lazarsfeld, Paul, and W. Thielens Jr. *The Academic Mind*. New York: Columbia University Press, 1955.

Lewis, Lionel S. *The Cold War and Academic Governance: The Lattimore Case*. New York: New York State University Press, 1993.

Machlup, Fritz. "On Some Misconceptions Concerning Academic Freedom." *Bulletin of the AAUP* 41 (Winter 1955): 753–84.

Maciver, Robert M. *Academic Freedom in Our Time*. New York: Columbia University Press, 1955.

Metzger, Walter P. "Academic Freedom in Delocalized Academic Institutions." In *Dimensions of Academic Freedom*, edited by Walter P. Metzger et al. Urbana: University of Illinois Press, 1969.

Metzger, Walter P. "The First Investigation." *Bulletin of the AAUP* 37 (Autumn 1961): 206–10.

Metzger, Walter P. "Academic Tenure in America: An Historical Essay." In *Faculty Tenure: A Report and Recommendation by the Commission on Academic Tenure in Higher Education*. W. R. Keast, Chairman. San Francisco: Josey Bass, 1973.

Metzger, Walter P. "Profession and Constitution: Two Dimensions of Academic Freedom." *Texas Law Review* 66 (1988).

Nourse, Edwin G. *Economics in the Public Service*. New York: Harcourt Brace, 1953.

Pincoffs, Edmund L., ed. *The Concept of Academic Freedom*. Austin: University of Texas Press, 1972.

Rader, Benjamin G. *The Academic Mind and Reform: The Influence of Richard T. Ely in American Life*. Lexington: University of Kentucky Press, 1966.

Ross, Edward Alsworth. *Seventy Years of It*. New York: Appleton Century, 1936.

Schrecker, Ellen W. "Academic Freedom: The Historical View." In *Regulating the Intellectuals: Perspectives on Academic Freedom in the 1880's*, edited by Craig Kaplan and Ellen W. Schrecker, 25–43. New York: Praeger Scientific, 1983.

Schrecker, Ellen W. *No Ivory Tower: McCarthyism and the Universities*. New York: Oxford University Press, 1986.

Sedlak, Michael W. *The Emergence and Development of Collegiate Business Education in the United States, 1881–1974: Northwestern as a Case Study*. Ph.D. diss., Northwestern University, 1977.

Van Alstyne, W. W. "Academic Freedom and the First Amendment in the Supreme Court of the United States, An Unhurried Review." In *Freedom and Tenure in the Academy*, edited by W. W. Van Alstyne. Durham, N.C.: Duke University Press, 1993.

Veysey, Laurence. *The Emergence of the American University*. Chicago: University of Chicago Press, 1965.

Wilson, Daniel J. *Arthur O. Lovejoy and the Quest for Intelligibility*. Chapel Hill: University of North Carolina Press, 1980.

Notes

1. The letters and resolutions to appoint a committee are in the *AER, P&P* 3 (March 1913): 255–58; 4 (March 1914): 197, 199; and 4 (December 1914): 534. For the context, see Metzger 1973, pp. 146–48. The editor of the *AER*, Davis R. Dewey, of MIT, apparently took the initiative in publishing the letters, assuming the case would be of interest to his readers. He may have been influenced by his contact with a member of the Wesleyan faculty.

2. The initial Joint Committee comprised Seligman (Chairman), Ely, and Frank A. Fetter, of the AEA; F. N. Judson (Chairman), J. Q. Dealey, and Herbert Croly of the APSA; and U. G. Weatherly (Chairman), P. Lichtenberger, and Roscoe Pound of the ASS. The expanded committee included: Seligman, Dealey, Ely, Pound, Weatherly, Henry W. Farnam (the economist), and F. H. Giddings, Charles A. Kofoid, Arthur O. Lovejoy (Secretary of the AAUP), Frederick W. Pudelford, and Howard C. Warren. Its report was published in the *Bulletin of the AAUP*. The first Committee A report did not appear in the *Bulletin* until Vol. 4 (February–March, 1918, pp. 16–28), and was immediately followed by the controversial *Report of a Special Committee on Academic Freedom in Wartime*. (Ibid., pp. 29–47). The three signatories to this latter report were Lovejoy, Edward Capps (of Princeton), and A. A. Young, secretary of the AEA and chairman of the AAUP's General Committee on Academic Freedom and Academic Tenure. Young was, in effect, Seligman's successor.

3. For a vivid account of the situation, see Walter P. Metzger, "The First Investigation," *Bulletin of the AAUP* 37 (Autumn 1961): 206–10. For example, "Expecting to play the detective, Lovejoy [the prime mover, and host Secretary] found that he had to be as well a critic of academic management, a human relations counselor, and a judge of the involved problems of internal academic discipline" (p. 208). As for Lovejoy's most prominent allies,

"Having made an orderly ascent to the peak of their several disciplines, the John Deweys, the ERA Seligmans, and the Roscoe Pounds were strongly inclined to assume that the academic world as a whole was conforming to a law of progress and that the worst examples of executive encroachment on the rights of university professors—such dark instances, for example, as the attacks on academic evolutionists by religious fundamentalists or the silencing of radical economists by wealthy, intolerant trustees—belonged to a period forever past" (p. 206). See also the account of Lovejoy's activities in Wilson, 1980.

4. Barrow, 1990, p. 60. See also the standard account of the processes Barrow characterizes in Laurence Veysey, 1965.

5. For a valuable review of the period see Gruber, 1975; also Metzger, 1955, p. 495 ff. Some leading economists, like Arthur T. Hadley and Henry W. Farnam, both of Yale, were ambivalent, but they unequivocally declared their support for the allies despite their personal ties with Germany and their indebtedness to their German educational experience.

The AAUP report, *Academic Freedom in Wartime*, warned against the dangers to freedom of thought, "since the forces of obscurantism and reaction may seize the opportunity to remove secretly some of the established landmarks of liberty," and sought to define "the legitimate causes of dismissal from academic office which are consequences of a state of war" (pp. 32, 42). Nevertheless, the general thrust of the report was highly restrictive.

6. There was a considerable debate about the desirability of this state of affairs. For earlier examples see R. L. Church, "Economists as Experts: The Rise of an Academic Profession in the United States, 1870–1920," in Stone, 1974. Joseph Dorfman reveals that in the period 1918–29 more than sixty economists were employed as specialist advisers or technical experts by leading politicians, Congress, government agencies, and a number of other bodies. No doubt systematic inquiries would reveal many more examples. There is useful general review of pre–1946 "precedents" for economic advisership in Edwin G. Nourse, 1953, chapter 6.

7. These comments are based on the detailed investigation in Michael W. Sedlak's 1977 Northwestern University Ph.D. dissertation: "The Emergence and Development of Collegiate Business Education in the United States, 1881–1974, pp. 184–201, especially pp. 203–4. For several papers on the problems of public utilities, including the charge that the use of experts by the rival parties in the dispute "tends to prostitute the entire process of regulation," see the *AER*.

8. The report distinguished between three types of cases: a) purely technical or scientific research in the natural and applied sciences; b) technical economic problems, like scientific management, which are close to engineering; and c) highly controversial economic questions like public ownership, criteria of valuation, equitable taxation, the respective merits of reproduction and actual or prudent cost as the basis for rate control, or the influence to be ascribed to depreciation and obsolescence in the fields of valuation. In these matters "no funds at all ought to be solicited or accepted from individuals or business concerns, whether earmarked for, or utilized in, the prosecution of such researches." With the utility corporations, soliciting always came from the beneficiary. Whatever the circumstances, the man in the street will be suspicious, and this "must impair the influence of scholars' contributions and go far towards discrediting the academic or other institute that stands sponsor for the research project." *AAUP Bulletin* 14 (May 1930): 364–65.

9. Metzger, speaking of an earlier period, has described the AAUP's functions as "to warn and to illustrate, rather to avenge or redress" (cf. 1955, p. 492). The AAUP's increasing emphasis on "bureaucratic safeguards—partly owing to the difficulty of" formulating principles of academic freedom—was, of course, in harmony with the increasing bureaucratization of American universities. The AAUP was essentially designed to influence institutions at or near the top of the higher educational hierarchy, in the hope that competitive cultural emulation would be effective in spreading desirable practices.

10. For a brief review see Coats, 1992, p. 444 ff.

11. In this and the next four paragraphs I have drawn heavily on Ellen W. Schrecker's impressive study: *No Ivory Tower*, 1968.

12. There is a large literature on the Berkeley episode. For a recent discussion, with ample references, see Nancy K. Innis, "Lessons from the Controversy over the Loyalty Oath at the University of California." I am indebted to Professor Innis for helpful advice about this section of my paper.

13. The AAUP collaborated with the opposition by adopting a new professional requirement: complete candor. Loyalty to one's institution was to have priority over loyalty to one's current or former friends, and the traditional definition of academic freedom was reformulated to make membership of an unpopular but legal organization sufficient grounds for dismissal (Schrecker, 1983, pp. 38, 34, 30). In practice, a minority of individuals was sacrificed in the collective interest, while for the majority, "The freedom of the profession as a whole, its control over its own employment, remained pretty much intact" (Ibid., p. 40).

14. The protest was to be published in the *American Historical Review*.

15. McConagha to Bell, 26 Sept. 1946; Bell to McConagha, 3 Oct. 1946; Bell to Davis, 3 Oct. 1946. All in AEA Archives.

16. *AER, P&P* (1952): 718. The original committee was composed of three past presidents of the AEA—initially J. S. Davis, I. L. Sharfman, and S. H. Slichter. Subsequently, Davis and Slichter were replaced by A. Goldenweiser and F. C. Mills, Chairman. The reports are of no interest, though at one point it was suggested that the absence of complaints submitted might be a favorable sign. In March and December of 1950 the Executive Committee discussed the California Loyalty Oath situation. No formal action was taken, but a resolution conveying "the sense of the members present" was sent to the Berkeley Department of Economics and the relevant dean, an economist. (Cf. *AER, P&P* [1951]: 765, 767.)

17. The Committee cited strong statements from the American Psychological Association criticizing limitations on freedom of thought "other than limitations imposed by the psychologist's social responsibilities and considerations of public welfare" and promising "every feasible assistance" to any responsible member subject to such unwarranted limitations. It also asserted the association's "duty . . . to ascertain the facts and come to his [i.e., the psychologist's] defense if it appears that his rights as a psychologist have been abrogated." (*AER, P&P* [1954]: 734.)

18. It was "charged with the responsibility of reviewing alleged infringements upon the academic freedom or civil liberties of economists and to submit reports which may be supplemented by such general observations and recommendations concerning the status of the profession and the Association's relation thereto as might promise to be fruitful" (*AER, P&P* [1957]: 698). This repetition of past phraseology suggests that no radical new departures were envisaged.

19. See, for example, his impressive article in the *Bulletin* of the AAUP (1955): 753–84. He was also a courageous and effective defender of his Johns Hopkins colleague, Owen Lattimore. For a recent study of this topic see Lewis, 1993. The other members of the committee were Howard R. Bowen and Richard H. Heflebower.

20. *AER, P&P* (1958): 652. The concept of academic freedom had not received constitutional recognition until 1952, by Federal Supreme Court Justice William Douglas and Justice Hugo Black, in the case of *Adler* v. *the Board of Education of the City of New York*. Douglas was in fact a former academic. Cf. Van Alstyne, 1993, p. 105. Metzger (1988) has emphasized the distinction, if not incompatibility, between the "professional" and the "constitutional" definitions of academic freedom.

21. *AER, P&P* (1975): 443; (1976): 467; (1977): 438; (1978): 447, 450; (1982): 402.

Clarifying the Issues:
Free Speech, Hate Speech Codes, and Academic Freedom

Speech Codes and the Mission of the University

DONALD A. DOWNS, JR.

Let me begin this piece about freedom of speech and the university with two victimization narratives that relate real experiences. In scenario 1, an eighteen-year-old freshman woman, who is black, arrives on the Madison campus and embarks on her first trip to the library. At its entrance, she confronts a group of burly white male students who greet her with threatening racial slurs and the message that "we don't want your kind here." Because of this and other encounters, she begins to feel intimidated and to feel that the Madison environment is hostile. She soon leaves the campus.[1] Similar incidents have occurred on American campuses over the last decade, leading administrations and students to press for campus speech codes and other measures to discourage various forms of discrimination and hate speech. By 1990, 60 percent of all colleges and universities had policies against bigotry or racial harassment, and many more policies were under consideration. Many or most of these included restrictions on harassing or even offensive speech, including those at Michigan, Stanford, Wisconsin, Emory, and others.[2]

Scenario 2 is drawn from an incident at Oberlin University. It was related to me by an Oberlin instructor to a student group with whom I have worked. In a class discussion of sexuality and homosexuality, a conservative student with traditional religious values came out of his shell and confessed to the group that although he intellectually agreed with the class's consensus that gays should have equal rights across the board, he could not reconcile this proposition with his moral training and beliefs. Rather than using this remark as an occasion for pursuing the issue further, the class resorted to anger, censure, and ostracism. Within a week, the ostracism had spread to the entire campus, turning the dissenter into a ritualistic pariah.

We are too familiar with incidents on both sides of this ledger. Each episode is unacceptable to university life. The question that confronts us is how to promote a university climate that protects students' needs for security and basic respect without sacrificing the intellectual freedom and

---

Donald A. Downs, Jr. is professor of political science at the University of Wisconsin–Madison.

respect for diversity of ideas that is (or should be) the university's raison d'être. In this paper I will explore this portentous question. I will argue that there are two fundamental types of speech codes: codes that are limited and consistent with the missions of the university, and those that are broad and detrimental to that mission. Much is at stake, including the nature of the university and constitutional citizenship. Although this paper deals specifically with speech codes and free speech in the university, we must recognize two facts. First, the problems of sexual and racial conflict that the codes attempt to ameliorate are too intractable for codes to rectify on their own. Indeed, codes might even exacerbate such conflicts by producing resentments. Second, the problems in thinking that have led to improper codes will not disappear simply because courts have ruled such codes unconstitutional. A proper understanding of speech codes is but a first step in correcting what afflicts the contemporary university. To begin this quest, we must first grasp what the missions of the university properly are.

The Missions of the University

Like so many other institutions today, the university is struggling to define what it should be. Given the varieties of institutions and philosophies in higher education, I feel some trepidation in presenting my own view of what the university should be. I can only speak in terms of my own experience as a scholar and a teacher. But I believe in a set of purposes that is essential to the calling of being a professor.

Any definition of purpose must get at what is essential. Like other institutions and activities in the world, the university has practical and higher purposes that are distinct yet interdependent. Our practical obligation is to prepare students for making their livings and succeeding in life after college. We train professionals and prepare undergraduates for graduate and professional schools. To accomplish this goal we must know our fields and convey the relevant knowledge to students. At this level the university is a kind of business enterprise. Those faculty and administrators who claim that speech codes are justified (or required) under Title VII of the Civil Rights Act typically envision the university in this light. Title VII prohibits discrimination and harassment in employment in various enterprises, including forms of expression that create a "hostile environment."[3]

But great universities are more than trade schools. The next purpose is vital engagement with the important issues in the world. Jose Ortega Y Gasset states the matter well in *Mission of the University*: "Not only does it [the university] need perpetual contact with science [Ortega construes science as the spirit and method of inquiry in a broad sense], on pain of atrophy, it needs contact, likewise, with the public life, with historical reality, with the present, which is essentially a whole to be dealt with only in its totality . . . The university must be in the midst of real life, and saturated with it."[4] In this realm the university participates in what the great political theorist Hannah Arendt called the *vita activa*, the realm of active public life in which thought and speech contribute to social and historical action. Commitment to the *vita activa* can send electric charges through research and teaching, as teachers and students engage the vital issues of the day in various fields of endeavor. I recall the excitement I felt as a freshman when I began to fathom the relationships between my studies in history, political science, and economics and the vital public questions of the late 1960s and early 1970s. This connection seduced me to become a professor more than any single factor, and to specialize in public and constitutional law, fields in which ideas about justice, equality, liberty, legality, and public philosophy clash. Today, the opening of the university to more racial and cultural diversity promises to revitalize the *vita activa*, if only we proceed in the right way.

Thus, the *vita activa* role of the university is important, and I confess that it is the realm in which I am most at home. But under the wrong circumstances it offers a Faustian bargain that exchanges intellectual obligation for political obligation or politicization. The temptation is greatest in those disciplines that deal with society, culture, politics, and law, and in those areas of university life that involve these domains, such as public lectures and related interactions. We have witnessed how tense things can get when politically unwelcome speakers come to prominent campuses to speak. This problem intensifies when universities become as ideologically one-sided as they are today, in a left-liberal direction. Those who question the presence of such orthodoxy need only consider the telling fact that the conservative National Association of Scholars believes it necessary to keep its members' names secret, hidden behind lock and key.

Political orthodoxy like that at Oberlin casts a pall over intellectual life. In order to be vibrant and thoughtful, the *vita activa* requires meaningful interchange of differing viewpoints, and a commitment to truth that either transcends political commitment or entertains a sense of irony about political commitments. A vital public realm involves a plurality of voices that are animated by common purposes, a balance that reflects the "uni" and "versity" aspects of the concept of the university. Real intellectual diversity and a sense of humor are necessary to keep the *vita activa* honest.

In her famous essay "Truth and Politics," Arendt, the noted champion of politics and commitment to "the political," demonstrates how truth and politics can conflict. Speech in the political realm is different from the commitment to truth because it is often motivated by power and the desire to mold opinion rather than by the desire to pursue the truth through inquiry. Arendt's depiction of political orthodoxy is germane to the contemporary university:

> But such a power monopoly is far from being inconceivable, and it is not difficult to imagine what the fate of factual truth would be if power interests, national or social, had the last say in these matters. Which brings us back to our suspicion that it may be in the nature of the political realm to be at war with truth in all its forms, and hence to the question why a commitment even to factual truth [distinguished from such inherently less objective sources of truth as interpretation and opinion] is felt to be an anti-political attitude.[5]

Arendt's observation points us toward the highest purpose of the university, which anyone who loves teaching and research appreciates. It consists of two intimately related objectives: the pursuit of truth and knowledge, and the pursuit of the mind. Though the other purposes are important, this set of objectives constitutes the very soul of the university, distinguishing it from the other projects and institutions in society.

Furthermore, it is obvious that social, moral, and political truths are shaped by historical experience, interpretations within relevant discourses or language, and power. But recognizing this truism does not mean that truth is nothing but a function of these forces. If there is no truth beyond historical relativism, social construction, power, and language, there is no objective means by which to refute Holocaust deniers or others who make fraudulent claims. Nor is there a basis for standing against or outside of conventionality.[7]

The pursuit of truth is different from the attainment of knowledge per se, which involves mainly conveying what has been learned through the inquiry of others. This constitutes the *practice by which we seek knowledge*, a process that encompasses research, critical thinking, and philosophical inquiry, depending on the type of knowledge and the spirit of investigation:

To know is not to investigate. To investigate is to discover a truth, or inversely, to demonstrate an error. To know means to assimilate a truth into one's consciousness, to possess a fact after it has been attained and secured . . . The words [the Greeks] used to designate science exposed its identity with inquiry, creative work, investigation . . . The name *philo-sophia* arose, comparatively late, from the effort to distinguish from the usual learning that novel activity which was not to be learned, but *to seek* knowledge.[6]

The pursuit of truth requires standards of inquiry that are shared as well as contested in a community of inquiry;[8] in the end, however, the integrity and distinctiveness of the individual and the individual mind are essential to this pursuit. First, truth is often shaded and enigmatic, requiring a true plurality of perspectives. Second, to pursue truth is to think and to think is to engage in dialogue with a community of thinkers and to commence, in Arendt's words, the universal "soundless dialogue we carry on with ourselves." It involves a kind of "homelessness," meaning that thinking points beyond the world of the *vita activa*.[9] There will always be something subversive about freedom of thought and education. Though good education should transmit what is excellent about tradition, it also creates a capacity to question, to criticize, to be homeless. Established moral and political orders instinctively distrust thinking, which, as Nietzsche knew so well, will always possess a quality of being "beyond good and evil." Thinking resists moral shrillness or simplicitude (what Stephen Carter calls "shibboleths"), whether cloaked in the imperatives of the Right or the Left.[10]

The inquiry purpose of the university is compromised when the university loses sight of the importance of independent thinking. This happened in the case of the eastern college dean who corrected student papers in which the word "individual" appeared, claiming that such a word is a code word for "oppression"; and it prevailed when an instructor in a class on women and the law at a school with which I am acquainted began the class by informing the students that they would not be allowed to even discuss the potential criminal culpability of battered women for criminal acts. Many individuals, including me, consider this one of the single most important questions in this area of law.[11] And teaching "workshops" for teaching assistants and others too often turn into "thought control" sessions, according to sources who have confided in me.

The movement toward "political relevance," which began with the student revolts of the 1960s, wrought an imbalance between the *vita activa* and the spirit of inquiry in many institutions. This problem was compounded by the mushrooming of federal influence during the Cold War and with the many "mandates" that arose during and after the sixties with federal funding of projects and student aid. Then, when the sixties generation assumed professorial and (more importantly) administrative roles in the 1980s, the stage for "political correctness" was set. As Alan Wolfe recently argued, "Some of the more notorious of the stories recounted in the political correctness debates have involved academic administrators more than English professors."[12] Many of the leading administrators of major research universities in recent years have brought less-than-distinguished intellectual credentials to their positions, but this has not deterred them from espousing social and political agendas upon assuming office. (Donna Shalala of Wisconsin, Sheldon Hackney of Penn, and James Duderstadt of Michigan are examples.) When Shalala assumed the chancellorship at Madison, she told the press that "the mission of the university is social justice," by which she meant the elimination of racism, sexism, and related forms of discrimination. This espousal fuels the tension between truth and politics, and places the power and prestige of the chancellor's office behind a particular conception of social justice or a particular means to achieve it. Such action encourages a "monopoly" on truth rather than the dialogue and vital debate among different viewpoints that save the *vita activa* from the seduction of orthodoxy.

The rise of a new kind of group consciousness (known as "identity politics") based on such ascriptive characteristics as race, gender, sex, ethnicity, and related factors has also contributed to the deindividuation of minds. This type of consciousness is natural and potentially beneficial. But if it is not tempered by broader knowledge and critical thinking, it jeopardizes individualism and the pursuit of truth. The civil rights movement, under the leadership of Martin Luther King, Jr., sought to achieve a common sense of citizenship and equality by transcending ascriptive definitions of the self and making it possible for all citizens to share in the responsibilities that accrue to the *vita activa*; the movement considered judgments based on race and related immutable characteristics as presumptively unconstitutional and immoral because they deny the moral autonomy and independent consciousness of the individual. Constitutional law endorsed this Kantian understanding of individuality in the set of cases stemming from the famous *Carolene Products* footnote of 1938.[13]

But identity politics in its various incarnations turns this logic inside out, making ascriptive characteristics essential (even primary) ingredients of self-definition, as Henry Louis Gates, Jr., has shown in a recent brilliant article. While King stressed the importance of free speech in active citizenship, identity politics is based on drawing protective lines around group notions of the self.[14] Also, identity politics fits a university mission that emphasizes emotion and redemption through admitting oppressiveness rather than thinking. Wolfe states that it involves "a battle between those who claim that the university should be about ideas and those who believe that the university should be about suffering and redemption . . . The period when political correctness achieved its high purpose was a period of emotion, not one of reason."[15] Accordingly, speech that *offends* existential notions of self on the basis of ascriptive characteristics constitutes a threat to identity. Identity politics dissolves the distinction between being offended or criticized and being threatened, making it more difficult to speak honestly and courageously about crucial and complex issues that have implications for race, gender, and sexual choice. As an example, notice how difficult it is to name one university that has had a vital public debate about affirmative action.

Another consequence of the thinking and inquiry role of the university is the creation of a perspective that is broader and less time-bound than the call of the *vita activa* per se. Jacques Barzun voices this effect in holding that education should instill an appreciation of the universal "difficulties" of the human condition, which he distinguishes from "problems," which are more immediate and pressing.[16]

The spirit of inquiry seeks to develop educated individuals who possess qualities of critical thoughtfulness through their familiarity with great minds. Such qualities are important to constitutional citizenship. From this perspective, the university should strive to make the notion of social justice a problem and a difficulty—like anything else that falls under the critical eye of the pursuit of truth. The *vita activa* challenges us with the vital issues of our time, yet the pursuit of truth problematizes such commitments and compels us to pursue them with intellectual responsibility. Abandoning this tension is to surrender to thoughtlessness and to the evils that ineluctably follow in surrender's wake. As Arendt discovered after a life of active intellectual and political engagement, "absence of thought is not stupidity; it can be found in highly intelligent people, and a wicked heart is not its cause; it is probably the other way round, that wickedness may be caused by the absence of thought."[17] If we abandon our commitment to the pursuit of truth and the individualism such commitment entails, we will encourage zealotry rather than responsible commitment. "Political correctness" is ultimately the result of a mentality that disdains deeper knowledge and critical thinking in favor of the instant gratification that comes from the feeling of moral and political redemption. Such feelings are not thoughtfulness, and by an ancient psychological and social process they inexorably lead to the ritualistic censure of nonconforming ideas.

In the end, the university can remain a vital institution only it if maintains a delicate balance between the realms of *vita activa* and critical thinking and inquiry. As Ortega concludes *The Mission of the University*: "In the thick of life's urgencies and its passions, the university must assert itself as a major 'spiritual power,' higher than the press, standing for serenity in the midst of frenzy, for seriousness and the grasp of intellect in the face of frivolity and unashamed stupidity. Then the university, once again, will come to be what it was in its grand hour: an uplifting principle in the history of the western world."[18]

The Role of Free Speech and the First Amendment

Treatises have been written about the reasons for freedom of speech, and since my space is limited, I will stress what I consider to be the major roles free speech plays at the university. On one level the matter is exceedingly simple yet important. Without freedom of speech there can be no freedom of thought and common pursuit of truth and meaning. Freedom of speech is a necessary ingredient of the freedom of thought that is our life blood.[19] Furthermore, censorship or punishment for inappropriate speech has to be inflicted by actual administrators, who too often possess little sense of what is at stake, as so tellingly revealed by the remarkable "water buffalo" incident at Penn in 1993 and in the administrative determination of what was forbidden by the University of Michigan speech code (see below).

First Amendment theory and law also point to the type of intellectual character that is consistent with the portrayal of critical, independent thinking discussed above. The theories of thinkers like Alexander Meiklejohn and Justice Louis Brandeis (whose theories of citizenship resemble Arendt's) pay tribute to the pursuit of truth, but they also champion the type of character who can "think against the tides" (Octavio Paz's foremost recommendation to young writers) with intellectual courage and critical reason. The lack of courage on the part of the believers in freedom is no small part of our problem. At this and many other universities, faculty (especially in law-related fields) have been remiss in challenging codes and related measures that many knew were illegitimate on legal or intellectual grounds. It is in this area that Arendt's notion of the *vita activa* serves freedom of thought, for the failure to defend intellectual freedom in the public forum (the essence of a healthy *vita activa*) has contributed to our present predicament as much as any single factor. In a case that was a harbinger of First Amendment doctrine that was to come, Brandeis stated:

> Those who won our independence believed that the final end of the state was to make men free to develop their faculties, and that in its government the deliberative forces should prevail over the arbitrary . . . They believed that freedom to think as you will and to speak as you think are means indispensable to the discovery and spread of political truth . . . that the greatest menace to freedom is an inert people; that public discussion is a political duty . . . Believing in the power of reason as applied through public discussion, they eschewed silence coerced by law—the argument of force in its worse form . . .
>
> Fear of serious injury cannot alone justify suppression of free speech and assembly. Men feared witches and burnt women. It is the function of speech to free men from the bondage of irrational fear . . . Those who won our independence by revolution were not cowards.[20]

Lee Bollinger, a noted constitutional scholar and former dean of the University of Michigan Law School, provides a powerful theory that highlights the connection between free speech and intellectual character. His argument for legally tolerating hate speech boils down to the type of character such tolerance engenders: a character that exercises self-control in the face of upsetting doctrine, and marshals reason and courage to refute it. Bollinger ingeniously links the First Amendment's lesson of tolerance to other constitutional norms and provisions that counsel reason over irrational fear:

> Under the general tolerance function, free speech is not concerned exclusively with the preservation of a freedom to do whatever we wish, or with the advancement of truth or of democracy as those terms are generally used, but with the development of a capacity of mind, with a way of thinking; it is concerned with facing up to a perceived bias of mind, one that interferes with all of those objectives, as well as others, and also encountered in the decisions

over regulation of speech. [Many have] failed to see the importance of free speech in helping control the impulse that may lead us to "smite on the mouth" those who go among us advocating and acting on views we dislike, even legitimately so.

Free speech in this sense, then, is not inconsistent with what we do toward speech in other areas, like juries. There we seek means of controlling the impulse just as we do with the principle of free speech . . .

The "principle" is the choice to exercise extraordinary self-restraint toward injurious behavior as a means of symbolically demonstrating a capacity for self-control toward feelings that necessarily must play a role throughout social interaction, but which also have a tendency to get out of hand . . .

Meiklejohn's concern, therefore, is with the intellectual attitudes of the general public, not just with protecting speech activity thought to have important informational value . . . [It is about] creating a kind of democratic personality . . . Insistence that the speech—even extremist speech—be tolerated becomes a display of mastery over the "fears" about ideas, for to "be afraid of ideas, any idea, is to be unfit for self-government."[21]

Modern First Amendment doctrine, forged in reaction to McCarthyism and repression during the civil rights movement, is dedicated to distinguishing rational from irrational fear, to the courageous confrontation of all ideas. Today, we are busy teaching people to revel in their victimization rather than to develop the capacities of thoughtfulness and courage. The danger of over-expansive speech codes is that, in the name of protection and victim ideology, they stifle the thinking process. They betray a fear of ideas. The result is the death of the thinking process at Oberlin, portrayed at the beginning of this essay.

But let us now return to the scenario of hate speech with which we began this essay. The thinking process cannot prevail in environments of intimidation. There is a need for basic security that we are obligated to protect. Although we cannot brook fear of ideas, even very unpleasant or upsetting ones, we must protect those who are targets of objectively demonstrable intimidation. Violence and the threat of violence undermine the very integrity and viability of the *vita activa*. Consider the case of Vietnamese fishermen in Galveston Bay, Texas, in the mid–1980s. It is one of the few such legal cases on the books, and it is seldom cited in the literature; yet, it stands as an example of hate-mongers forfeiting their speech rights in a manner that does not endanger the freedom of speech and thought. In the early 1980s the Knights of the Ku Klux Klan commenced a campaign of intimidating Vietnamese fishermen in the Bay. On one occasion, the Klan and its affiliates took a boat ride near Vietnamese fishermen, wearing military regalia and brandishing weapons. They circled the boat and hung an effigy of a Vietnamese fisherman. The Vietnamese sued for injunctive relief citing intimidation and distress, contractual interferences, and the violation of property and personal rights. They won. The federal district court's decision against the Klan's free speech claim stressed that the Klan's expression amounted to "conduct," not speech, and the Klan's provocative expressive acts constituted intimidating "fighting words."[22]

Speech Codes

A speech code devoted to protecting students from clear intimidation (as opposed to embarrassment, being offended, or fearing ideas) is consistent with free speech principles and the university's mission. But because restrictions on speech, especially in today's environment, are so rife with broader potential, we must craft them with care.

Codes must be directed at rational fear, and they must be cast in content-neutral terms that apply to all students and members of the university community, not just politically preferred groups. Group-based protection ineluctably raises the specter of idea-based censorship. Of course, most intimidation will probably be of a racial, ethnic, or gendered nature, so the law will likely be differentially applied. But such a result simply accounts for sexism and racism in American society in legal application, rather than building special protections based on political ideology. Speech codes directed to speech about sex, gender, race, etc., seek to control ideas, not intimidation.

The scope and depth of the codes has varied widely. The University of Wisconsin policy was relatively limited, specifically exempting classrooms in order to protect freedom of discussion. Stanford's code (which has not been tested in court) was crafted with care, and it is limited to insults directed at individuals that amount to "fighting words" (which have always been an exception to free speech, though the Supreme Court has not upheld a fighting-words conviction since 1942). Others, however, succumbed to overkill and lack of precision. Michigan's speech code did not exclude the classroom and was supported by a set of administrative interpretations that constituted thought control. Michigan's code prohibited "any behavior, verbal or physical, that stigmatizes an individual on the basis of race, ethnicity, religion, sex, sexual orientation, creed, national origin, ancestry, age, marital status [no jokes about "old maids"], handicap or Vietnam-era status."[23] In fall of 1989 Michigan's Office of Affirmative Action published an interpretive guideline entitled *What Students Should Know about Discrimination and Discriminatory Harrassment by Students in the University Environment.* Some of its examples of code violations include: distributing a racist leaflet; commenting in class that "women students just aren't as good in this field as men;" lesbians not being invited to a dorm party.[24] In fall of 1989 the federal district court ruled the code unconstitutional for being over broad and vague. The court focused on three administrative actions against classroom comments, and made it clear that the code constituted a deep threat to the modern doctrine of speech and intellectual freedom at the university. In the end, the court concluded that "the University had no idea what the limits of the Policy were and . . . was essentially making up the rules as it went along."[25]

The University of Connecticut proscribed "inappropriately directed laughter [and] inconsiderate jokes" and the "conspicuous exclusion" of people from conversations. Some advocates, like Charles Lawrence at Stanford and Richard Delgado at Wisconsin, argued that the Fourteenth Amendment required that hate speech be restricted.[26] As Samuel Walker points out, "Civil libertarians . . . asked whether it would be possible to discuss any sensitive issue related to race or gender without fear of offending someone and facing possible charges. Would it be possible to discuss theories of race or gender differences in intelligence?"[27]

The University of Wisconsin system adopted its speech code in the summer of 1989. A federal court ruled it unconstitutional in 1991, and a new committee convened to redraft the code along narrower grounds to conform to the "fighting-words" exception to free speech. I opposed this new effort as a consultant to the committee and in the public hearings and politics surrounding the code. Though the university voted to adopt the code, the *R.A.V.* decision (see below) forced the university Board of Regents to balk at final approval.

The first code prohibited "racist or discriminatory comments, epithets or other expressive behavior directed at an individual" when such comments "demean the race, sex, religion, color, creed, disability, sexual orientation, national origin, ancestry or age of the individual or individuals" or "creates an intimidating, hostile, or demeaning environment for education."[28] The guidelines for the policy made it clear that classroom opinions, including derogatory comments, did not violate the policy. But the university did refer to the *Meritor* (Title VII) notion of hostile working environment to justify the employment of the code in all areas outside of the classroom.

Nonetheless, the district court declared the policy unconstitutional, largely because it did not conform tightly enough to the fighting-words doctrine as it presently stands. The original fighting-words doctrine arose in 1942 in *Chaplinsky v. New Hampshire*. The Supreme Court declared that fighting words and some other "narrowly defined" types of expression like libel, obscenity, and profanity were not protected by the First Amendment because "Such utterances are no essential part of any exposition of ideas, and are of such slight social value as a step to truth that any benefit that may be derived from them is clearly outweighed by the social interest in order and morality." The Court then proceeded to define fighting words as "those which by their very utterance inflict injury *or* tend to incite an immediate breach of the peace."[29]

In the wake of the civil rights and antiwar movements, however, the Supreme Court grew suspicious of the *Chaplinsky* doctrine. Authorities too readily punished or prevented speech because of its possible effects on overly sensitive audiences, especially those who disagreed with civil rights protesters (what came to be called the "heckler's veto.")[30] In *Cohen v. California*, in 1971, the Court reversed the conviction of a young man in Los Angeles for wearing a jacket that had "Fuck the Draft" emblazoned on its back. In so doing, the Court applied the tenets of the modern doctrine of speech and held that the speech had to inflict injury and be likely to trigger a violent reaction.[31]

The district court in *UWM Post* carried *Cohen*'s move one step further. It ruled that the Wisconsin policy was invalid because the first part of *Chaplinsky*'s test for fighting words was now "defunct," and the policy did not narrowly cover speech likely to trigger a violent reaction. In addition, the court held that the policy was not content-neutral in that it singled out racist speech for proscription (foreshadowing *R.A.V.*). The court also rejected Wisconsin's claim that the Fourteenth Amendment required such limits on speech, and said that the *Meritor* notion of hostile work environment applied to employment, not education. The latter point highlighted the crucial distinction between the mission of the workplace and the mission of the university, except in certain quarters (narrowly defined domains of the university could be seen as employment contexts).[32]

In response, Wisconsin modified its code to apply to the fighting-words doctrine as articulated by the *Post* decision. However, the code still applied only to racist, sexist, etc., speech, not all forms of hate speech or fighting words. The university simply ignored the district court's warning about content neutrality. This decision would prove fatal when the *R.A.V.* decision came down in June 1992, just days after the legislature adopted the revised code and sent it to the Board of Regents for approval.

The St. Paul Bias-Motivated Crime Ordinance at issue in *R.A.V. v. St. Paul* made it a misdemeanor to place "on public or private property a symbol, object, appellation, characterization or graffiti" that "arouses anger, alarm or resentment in others on the basis of race, color, creed, religion or gender." The ordinance was very broad because it did not require that the display lead to disturbance of the peace, and it applied to speech made on one's private property. I do not think that *R.A.V.*'s speech act should be protected by the Constitution, but the issue in the case was the validity of the ordinance as it was written.

The case arose when Robert Viktora and friends burned a cross on the yard of a black family who lived across the street. Viktora was convicted of violating the ordinance. The Supreme Court reversed the conviction unanimously. Justice Scalia ruled the ordinance in violation of free speech because it engaged in content or viewpoint discrimination within the erstwhile unprotected category of fighting words. For instance, fighting words related to "political affiliation, union membership, or homosexuality" were not punished. The content neutrality doctrine obligates the state to treat all fighting words the same way in order to comply with the norm of nonpreferential treatment. Obscenity and threatening the life of the president are not protected by the First Amendment because of their harmful nature and lack of value, but if the state punishes such expression selectively for clearly political or idea-laden reasons, then the censorship is directed at ideas, not the idea-neutral harms normally associated with obscenity and threats on the president. Scalia states:

> When the basis for the content discrimination consists entirely of the very reason the entire class of speech at issue is proscribable, no significant danger of idea or viewpoint discrimination exists. Such a reason, having been adjudged neutral enough to support exclusion of the entire class of speech, is also neutral enough to form the basis of distinction within the class. To illustrate: A State might choose to prohibit only that obscenity which is the most patently offensive *in its prurience* [prurience is the major rationale for the exclusion of obscenity from First Amendment protection in the first place] . . . But it may not prohibit, for example, only that obscenity which includes offensive *political*

messages . . . the Federal Government may not criminalize only those threats against the President that mention his policy on aid to inner cities.[33]

R.A.V.'s holding concerning viewpoint discrimination within the confines of otherwise unprotected speech seriously jeopardizes many or most campus speech codes, for they (following the logic and categories of heightened judicial scrutiny in equal protection law) single out politically preferred groups for special protection against hate speech and fighting words. In this sense, they grant special protections from offensive or threatening speech to certain groups, but not others, thereby leading to differential treatment based on the ideas expressed. This understanding of the codes is supported by the fact that most institutions of higher education (including Wisconsin) already have had rules in place against harassment or threatening other students. Such rules have typically covered all forms of harassment or threatening speech, not just those against certain groups. By passing new laws that go further, in that they single out certain groups for protection over others, the speech codes raise the suspicion that they are political measures designed to prevent certain kinds of ideas as much as measures designed to protect students from discrete and significant harm.

A Speech Code That Protects University Citizens from Intimidation Without Leading to or Supporting Thought Control

A restriction that protects vulnerable individuals without engaging in group-based justice is reconcilable with *R.A.V.* Also, the theory of constitutional citizenship I have broached entails the exercise of courage in the public realm; but individuals need sufficient social or state protection and a sense of security in order to feel enabled or empowered to enter this realm.[34] Clearly threatening or intimidating speech crosses a line between advocating a noxious idea and actually instilling fear in individuals. Arendt's theory of the *vita activa* makes no pact with violence. Violence is the antithesis of the *vita activa*, as it is mute and brutal.[35] Also, violence instills fear, which Hobbes teaches us is a primordial and universal emotion. The First Amendment is designed to distinguish rational and irrational fear, not to turn its back on legitimate fear. Accordingly, speech that is targeted at individuals or small, discrete groups and that instills fear of violence crosses a line. The speech act in *R.A.V.* provides an example. Serious threats would constitute fighting words under this logic; or perhaps it would be better to simply depend on the fact that realistic threats have never constituted protected speech regardless of any "unprotected categories" to which they might be attached.[36] Such fear must be about bodily harm (deadly, serious, or lesser physical harm), but it need not be imminent in nature, for then the criminal law of self-defense would become operative. Such rhetorical threats as "the President oughta be shot if the crime bill passes" do not qualify, for they do not present realistic beliefs in danger.[37]

The concept of fear is important in this regard because of the seriousness of the harm, the clear legitimacy of the state's role, and the clearly low value of the speech in terms of First Amendment values. In addition, a focus on fear most adequately avoids the problems that arise in the context of the new politics of censorship: viewpoint discrimination (content non-neutrality), balkanization of the First Amendment stemming from group claims for special protection, thought control, and victim ideology. Meaningful threats to another's security hardly constitute an idea, so Bollinger's and Meiklejohn's emphasis on protecting all ideas in the name of constitutional citizenship is not sacrificed. General hate speech and other forms of pernicious speech in nontargeted contexts would be protected. Speech in politics bears the potential for evil as well as good, and it can serve the Big Lie as well as the truth (e.g., Holocaust denial; hate speech; the two potentials of the *vita activa* discussed above).[38]

But when it comes to pernicious lies and hatred of this nature, the remedy is Brandeis's: the political obligation of counterspeech. All political and historical truths and facts (not the stubborn facts themselves, but our recognitions and interpretations of the facts) are like our lives: contingent and subject to distortion. As Mill asserts in *On Liberty*, we are obliged to renew their political relevance through speech and persuasion.[39] This is the proper way to handle hate speech when it does not single out individuals for intimidation. Though general hate speech represents pernicious ideas, it is made up of ideas, not distinct, individuated threats that possess a strong possibility of being carried out.

The standard would apply to all specifically targeted individuals who reasonably felt threatened, not just those in protected categories. The principle and doctrine must protect only individuals, not groups or communities per se. If the speech were made in a public forum or in class, targeting, by definition, would not exist.[40]

Such a rule would conform to *U.W.M. Post* and *Cohen*, but with one exception. The reasonable feeling of fear would justify proscription, regardless of the presence or likelihood of a hostile, fighting reaction by the target of the speech. Wisconsin's abandoned revised code attempted to account for this type of harm.[41] If the reasonable state of fear is the key reaction, whether the target is likely to strike against the targeter is irrelevant. Requiring a likely hostile reaction is also unfair to those targets who are too weak or vulnerable to risk attacking back. Recall the incident at Wisconsin with which we began. Depending on the facts, the young woman could have felt very threatened, yet she posed no threat of retaliation. To disqualify her from the protections of an intimidation rule would be cruel and unjust.

Recommended Policy

Thus, an "intimidation doctrine" can be fashioned that avoids the pitfalls of balkanized justice and thought control. Following *R.A.V.*, it must be neutral as to the protected targets, it must deal with realistic or reasonable fear of future violence, it must protect individuals rather than groups, and it must distinguish speech that is threatening and clearly intimidating from speech that is simply highly offensive and upsetting by virtue of its ideas. I propose the following standard:

Speech that is directly targeted at individuals or small groups and is intended to threaten that person's physical safety, and which instills in that person the reasonable belief that he or she is in danger of being inflicted with deadly or physical harm at the hands of the speaker(s) now or in the future.

In the end, this standard is built along the boundary that distinguishes rational, clearly delineated fear from generalized fear that slides easily into irrationality and ideological distortion. It also embraces a return to the notion that the law should protect all citizens equally, regardless of their race, gender, or other ascriptive qualities. If applied in good faith (an issue meriting further debate), it would protect vulnerable individuals without sacrificing the missions to which the university should be dedicated.

Notes

1. An incident related by Mary Rouse, dean of students at UW–Madison, in public hearings and to the author.

2. See, e.g., Samuel Walker, *Hate Speech: The History of an American Controversy* (Lincoln: University of Nebraska Press, 1994), ch. 7.

3. See, e.g., *Meritor Savings Bank, FSB v. Vinson*, 477 U.S. 57 (1986).

4. Jose Ortega, *Mission of the University* (New York: Norton, 1966), pp. 88–89.

5. Hannah Arendt, "Truth and Politics," in Peter Laslett and W. G. Runciman, eds., *Philosophy, Politics and Society* (London: Basil Blackwell, 1967), p. 113.

6. Ortega, *Mission of the University*, p. 61. Emphasis in original.

7. In an extreme example of this dilemma, we witness the godfather of American deconstruction, Paul de Man, eschewing any notion of the truth being "out there" and engaging in propaganda for the Nazis during World War II in France. See, e.g., the excellent critique of deconstruction by David Lehman, *Signs of the Times: Deconstruction and the Fall of Paul de Man* (Poseidon Press, 1991). On Holocaust denial, see Deborah E. Lipstadt, *Denying the Holocaust: The Growing Assault on Truth and Memory* (Free Press, 1993).

8. On the interplay between community standards of inquiry and individual discretion and creativity, see Richard J. Bernstein, *Beyond Objectivism and Relativism: Science, Hermeneutics, and Praxis* (Philadelphia: University of Pennsylvania Press, 1983).

9. See Arendt, "Thinking," in *The Life of the Mind* (New York: Harcourt Brace Jovanovich, 1977), pp. 7, 199.

10. Stephen Carter, *Reflections of an Affirmative Action Baby* (New York: Basic Books, 1991).

11. See Donald A. Downs, *More Than Victims: Battered Women, the Syndrome Society, and the Law* (Chicago: University of Chicago Press, 1996).

12. Alan Wolfe, "The New Class Comes Home," Partisan Review 60 (1993): 729–30.

13. *U.S. v. Carolene Products*, 304 U.S. 144 (1941), at 152–53, fn. 4. Kant, *Groundwork of the Metaphysic of Morals* (New York: Harper, 1964), pp. 95–96.

14. Henry Louis Gates, Jr., "Let Them Talk: Why Civil Liberties Pose No Threat to Civil Rights," *New Republic*, (September 20 & 27, 1993), pp. 37–49.

15. Wolfe, "The New Class Comes Home," p. 734.

16. Jacques Barzun, *Begin Here: The Forgotten Conditions of Teaching and Learning* (Chicago: University of Chicago Press, 1991), pp. 5, 13–15.

17. Arendt, "Thinking," in *The Life of the Mind*, p. 13.

18. Ortega, *Mission of the University*, p. 91.

19. On the relationships between freedom of speech, freedom of thought, and the "liberal model of science," see Jonathan Rauch, *Kindly Inquisitors: The New Attacks on Free Thought* (Chicago: University of Chicago Press, 1993).

20. Louis Brandeis, in *Whitney v. California*, 274 U.S. 357 (1927).

21. Lee C. Bollinger, *The Tolerant Society: Freedom of Speech and Extremist Speech in America* (New York: Oxford University Press, 1986), pp. 142, 155, quoting Meiklejohn.

22. *Vietnamese Fishermen's Association v. Knights of the Ku Klux Klan*, 543 F. Supp. 198 (S.D. Tex. 1982), at 206–8.

23. *Doe v. University of Michigan*, 721 F. Supp. 852 (E.D. Mich. 1989).

24. *Doe v. University of Michigan*; Walker, *Hate Speech*, p. 151.

25. *Doe V. University of Michigan*, at 868. Discussion with Robert Sedler, ACLU attorney for the plaintiff, April 1990.

26. Charles Lawrence, "If He Hollers Let Him Go: Regulating Racist Speech on Campus," in Mari J. Matsuda et al., *Words That Wound: Critical Race Theory, Assaultive Speech, and the First Amendment* (Boulder: Westview Press, 1993).

27. Walker, *Hate Speech*, p. 128.

28. *UWM Post v. Board of Regents of the University of Wisconsin*, 774 F. Supp. 1163 (E.D. Wis. 1991).

29. *Chaplinsky v. New Hampshire*, 315 U.S. 568n (1942).

30. See, e.g., *Edwards v. South Carolina*, 372 U.S. 229 (1963).

31. *Cohen v. California*, 403 U.S. 15 (1971).

32. *UWM Post v. Board of Regents of the University of Wisconsin*, 774 F. Supp. 1163 (E.D. Wis. 1991).

33. *R.A.V. v. St. Paul*, 112 Sup. Ct. 2538 (1992). I made a similar point in speaking against the new UW–Madison speech code in April 1992, and in *The New Politics of Pornography* (Chicago: University of Chicago Press, 1989), pp. 153–54, paying special attention to *Schact v. U.S.*, 398 U.S. 58 (1970).

34. Arendt maintains in *The Human Condition* (Chicago: University of Chicago Press, 1958) that an ordered private realm is necessary to support a vibrant public realm. My graduate student Paul Passavant has also made this argument to me, and I thank him for this idea here.

35. See also Arendt's "On Violence," in *Crises of the Republic* (New York: Harcourt Brace Jovanovich, 1972).

36. I owe this idea to another graduate student, Evan Gerstman.

37. See, e.g., *Watts. v. U.S.*, 394 U.S. 705 (1969).

38. See Arendt, "Truth and Politics." On Holocaust denial, see Deborah E. Lipstadt, *Denying the Holocaust: The Growing Assault on Truth and Memory* (New York: Free Press, 1993). Lipstadt's logic about the importance of historical memory is very similar to Arendt's in "Truth and Politics," though she does not recognize or acknowledge this connection.

39. John Stuart Mill, *On Liberty* (New York: Appleton-Century-Crofts, 1947).

40. On the constitutional doctrine of the public forum, see, e.g., *Perry Educ. Assn. v. Perry Local Educators' Assn.*, 460 U.S. 37 (1983).

41. It spoke of reactions by reasonable or typical targets, thereby accommodating the vulnerable few who would be afraid to retaliate. Ted Finman explained this logic to me in a discussion. My doctrine, however, deals with this problem or matter more directly.

Hate in the Cloak of Liberty

LINDA S. GREENE

Perhaps the most recent civil rights movement, and our observation of film footage that graphically portrayed the violence associated with racist epithets, helped us to understand the relationship between hate speech and the question of equality. Soundbites of racial epithets accompanied by graphic portrayals of violence helped us to understand this relationship both emotionally and intellectually. We were officially embarrassed and ashamed of these frank demonstration of hate. And we seemed to understand that words as well as actions played a key role in a regime of separation and subordination. We knew that certain words were audible reminders of an ideology of racial supremacy and inferiority, and that such language signaled a rejection of the ideal of equality we hope to belatedly embrace.

And so it seemed for a moment that we were clear about racist hate speech.[1] We concluded that it was the expression of the ideology of racial inferiority that had been so central to our constitutional and popular culture. Pursuant to new civil rights statutes our judges ruled that racially hostile environments violated the law. Official rules as well as customs eradicated the use of racial epithets from public life and required the punishment of public figures if their private verbal indiscretions were broadcast to society. There was no public argument, on any ground, that racist speech was harmless or useful. Or perhaps there was no one willing to make that case.

Now, however, we do have a public argument about the permissibility of racist speech. The pre–1965 public argument was that racist speech conveyed truthful and appropriate messages about the worth of those maligned. The old public argument was fairly similar to the private argument. But the new public argument eschewed the endorsement of specific language and the endorsement of racial inequality. The new public argument is that our expressed liberty—our expressive freedom—is threatened by any curtailment or punishment of—racist speech. The argument is that any curtailment or punishment of racist speech would not only violate First Amendment principles but would also have a chilling effect on freedom of expression.

Linda S. Greene is professor of law, University of Wisconsin–Madison.

The new public argument is much more attractive than the old ones. In the first place, the new argument appropriates a major premise difficult to refute—that personal liberty in every aspect of our lives, including speech, is fundamental. The new public argument avoids the messy and embarrassing discussion of the particular words that racist-speech users hurl to remind certain people that they are not equal and are still at risk. The new public argument is also attractive to a wider range of people, some of whom are prominent and above reproach, and it provides the proponents of racist ideology some new and respectful bedfellows. The public argument does everything a good public argument should do—it provides a lofty and unassailable rationale for behavior that one could not directly defend. Moreover, it may be asserted without discussing the particular behavior at all. The new public argument "spins" the arguments against racist speech into an argument against liberty, choice, and freedom.

How ironic it is that images of the flag and the First Amendment have precluded a discussion of the dangers presented by hate in the cloak of liberty. Is it possible that we have allowed the discussion of laws and hate speech to take place in such general terms that we have failed to expose the particular dangers presented when abstract ideas and fundamental values are offered in support of words and actions that pose a great threat to our society, the university, and to certain individuals and groups? While it is truly the responsibility of the university to respond vigorously to any challenge to liberty, we do not discharge this responsibility by automatically rejecting any limitation on expressive liberty. We appropriately discharge our responsibility when we determine the conditions under which a society and all its people may flourish. In particular, we have a responsibility to look closely at any claim of liberty to determine whether we abdicate our societal responsibilities by treating hate, and, in particular, racial hate, as just another idea.

I have deliberately chosen not to focus on what the Constitution permits because I do not believe that the values we hold at the university turn on constitutional restraint. However, some of you may have heard that a recent Supreme Court decision[2] renders moot any discussion of hate speech and hate speech suppression. The decision in *RAV v. City of St. Paul* does not do that, but since all members of the Court (albeit pursuant to different rationales) found unconstitutional a statute that punished a Klan-type cross burning on the property of a black family, there is legitimate concern about the future constitutionality of any code or law that punishes hate speech.

The five-justice majority opinion in *RAV*—written by Justice Scalia—said that racist hate speech, in this case personalized cross burning, could not be singled out for suppression while the government permitted other kinds of invective that might provoke violence. In the words of the opinion, "the First Amendment imposes . . . a 'content discrimination' limitation upon the State's prohibition of prescribable speech."[3] According to the Court, the problem with the ordinance was that it applied only to fighting words on the basis of race, color, creed, or religion, and that this limitation embodied both content discrimination as well as viewpoint discrimination. However, the majority decision did suggest that the state might criminalize threats of violence as long as it did not select the threat of violence to be criminalized on the basis of the content of speech utilized.[4] The majority decision also suggested that the state might criminalize or punish a type of conduct—such as sex discrimination—and decide that sexually derogatory words violate the prohibition against sex discrimination.[5]

The remaining four justices agreed that the ordinance was unconstitutional but on different grounds. Justice White (with Blackmun, O'Connor, and Stevens) wrote both to express disagreement with the majority rationale as well as to suggest another theory upon which the statute was unconstitutional. Justice White's opinion concluded that the statute was unconstitutional because it punished both protected speech—that which simply hurt feelings and did not provoke violence—and unprotected speech—speech that provoked violence known as "malicious" in First Amendment doctrine. The specific theory—that of unconstitutional overbreadth—prohibits laws that sweep protected and unprotected speech up in one prohibition.[6] Thus, these justices suggested that a law or code focused on fighting words that provoked violence would be constitutional. And though Justice Stevens agreed with Justice White that the ordinance was unconstitutionally overbroad, he wrote separately to emphasize his view that the "scope of protection provided expressive activity depends in part upon its content and character[7] . . . as well as on the context of the regulated speech. The distinctive character of a university environment, or a secondary school environment, influences our First Amendment analysis."[8] A close reading of these opinions reveals that there may be ample room for debate about the constitutionality of hate speech codes and laws, and the *RAV* case did not categorically foreclose them.

Regardless of the conclusions legal scholars may arrive at about the permissibility of punishing cross burning or swastika inscribing after the Supreme

Court decision in the *RAV* case, the university must, nevertheless, sort out its own role and responsibilities. The Supreme Court decisions, as divided as they are, provide some guidance. Even if an argument may be made that the Supreme Court foreclosed the curtailment of racist speech in the community at large, the Supreme Court has not spoken directly to the question of the curtailment of hate speech in the academy. Whatever the Court may say when this question is squarely presented, its decisions cannot supply our values or supplant our traditions. For example, the Court cannot decide whether we want to challenge racist speech, suppress it to the full extent permissible, or watch it from a comfortable distance with wrinkled brow and wringing hands. Court decisions do not help us to evaluate what we have done to make the expression of hate feasible and tolerable, or what we have failed to do to deter its expression. Court decisions do not tell us how hate might flourish under our protection or wither or fade without it. The Court cannot supplant our own responsibility to sort out the dangers and benefits hate speech offers. The Court may limit our weapons if it should decide that hate speech poses a danger. But judicial institutions can never absolve us of our responsibility to clarify the role racial hate has played in our society and to decide what role we will permit it to play in our educational institutions.

Arguments in favor of permitting hate speech now find their justifications in acceptable ideas. It is no longer acceptable—nor politically correct— to seek refuge in explicit claims of inferiority and inequality. Yet, even if we assume that those who oppose limits on the distribution of hate are acting on the basis of generally agreeable principles, we should not end our investigation of the current cultural justification that cloaks hate in glorious garb.

As scholars grounded in history, we ought to be exceedingly curious about new manifestations of hate justification. Several questions demand rigorous investigation. What accounts for the roles that leading intellectuals play in the effort to offer arguments in favor of racist hate-speech tolerance in other nations, and what have been the consequences? How does the resurgence of racist hate speech affect the willingness of minority group members to participate in historically white institutions or, conversely, their attractions to historically black institutions? Is there a relationship between the availability of official sanctions for racist hate speech and the incidence of racist hate speech? What motivates those who choose this language, and are there corrective possibilities? As scholars, it is our responsibility to investigate how racism may have reformulated itself to survive and flourish anew.

We know that many distressing historical phenomena have found resilient justification in higher values and ideals.

The conquest of Native Americans was justified by arguments of manifest destiny and cultural superiority, slavery on the grounds of black racial inferiority and state sovereignty, the subordination of females on the ground that it was necessary to preserve white female purity, and resistance to racial integration on the ground of states' rights. In each case, too, constitutional principles played a role in arguments that either legitimated these efforts or limited judicial interference.[9] Opposition to hate speech suppression is too often viewed as an effort to denigrate the importance of liberty and First Amendment claims. Rather, it is an effort to show how broad value-claims are often offered in support of questionable and subordinating practices.

It is not necessary to agree that speech freedom should be curtailed to conclude that the free expression of ideas is not necessarily associated with liberty. Just who is likely to be hurt or victimized by this invocation of liberty? Indeed, it is possible to conclude that the free expression of certain ideas is not necessarily associated with liberty, and that a more studious examination of the impact of this invocation of liberty would reveal that selective disadvantage flows from this invocation of liberty. Here I define liberty as a state of society where all people may enjoy the benefits of that society. Liberty, as I would define it, includes the opportunity to take full advantage of legal rights such as access to a university education or the right to enjoy the opportunities that accompany full personhood and citizenship, as well as a more generalized opportunity to fully develop one's potential. Those who argue that liberty is thwarted when speech is constrained implicitly and explicitly argue that speech is a first freedom upon which the opportunity to exercise all other rights and opportunities is based and that therefore the constraint of speech is a necessary constraint of all other opportunities, political and personal. As an abstract argument this point has great force, but we must examine the risks that attend racist hate speech. Just who is likely to be hurt or victimized by this particular invocation of liberty? The purveyors of racist hate speech intend to damage and undermine the spirit of individuals and racial groups and to send the message that they do not deserve to be full and equal persons in society. The individuals targeted know that violence has often accompanied the use of certain words toward them and they fear the renewal of violence as a result. In short, these racist speech acts deprive the targeted individual of confident and effective participation in society.

Moreover, even though the racist hate speech targets a specific individual or family, we are all affected. When we swiftly embrace the argument that our liberty is threatened by any constraint on speech, we forget how racist speech has conditioned our perceptions of individuals and groups. Framing the question as one of abstract liberty or freedom has obscured the importance of this inquiry. What is the significance and message of a cross burning and how are our associations with blacks, even those not directly targeted, affected by the valence of that symbolism? What reminders do swastikas and Nazi uniforms suggest? How might we view Jewish people differently in the absence of the Holocaust? Are not these phenomena current reminders that continue to threaten our ability to treat religious faith or physical characteristics neutrally? We know the difference slavery and the Holocaust have made in our lives generally, and we also know the role rhetoric and the ideology of liberty played in permitting these phenomena to flourish. We know too much to let generalized ideological claims, however attractive in the abstract, decide this kind of question for us.

This is not, however, an argument in favor of the proposition that generalizable values are irrelevant to this debate about the university's posture vis à vis hate speech. On the contrary, such values are important to articulate and examine. I have noted that the mere invocation of liberty (and its related ideal in this context, academic freedom) does not resolve the problem of whether hate speech contributes to liberty or academic freedom.

There are other free-expression related values that must also be evaluated in the context of the general claim that we give up too much when we permit any speech to be curtailed. Among the values invoked in favor of freedom of expression are the value of promoting the search for truth (or importance of preserving the market place of ideas),[10] the importance of individual autonomy in the choice of words and in the development of conscience,[11] the importance of public debate to political self-governance,[12] and the general idea of tolerance as a fundamental norm of American constitutional culture.[13] Each of these values might form the basis of arguments against the curtailment of racist hate speech. On closer examination, however, we might conclude that tolerance of hate speech does not further any of these values, and moreover that the risk posed to these values by embracing racist hate speech is too great to tolerate.[14]

In the university setting, several important values may be compromised if we remain neutral on the question of hate speech. In general, we have an interest in the preservation of a peaceful environment in which our students and faculty feel secure and welcome. As important, hate speech is a phenomenon most frequently directed toward historically powerless and excluded groups, the same groups who have had unequal educational opportunity and exposure. Hate speech poses the risk that these individuals will be deterred from attending our university or will fail to take advantage of its benefits as a result of fear. Hate speech is also an explicit devaluation of the targeted group and a challenge to our vision of a diverse university population.

Some argue that we cannot reshape the society, while others argue that the university is a microcosm of the world and that exposure to that world, good and bad, is important preparation for adult life. Nonetheless, we protect our students and faculty from many risks that abound in the world because we aim to create a special place here where we may not only prepare for the world but also decide what we want to make of it. The years our students spend here are a special time, and this is a special place. We can decide that we want to create an environment in which all may participate in the free exchange of ideas without fear and denigration. This is a liberty-related interest of the highest order that must be furthered actively lest it be eroded insidiously. Our interest in liberty and participation for all our students and faculty is just as important as the grass on Bascom Hill, the ice in the hockey rink, and the flowers along Observatory Drive. None flourishes unmaintained.

Moreover, the matter of speech at the university is very complicated and textured. In a debate framed in terms of liberty and freedom of speech, we tend to express our support for untrammeled expression without thinking about the critical approach to speech that is an integral part of our lives here. We grade—pass and fail—our students on the basis of their expression.

Thus, the drafters of the 1989 rule sought to preserve the possibility of free discussion that might be offensive while preserving the opportunity of individual students to be free of menacing and emotionally harmful statements. However, the federal district court struck down the 1989 rule on First Amendment grounds.[15] The court found certain language in the rule vague, but, more importantly, concluded that the rule was unconstitutionally overbroad because it was not limited to fighting words.

Thereafter, the chancellor asked the dean of the Law School to head an advisory committee to advise her and university counsel on a response to the court decision. The committee, which included some of the advisers on the 1989 rule, as well as others[16] concluded that the district court opinion had offered clear guidance on the drafting of a rule that would meet constitutional standards, and that an effort to redraft the old rule might be more productive than a costly, combative, and risky appeal. The committee then proposed a new rule, which was later adopted by the UW Faculty Senate and then adopted but later rescinded by the Board of Regents.[17]

The new rule would have limited the sanctionable language in an "epithet," defined as ". . . a word, phrase, or symbol that reasonable persons recognize to grievously insult or threaten persons because of their race, sex, religion, color, etc., and that make the educational environment hostile or threatening for a person to whom the word, phrase, or symbol is directly addressed; and (2). . . would tend to provoke an immediate violent response when addressed directly to a person . . . who is a member of the group that the word, phrase, or symbol insults or threatens." The rule explicitly provided that "the use of epithets in statements addressed to a general audience rather then directly to a specific individual, or specific individuals, shall not be a violation of this subsection even though the speaker's intent is to demean and create a hostile environment and even though a member, or members, of the group demeaned by the epithet constitute part of that audience."[18] The rule, therefore, would have permitted wide-ranging, if offensive, discussion and debate and yet would have permitted punishment for verbal assaults posing the risk of both emotional harm as well as violent response. It should be noted that the rule did not provide for advance censorship or any prior restraint on speech.[19]

Our committee implicitly rejected the argument that it is inappropriate for the state—here the university—to interfere in the "private" communications or interactions between individuals. The university undertakes a general commitment to provide a safe and nurturing environment for our students. We provide security, light, clean water, recreational activities, sports entertainment, parking, and other amenities so that these years will be both productive and memorable. We have adopted codes of conduct to govern students' behavior that give clear notice of that conduct—such as the destruction of property, physical assault, or academic dishonesty—which we believe harms others and the community at large. Though our students are relatively free—evidenced by the mood on campus and State Street on the night and morning before a Big Game—we do not leave all matters of judgment entirely to them. Our response to the problem of hate speech should be understood in the context of our overall responsibility to all students to provide a tolerant and relatively safe community during their special time here at Wisconsin.

Maintenance of the status quo is not the role of a great university. The role of a great university is to prepare the next generation for the future, not to mire it in the useless paradigms of the past. That role requires a sifting and winnowing among our traditions and values to separate out that which is useful from that which is not. We have an affirmative duty to learn what role racism and other hate phenomena have played in our history and how these phenomena have harmed or benefited us. Just as we have duty to share with our students what we have learned about biochemical hazards and persistent viruses, we also have a duty to share with our students what we have learned about racism and its associated phenomena. We are just forty years removed from South Africa if we count from *Brown v. Board*, and only twenty-five years removed if our reference point is the enforcement of *Brown*'s principles. The roots of racism run deep in our society.

Horticultural logic suggests that these roots, given their longevity, would be difficult to remove or contain, and that we might find among our crops the product of this weed. What shall we do when it appears among our desired crops? Gather it up and consume it, sell it as if we had planted it deliberately, or separate it from the desired produce and burn it to destroy its seed? Each decision has consequences for the future.

We cannot embrace hate speech simply because it appears in the cloak of liberty. An uncritical stance is at odds with our tradition of sifting and winnowing and at odds with what we know about the history of race in our country. Our responsibility is to be much more critical, to look more closely at this phenomenon, to find its roots, to study its present appearances, and to understand its current and future consequences. Our responsibility is to decide whether the embrace or tolerance of racist hate speech is consistent or inconsistent with our university's traditions of liberty. And that decision should not be made in an abstract or detached manner. Rather, it must be made in light of the impact of racist hate speech on the liberty and prosperity of an emerging university community that is, and will be, far more inclusive and diverse than it has been in the past.

Notes

1. Here I define racist hate speech as the use of epithets and similar words that the speaker intends to cause a grievous insult to the listener and that are akin to an effort to inflict emotional distress on the individual to whom the words are addressed. Words that may be

characterized as racist speech may be employed in other contexts, but I do not address those issues in this paper.

2. *RAV v City of St. Paul*, 112 Sup. Ct. at 2538 (1992).

3. *RAV*, 112 Sup. Ct. at 2538, 2545 (1991).

4. *RAV*, 112 Sup. Ct. at 2545–2546 (1992).

5. *RAV*, 112 Sup. Ct. at 2546 (1992).

6. *RAV*, 112 Sup. Ct. at 2556, 2558.

7. *RAV*, 112 Sup. Ct. at 2567.

8. *RAV*, 112 Sup. Ct. at 2568.

9. See, e.g. *Johnson v McIntosh*, 21 U.S. 543 (1823); and *Lone Wolf v Hitchcock*, 187 U.S. 553 (1903); *Dred Scott v Sandford*, 19 How. (60 U.S.) 393 (1857) (Constitution embodies principles that blacks are an inferior race with no rights whites are bound to respect); *Bradwell v State*, 16 Wall (83 U.S.) 130 (1873) (women denied right to practice law due to timidity and delicacy); and *Muller v Oregon*, 208 U.S. 412 (1908) (women barred from employment due to need for physical structure and maternal functions); *U.S. v Harris*, 106 U.S. 629 (1882) (no prosecution for lynching because state not sufficiently involved); *Brown v Board*, 359 U.S. 294 (1955) (stating numerous grounds upon which states might petition for delay of implementation of *Brown*).

10. See J. Mill, *On Liberty* (1859); *Abrams v United States*, 250 U.S. 616, 630 (1919) (Holmes, J., dissenting).

11. Meiklejohn, *Free Speech and Its Relation to Self Government* 15–16, 24–27 (New York: Harper, 1948). See *NAACP v Clairborne Hardware*, 458 U.S. 886, 911–13 (1982).

12. See Richards, *Free Speech and Obscenity Law: Toward a Moral Theory of the First Amendment*, 123 U. Pa. Law Rev 45, 62 (1974); and Scanlon, *A Theory of Freedom of Expression*, 1 *Philosophy and Public Affairs*, 204, 213–18 (1972). See also *NAACP v Clairborne*, 458 U.S. 886, 928 (1982) and *Cohen v California*, 403 U.S. 15 (1981).

13. See L. Bollinger, *The Tolerant Society: Freedom of Speech and Extremist Speech in America*, 9–10 (New York: Oxford University Press, 1986).

14. For example, what is the claim of truth to be embodied in a racial epithet? Would those who defend the rights of racist hate-speech purveyors be willing to specifically state and invoke that claim? Or similarly, how is the idea of tolerance furthered by protecting these semiviolent verbal assaults. On the other hand, one might concede the value of protecting open and free expression, yet conclude that the price of curtailing epithets under limited circumstances—in the context of the college campus—is a small price to pay to guarantee the effectiveness of all members of the community and to promote tolerance in an institution whose primary purpose is the inculcation of important values.

15. *UWM v Post*, 774 F. Supp. 1163 (E.D. Wis. 1991). "Fighting words" are words that would provoke an immediate violent reaction and are a category of speech which the Supreme Court has historically denied protection.

16. I was a member of the committee.

17. 1992 revised UWS 17.06(2) with Admin Code (1992), repealed, Sept. 11, 1992, Board of Regents' minutes, p. 7–11 (Sept 30, 1992).

18. *Id.*

19. *Id.*

"Hate Speech" Codes in Theory and Practice

TED FINMAN

While the protective umbrella spread by the First Amendment and Academic Freedom shelters a vast array of expressive activity,[1] its coverage is not complete. Some speech, indeed, can be totally banned. Many lesser regulations have long been recognized as wholly proper. The critical question—the dividing line between permissible and impermissible restrictions—is whether a limitation on speech would violate the very purposes, principles, and values of Academic Freedom and the First Amendment. Thus any intelligent discussion of "hate speech codes" must carefully specify the communicative activity that various codes would ban, identify the values that stand behind the First Amendment and Academic Freedom, and consider the impact on those values of different kinds of codes.

Initially, however, it is vital to examine the premise that lies behind all such codes, namely that the speech they ban makes a university campus hostile and threatening for the students that the speech attacks, and, therefore, substantially impairs their ability to study and learn effectively. That will be the focus of part 1 of this paper. Part 2 will set out briefly the generally recognized justifications for protecting speech. Part 3 identifies the common characteristic of the various rules and regulations commonly called "hate speech codes," and then draws a critical distinction between two types of codes. Part 4 considers whether each type would violate the basic principles of Academic Freedom and of the First Amendment.

I will argue that although some codes ban speech that is clearly entitled to protection, the expressive activity covered by others, like the Wisconsin code, has little or nothing to do with the purposes of Academic Freedom or the First Amendment and, therefore, is not entitled to protection. Thus a prohibition on such speech does not *in itself* violate free speech values. In various ways, however, the adoption and enforcement of these codes may *indirectly* lead to limitations on speech clearly entitled to protection.[2] Thus the truly serious problems raised by a Wisconsin-type code have to do with its possible indirect consequences: How likely are they? How serious? Can efforts to prevent them be effective?

Ted Finman is professor of law at the University of Wisconsin–Madison.

1. The Harms of Hate Speech

All of us would agree, I think, that universities have some duty to provide an environment conducive to learning, or, at the least, to take appropriate measures to prevent conditions that seriously impair learning. Racial epithets poison the atmosphere for many minority students and substantially undermine their ability to study and learn. This point needs and deserves elaboration. First, however, I want to clarify the implication of the proposition that hate speech (or any speech, for that matter) has harmful consequences.

While harm is a *necessary* condition for restricting speech, it is not *sufficient*. It is also essential that a restriction not infringe on the very principles and values that underlie speech's privileged status. If harm were in itself a sufficient basis for censoring speech, it would surely be proper to ban racist tracts, for they spread belief in racial inferiority and encourage racial discrimination. Despite these harmful effects, however, such publications receive protection, because to ban them would violate the bedrock free-speech principle prohibiting censorship of ideas. Whether a Wisconsin-type code would constitute such a violation will be considered below. I return now to consider how hate speech affects the students it attacks.

To some extent, any effort to make this fully understandable is doomed to fail. It is not difficult to communicate a conceptual understanding of how racial epithets work. But many things in life—and this is one of them—can be fully understood only through experience. A medical textbook, for example, can explain the physiological mechanisms involved in the production of physical pain, and in one sense, the reader will come to "know" that phenomenon. But, in another important sense, someone who has never *felt* pain cannot know it.

The same holds true for psychological pain. If you have never been depressed, you cannot fully understand depression. More to the point: Unless one belongs to a racial or ethnic or religious group that the larger society has viewed as hateful or inferior (or both), it is difficult (if not impossible) to comprehend fully the damage done by epithets that embody this vision and serve to justify the abuse, the indignities and humiliation, and the discrimination that members of the group still encounter in modern day America.[3]

Generally speaking, I am not what you would call "thin skinned" or "over sensitive." Yet at sixty-three years of age I still recall the emotional turmoil evoked by anti-Semitic remarks heard during my childhood: anger and frustration, because there is no way to argue with irrational hate; self-doubt, since these epithets represent widespread attitudes and cannot be passed off as the ravings of some "nut;" guilt, deep long-lasting guilt, when, out of fear of further hurt, one turns silently away instead of standing up for oneself and one's people. These feelings are not fleeting or momentary. These things I heard long ago still produce psychological upheaval—sometimes leave me close to tears—when, as now, I find it necessary to think and talk about them.

A substantial body of scholarly study and writing indicates that my experience is hardly unique. These materials explore and explain the psychological mechanisms at work and report that emotional turmoil and injury caused by racial epithets are common among African-Americans and members of other minority groups.[4] This is not to say that racist epithets deeply scar each and every minority person. But laws are commonly based on the premise that the prohibited acts will usually, though not invariably, cause harm. A university rule against using epithets as personal assaults would certainly pass that test.

As already noted, however, harm is not in itself sufficient to justify a limit on speech. The question remains, therefore, whether codes restricting "hate speech" are impermissible because they would violate the values and principles that Academic Freedom and the First Amendment are supposed to protect.

2. Freedom of Speech and Academic Freedom: The Underlying Values

In our society, expressive activity enjoys a privileged status. Other activity, if perceived to be socially harmful by a legislature or by the governing body of a university, can properly be prohibited. But harm is not a sufficient basis for banning protected speech. Volumes have been written on the rationales for this special treatment. Three ideas predominate and together constitute the generally accepted justification for granting special protection to expressive activity.

Truth. Perhaps best known of the three is the thesis that freedom of expression promotes the search for truth, i.e., our understanding of empirical phenomena and of moral, ethical, and political values. Considerable experience indicates that truth is more likely to emerge when the expression of ideas is unconstrained by fear of governmental sanctions or, in the academic context, by fear that the expression of unpopular views can appropriately be a basis for dismissal. The absence of such constraints, though not a guarantee of truth, maximizes the opportunity for exploration of conflicting ideas and thus increases the likelihood that we will come to valid conclusions.

Freedom from informal sanctions, it should be noted, does not mean total freedom. Informal constraints remain. Our normal reluctance to be perceived as deviant—weird, "off the wall," and so on—discourages dissent from generally accepted truths. Such pressures are not all bad. Life might well be too chaotic if everyone felt free to question everything. The presence of these informal pressures to conform, however, make it all the more important to maintain the protection afforded by Academic Freedom and the First Amendment. Thus, in academe informal pressures surely have some impact on innovation. Nonetheless, the principle that academic rewards and punishments should not turn on the political popularity of one's ideas provides critical protection and encouragement for original thinking.

Democratic decision-making. The right to advance any proposal for formal adoption into law or informal adoption as social custom constitutes an essential ingredient of political democracy. Indeed, the moral obligation to respect laws adopted by the majority rests on the freedom to seek to make one's own views those of the majority. That, of course, requires freedom to try and convince others of one's own views no matter how deviant or despicable society currently considers them to be.

Respect for individual dignity. Free speech is also seen as an inherent aspect of respect for the dignity of the individual. The capacity to think and express one's ideas is a constitutive characteristic of human beings. Thus, if we are to respect the dignity and autonomy of the individual, we must protect the individual's freedom to exercise his or her intellectual capacities, including freedom to engage in intellectual exchange with others.

3. Two Types of Hate Speech Codes

As commonly used, the phrase "hate speech codes" refers to a prohibition against expressive activity that attributes to members of a racial, religious, or ethnic group some characteristic—e.g., lower intelligence, avarice, a propensity for criminality, and so on—that society would take as making it appropriate to hate, or shun, or indiscriminately mistreat all members of the group. The codes differ substantially, however, in the scope of their prohibitions. While some condemn a broad range of expressive activity, others reach only a narrowly limited category of speech. For present purposes, the critical distinction is between codes that seek to suppress ideas and those that do not.

The code adopted at the University of Michigan some years ago is illustrative of those that strike at ideas. It prohibited "any behavior, verbal or physical, that stigmatizes an individual on the basis of race, ethnicity, religion, sex . . . or Vietnam-era status." On its face, this seems to bar any discussion, speech, or literature that includes derogatory views about, say, a race or gender. And, indeed, the university's interpretive guidelines included distribution of a racist leaflet in its list of prohibited activities.

At the other end of the spectrum lie codes such as those adopted at Stanford University and the University of Wisconsin.[5] These impose a sanction when one individual, in order to make the campus environment hostile or threatening for another,[6] addresses the other with epithets[7] commonly understood to express hatred and contempt for that person's race, religion, gender, etc. But no restraint is imposed on racist speeches or publications or other efforts to discuss or expound a viewpoint. In that context, epithets may be freely used. Even the hateful harangues we associate with KKK and neo-Nazi rallies are not prohibited.

4. The Codes and the Values Underlying Freedom of Speech and Academic Freedom

A. Prohibitions on Ideas: Michigan-Type Codes

The rationale behind a Michigan-type code is that certain ideas are wrong and harmful and therefore may properly be placed out of bounds. The test of "wrong" and "harmful," of course, is the majority opinion of the body vested with legislative authority.

Were this thesis deemed valid, little if anything would be left of Academic Freedom and the First Amendment's freedom of speech. Policy proposals deemed racist or sexist could be barred from the political arena. Academics would not be free to explore and discuss genetic differences that might be seen to stigmatize one group or another. And, of course, the respect for an individual's intellectual freedom could be denied to those who hold obnoxious viewpoints.

B. Prohibitions on the Use of Verbal Assaults to Create a Hostile, Threatening Campus Environment: The Wisconsin-Type Code

In my judgment, a code that prohibits only the use of racist, ethnic epithets and the like, addressed directly to an individual, and for the purpose of making the campus hostile or threatening for that individual does not *in itself* infringe on free speech or academic freedom values. The *indirect* impact of such a code is more problematic.

The direct effect on free speech values. Does a narrowly drawn prohibition that reaches only students who hurl epithets such as "spic," "nigger," and "kike" at their Hispanic, African-American and Jewish peers interfere with the search for truth, the democratic process, or respect for the dignity of the individual? For me, the question is almost rhetorical.

Such an encounter is neither intended nor likely to be a part of any search for truth. The speaker seeks to exclude the person addressed, not to initiate dialogue. There may well be an exchange of mutual insults and expressions of hatred. But the chances of an exchange in which people put forth conflicting ideas and try to convince one another of their points of view are surely exceedingly slim.

Similarly, the verbal assaults banned by a Wisconsin-type code cannot reasonably be viewed as part of the political process. There is no limit on public discourse, not even on the use of epithets in that context. The code comes into play only when one student uses epithets to verbally assault another. In that setting, it seems rather fanciful to suppose that the speaker is engaged in an effort to propagate a point of view.

What of the value we place on respect for the dignity of the individual? A moment's thought indicates that respect for this value does not imply that individuals are entitled to do whatever they want regardless of the consequences. We do not violate human dignity by prohibiting harmful activities that do not involve speech. What distinguishes speech is its relationship to the intellectual activity inherent in the very notion of a human being. Freedom to express ideas is an integral part of freedom to think and develop ideas. For it is by expressing and exchanging ideas that we fulfill our individual intellectual selves. Thus respect for individual dignity does not imply freedom for speech per se but, rather, freedom for speech that is part of the processes by which human beings acquire, evolve, and exchange ideas.

One can argue, of course, that hurling epithets expresses an idea. Such speech does communicate an idea. It tells the person addressed that the speaker views that person as inferior and hateful. But the communication has a very limited purpose: to hurt, not to put forth ideas for others to consider. Such conduct seems far removed from the intellectual activity that a society that respects the dignity of the individual is obliged to leave free.

Long ago, in *Chaplinsky v. New Hampshire*,[8] the United States Supreme Court recognized that person-to-person insults that are likely to provoke a violent response—what the Court called "fighting words"—have little to do with the values the First Amendment is supposed to protect. Such utterances, the Court said,

> are no essential part of any exposition of ideas, and are of such slight social value as a step to truth that any benefit that may be derived from them is clearly outweighed by the social interest in order. . . .[9]

Indeed, the rationale of the *Chaplinsky* decision amply supports the constitutional validity of the Wisconsin codes.[10] However, in a recent case, *R.A.V. v. City of St. Paul*,[11] five members of the Court held an ordinance invalid because it prohibited only "fighting words" that attacked race, religion, and gender. This, these Justices said, violated the principle that government may not discriminate against speech on the basis of its content. This case, it is argued, precludes a university code that bans only epithets aimed at race, religion, and the like. That argument, however, overlooks a critical portion of the Court's opinion.

When an entire class of speech (such as "fighting words") can be prohibited, the Court said, the vice of content discrimination (banning only a *subclass*) is that it poses a threat of governmental censorship of ideas. "But," the opinion continued, "content discrimination among various instances of a class of proscribable speech often does not pose this threat."[12] Then, after noting several specific examples of permissible content discrimination, the Court states broadly that "where totally proscribable speech is at issue," a selective prohibition is permissible

> so long as the nature of the content discrimination is such that there is no realistic possibility that official suppression of ideas is afoot. . . . Save for that limitation, the regulation of "fighting words," like the regulation of noisy speech, may address some offensive instances and leave other, equally offensive, instances alone.[13]

The Wisconsin code,[14] though drafted well before the *R.A.V.* decision, was sensitive to the concerns that moved the Court in that case. It contained the following provision, clearly negating any intent to suppress ideas:

The use of epithets in statements addressed to a general audience rather than directly to a specific individual (or specific individuals) shall not be a violation of this rule even though the speaker's intent is to demean and create a hostile environment and even though a member or members of the groups demeaned by the epithet constitute part of that audience.

In sum, since the conduct it covers has little if any relationship to free speech values, a Wisconsin-type code does not directly offend either Academic Freedom or the First Amendment. In judging whether such a code would be wise or constitutional, however, we must also take into account whether its enactment and enforcement would indirectly dampen speech that ought to be protected.

The indirect impact on free speech values. Though unobjectionable on its face, even a narrow Wisconsin-type code can have troublesome indirect consequences. Misperceptions of what the code covers can lead to overbroad enforcement as well as self-censorship. In addition, the enactment of such a code may lend legitimacy to proposals that strike at the very heart of the First Amendment and Academic Freedom.

Experience in the UW System and at other academic institutions indicates that a narrowly drawn code covering only epithets used as personal insults is often perceived as prohibiting a far broader range of expressive activity. This results in administrative action against speech that the code does not in fact prohibit. These misapplications resulting from administrative misperceptions reinforce similar misperceptions by faculty and students. Faculty and students see the code as aimed not only at individual verbal assaults but at any speech that might be viewed as racist, sexist, etc. The net result is self-censorship. Open discussion is dampened by a reluctance to say things that challenge academe's current conventional wisdom concerning race, gender, homosexuality, and so on.

This unfortunate impact on Academic Freedom occurs even when the limits of the code are spelled out in clear, uncomplicated terms. We can readily understand how administrative overapplication would reinforce the misperceptions of faculty and students. But what accounts for the misperceptions of administrators and the initial misperceptions of faculty and students?

One factor may well be the role and training of the administrators charged with enforcement. Quite appropriately, their responsibilities include concern for the welfare of minority students. From training and sometimes from personal experience they understand that racist talk, whether directed to a specific individual or included in a public address, can seriously impair the ability of those students to study and learn effectively. Indeed, as most of us do, they find such speech obnoxious. The importance of protecting the free exchange of even obnoxious ideas may not be so well understood. It may be, then, that administrative concern with the harm caused by speech plays a more powerful role in code enforcement than do free speech values, and this concern provides at least a partial explanation for overapplication of a code.

The focus of the arguments commonly advanced in support of codes reinforces the tendency of administrators and others to misperceive the reach of the code. Code proponents seldom make the point that a ban on epithets used as personal insults would not violate free speech values. They concentrate instead on the harm caused by "hate speech." This argumentative focus, I think, creates the impression that harm is a sufficient condition for suppression of speech, and makes students and faculty wary of expressing ideas likely to offend others.

This reaction to the focus on harm, while understandable, is ill-founded. The reason a Wisconsin-type code can withstand First Amendment and Academic Freedom challenges is that the rationales for protecting speech are inapplicable to epithets used as personal insults. Those rationales, however, do apply when speech is part of discourse even though the speech has harmful effects. As a rational matter, therefore, a Wisconsin-type code should not inhibit open discussion among faculty and students. Rational or not, however, the first Wisconsin code seems to have had this inhibiting effect.

The second Wisconsin code addressed these problems. One provision required campus-level administrators to check with the UW System legal staff before commencing proceedings to impose discipline for an alleged code violation. Another provision, quoted above, stated explicitly that speech addressed to a general audience, including epithets, could not constitute a violation of the code. The Board of Regents, after first adopting this code, ultimately rejected it. Thus we will never know whether the code's safeguards against misapplication and misperception would have solved the problems thus far discussed.

There is yet a further difficulty, another way in which support for even a narrowly drafted code can threaten speech entitled to the full protection of Academic Freedom and the First Amendment. Recent years have seen various proposals that would limit speech that expresses ideas deemed racist, sexist, homophobic, etc. The proponents of these proposals argue that the speech in question will lead to acceptance of the ideas, which in turn will lead to antisocial conduct.

Perhaps the most publicized of these proposals are those that come from certain feminists—staunchly opposed, it should be noted, by many other feminists. Indianapolis adopted an ordinance based on these proposals, only to have it held unconstitutional in federal court.[15] In addition, several law professors, in articles published in law reviews and elsewhere, advocate a ban on "persecutory, hateful, and degrading" messages of "racial inferiority."[16] As they explain it, the messages subject to censorship include not only those that use racist epithets but also those that express hateful ideas. Thus they would ban anti-Semitic tracts espousing "monetary conspiracy theories" and the claim that the Nazi holocaust is a hoax, even when such tracts are "devoid of explicit hate language."[17]

In effect, in recent years a sort of sociopolitical movement has emerged that seeks to deal with social evils such as racism and sexism by prohibiting messages that spread these ideas. One cannot combat racism and sexism in this manner, however, without abandoning the most fundamental free speech values. To ban an idea because we currently know it to be false makes conventional wisdom an acceptable limit on the search for truth. To exclude viewpoints from the political process because we consider them obnoxious violates the right to participate in the democratic process. To punish racists for presenting their ideas to the public denies their rights as autonomous individuals. Consequently, though I identify both intellectually and emotionally with the goals of this movement, I cannot help but see it as a threat to the First Amendment and Academic Freedom.

The individuals who constitute this movement have also been among the most visible and prominent advocates of Wisconsin-type codes aimed only at individual verbal assaults. In supporting such codes, they stress the harm of racist speech. That is also the focal point of their argumentation for censoring racist ideas. Indeed, telling stories that illustrate how individuals are victimized by racism is part of the analytic method that they identify with their movement. This focus on harm, especially by the advocates of censorship, poses a twofold risk that support for Wisconsin-type codes may indirectly promote censorship of ideas.

The public understands quite well that bad ideas can cause harmful behavior. When the ideas and the behavior clash with deeply held convictions, the urge to censor is strong and powerful. Fortunately, a widespread but nebulous belief in "free speech" acts as a check on this impulse. Adoption of even a narrow, Wisconsin-type code may put this check at risk. The danger lies in the natural tendency to interpret approval of the code as validating the dominant argument advanced on its behalf: that speech can properly be suppressed when it induces bad beliefs that lead to bad behavior. If this thesis became part of the common conception of the appropriate limits on free speech, the public's commitment to freedom of speech would cease to function as a check on the urge to censor.

A second, related risk is this: The same movement that sponsors broad-based censorship of racist ideas is also prominent in support of narrow, Wisconsin-type codes. If we make common cause with them when the question is whether to adopt a limited code, will this add to their standing and legitimacy, and thus enhance their chances of marshaling support for broader measures that violate fundamental free speech values? If so, how is one to balance this risk to freedom of expression against the benefits that might be gained from supporting a Wisconsin-type code?

Politics, to be sure, makes strange bedfellows. And, generally speaking, we ought be reluctant to withhold support from sound policies simply because they attract supporters with whom we disagree on other matters. But if in making common cause we would lend support, albeit unintentionally, to attacks on fundamental free speech values, perhaps the wisest course would be to look for other sleeping accommodations.

Where all this leaves us is unclear. Though a Wisconsin-type code can help to improve the educational environment, and though the limits it directly imposes on expression are unobjectionable, its indirect, harmful effects could be substantial. As is so often the case, the cost-benefit balance is difficult to calculate. What seems clear, however, is that those who would censor ideas are attacking the very foundations of the First Amendment and Academic Freedom. Whether this attack is likely to succeed is another matter. Given what's at stake, I am not inclined to gamble.

One final point. The fundamental evil is not epithets or other speech that attacks race, gender, ethnicity, and the like, but prejudice and discrimination themselves. Whether a Wisconsin-type code (or any other) would have much effect on underlying beliefs and attitudes is problematic. Perhaps, then, we should focus on peoples' minds rather than on their mouths. Perhaps the efforts we might spend on passing and enforcing codes would be better spent on developing courses and forums that would promote truly free and open discussion of the beliefs and behaviors that have so long bedeviled our nation.

Appendix

The First University of Wisconsin Code

Under the code adopted by University of Wisconsin System in 1989, a student was subject to discipline

(a) For racist or discriminatory comments, epithets or other expressive behavior directed at an individual or on separate occasions at different individuals . . . if such comments, epithets, [or] other expressive behavior . . . intentionally

1. Demean the race, sex, religion, color, creed, disability, sexual orientation, national origin, ancestry or age of the individual or individuals; and

2. Create an intimidating, hostile or demeaning environment for education. . . .

The code went on to give illustrations of conduct that was and was not covered. It noted that a derogatory opinion concerning race, made during a class discussion, would not be a violation, since it was addressed to the class, not to an individual, and since there seemed to be no evidence of an intent to create a hostile environment.

This code was held unconstitutional. *UWM Post v. Board of Regents*, 774 F. Supp. 1163 (E.D. Wis. 1991).[18]

The Second University of Wisconsin Code

In 1992, the Board of Regents adopted but later revoked the second University of Wisconsin code. This code was explicitly based on the "fighting words" rule. The provisions defining punishable expressive activity read as follows:

The University may discipline a student . . .

(a) For addressing directly to a specific member, or specific members, of the University of Wisconsin system student body an epithet, as defined in par. (b), that is:

1. Intended to demean the race, sex, religion, color, creed, disability, sexual orientation, national origin, ancestry or age of the person addressed; and

2. Intended to make the environment at the university hostile or threatening for the person addressed . . .

(b) In this subsection, "epithet" means a word, phrase or symbol that reasonable persons recognize to grievously insult or threaten persons because of their race, sex, religion, color, creed, disability, sexual orientation, national origin, ancestry or age, and that:

1. Would make the educational environment hostile or threatening for a person to whom the word, phrase or symbol is directly addressed; and

2. Without regard to the gender or other physical characteristics of the individuals involved, would tend to provoke an immediate violent response when addressed directly to a person of average sensibility who is a member of the group that the word, phrase or symbol insults or threatens.

(c) The use of epithets in statements addressed to a general audience rather than directly to a specific individual, or specific individuals, shall not be a violation of this subsection even though the speaker's intent is to demean and create a hostile environment and even though a member or members of the group demeaned by the epithet constitute part of that audience.

Notes

1. The phrase "expressive activity" as commonly used, and used here, includes speech as well as other activities used to communicate a message, e.g., cartoons, parades, nonverbal symbols.

2. Whether these indirect effects would play a significant role in the determination of a code's constitutionality is problematic. This paper will not address that somewhat complex issue. Assuming constitutionality, however, the question of wisdom remains, and I will consider the indirect impact of a Wisconsin-type code in that context.

3. I find the proposal of my friend and colleague, Professor Downs, interesting and perhaps illustrative. He considers it permissible to ban speech that is directed at an individual and causes that person to fear physical violence now or at some future time.

   If we ask, "What is it about such fear that justifies the suppression of speech?" the answer must be that the fear has harmful psychological consequences, since Professor Downs requires only a "reasonable feeling of fear," not an objective likelihood that violence will actually be committed. He does not consider, however, that the psychological harm of racist epithets can be as debilitating as fear of violence, and thus deserves equal weight in deciding whether speech can properly be banned. Why this omission?

   The answer is not that threats of violence cause more psychological damage than racist epithets. And it surely is not that Professor Downs is insensitive to or unconcerned about racism. The answer, I suggest, lies in the emotional knowledge he has of the one experience but not of the other. At some time in his life, Professor Downs has probably felt fear of violence; he knows from experience what that fear can do. If, as appearances indicate, he is not a member of a hated racial, religious, or ethnic group, he has not had the experience necessary to fully comprehend the feelings that racist epithets induce in the people at whom they are hurled.

4. For references to studies of the effects of racism and racial insults, and a "hate speech" code advocate's description of the findings of those studies, see R. Delgado, "Words That Wound: A Tort Action for Racial Insults, Epithets, and Name-Calling, 17 *Harvard Civil Rights-Civil Liberties Law Review* 133, 136–47 (1982), reprinted in M. Matsuda, C. Lawrence III, R. Delgado, and K. Crenshaw, *Words That Wound* (Boulder, CO: Westview Press, 1993).

5. See the appendix for the provisions of the two codes adopted at the University of Wisconsin.

6. Whether a speaker intends to create a hostile environment must be inferred from the circumstances. While such determinations can be difficult, the problem here is no greater than in the many other situations in which legal consequences depend on a person's state of mind.

7. As used here, "epithet" means "a disparaging or abusive word," one of several definitions given in *Webster's Third International Dictionary*.

8. *Chaplinsky v. New Hampshire*, 315 U.S. 568 (1942)

9. Ibid. at 572.

10. The second Wisconsin code explicitly invokes the *Chaplinsky* holding that "fighting words" can be banned. The argument for the first code invokes the principle from which the Court derived its holding. A narrow reading of *Chaplinsky* would say that it stands for the limited proposition that the state may ban "fighting words," i.e., personal insults likely to provoke a violent response. But such a reading ignores the rationale of the decision: talk that causes harm and that is unrelated to the values underlying the First Amendment can be banned. The Wisconsin code prohibited racial and religious epithets and the like, when used as personal insults, because they made the campus a hostile, threatening place for the person addressed. Thus the code, just like the law in *Chaplinsky*, sought to prevent a serious harm. And, as in *Chaplinsky*, the speech covered by the code was prohibited only when used as a personal insult, not when used as part of public discourse. Thus, the prohibited speech had no more First Amendment value than the speech involved in *Chaplinsky*.

11. 112B Sup. Ct. Rept. 2538 (interim ed., 1992)

12. Ibid. at 2545.

13. Ibid. at 2547.

14. The code referred to here is the code drafted following the federal district court decision holding the first code invalid. See appendix.

15. See *American Booksellers Ass'n v. Hudnut*, 771 F. 2d 323 (7th Cir. 1985).

16. See *Words That Wound*, 17, 35–36.

17. Ibid., 41–42.

18. This decision was based in part on the court's view that personal epithets could be prohibited only if they were likely to provoke an immediate violent response. For the reasons stated in note 9, I believe this to be mistaken.

A Student's Perspective on
University Hate Speech Codes

REBECCA SCHAEFER

Picture a typical elementary school playground. Children run around, climb jungle gyms, and toss balls. Songs are sung, baseball cards traded, and games of tag and kickball are played. In one corner, two children are not getting along. Suddenly, one child turns and screams, "I can't stand you! You are so ugly!" The other replies, "Oh, yeah? Well, sticks and stones may break my bones, but words can never hurt me!"

I remember singing that chant as a child. I am sure many others sang it too. Isn't it interesting, that as children, we said that words could not hurt us? Now, as mature and rational adults, we are told that words can hurt us. In fact, we are told that words can hurt so much that we need protection from them. Indeed, some say we need rules to limit speech to ensure that people are not hurt. These rules are what we call hate speech codes.

Isn't it strange that at a conference celebrating one hundred years of academic freedom, we are questioning whether or not hate speech codes infringe upon learning? Isn't it odd, that at this conference, we are discussing any codes that limit speech? Yet speech codes continue to be a major issue on this campus and on campuses throughout the country. Speech codes have become the politically correct movement of choice today. At one American university, a student came close to being kicked out of school for referring to a group of women as "water buffalo." At another university, a student was almost expelled for making fun of a Gay, Lesbian, and Bisexual Celebration week. Most people would agree that these students acted in thoughtless ways and showed bad manners. Most people would also agree that these students need to be taught that their actions may have hurt others. But, should these students be punished because what they said allegedly hurts and demeans others? Should their right to speech be limited?

As with any important freedom, there are opposing views on how to uphold freedom of speech. Today, I am responding to the views of three

Rebecca S. Schaefer is a 1994 graduate of the University of Wisconsin–Madison who majored in economics.

professors, Professor Greene, Professor Finman, and Professor Downs. It is my view that hate speech codes are unwarranted on a college campus. Hate speech codes limit the effectiveness of education, find their basis in racist beliefs, and deny students the chance to learn tolerance of opposing views. Although I condemn hate speech, any insult or word that hurts another person, I believe that hate speech codes should not exist at a public university.

According to Professor Greene, a university should, "create an environment in which all may participate in the free exchange of ideas without fear and denigration." She believes that hate speech codes enhance learning because they allow all "to take full advantage of [university] benefits [without] fear." I disagree. In my view, hate speech codes do not enhance learning, they hinder it, and for two reasons. First, an opportunity is lost to educate students so they will no longer want to use hate speech. How can a university expect to educate students on the ills of hate speech if the university does not allow all speech, including hate speech, to occur? How is the university to identify which students hold biased thoughts so it can then challenge the thinking and reasoning behind those thoughts? By banning hate speech, the university denies itself an opportunity to educate its students. This means that the hateful thoughts will hover in the shadows rather than be out in the open, to be debated and contested. This is antithetical to the purpose of a university.

Second, an opportunity is lost to hear varied opinions, as students become afraid to say what they think. They worry they may say the wrong thing, or that others may misinterpret what they say. Students will begin to worry that any time they mention an idea that involves a minority group, they may be chastised. This is already happening in our classrooms. Students are afraid to say what they think or to challenge others because they fear they will be labelled as a racist or bigot. This fear limits the free exchange of ideas, and it impairs the effectiveness of education. This is sad, since it is the free exchange of ideas that forms the basis of the university. A university should not foster fear of expression. Rather, it should encourage free expression so that all may learn new ideas, and develop a greater tolerance for opposing ideas.

Professor Greene advocates hate speech codes because she believes hate speech poses an educational risk. She believes that victims of hate speech will fail to take full advantage of university benefits because of fear. It is wonderful to be empathetic to other people's feelings. However, to ban speech is to move in the wrong direction. To ban hate speech is to transfer fear from the previous "victim" to the minds of speakers. To ban hate speech is to deny people the opportunity to educate the ignorant speaker. To ban hate speech is to take away an opportunity for minority groups to defend themselves in the face of hateful ideas. To ban hate speech is to deny minority groups many opportunities to combat hate. This is wrong, since it is these kinds of opportunities that make universities our society's most unique and important places of learning.

Professor Finman justifies hate speech codes that "prohibit only the use of racist, ethnic epithets . . . when addressed directly to an individual, and for the purpose of insulting that individual." However, even this code is indefensible. Professor Finman notes that overzealous administrators would misinterpret and too broadly apply the code, as past evidence shows. Administrators will come to apply the code to show their concern for minority groups and for those offended by speech. Although it is admirable to show such concern for these causes, to show concern and display support does not require administrators to limit speech. Moreover, showing concern for these students may, as author Nat Hentoff puts it, actually turn the offending speaker into a free speech martyr, as people rush to the side of the speaker to defend his First Amendment rights. Although I agree that the speaker's rights should be defended, this type of reaction actually turns the focus to the offender and away from the hate speech and the harm it causes. What results is a lost opportunity to educate not only the speaker, but also others who may share his point of view.

Nevertheless, Professor Finman misses a more important problem inherent in his code. He supports this code by saying "it is difficult for people who are not members of minority groups to comprehend the psychological impact of [hateful] epithets." He continues to defend his code because it protects those who are "deeply and personally injured in a manner that has profound and lasting effects." If these are the bases for Professor Finman's code, then why stop with racial and ethnic epithets? Why not include in the code all hurtful words and insults? There is no justifiable reason to call someone an "idiot" or a "geek" or a "dumb jock" in an academic setting. These words, too, may have profound and lasting psychological effects on students. These words, too, may deeply and personally injure students. And, unfortunately, there are no easy ways for one to fairly judge the effects of these words on students. By Professor Finman's own criteria, the university would ban these words as well. However, most people would agree that banning "idiot," "geek," and "dumb jock" would be ridiculous. Just as it is ridiculous to ban any word.

The above example shows the dangers of implementing any hate speech code, regardless of how precise it is. We all wish we lived in a world where everyone got along. We wish we lived in a world where all would feel free "to take full advantage of all university benefits without fear." It would be wonderful to live in a world where no one would ridicule or make fun of others because of race, or sexuality, or gender. However, hate speech codes try to impose this type of world. They try to create what they believe is a much more understanding world by eliminating any word that may hurt someone. Although the goal is noble and desired by many, banning speech is not the way to teach tolerance and acceptance of others. Banning speech leads to a false, "understanding" world. This world would only have the appearance of tolerance and acceptance. In reality, all the hateful and racist thoughts would still exist; they just would not be openly expressed. These thoughts would persist and fester. They would be secretly passed along to others. How could one debate or combat these hateful thoughts in a world where hatred would appear to be dead? By limiting speech, we create a world where hate can live and grow in secret rather than be confronted and defeated in public.

It must be recognized, as Eleanor Roosevelt said, that no one, no one, can make one feel inferior without his permission. This is the key idea that defenders of hate speech codes miss. Not all people in minority groups allow themselves to become victims. Not all people in minority groups are hurt by words. Not all people in minority groups need rules to protect them from words. Hate speech codes inherently make these assumptions. These assumptions, in turn, make hate speech codes just as racist as the hate speech they condemn.

I agree with Professor Downs that a university's practical obligation is to prepare students to succeed in life after college. Perhaps the most important skills to teach are how to articulate and defend one's views and how to respond to opposing views with composure and rationality. When students hear hateful speech, they have three options. First, they can attack the speaker, from behind the armor of a university hate speech code. Second, they can ignore the comments as unworthy and discount the speaker as ignorant. Or third, they can disprove the speech, through articulate reasoning, impressive action, or persuasive dialogue. The university should not promote the first option; rather, it should support the second option, and it should advocate and champion the third. It is the third choice that makes the biggest difference for both the speaker and the student. It forces both to confront why the speech is hurtful and why it should not be used. It forces both speaker and student to learn to articulate and defend their views. It forces both to become critical thinkers and to learn to respond to the world around them with rationality rather than simply with "politically correct" ideas. It forces all to learn, which is the primary reason for a university's existence.

The university succeeds when it develops conscientious and critical-thinking students. It succeeds when its students acquire understanding and tolerance. This tolerance is the key to truth-finding. It allows all to express ideas without fear. Students striving to grow and develop their beliefs should not fear their own thoughts. Students should feel they have a right to express whatever thoughts they have, but they should also be prepared to defend any of these thoughts and their expression of these thoughts. Hate speech codes form a barrier to free expression, tolerance, critical thinking, and growth. A public university is the last place a hate speech code should be implemented.

I believe hate speech is the vernacular of the ignorant. I believe uneducated individuals use hate speech. I believe unfounded ideas support hate speech. I believe hate speech discolors arguments that might otherwise be intelligent and widely shared. Countless ills are intrinsic to hate speech, yet I believe efforts to ban or limit hate speech are wrong. Hate speech codes stifle the free exchange of ideas, they fail to combat racist beliefs, and they restrict efforts to produce tolerant and critical-thinking students. Only by allowing all speech and supporting the "continual and fearless sifting and winnowing" of all ideas "can the truth be found."

A Faculty Member's Perspective on Hate Speech Regulation

Cyrena N. Pondrom

I want to turn back specifically to the title of this session in my remarks: "Clarifying the Issues: Free Speech, Hate Speech Codes, and Academic Freedom." A listener could understandably be unclear about how the issues have been clarified, for we have heard three speakers (who obviously, I believe, do not think they agree with each other) endorse versions of hate speech codes that are remarkably similar. What's the debate all about, and why were the remarks of one speaker denouncing the "politically correct" laden with dismissive allusions to people who decide issues on emotion rather than reason and similarly dismissive references to the "thought police"? It sounds as if something really fundamental is being threatened here.

I think that is correct, and I am not ready to predict how the argument is going to come out. But to see the fundamental issues, we must look beyond the narrow, constitutionally grounded proposals for specific hate speech codes and look at the values to which appeal has been made to justify these positions and the rigorous and animated intellectual debate that rages today over the sustainability of those values. This *is* an intellectual debate of the basic and momentous sort that our commitment to sifting and winnowing was intended to support, and it is made the more poignant and, to many, frightening, because it reexamines and makes a problem of the very descriptions of the perceiving self and the process of gaining knowledge that underlie the construction of the sifting and winnowing injunction. The hate speech debate—along with many changes in the university curriculum and many of the university's actions to ensure education equity—have become the proxy battles by which the more fundamental debate is engaged.

Because these current debates are sometimes very harshly engaged, I want to interpolate a disclaimer. I am a literary critic, a member of the field in which these debates have swirled most intently and with, very probably, the greatest rigor and inspiration. I teach and use poststructuralist/deconstructive methods *and* the more traditional methods associated with liberal

---

Cyrena Pondrom is professor of English at the University of Wisconsin–Madison.

humanism and one of its many literary critical methods, the now-old "new criticism." I do not intend these remarks to be a brief for any of these positions, but an explanation of why the issues are so bitterly and momentously engaged.

All three speakers aligned themselves with all or most of the values that, for lack of a better short label, I will designate "liberal humanism." Specifically, they share allusions to the following description of the acts of perceiving and learning: there exists a discrete self, defined as an isolated individual, capable of acting freely and without compulsion by cultural currents beyond the self's control, able to offer disinterested and dispassionate assessments of data. Language is treated as transparently referential (having the same meaning for all appropriately credentialed users), and knowledge is treated as separate from interpretation and subject to objective validation that could be agreed to by a consensus of all (appropriately credentialed) users. The university itself is seen as a place apart from the currents of political power, to which the self could have recourse to offer a dispassionate evaluation of the political realm, or the *vita activa*, to use Don Downs's phrase.

Now I believe that Don Downs made almost all of those assumptions explicit, and that Ted Finman made it clear that he subscribed to most of them—indeed, that one of his reasons for hesitating in developing any kind of speech code was the fear that it would give aid and comfort to those who do not subscribe to the guarantees of academic freedom in intellectual debate. Linda Greene made clear her recourse to *some* of those assumptions, but, I believe deliberately, left unclear how she would judge others of them. In sum, all of these speakers sought to ground their proposals on speech codes on the assumptions of liberal humanism—when in fact the debate that has made this issue so hot involves an interrogation of those very founding assumptions. The interrogation was launched—not by the "emotional," or by the political proponents of identity politics—but by philosophers of language, history, and knowledge. (Since Socrates, I guess, philosophers have been the real threats to the established order.)

The critique of these assumptions goes this way: there is no such thing as the isolated, dispassionate, knowing individual—indeed the very conception of the self as a discrete entity is an error. Instead, we are embedded in our moment in time and all of the practices that that moment makes available to us. One of those practices is language. We did not build it, but we cannot know the world without it. But the meaning of language is dependent upon the precise situatedness of its users. For example, others of the "practices" in which we may be embedded are the praxis of professors at a great research university founded on liberal principles—and the cultural practices associated with skin color, gender, religion. Those cultural practices (or discourses) specify power relations. There is no such thing as a neutral place from which to observe the practice of power by others. Our precise position in the intersection of those multiple power structures that we occupy gives us interests, which we serve even when we do not know it, and declare our values to be universal, validated, and neutral. Any analysis of, let us say, a policy on hate speech, must not omit subtle consideration of such questions as "what is the meaning of this speech to each of those who is a party to it," and "whose interests does this policy serve, and how?"

Let me make this more concrete. An African American student newly arrived from a blindingly poor section of Milwaukee is unlikely to hear the words of (say) a discussion of genetic influences on intelligence the same way that a zoologist with a forty-year history of university writing will hear them. The words do not mean the same thing. When we say that "the real meaning of the words is . . ." we are actually talking about whose view of the world we will privilege, and why; we are talking about who will have the right to stipulate meanings. When a professor talks about the need to tolerate that which is "merely offensive" in the interests of academic freedom, he or she is certainly defending a structure of privilege for academic discourse in which he or she is deeply interested. Or when an editor demands freedom of information so that the people may know the "truth," he is surely speaking on behalf of a structure in which both his economic and status interests are profound. Even the issue of what constitutes truth is deeply exercised, for if knowledge is accessible only through language, we cannot overlook the way language works. The very act of bringing knowledge into words structures that knowledge, and structure confers interpretation.

In short, the new philosophical discourse about knowledge has called into question the position of dispassionate neutrality within which isolated individuals would sift and winnow conflicting ideas free from cultural interests and confident of the validating authority of their method. As a consequence, we are in a period of sometimes tumultuous conflict in which we are retheorizing what we are all about. I said at the outset that I would not predict how this debate will come out—but I will hazard at least this guess. I believe if this panel were held again in ten or twenty years, we would still have a substantial consensus on the value of "free speech" and untrammeled academic inquiry, but we would ground that choice not on the assumption of the transcendent meaning of language and the dispassionate and unproblematic knowledge of the isolated self, but on a subtle argument about the capacity of those practices to serve the diverse interests of the cultural communities of Wisconsin.

An Alum's Perspective on
Hate Speech and Academic Freedom

MORDECAI LEE

Introduction

My assigned role is to provide an alum's perspective. But there probably isn't such a person as a "typical" alum. As an "atypical" alum, I will confess to some particular biases:

I am from the only class that did not have a graduation ceremony, or, for that matter, any final exams for our last semester on campus—the Class of '70. After Cambodia and Kent State, the chancellor simply shut down the campus and sent everyone home, saying that their semester grade would be the grade they were at when the rest of the school year was canceled. It was my best semester yet. So, I am from the generation of the 1960s that questioned the status quo. I still have an SDS poster that had been posted on the bulletin board in front of the Union saying "Off the Ruling Class."

I am an alum that went on to get a doctorate, a credential that I hope gives me some credibility when discussing the problems of the academy.

I went on to serve for thirteen years in the Wisconsin legislature, including cochairing the Joint Audit Committee. That committee has been at the fulcrum of the increasing legislative disenchantment with the university.

Last, but not least, I am Jewish. For me, being Jewish is not simply what I fill out on the line on forms that ask for a person's religious affiliation. Rather, for me, Judaism is my North Star. It provides me with an absolute and fixed point of reference, to be used when evaluating the big and little issues one deals with in life.

Hate Speech Codes

The topic for this panel covers three distinct, though related, topics: free speech, hate speech codes, and academic freedom. I don't understand why the three major presentations focused on only one of the three: hate speech codes.

Mordecai Lee is director of the Milwaukee Jewish Council for Community Relations, and a former Wisconsin state legislator.

It is also extremely interesting that the three papers made no significant distinction between hate speech codes in public universities and those of private universities. Yet these are enormously significant distinctions, both constitutionally and politically. Specifically, Professor Cass Sunstein of the University of Chicago Law School, in discussing hate speech codes, stated:

> To the extent that we are dealing with private universities, the Constitution is not implicated at all, and hence all such restrictions are permissible. This is an exceptionally important point. Private universities can do whatever they like. (P. 18, "Liberalism, Speech Codes, and Related Problems," *Academe*, July–August 1993.)

I cannot understand why the papers would gloss over this distinction. Professor Downs's paper began with two narratives, one from Madison and the other from Oberlin. He never called attention to the fact that one is a public university and the other is private. Later in his paper, when reviewing speech codes, he lumps a discussion of the University of Wisconsin–Madison, Michigan, and Stanford codes in the same paragraph, as though the different status of Stanford is irrelevant.

I will come back to the importance of the difference between public and private universities when I discuss the other two subjects of the panel: free speech and academic freedom.

As an outsider, I am somewhat baffled by the academic obsession with hate speech codes. This is a regulatory, administrative, and enforcement approach that seems understandable to a bureaucrat, but seems to be such a misdirected response for an educational institution. After all, the job of an educational institution is to teach. So why not focus on teaching tolerance, antidefamation, antiracism, and so on rather than regulating it?

All of the university's degrees have certain course requirements. In the College of Letters and Science students cannot matriculate until they demonstrate a proficiency in core curricula, by accumulating a certain number of credits in such areas as humanities, social sciences, natural sciences, communications, and quantitative skills.

All students in Madison—regardless of their college or school—must have taken a 3-credit course in "ethnic studies." The course must deal with the problems that a racial or cultural group has faced. There are 130 courses on the Madison campus that have been approved as meeting that criterion! To an outsider, this appears to be an absurdity, a result of the typical university decision-making process where all faculty members end up being able to continue doing what they want to do and yet have the appearance of compliance and cohesion. Any 3-credit educational requirement that can be met with 130 courses is a fraud. Clearly, there is no single "content" that is taught. Just like in the bad old days when every student had to pass the same course in English composition, perhaps every student should now be required to pass the same course (or courses) regarding social diversity and antibias.

Generally speaking, the consensus within the organized Jewish community is not to support broad hate speech codes that focus on—and punish— words. As the "people of the book" we value the importance of education and free speech, and are very leery about regulating speech. Rather, our reaction to hate incidents is to focus on the behavior that can be regulated and punished.

That is why Wisconsin's Jewish community pushed for adoption of a hate crimes law in the state legislature. Under that approach, any criminal act that also included the intentional selection of a victim based on race, religion, etc., was subject to a penalty enhancement. This approach was explicitly content neutral. For example, the test case that went all the way to the U.S. Supreme Court concerned an African American who instigated an attack on a white, because of the victim's race.

Proving "intentional selection" often requires a prosecutor to put into evidence the accused's statements, words, writings, etc. The simplistic criticism of our bill was that this meant we were punishing people for their words, and therefore that the bill was an unconstitutional violation of the First Amendment. Our response was that in criminal courts every day, prosecutors prove intent with evidence including words. In a first-degree murder trial, using a person's words to prove that he or she intentionally acted to kill someone is not a violation of the free speech rights of the accused.

And the U.S. Supreme Court affirmed our approach, reversing the mistaken decision of the Wisconsin Supreme Court.

So, our support for hate speech codes is limited to those that are content neutral and that focus on behavior and action. This means that words are involved only when directly related to the behavior and action in question. Therefore, we are sympathetic only to those restrictive codes that focus on fighting words, threats, intimidation, and harassment, such as outlined by Professor Downs and Professor Finman.

Free Speech

The rise of Holocaust deniers and the rhetoric of hate from the Louis Far-rakhan's Nation of Islam has been very trying for the Jewish community. We viscerally understand the trap entailed in regulating free speech. But an enormous difference exists between the right of freedom of speech that an individual possesses and the appropriate response by a *public* university.

First, while every individual has a right to freedom of speech, there is no concomitant obligation to listen. For example, Holocaust deniers have been able to manipulate the naifs and simpletons of the academy by asking whether people ought not hear both points of view. This is an enormously seductive argument. After all, shouldn't we listen to both sides? But there are some areas where there are not two sides. (Just as there are some issues that have more than two sides. American culture assumes that everything has only two sides—never more and never less.) We did not say that doctors must give consideration to the quacks selling laetrile as a cancer treatment. We do not say that so-called "creationism" must be taught side by side with evolution. The same applies to the Holocaust deniers—there is no other side. They are no different from the "flat earth society" except that the flat-earthers are merely ridiculous while the Holocaust deniers have an anti-Semitic agenda. That is why we feel comfortable saying that a student newspaper does not have an obligation to publish an ad from a Holocaust denier.

Second, a public university by definition is different from a private one. A public university is the beneficiary of the coercive power of the state to tax, and in return the taxpayers have the right to certain expectations and restrictions. In this case, the taxpayers have the right that their funds—whether directly or indirectly—not be used to recompense, pay, reimburse, or subsidize the public appearances of hate speakers. Khallid Muhammad has the right to speak on campus. But, public funds cannot be expected in any way to subsidize his appearance.

Third, no speaker on a public campus should have the power to restrict who can or cannot attend. All such events must be open to the entire public. Similarly, security at the event must be exclusively handled by the university. Hate speakers should not be allowed to use trumped-up security considera-tions and their own entourage to limit access to the hall, frisk students, intimidate the audience, and so on. Finally, the freedoms that the haters take advantage of in order to speak apply to their audience as well. I'm not talking about heckling, but rather about tactics used by the speaker's entourage to intimidate members of an audience from asking critical questions of the speaker, etc.

Fourth, what is the role of the university administration? Certainly, a chancellor sets the tone regarding freedom of speech, even for hateful speakers. But, the chancellor also has the duty to condemn those hateful speakers at the same time that he or she defends their right to freedom of speech. Some speakers and ideas are simply beyond the pale. I do not see the chancellor as a eunuch with a limited role. Defense of freedom of speech is a sterile educational lesson when it is not accompanied by a denunciation of ideas and speakers who promote hate, bigotry, and prejudice.

Academic Freedom

Perhaps an operative definition of academic freedom is the freedom of faculty to spend their time as they wish and on the subjects they choose. I suggest that the underlying premise of this view of academic freedom is the ability to attract funding to permit this professional and professorial life. The dynamics of attracting the funding to permit the kind of academic freedom that faculty seek is different in public than in private universities.

The scope of academic freedom in a private university is based on the ability to attract private funding. If at Harvard, Princeton, Stanford, Cornell, or Yale, they can afford to have a tenured faculty member who only teaches one graduate seminar a semester on the differences between early medieval and late medieval Latin, and spends the rest of his or her time doing research—well, more power to that professor and that private university.

But a public university exists in a totally different context. And it is that context that gives the concept of academic freedom a different meaning.

The University of Wisconsin is part of state government. Enormous amounts of its funding derive from the coercive power of state government to force individuals to pay money to it. Perhaps even some of the grounds of its campuses may have been acquired with the threat of the power of eminent domain lurking in the background—the power of government to take someone's private property, whether they want to sell or not.

What's happening at the other end of State Street, in the legislature and the executive branch, is a questioning of the basic compact between state government and UW. In the past, the assumption was that somehow the residents of Wisconsin benefited from the enormous subsidy they provided to cover the costs of running the university. Now, increasingly, this compact is seen as an empty one, a self-serving "give and take" relationship: the legislature gives enormous amounts of money to the UW and the university takes it.

The benefits and logic of the relationship are increasingly obscure to the legislature and the taxpayers. What really is the benefit to the taxpayers? The benefits accrue essentially to the faculty who have created an instrument that benefits them: a zone of academic freedom that is used to bar virtually any attempt by the legislature and the executive branch at accountability, at evaluating the costs and benefits of financing a world-class research institution, at increasing the hours a professor is expected to teach, and at expanding the amount of real contact professors have with students.

What is the state getting in return for providing the funding for academic freedom and a world-class research institution?

In the field of political science, for example, what relevance does it have to the real-world issues of improving government? Very limited. The main relevance of political science is to other political scientists. It is essentially a closed world, with its activities having significance and importance only within the profession. But for the taxpayers, what is the benefit?

The concept of academic freedom that faculty assert to fend off the legitimate inquiries and concerns of the legislature is increasingly being called into question. The new buzz-word, both in the private sector and increasingly in the public sector, is that of "value." State legislators are wondering more and more if the taxpayers are getting the best "value" from their investment in the university.

Take one example. State government invests significant amounts of money to fund the medical school. Yet what is the value to the state's taxpayers? After all, the students who turn into doctors are free to practice anywhere. What is the benefit to Wisconsin's taxpayers to training doctors when the local taxpayers do not get the benefit that comes from paying for that training? Taking this perspective to its extreme, the legislature should de-fund the medical school, and simply rely on the free market to attract already-trained graduates of other medical schools to practice in Wisconsin.

These kinds of questions are going to be asked with increasing frequency.

Some legislators mutter that the university is Wisconsin's Pentagon, a bottomless pit that sucks money with virtually no measurement of value. Just as the critics of Pentagon spending ask "how much is enough" to spend to underwrite an appropriate national defense for our country; the same question is now being asked about the university.

The UW–Madison faculty may wish for the academic freedom of their counterparts in private institutions. But, the context of their academic freedom, as part of a state government, means that the academic freedom they get is somewhat different. The UW faculty needs to recognize this reality of being part of state government and develop a concept of academic freedom consistent with it.

Quality teaching, community service, and applied research are what the taxpayers want in return for their investment. The cry for the "relevance" that typified the student protest movement in the sixties is returning, and now it is coming from the people who hold the purse strings. It is time to redefine what academic freedom means in a public university in the 1990s.

A Perspective from the Press

Thomas A. Still

I would like to congratulate all three of our presenters and our reactor panel today for their very thoughtful remarks. And a special note of admiration for Professor Grossman, who read Linda Greene's piece and edited it on the fly. As a newspaper editor I have a special respect and admiration for that skill. A few remarks first about what brings us all together today.

I think that it's important, whether we agree or disagree, that this group has been assembled, along with other groups throughout today and tomorrow, to investigate, chew on, look at, and review the sifting and winnowing ideal, which has guided this university for many years. I think it is important, too, that in less than an hour, the bronze plaque bolted to the front of Bascom Hall is going to be rededicated.

It is important to note that while the inscription was written in 1894, the plaque itself didn't materialize until 1910; it originated as a class project of the UW graduation class that year. But it was not actually mounted until 1915 because of some snubs and insults involving the Board of Regents. In 1956, the plaque was actually stolen and it disappeared for several weeks, perhaps because of a prank or perhaps for some other reason, before it was located and remounted. These events are symbolic of the discussion that is taking place over the course of today and tomorrow. There will always be those who want to delay doing what is right regarding free speech. There will be those who will want to come and steal away our symbols of freedom in the night. We have seen both, and I think we can discuss the ramifications of both.

As a newspaper editor, I have observed the effect of this great university on our community and our state. During that "Hate Speech" period when the code was written in 1989, and then revised later on, I sensed a chilling effect on public discourse at all levels. People were looking over their shoulders, and legislators and others were emboldened to chip away at the Wisconsin Open Meetings Law and Open Records Law at a pace we were not accustomed to. I believe the UW–Madison, in its hate speech efforts, inad-

---

Thomas A. Still is the editorial page editor of the Wisconsin State Journal, Madison, Wisconsin.

vertently contributed to that climate. The UW is not a closed universe, and the 1989 Hate Speech Code tried to pretend it was. It had the effect of widening the gap in the statewide town-and-gown relationship. This is inconsistent with the "Wisconsin Idea" that the borders of the university should indeed be the borders of the state.

It is also inconsistent with the *vita activa* principle outlined by Professor Downs. A university, especially a public university (and the distinction made by Mordecai Lee is important) should be as open and reflective a part of the greater community as it can be.

The Hate Speech Code, especially the first attempt in 1989, had the effect of eroding that atmosphere. You can suppress certain types of speech here on campus, but they will pop out elsewhere in society. The information age has created many new ports of entry for people with ideas, whether they be obnoxious, offensive, or otherwise. There are many ways for those ideas to come out. Knowing the strength of this university, this community, and how affairs are conducted here, I would rather see those ideas come out here and be debated fully on this campus in an open setting where there are many ideas, a diversity of ideas, and some strong opinions to react to those ideas and speech that is truly hateful. I would rather see that done here than in other forums. You cannot sift and winnow noxious weeds from the garden of ideas unless they first pop up in the form of seedlings.

In reviewing the presentations themselves, I felt that Professor Greene's proposal would create a greater level of comfort for many here on campus but generate a rising level of discomfort for the majority. Her effort seems intended to blur the line between speech and actions, and speech and behavior; no clear distinction was made. It was obvious from Professor Finman's paper that indeed he has undertaken a long journey; he has come a long way from where the 1989 debate originated. The flaw, I believe, in his approach continues to be the listing of types of speech that can be prohibited and proscribed. This was the strength of Downs proposal. It was broadly written, but that is a strength in this case, not a weakness. I believe there is no list long enough to cover the many types of epithets and slurs in hate speech. It becomes a judgment of what is going to make the list and what is not. For example, what about crude statements? Are they impermissible? The chant (at UW–Madison football games) from section O or the chant from section P?

The Downs proposal, I think, also ties in with the spirit of the hate crimes law here in Wisconsin, which has been upheld. Again, it was based on action. I'll read it once more for those who may not recall it. "Speech that is directly targeted at individuals or small groups and is intended to threaten that person's physical safety, which instills in that person the reasonable belief that he or she is in danger of being inflicted with deadly physical harm at the hands of the speaker now or in the future."

Academic Freedom: The Indivisibility of Due Process

Nat Hentoff

A few years ago, I was in Jerusalem for a conference on the ethics of the press—a boundless subject. Among those present was a widely respected Israeli philosopher, David Hartman. I had never met him. During a break, I was walking down a corridor, and he was coming at me from the other end.

The philosopher stopped me and without introducing himself, asked, "What is the greatest achievement in the history of mankind?"

For once, I didn't have to grope for an answer.

"Due process," I said.

"Absolutely correct," the philosopher nodded and walked on. That was the only conversation we had.

It's obvious that there can be no academic freedom without due process, but a point I want to make early on is that due process is indivisible. If, on a college or university campus, there is no substantive due process for students, the ambience—the atmosphere—is hardly likely to be supportive of substantive due process for professors.

And since academic freedom, protected by due process, is primarily freedom of speech, a campus that violates students' free speech is not a healthy environment for the free speech of teachers.

This is a university—a public university—where not long ago, the then chancellor, Donna Shalala—after assuring me that she would not countenance a speech code here—vigorously supported a speech code. And several distinguished members of the University of Wisconsin's law faculty designed such a code as if the First Amendment did not apply to a *public* university.

Your speech code was justifiedly declared unconstitutional by Federal District Judge Robert Warren. This is the same judge who, years before, placed the longest prior restraint on a publication in American history. The magazine, which is still published here in Madison, was the *Progressive*. It was targeted for an article on the making of an H-bomb. Not a word in the

---

Nat Hentoff is a New York–based writer and columnist, and author of the 1992 book, Free Speech for Thee, But Not for Me.

piece had been classified. I mention the case to indicate that your speech code had to be in particularly egregious violation of the First Amendment to earn the condemnation of Judge Warren. The editor who defied the United States government and a majority of open newspapers, including the *Washington Post*, was Erwin Knoll. He said, while being besieged: "If there is no First Amendment for the *Progressive*, there is no First Amendment for anyone. If the founders had intended the First Amendment to be negotiable, they would have written a mediation clause into the constitution."

In his opinion, Judge Warren noted that the aim of the university was to encourage diversity among its student body and therefore to *discourage* the kinds of language that could create a hostile learning environment for blacks and others underrepresented here. Warren went on to point out, however, that the university's *speech code* "does as much to hurt diversity on Wisconsin campuses as it does to help it."

"By establishing content-based restrictions on speech, the rule limits *the diversity of ideas* among students and thereby prevents the 'robust exchange of ideas' which intellectually diverse campuses provide."

The judge also used a phrase to describe this university's failed speech code. He called it "government thought control."

How could this have happened at a university where the memory of Professor Richard T. Ely—and his trial for having engaged in robust exchange of ideas—still reverberates?

Also still much prized here are these words from the 1894 report on the trial by the Board of Regents: "Whatever may be the limitations which trammel inquiry elsewhere, we believe that the great State University of Wisconsin should ever encourage that continual and fearless sifting and winnowing by which alone the truth can be found."

I assume those words used to be meant to apply only to professors— otherwise how could this university have tried to enact a speech code for students?

Yale University did better in creating an environment in which freedom of expression is protected for *everybody* on campus. Its 1975 report, under the name of C. Vann Woodward, is still in effect at Yale, and it says: "No member of the community with a decent respect for others should use, or encourage others to use, slurs and epithets intended to discredit another's race, ethnic group, religion, or sex. [Yet] it may sometimes be necessary in a university for civility and mutual respect to be superseded by the need to guarantee free expression. . . . If the university's overriding commitment to free expression is to be sustained, secondary social and ethical responsibilities must be left to the informal processes of suasion, example, and argument."

I am including students in this lecture because—to repeat the point— due process, as well as its corollary, freedom of speech, does not flourish in a fragmented community. That is, a community where it is guaranteed, supposedly, to some and only marginally to others.

Over the years, I have covered many stories of disciplinary cases on campuses around the country where students accused of various violations appear before alleged judicial bodies composed of faculty members, administrators, and other students. With very few exceptions, the students' due process rights are closer to those accorded by the Star Chamber in seventeenth-century England than provided in the Bill of Rights for the rest of us outside the university.

A faculty member may be of counsel but cannot question prosecution witnesses. Often, neither can the accused. Indeed, the adversary protections of a real trial are almost entirely absent on many campuses. But—I am told by university presidents and provosts I've talked to—"this is a family affair." By not having adversary proceedings, the student is being protected. But if the result of the "family" trial is that the student is suspended or expelled, the punishment can be as severe and permanent as in a trial in the "real world."

I have come across a few professors—more in the general faculty than in law schools—who have protested this bizarre notion of due process, but not many.

So, in a large number of colleges and universities, some members of the community are considered more worthy of due process than others. And even the former often find that they too—tenured or not—come to be treated by campus judicial bodies and administrators as if they were before a congressional committee chaired by Jesse Helms.

That may sound like hyperbole, but I've been at some judicial sessions within the university "family."

Here, within the University of Wisconsin system, last October, a county circuit judge in Milwaukee ordered the University of Wisconsin at Milwaukee to pay a penalty of $2,240 to three professors—charged with sexual discrimination—because they had not been allowed to look at *their own personnel records* in preparing a defense. The professors asked for that information in March of last year, but—said the judge—the UWM stalled for 112 days.

Why did they have to go to court? It's all in the family, right? The professors—if anybody wants to find out more about the case—are Carl Pope, Stan Stojkovic, and Rickie Lovell, all in the Criminal Justice Department of the School of Social Welfare at Milwaukee.

Then there is Doug Eamon, sort-of-outgoing chair of the Department of Psychology at the University of Wisconsin–Whitewater. His account of what is happening to him would, I think, remind some people of Franz Kafka's *The Trial*:

"Upon receiving the results of an investigation of complaints of sex discrimination against my department (not me personally), the University disciplined *me* without any hearing of any kind. After I documented some 60 falsifications of facts and falsifications of record by the Affirmative Action Officer 'investigator' and demanded a hearing, the administration decided, apparently fearing a lawsuit and the attendant publicity, that, well, maybe a 'review' of the Affirmative Action Officer's report might be appropriate— but I was not permitted to be present at the review."

Professor Eamon is tenured, but apparently tenure does not guarantee actual due process. For the past year, he continued teaching, but all the rest of his time is taken up, including his wife's time, with documenting answers to charges and more charges. He has not published any new work for the past year, unless you consider rebuttals a new work in progress. Finally, Eamon's case was "sort of " resolved. That is, he was "sort of " cleared and a university official told him he had taken all of this much too seriously.

There was a time, many years ago, when I was studying at Harvard under F. O. Mathiessen, when I wanted, more than anything else, to be a college professor. I had done some teaching and liked it very much. To spend many hours, for many years in a research library like Widener would be a wondrous way to grow. And there was the grail of tenure.

The more I cover stories of accused professors, the more I do not regret having abandoned that road. Especially knowing that the atmosphere in many colleges is so righteously poisonous that, as in *Alice in Wonderland*, a verdict of guilty is reached before there is a trial. Or, "fearless sifting and winnowing of ideas" is condemned as racist or sexist or homophobic.

There is the case of Louis A. Jacobs, professor of law at Ohio State University. In 1992, he had been using a text, *Evidence in the Nineties*. As he noted in a report from the battlefront in the spring 1993 *Academic Questions*, "the text uses a problem method to study the law governing what testimony and items may be admitted to sway a jury . . . One case file involves the rape of a woman, and several students vigorously criticized the text for creating a hostile learning environment."

It was the text—not Jacobs himself—that initially created a furor. "As a card-carrying member of—and active cooperating attorney with—the American Civil Liberties Union, and a moonlighting plaintiffs' employment lawyer with several successful sexual harassment cases, my reputation had been that of a flaming liberal," he writes. Also, he had "a career-long commitment to issues traditionally associated with feminism."

At a forum to discuss the complaints by a number of women students that the text be abandoned, a black male law professor and a female member of the department argued fiercely that Jacobs, being male, was not qualified to determine whether the text should be used. They maintained that only a woman could determine whether *Evidence in the Nineties* did indeed create a hostile learning environment.

"The mood of the crowd," Jacobs wrote, "turned to lynching." Not lynching the text, but lynching the professor. "The difference in my classroom from before the forum was palpable . . . Male students seemed silenced for fear of misstatement." And female students so reacted to the word "rape" that the legal and educational issues were sidetracked. "A hostile learning environment had, in fact, developed," said Jacobs. He selected a different text for the next semester.

Interestingly, "the *anonymous* student evaluations were nearly universally opposed to dropping the text." But the professor yielded to the overt hostility of some students and colleagues.

Jacobs does not refer in his article to the real possibility—as I see it—that he has strengthened the "politically correct" forces of suppression in the law school. Nor does he indicate the degree to which he tried to teach the objectors in that class how vital it is for a law student to learn how to deal with fact patterns and feelings they find repellent. Unless they intend to be lawyers who will take only clients and cases with which they feel entirely comfortable.

I wonder whether Jacobs had received any support from colleagues or from the administration before he decided to surrender the text.

I asked a colleague of his, on that law school faculty. "The professors who agreed with his initial decision to use the text," he told me, "let him hang once the attacks began. At that forum, I did say something from the back of the room, but I didn't pursue it. I had a brief to write, and besides this wasn't the only case at the law school where a professor has been harassed by students for being insufficiently 'sensitive.'"

"What about the president of the university? Did he say anything?"

Another law professor laughed mordantly. "Oh, he's like Mussolini at the end of the Second World War. He's running around trying to figure out whom to surrender to first."

There was no formal due process in this case because the professor didn't ask for it. If he had, it's doubtful whether it would have done him any good. Nor was there academic freedom for him. He didn't fight for that either. He was intimidated.

So are many other professors—particularly when the charges involve sexual harassment. But a growing number of professors, caught in this epidemic of accusations of sexual harassment, are fighting back.

Graydon Snyder, for example. He is a biblical scholar on the faculty of the Chicago Theological Seminary, which takes pride in its tradition—it says—of free speech. During an evening class, Snyder was trying to show the differences between Judaism and Christianity on certain ethical and legal questions. As he has done for years, he took a story from the Talmud to begin to illustrate his point. From that centuries-old repository of Jewish law and commentary, Snyder cited a section of the book of ethics in which a rabbi tells of a roofer who took his clothes off because it was so hot that day. In the courtyard below, a woman also removed many of her clothes because of the heat.

The roofer suddenly lost his footing and fell on top of the woman. Through the forces of the fall, he accidentally penetrated her with his penis. The result was sexual intercourse.

According to the verdict in the Talmud, the roofer must pay the woman "for bodily injury, for pain inflicted, for enforced unemployment, and for medical expenses." *But* the roofer is not liable for damages for the "degradation" the woman suffered as a result of the sexual act. "One is not liable," says the Talmud, "to pay any indemnity for indignity unless it was intentionally caused."

Therefore, unintentionally falling from the roof and unintentionally having brief intimate contact with the woman did not signify an *intent* to have sex with her.

By contrast, Professor Snyder noted in that fateful lecture, Jesus—in the Sermon on the Mount—said, "Anyone who so much as *looks* with lust on a woman has already committed adultery with that woman." Accordingly, Snyder went on, the New Testament "says that if you *think* about doing the act," you've done it.

Just like Professor Catharine MacKinnon says.

I should say here that there are scholars, Alan Watt, for one, who claim that Jesus, in that sentence, was being ironic. He was discussing the rigid legal righteousness of the Pharisees.

Even if Professor Snyder had mentioned that, he would not have been spared his ordeal. It was the Talmud that got him into great trouble.

A woman student who had tape-recorded that lecture filed a formal complaint with the seminary's Sexual Harassment Task Force. The student charged that she had been sexually harassed by the Talmud, with Professor Snyder as its agent.

Later, Professor Snyder had a talk with the student. He was naturally curious as to how she felt he had harmed her. She told him, as he later told me, that she had found that part of his lecture so offensive because men in her life, and men generally, say that they don't *intend* to do anything. And then they do it anyway. By presenting that story from the Talmud, Snyder, the student said, has given support to those men who—without *intending* to harm women—abuse and hurt them anyway.

Meanwhile, the Sexual Harassment Task Force had gone to work. Without providing Professor Snyder with a formal charge or the right to cross-examine witnesses, the Task Force found that in that lecture, he had "engaged in verbal conduct of a sexual nature" that "has the purpose or effect of unreasonably interfering with an individual's work or academic performance or creating an intimidating, hostile, or offensive working or academic environment. Until that moment, Snyder, in his long career as a professor, had never been charged with sexual harassment or anything like it.

The Chicago Theological Seminary issued "a formal reprimand for sexual harassment," placed Snyder on probation, urged him strongly to take psychiatric counseling, and ordered him not to be alone with students or staff members. Furthermore, a member of the administration now monitors all his classroom lectures with a tape recorder. So much for being a tenured faculty member at the Chicago Theological Seminary.

Snyder has filed a defamation suit against the seminary. It is based on the fact that an official memorandum detailing the verbal sins of Snyder and the Talmud was "placed in the mailboxes of all 250 faculty members, staff and students of the seminary. Because of that distribution of the memorandum, Snyder's lawyer claims that the professor "has suffered substantial damages, including but not limiting to personal humiliation and mental anguish."

Meanwhile, Snyder continues teaching at the seminary and is still on probation. He has no support from the cowardly faculty, but the students—including the women students—have been very supportive, even to the point of sending petitions to the administration.

"If the students had been against me," Snyder told me, "it would have been too painful, and I would have left. But it has also helped that the staff—the maintenance people and the secretaries—are also for me."

But not the faculty. And, of course, not the administration.

A dismayingly illuminating footnote to the punishment of Professor Snyder and the Talmud is the reaction of Bernice R. Sandler, a senior associate at the Center for Women's Policy Studies in Washington. She told Edward Walsh of the *Washington Post* that she was not familiar with Professor Snyder's particular case, but then she added:

"It's very hard to get women to file a formal charge. They file because the [verbal harassment] has been repeated and repeated, and I'd bet my bottom dollar that is the case here . . . It's because [men like Snyder] have made remark after remark that are offensive to women. *There's got to be a pattern there in this case.* But from his point of view, he just doesn't get it."

And in the *National Law Journal,* Bernice Sandler added that since Anita Hill's allegations of sexual harassment against Clarence Thomas, "We are re-evaluating our idea of justice in the classroom."

We?

Bernice Sandler's vengeful approach to due process is not unique. Increasingly, in the academy—and in other workplaces—charges of sexual harassment almost instantly generates the view of the Red Queen in *Alice in Wonderland*—whom I invoke again—verdict first, trial afterwards. The making of the charge is proof of guilt.

On the other hand, there are *professors* who also discover and punish hostile learning environments, or variations thereof, with remarkable resourcefulness.

Roland Rotunda is a law professor at the University of Illinois, and he sent me this epiphany of the learning process on some contemporary campuses. It also bears on when professors' academic freedom is used to mistreat students.

Shawn Brown is a sophomore at the University of Michigan. For his assignment in Political Science 111, he wrote a term paper on possible inherent flaws in political polling data. It contained the following passage:

"Another problem with sampling polls is that some people desire their privacy and don't want to be bothered by a pollster. Let's say Dave Stud is entertaining three beautiful ladies in his penthouse when the phone rings. A pollster on the other end wants to know if we should eliminate the capital gains tax. Now Dave is a knowledgeable business person who cares a lot about this issue. But since Dave is 'tied up' at the moment, he tells the pollster to 'bother' someone else. Now this is perhaps a ludicrous example, but there is simply a segment of the population who wish to be left alone. The have more important things to be concerned about—jobs, family, school, etc. If this segment of the population is never actually polled, then the results of the poll could be skewed."

Mr. Brown's teacher, Ms. Debbie Meizlish, may have been pleased to see the sex-neutral term, "business person," but was otherwise appalled. She interpreted Mr. Brown's term papers as sexual harassment directed against her. She wrote the following to Mr. Brown:

"This is ridiculous & inappropriate & OFFENSIVE. This is completely inappropriate for a serious political science paper. It completely violates the standard of non-sexist writing. Professor Ronsenstone [a colleague on a higher level] has encouraged me to interpret this comment as an example of sexual harassment and to take the appropriate formal steps. I have chosen not to do so in this instance. However, any future comments in a paper, in a class or in any dealing w/me will be interpreted as sexual harassment, and formal steps will be taken. Professor Rosenstone is aware of these comments–& is prepared to intervene. You are forewarned."

The student, Shawn Brown, did not need another warning. He dropped the course.

George Orwell was also forewarned. In *1984*, he said, "Orthodoxy means not thinking."

Of all the stories I've covered concerning the ascent of the relentlessly orthodox on or off college campuses, one of the most dismaying has been the initiation into the modern times of Murray Dolfman, legal studies senior lecturer at the Wharton School, University of Pennsylvania.

These events began in February 1985, but to this day, Sheldon Hackney, the then-president of the University of Pennsylvania, says that Dolfman was treated fairly in view of his remarks in class, which, the university points out, grievously offended black students.

At the time of the incident, Dolfman had been a part-time lecturer in the legal studies department for twenty-two years. He is a practicing lawyer in Philadelphia but, as he has told me, he likes to teach. And he teaches so well that even the university committee that found him guilty of "offensive speech" noted that no previous complaint had ever been made against Dolfman. It also noted that he was an "extremely popular teacher" with "outstanding course evaluations," and that students competed vigorously to get into his classes.

So what did Dolfman do to create a campuswide demonstration against him—led by black professors and students—in which one distinguished black academic charged that Dolfman had turned his classroom "into a cesspool?"

What had Dolfman done to lead the university's Committee on Academic Freedom and Responsibility (strangely named in this case) to condemn him for behavior that should not take place at the University of Pennsylvania?

Murray Dolfman teaches the way Charles Kingsley (portrayed by John Houseman) taught in the television series "Paper Chase." He makes demands of his students. He challenges them. He will single out a student—of whatever color or creed—and drill him in a point of law or a section of the Constitution. If you come unprepared to Dolfman's class, you are in peril.

On the fateful day that was to make Murray Dolfman a pariah on the University of Pennsylvania campus, he was lecturing about personal service contracts. Dolfman was making the point that no one can be forced to work against his or her will, even if a contract has been signed. A court may prevent you from working for someone else so long as the contract you signed is in effect, but, said Dolfman, there can "be nothing that smacks of involuntary servitude."

Okay, said the professor, where does this concept come from in American law? Silence. Finally, a student screwed up his courage and said, "the Constitution?"

"Where in the Constitution?"

Silence.

Dolfman finally told them where it came from, the Thirteenth Amendment. "What does that Amendment say?" he asked. No one knew.

Dolfman often tells his students, "We will lose our freedoms if we don't know what they are." He tried to bring in a personal note. As a Jew, he said, and as an ex-slave, he and other Jews began Passover every year by celebrating the release of Jews from bondage under Pharaoh.

"We have ex-slaves in this class," Dolfman said, "who should know about, and celebrate, the Thirteenth Amendment."

Dolfman later told me, "I used that approach because I wanted them to think about that Amendment and know its history. You're better equipped to fight racism if you know all about those post–Civil War amendments and civil rights laws."

He started asking black students in the class if they could tell him what's in the Thirteenth Amendment. None could.

The Thirteenth Amendment, he said, provides that "neither slavery nor involuntary servitude . . . shall exist within the United States." He asked a black student to stand and read the Amendment and to repeat it.

Four black students later complained to higher authorities that they had been hurt and humiliated by the way Dolfman had taught them the Thirteenth Amendment. They resented being called "ex-slaves." Furthermore, they said, why should they be grateful for an Amendment that gave them rights that should never have been denied them, and that gave them little else?

They had made none of these points in Dolfman's class.

Three of them went to see Dolfman later. He said he certainly had not meant to offend them and apologized if he had. He added that he should have said "descendants of slaves" rather than "ex-slaves." The students did not accept his apology.

Charges were filed, and university committees conducted a probe. One thing they came up with was that Dolfman had always taught this way. He had always zeroed in on students, not only blacks, to force them to think. But the university had to set an example, all the more since there were rising black-Jewish tensions on campus on other matters. A sacrifice was needed, and who better than Dolfman? He was part-time, with a contract, and without a union.

Dolfman's class was disrupted on February 13. Seven days later, there was a rally at which Houston Baker, Albert M. Greenfield Professor of Human Relations and director of the Center for the Study of Black Literature and Culture, declared: "We have people here who are unqualified to teach dogs, let alone students, and they should be instantly fired."

Four days later, a vigil and rally took place in front of the home of the president of the university. According to the *Daily Pennsylvanian*, Professor Baker thundered: "We are in the forefront because some asshole decided that his classroom is going to be turned into a cesspool. . . . This administration is bull shit." To spell Professor Baker and other speakers, recordings of speeches by Martin Luther King and Malcolm X were played. And Ralph Smith, associate professor in the law school, declared, "Dolfman must go!" Both professors are black.

The Black Student League called Dolfman "a racist," adding, "we will not be satisfied until we are convinced that actions such as those undertaken by Senior Lecturer Murray Dolfman will NEVER, NEVER take place again at this university."

University President Sheldon Hackney did not defend academic freedom, free inquiry, common sense, or Murray Dolfman. And Dolfman said to President Hackney: "If a part-time professor can be punished on this kind of charge, a tenured professor can eventually be booted out, then a dean, and then a president."

Having no epaulets that could be stripped from him, Dolfman had to make a public apology to the entire university. It was, he told me, a forced apology. He also had to attend "a sensitivity and racial awareness" session, sort of like a Vietnamese reeducation camp. But that wasn't punishment enough. He was exiled from the campus for a year. A good many of the faculty, black and white, were sorely disappointed. They thought he should be fired.

June Axinn, professor of social work and former Faculty Senate chairman, observed that the punishment was fair. "They found that Mr. Dolfman made racist remarks and was insensitive, and I hope an educational institution would find a way to educate him."

It is worth noting that, so far as I can find out, none of the law school professors, including those specializing in civil liberties, defended Dolfman. Nor did the liberals elsewhere on the faculty. If they had, they might have been called racists! And only a few conservative professors supported him.

Nor, I might add, did the American Civil Liberties Union of Pennsylvania get involved. But other ACLU affiliates are likely to have defended Dolfman's free speech rights.

I have left out one of the charges leveled against Dolfman. It was held against him that he had told a black student to change his pronunciation from "de" to "the." He also corrected the speech of white students, and had routinely instructed students to omit the repetitive "you know" from their ways of speech, and to get their hands out of their pockets when they talk. But it was the correcting of "de" to "the" in the black student's speech that offended the University's Academic Freedom and Responsibility Committee.

When Dolfman was finally permitted to teach again, he took his students—as he had previous classes—to hear oral arguments in Pennsylvania Supreme Court. On that day, the diction of one of the lawyers was so bad—full of "deses" and "doses"—that the students found it difficult to concentrate on his argument.

When they were outside the courtroom, Murray Dolfman told the class, "Now you see why I stress the need to speak well." The lawyer in the courtroom who had been using all those "deses" and "doses" was white.

Later, when Louis Farrakhan was invited by black groups to speak at the University of Pennsylvania, the student newspaper urged that the invitation be withdrawn. President Sheldon Hackney demurred: "Open expression is the fundamental principle of a university," he said. Of course it is in defending the politics of open expressions in that university.

At the University of Wisconsin at Madison, minority and nonminority students do not compete for the same slots. Millard Storey, director of undergraduate admissions, said that all minority students who are capable of succeeding at Madison are admitted. White applicants then compete for the remaining places. Minority students, Mr. Storey said, "are admitted on a somewhat lower level and on a noncompetitive basis." Many white applicants who could succeed at Madison are rejected, he added. This is due process?

PART 3

Reinterpreting the Meaning of "Sifting and Winnowing"

Sifting and Winnowing:
Its Meaning and Significance to
Faculty and to Freedom of Research

WACLAW SZYBALSKI

When I joined the faculty of the University of Wisconsin in the winter of 1959–60, I was not aware of the existence of the "sifting and winnowing" resolution on the bronze plaque located on the outside wall of Bascom Hall. Its representation was not included with the university offer extended to me, and nobody took me for a stroll to see it and to read its message during my visits here in 1959 or later, in 1960. It would have been such a touching and meaningful start for my transformation into a Wisconsinite.

I hope that at present every new faculty and staff member, postdoctoral fellow, and student is alerted to the message on the plaque. If not, the university should start doing so as a result of this conference. It should also be on the letterhead of all UW stationery.

Why is this "sifting and winnowing" statement so important? Because it so clearly and poetically states the principle of the freedom of teaching and research, because it is unique, because it stresses that the University of Wisconsin will not be swayed by temporary vogues or political trends, even if they should prevail at other institutions, and because this declaration is expressed in such beautiful and moving language. Maybe I am an incorrigible idealist and romantic, even at my age, but each time I read it, I feel a tingle go down my spine and I feel somewhat emotional, I am embarrassed to admit. I am certainly a devotee of this plaque, and I walk all my visitors and collaborators to Bascom Hill, to let them read it and be inspired.

I noticed the bronze plaque for the first time on my way to an appointment with President Elvehjem at his office in Bascom Hall. Both he and President Fred Harrington were very fond and proud of this emblem. The plaque refers to the freedoms of *teaching* and of *research*. During my forty-five years at the university, I have not experienced any limitations imposed on my teaching. Apparently, times have changed since the views of Profes-

Waclaw T. Szybalski is professor of oncology at the University of Wisconsin–Madison.

sors Ely and Ross were censored 100 and 84 years ago, respectively. All of that is now a part of the history and lore of the bronze plaque.

However, I have experienced unfortunate attempts to "trammel inquiry" in my own field of research, as related to modern genetics. It all started with a simple but insidious theme that scientists could not be trusted, and therefore their research must be legislated, regulated, and controlled by "Government" or by some other "Big Brother." Many kinds of legislation were proposed between 1975 and 1980, proposals that would have trammeled recombinant DNA research. Fortunately with the nationwide help of several fellow scientists, including those at our own institution, all such misbegotten legislative attempts were defeated or derailed. This was not easy, because scientists seemed to be quite complacent about the legislation, preferring not to be distracted, and believing that they could get around such onerous regulations by switching their research to different fields or carrying it abroad. But some scientists undertook the fight and won, mainly because the legislators and their aides became properly educated during numerous congressional hearings, and soon realized that the proposed legislation was unjustified and ill-founded. In the absence of any true dangers, one cannot legislate imaginary risks or other scenarios!

Actually, the anti-recombinant DNA legislation might have been almost equivalent to the suppression of the science of genetics in the Soviet Union in the forties and fifties by Stalin and his henchman, Trofim Lysenko—something I unfortunately remember all too well. Russian geneticists were not shielded by our bronze plaque! On the other hand, a slide presenting our "sifting and winnowing" plaque was often shown during various congressional hearings. I remember hearing much applause when I showed this slide during Senate hearings in Washington, and during analogous hearings at the Bundestag in Bonn, Germany. I was so proud to be from Wisconsin, where the regents had conceived these wise words, now already a century old.

Plaques and wise words should be placed on many buildings where they might influence the convictions and lives of students who, while passing by, might read the statements. I still remember, from my own student days, the imposing frieze on the library building of the Institute of Technology in Lvov, Poland, which espoused: "Hic mortui vivunt et muti loquuntur," which translates from Latin to: "Here, the deceased are alive and the mute are talking." I still remember well these engraved words, even though so much has happened in the intervening years. Lvov, the city of my birth, a university town much like Madison, but nearly one thousand years old, was first overrun by Stalin's army in 1939, then by Hitler in 1941, then again by Stalin in 1943. Finally it was presented to Stalin by President Roosevelt, with his informal blessing to be ethnically cleansed, with a brutal displacement of nearly half a million predominantly Polish residents, including myself. Of my chemical engineering class of 120 students, only 14 survived the 1939–44 war, all others being victims of the atrocities of the communist and Nazi invaders.

So, I learned the hard way to appreciate what freedom means, and when we stand before the "sifting and winnowing" plaque, it is clear that the regents of 1894, and President Adams among them, are "vivunt et loquuntur" (alive and talking). We should carefully listen to their poetic message about freedom, and we should profit from their wisdom.

Academic Freedom from a Student's Perspective

RAYMOND J. KOTWICKI

S tereotypical first-year college students travel in packs. That is, in groups averaging six to eight members, each member dressed in tattered, faded blue jeans, Rose Bowl sweatshirts, and Badgers caps on backwards, who slink along campus walkways. The amoebalike pack consumes objects and envelops other students who happen to block its carefully orchestrated, yet random, course. Such groups despise individuality and autonomy. Mass action governs; few group members dare to step out of the clique's implicit, pulsating rules into the beat of Thoreau's metaphorical drummer.

Observers from both outside and within the university often generalize this sheeplike social caricature to all aspects of undergraduate students' lives. Some cynics assume that cookie-cutter kids ambling aimlessly about in pursuit of good times on a Friday night also stumble directionless through the pursuit of an education in the classroom. Unfortunately, some cynics are right. Few undergraduate students believe they are capable of challenging entrenched ideals, safe to speak out against the norm, or even smart enough to reach new, valid conclusions. Consequently, some students forfeit their opportunities to explore new ideas and ways of thinking as undergraduates and simply memorize their Latin verbs and organic chemistry reactions without ever exploiting the academic freedom that frames a university education. In light of this observation, might one conclude that the academic freedom for which our predecessors, including Professor Ely, fought has been wasted on the silent, unappreciative, mass-produced "Generation X"?

This essay argues that current university undergraduate students must be encouraged to sift and winnow in the classroom unlike any past generation of students. This essay identifies an intimate link between undergraduate students' and professors' academic freedom. It itemizes reasons why the education of contemporary undergraduate students must always maintain roots in academic freedom. Most important, this essay suggests ways to ensure that plenty of sifting and winnowing occurs within university class-

Raymond J. Kotwicki is a 1994 graduate of the University of Wisconsin–Madison who majored in the history of science.

rooms. Undergraduates from the "Generation X" do not only possess the privilege but also the responsibility to continuously sift and winnow in pursuit of truth and individuality.

Whether they know it or not, undergraduates, like students from every level of education, maintain an intimate link with academic freedom in research. Students learn what professors teach. Professors teach what they research. Academic freedom undergirds research. Therefore, the ideas that teachers convey to students stem directly from the academic freedom that initially inspired and guided the research. Undergraduates must identify their dependency on professor's freedom to question accepted theories and conduct unadulterated, unbiased research. Academic freedom truly frames all university learning: the effects of professors' sifting and winnowing in the research lab trickles down to every seat in the lecture hall.

Students themselves necessarily need to sift and winnow through information at another level in the education process. Sifting and winnowing in the undergraduate classroom is important for many reasons, three of which appear below. First, sifting and winnowing is a result of sheer volume. Students must sift through unimportant and ludicrous information in order to savor meaty ideas and conclusions. As a medical student, this is one aspect of sifting and winnowing that I have perfected. Spending less time on the formalities of education and more time absorbing thoughts and extending their implications to other problems enhances students' thought processes. Heinrich Heine underscored this sentiment when he asserted that "the Romans would never have found time to conquer the world if they had been obliged to learn Latin first." Sifting and winnowing within the classroom ensures that students will have time to conquer the world.

The second reason why undergraduate sifting and winnowing is invaluable centers on students needing to integrate important ideas from one discipline with ideas in other disciplines. Sifting through many unique ideas enables students to match suppositions from eclectic sources and fields of study. Just as myopia may trap students in one course of study, thinking only one way might trap students in the prevailing social or university opinion. Sifting and winnowing from a variety of sources counters closed-minded thinking.

The third reason why students sift and winnow in the classroom focuses on ethics. Careful scrutiny of supposed facts may weed out facts that hold strong roots in nonfactual ground. In other words, students have the responsibility to challenge propaganda masqueraded as truisms. Often, this form of

sifting and winnowing requires a redefinition of the terms "sifting and winnowing." Rather than viewing the task of sifting and winnowing information
as a chore in excluding the useless, ludicrous, or painfully myopic information from the important information, one might look upon ethical sifting
and winnowing as an inclusionary task. For example, the 1994 Canadian
breast cancer study that published data heralding partial mastectomies as
treatment for the disease wrongly and deliberately excluded data that conflicted with the expected results. The breast cancer researchers *sifted out* true
results to fit their data. Students learning about this study, on the other
hand, need to sift and winnow *in* all data, so that truth—however messy or
bad for research funding—may be discovered.

Academic freedom rests at the core of a university education. It connects
students' educations to professors' research. Academic freedom allows students
to separate unimportant suppositions from important ideas. Academic freedom
encourages students to begin thinking for themselves, transcending prevailing
social opinions. Moreover, academic freedom challenges students to question
processes through which others distill "facts" from the world. Sifting and winnowing may consist of either excluding certain observations or including other
observations in testing theories. For all its importance, sifting and winnowing
is neither easy to define nor a static concept.

Author George Orwell modeled his novel *1984* after a society much like
the society that brought University of Wisconsin Professor Ely to trial in
the 1890s. Orwell constructed a state in which a free-thinking radical vied
for autonomy with the paternalistic government called Big Brother. Winston, the protagonist who set out to gain his intellectual, emotional, and
physical liberation, held unpopular beliefs rooted in intellectual independence. Big Brother attempted to screen out Winston's views through the
Thought Police, insiders who monitored the intellectual milieu of the state's
citizens. Such a world hyperbolized what occurs when authorities restrict
individuals' liberties. Professor Ely won his battle with Big Brother in 1894.
However, the educational war against the Thought Police remains at hand.

Recognizing the importance of sifting and winnowing in the classroom
and beyond, how might the students and the University of Wisconsin–
Madison ensure that ample sifting and winnowing occurs? Promotion of
academic freedom and free inquiry at the University of Wisconsin requires
two conditions: safety and encouragement. Undergraduate students who feel
threatened by professors who do not tolerate views other than their own are

at risk for acquiescing to Big Brother. Undergraduate students who become warehoused into traditional lectures emphasizing the white, male, Western, classic approach to academia face the Thought Police. Undergraduate students in discussion sections where questions are discouraged and where lecture dethrones discussion may feel like Winston felt in Orwell's *1984*. Student safety in challenging ideas, coupled with encouragement from professors and the administration to prompt students to think for themselves, discuss strange ideas, and integrate seemingly disparate thoughts, will undoubtedly drive Orwell's *1984* back into the world of the fantastic.

Safety in forwarding unpopular or progressive thoughts lies at the foundation of academic freedom. In his 1992 lecture, as part of the series entitled "Academic Freedom and the Future of the University," Louis Menand suggested that "it has always been assumed that conflicting views were precisely what the modern university was designed to accommodate." In fact, worthy professors enjoy tenure as a license for pursuing truth wherever it may lie without jeopardizing their jobs and sources of income. Tenure shields faculty from the possible ramifications of academic freedom. Furthermore, professors and other staff members research as they teach. Time to think independently through research and continuing education seminars or colloquia is a fundamental facet of a professor's career. In sum, professors feel safe and encouraged to strike out upon divergent paths of thought and academic inquiry.

To the contrary, many undergraduate students fear punishment upon subscription to a philosophy of academic freedom. Foremost, grades may reflect a professors disdain for free thought. Regardless of university ideals, professors' evaluations of students' performances may reflect the degree to which the authority figures agree or disagree with pupils' beliefs. To promote academic freedom in the classroom, professors must not use grades as weapons to polarize thoughts.

Undergraduate students also need to feel safe in challenging methods or assumptions behind the facts as taught. For instance, some medical schools across the country continue to teach about the course and related pathologies of syphilis based on the Tuskegee Syphilis Study that began in the 1930s. In that study, the United States Public Health Service followed and charted the effects of untreated syphilis on 399 black men in Macon County, Alabama. The United States Public Health Service denied the men treatment for the disease for forty years. Even after penicillin had been shown to

cure syphilis, the poor, black, uneducated men received absolutely no thera-
peutics for their syphilis. The Tuskegee Syphilis Study represented not only
a convenient way for the white public health service workers to obtain practice and notoriety, but also caustic, undiluted racism.

Despite the moral and scientific illegitimacy of the Tuskegee Study,
some schools persist in teaching its results. Students who blindly adopt conclusions based on the Tuskegee Study ignore the social context that devalues
the data. How researchers arrived at results are often as significant as the
final results themselves. Medical students who learn about syphilis from the
Tuskegee Study must understand what the biases and limitations of discrimination imposed upon the study's conclusions. Furthermore, students should
speak out against the study and others like it without fear of ostracism from
colleagues or jeering from faculty. In this instance, legitimate sifting and
winnowing mandates the inclusion of the research context and the exclusion
of results from the study without fear of retribution.

Beyond feeling protected from harm while reaching for academic freedom and autonomy, undergraduate students require encouragement to
develop their own thoughts and voices. Student discussions facilitate free
inquiry. In discussions, students need validation. That is, professors might
guide students through analyses of facts and origins of truisms, critiquing
underlying biases and assumptions together as a team. Moreover, a variety of
student perspectives might augment the goals and objectives for a course
that focuses on one way of thinking. Students need encouragement from
other students as well as from faculty in giving voice to their own ideas.

Successful music professors teach students to play instruments with
confidence. One of my band teachers assured me that playing a wrong note
loud and clear would be better than quietly squeaking out the right one.
Undergraduate students must apply this philosophy to all disciplines.
Although my parents told me that the band teacher asked me to leave the
band after I had fully subscribed to that philosophy, the advice to play even
wrong notes with strength and power served me well. Similarly, university
students deserve encouragement for giving their own ideas—however out-
landish they may first seem—a confident voice. The famous playwright
Anton Chekhov observed that "the university brings out all abilities including incapabilities." Undergraduate students may truly secure empowerment
in one area of study through experimentation and consequent elimination

of others. Such empowerment necessitates the academic freedom to fully embrace all subjects.

Clearly, academic freedom lays the foundation for a valuable university education. Sifting and winnowing ensures that students allocate appropriate amounts of time to intellectual necessities. Sifting and winnowing helps to integrate ideas from various disciplines, resulting in academic eclecticism. Sifting and winnowing also enables students to place theories that professors present as facts within the social, political, and economic contexts from which they arose. To ensure that plenty of sifting and winnowing occurs at the university, undergraduate students—vulnerable to the destructive forces of peer conformity, biased grading, and academic ostracism—need to feel safe and encouraged to challenge the establishment and formulate new hypotheses.

The trial of Professor Richard T. Ely epitomized Orwellian thought control. That the University of Wisconsin Board of Regents exonerated Professor Ely and adopted an academic freedom policy based upon the underlying principles that initially brought Professor Ely to interest, exemplifies the university's historical dedication to independence and unbridled inquiry. The 1894 sifting and winnowing decree loudly reverberates throughout the university. Let it now infuse the enigmatic "Generation X" of students who, for want of intellectual autonomy and freedom, reject the creation of a sequel to George Orwell's fantasy world.

Sifting and Winnowing Issues at the University of Wisconsin–Madison

E. DAVID CRONON

We have heard a fair amount of institutional self-congratulation in the past twenty-four hours. This is not surprising, for the centennial of the happy outcome of the Ely heresy trial—for that is what it was—is certainly worth celebrating. As President Lyall remarked, in rededicating the sifting and winnowing plaque we were recommitting ourselves and our university to that "continual and fearless" search for truth exemplified by the vindication of Professor Ely in 1894.

Even as we honor the 1894 regents for their forthright defense of academic freedom, however, honesty requires us to admit that our university has not always lived up to the ideal set before us in such powerful language. On the whole, the record is pretty good. Still, there have been times when the sifting and winnowing slogan has seemed something of an embarrassment to later boards of regents, university authorities, and even the faculty. So before we indulge in too much institutional self-congratulation this weekend, let us recall a few instances where the university did not always behave so fearlessly.

We probably should begin with the reluctance of a later Board of Regents to accept the gift of the graduating Class of 1910 of the bronze plaque quoting the sifting and winnowing sentence of the 1894 Ely verdict. More conservative than their predecessors, the regents in 1910 suspected (correctly) that the plaque was part of a larger political agenda, and some even disagreed with its freewheeling sentiment. Consequently, the board at first declined to accept the plaque. Unlike other class gifts, this one was relegated to the basement of Main Hall (now Bascom Hall), where it gathered dust and was largely forgotten for the next five years. In 1912 the board grudgingly accepted the gift, but did not authorize its display. Not until 1915, when the class officers raised the embarrassing issue of what had happened to their memorial when planning

---

E. David Cronon is professor emeritus of history at the University of Wisconsin–Madison, and author, with John W. Jenkins, of the 1994 book, A History of the University of Wisconsin: 1925–1949, *Volume 3.*

their class's five-year reunion, did the regents somewhat unenthusiastically agree to President Van Hise's recommendation that the plaque be mounted prominently on the front of the building.

This action would seem to suggest a renewed institutional commitment to free speech and ideas. If so, it was short-lived. American entry into the European war two years later brought a tidal wave of hysterical patriotism and intolerant conformity to the campus. The regents revoked the honorary degree they had awarded some years earlier to the German ambassador, Count Heinrich von Bernstorff, a noted man of letters who had similarly been recognized for his erudition by a number of major American universities. The regents also withheld the degrees of students who refused military service as conscientious objectors. Several UW faculty members eagerly produced anti-German propaganda for the national Committee on Public Information, works of such dubious scholarly integrity that they remain a continuing embarrassment. President Van Hise, all of the deans, and 93 percent of the faculty signed a round-robin manifesto denouncing the state's senior U.S. senator, Robert M. La Follette, for his antiwar views. In the most shameful manifestation of zealotry, a distinguished professor of German was dismissed for suggesting that an obnoxious colleague, who was, like himself, German born, should demonstrate his sudden American patriotism by wearing his Liberty Loan button on the seat of his pants. This was hardly a time of fearless sifting and winnowing on campus.

Happily, the university and the state had gained greater balance and maturity by the advent of World War II. This time there was no hysteria, only a quiet and largely unified determination to do as much as possible to support the war effort. The decisions make by student conscientious objectors were respected, though the objectors were not awarded the same academic credit given men who left for military service in mid-term. Student leaders and university administrators welcomed the relocation and enrollment of Japanese-American young people who had been interned in the west coast camps, and some of them were sponsored by UW faculty members.

Regular enrollment declined sharply during the war, but student housing remained tight as all but two campus dormitories were taken over for army and navy training programs. With considerable misgivings, in 1944 the Dean of Women, Louise Troxell, approved the formation of the first women's interracial cooperative living unit, Groves House, named for the group's faculty sponsor, economics professor Harold Groves. Student leaders and the *Daily Cardinal* were in fact ahead of university administrators in promoting open housing in Madison. They were quick to protest evidence of racial or religious discrimination in campus-area rooming houses. This, they pointed out, was in shameful denial of America's professed war aims. After a contingent of navy WAVES took over Barnard and Chadbourne Halls, one student found herself without a place in a campus dormitory at the start of her sophomore year. A half-century later she still remembers with indignation the humiliation of being continually rebuffed in her efforts to rent a room in one of the many private rooming houses, which rejected her because she was a New York Jew. She was about to leave Madison and go home when she got the inspired idea of approaching the German House, a university-sponsored private dormitory for women German majors that had been forced to close during the period of intolerance during World War I. "Look," she said. "You need me as much as I need you." The residents agreed, and she moved in.

Except for the aberration of World War I, the Ely case pretty much settled the issue of academic freedom for UW faculty members. There was never another heresy trial, nor any abridgment of the faculty's freedom to search for the truth, nor even any serious pressure for a faculty loyalty oath, as was common elsewhere during the McCarthy era. Indeed, when Governor Blaine demanded in 1926 that the university fire an extension professor whose book he found offensive, President Frank first ignored the call and then issued an eloquent defense of the faculty's academic freedom. That Frank waited several months until Blaine left office was a matter of political timing that did not undermine the force of his words.

Ironically, the university for many years was not willing to extend the sifting and winnowing ideal fully to its students. For example, before World War II, university policy required student groups to get official permission to bring outside speakers to the campus. The purpose was to protect the university from public criticism if the students were seen to be in danger of being swayed by unscrupulous demagogues or corrupted by unsuitable ideas. For many years these requests were reviewed by the president himself.

The policy gained a good deal of notoriety in 1928 when a student organization asked permission to sponsor a talk by Dora Russell, the free-thinking wife of the famous British philosopher, Bertrand Russell. Mrs. Russell was currently on a lecture tour of the United States, promoting among other issues her controversial views on free love and companionate marriage. The student request posed a dilemma for President Frank, who was a strong advocate of responsible student self-government. Rather than turn down the application, he conferred with the student organizers who then decided to withdraw their invitation. After the *Capital Times* accused Frank and the university of trying to censor Mrs. Russell, the local Unitarian church invited her to use its building for her talk, a talk that disappointed nearly everyone by its innocuous character.

Another worry for university authorities in the interwar years was the content of student publications, especially the *Daily Cardinal* and the irreverent humor magazine, the *Octopus*. Their youthful editors were not averse to testing the university's commitment to its sifting and winnowing ideal, not to mention the First Amendment. All of the student publications had faculty advisers who were supposed to keep an eye on their activities, but the supervision was usually more nominal than real. After the *Octopus* published a naughty cartoon in 1928, Dean of Men Goodnight ordered the offending page removed and for the next decade served as the publication's faculty adviser. In protest the editors thereupon included his name on their masthead, with the title "Censor."

The *Daily Cardinal* occasionally got into more serious trouble. In the spring of 1932 it published an anonymous letter entitled "Virginity—a Woman's View," signed simply "Junior Woman." Today's *Cardinal* readers would hardly be shocked by the letter, but in 1932 it created a sensation on campus and around the state. While not advocating promiscuity, Junior Woman argued that the decision to engage in premarital sex was a private one between the two consenting individuals and involved what she called "a natural and normal and wholesome method of rounding out their lives." The letter triggered angry denunciations from some of the pastors of campus-area churches and led one wrathful mother to call upon her counterparts to clean up the university, which she described as "a huge brothel," during the forthcoming Mothers' Weekend.

Other critics at this time were more concerned about the *Cardinal*'s (and the university's) alleged radicalism, atheism, and pacifism, the latter reflected in the paper's perennial campaign against compulsory ROTC. To quiet the uproar and reassure worried parents and alumni, President Frank dismissed classes and called an all-university convocation in the field house. His long address, entitled "Freedom, Education, and Morals in the Modern University," was a ringing defense of a free university, whose members must be free to study any political, social, economic, religious, or moral issue. "To do less," he declared, "is to commit suicide as a University." Still, he emphasized, with freedom comes responsibility. And recent experience ought to convince student editors that printing any student's views on sexual relations was not only a violation of good taste but gave ammunition to what the president called "the blatherskates and demagogues" who were seeking to attack the university for other reasons. As a former journalist himself, he was confident that student journalists could draw the line between good and bad taste. But if not, he cautioned, "I can draw this line and draw it without infringement of that authentic freedom of speech in which I believe profoundly." The president's address was broadcast over the university radio station, WHA, released to the press, and reprinted in the *Wisconsin Alumni Magazine*. For a time it seemed to quiet the furor.

The next year, however, the Board of Regents received two serious complaints about the *Daily Cardinal*. One, signed by 464 members of the ROTC Cadet Corps, complained about the continuing anti-ROTC bias of the *Cardinal*. The other, from the directors of the Alumni Association, with evident support from the University's Board of Visitors, probably reflected the continuing fallout from the uproar of the previous year. It urged the regents to establish an official campus newspaper under the School of Journalism to, as the petition put it, "promote the best interests of the University of Wisconsin and its student body and to secure for the University proper publicity."

The regents responded with a heavy hand. In the spring of 1933 they stripped the *Cardinal* of its status as the official campus newspaper and created a special high-powered committee to meet with the paper's editors and discuss what further controls might be necessary. When these discussions stalemated, the board directed its executive committee "to prepare plans for the creation of an official University newspaper designed to support the general University welfare and with opportunity for free expression of student opinion." This action could not silence the *Cardinal*, of course, because it was a financially secure private corporation that owned its printing press. The move was hardly in keeping with the sifting and winnowing ideal, however, and it struck many, including some editors around the state, as excessive. After further reflection, and very likely with the quiet intervention of Governor Philip La Follette, the board reversed itself. It abandoned the idea of a new university paper, restored the *Cardinal*'s designation as the official campus newspaper, and limited the regents' intervention to expanding the paper's Board of Control by two members, one to be appointed by the regents and the other by the president. It subsequently failed to carry out even this change.

The *Daily Cardinal* continued to infuriate at least some of its campus readers from time to time, especially after it took on a more radical and activist character in the 1960s. The paper's strident militancy inspired a rival conservative student paper, the *Badger Herald*, which appeared first as a weekly and eventually, as it prospered, a daily. The changed character of the *Cardinal* also led the campus administration to resurrect the 1934 idea of a university-sponsored newspaper to provide fuller and more accurate coverage of campus news, at least the kind of news considered of interest to UW staff members. Today's *Cardinal* editors probably don't realize their paternal responsibility, but their more radical predecessors in effect fathered the two rival campus papers of today, the *Badger Herald* and *Wisconsin Week*.

The foregoing suggests that some of the tarnish on the sifting and winnowing ideal over the past century resulted from the response to student activities of which university leaders or external critics disapproved of. The university was thus reluctant at times to extend to its students the unfettered right to engage in the same fearless sifting and winnowing that it expected of its faculty.

But the student body itself is also responsible for undermining the sifting and winnowing ideal. For nearly three decades since the turbulent protests against the Vietnam War, it has been risky and sometimes impossible to invite to the campus speakers whose unpopular ideas are opposed by one student group or another, lest they be heckled, shouted down, or even physically threatened. The result is a self-imposed censorship and conformity that denies the campus community the opportunity to hear all points of view. It makes a shameful mockery of the sifting and winnowing ideal.

What is more disturbing is that it has been a long time—decades, in fact—since the faculty as a body, or a top campus administrator, or a regent has spoken out forcefully and taken a strong stand against this form of censorship by student storm troopers.

Let me close by reminding you of what happened when a group of fraternity row athletes, many wearing their W sweaters, disrupted a student meeting in the Law School Auditorium in the spring of 1935. After heckling the speaker—a socialist organizer for the League for Industrial Democracy—they dragged him and others at the meeting down the hill and threw them into the lake. The Mendota dunking affair attracted great attention and outrage around the state and nation. The next day, philosophy professor Max Otto told his class of three hundred students, "If that was Americanism last night and I had been there I would have preferred to have been thrown into the lake." Dean Lloyd Garrison of the law school organized a Committee for Constitutional Rights. President Frank called an all-university convocation on a Friday evening that attracted an overflow audience of more than 1,200 to the large auditorium in Ag Hall. Frank's speech was a generalized defense of free speech and academic freedom, but another speaker, L&S Dean George Sellery, was much more impassioned and specific in denouncing the actions of the student mob, which he called "the most disgraceful thing ever perpetrated at the University." He heaped withering scorn on the athlete perpetrators and sarcastically questioned their right to wear the Wisconsin W. What the *Cardinal* headlined as "Sellery's Fiery Blast" was applauded wildly by the student audience, which gave him a tumultuous sky rocket cheer as he left the rostrum.

The sifting and winnowing ideal could have used the blunt-spoken defense of George Sellery in recent years.

PART 4.

New Challenges to Sifting and Winnowing

Academic Freedom: Threats and Limits

JOEL B. GROSSMAN

One can scarcely challenge either the force or the legitimacy of the basic principles of free academic inquiry set forth by the UW Board of Regents in 1894 and subsequently immortalized in our famous "sifting and winnowing" declaration. We take great pride in recognizing the UW–Madison's leadership not only in espousing these principles, but in living by them as well.[1] It is thus altogether fitting and proper that we mark the centennial of that declaration both by celebrating and by cerebrating, *thinking*, about academic freedom, about how it has become institutionalized,[2] how it operates and applies to the modern research university, and about its boundaries.

Periodic review and clarification of the role and function of academic freedom is always useful. But it is especially important and timely now when the role, mission, and autonomy of public academic institutions are under increasingly hostile external challenge. This principle, which we regard as the lifeblood of the university, is seen by some critics, tragically wrong in my view, as conferring self-serving license and unwarranted privilege that compromises the university's role as they define it, and undermining the public's confidence. Academic freedom and its corollary of faculty tenure are also viewed as a major impediment by those who seek to reinvent the university as a hypothetically efficient business organization whose main purpose is to supply and drive the economic system.[3] Unfortunately, they forget that just as the framers of the U.S. Constitution designed a government of separated powers not to promote efficiency but democracy and self-governance, so too universities cannot—and should not be expected to—fulfill their essential mission of creating and disseminating knowledge in a rigidly confining and inappropriate quasi-corporate structure.

It is therefore not sufficient merely for us to proclaim and reassert once again the primacy of academic freedom. Of course, scholarship needs sufficient breathing space to survive—and to flourish. Excellence in teaching, research, and public service cannot be achieved in a hostile and threatening

Joel B. Grossman is professor of political science and law, and the 1993–94 Chair of the University Committee at the University of Wisconsin–Madison. Author's note: *I am indebted to Robert O'Reilly for research assistance.*

environment. But we also must recognize that academic freedom is a dynamic concept subject to interpretation and capable of growth; that "sifting and winnowing in the search for truth" operates today in a more complex environment than the 1894 events that led to its articulation; that academic freedom is not absolute and must at times yield to other important values; and that as such it is a reasonable and responsible standard that serves the interests not only of the faculty and the university, but of the public as well.[4]

The idea of limits need not be threatening. Academic freedom, properly defined and understood in this context, helps to ensure that universities, unique and fragile institutions, are both responsive to public needs *and* able to fulfill their basic mission. My focus in these remarks on the *limits* of academic freedom is thus not designed to undermine the principle or comfort its critics, but rather to demonstrate the inevitability and utility of limits to its continued vitality and legitimacy.

Some definitions are in order. The basic idea of academic freedom has at least four substantive components: it protects the freedom of scholars and scientists to pursue untrammeled scholarly inquiry and publish the results without fear of institutional or public censorship; it protects the freedom of faculty to teach students, in whatever manner faculty choose, about the subjects of their expertise even if those teachings run counter to official dogma or popular belief; it protects the right of faculty to speak out on public issues without fear of official retaliation; and it protects the freedom of all members of the university community to listen and learn, and to seek the truth wherever it may lie and whatever the consequences.[5] There can be no compromise with these principles.

There is also a vital procedural component that at first glance appears paradoxical: academic freedom must be recognized at *both* the individual and institutional levels. Even though there is widespread consensus within the university about the governing principles of academic freedom, and an appreciation of the need for self-restraint in claiming their protections, some conflict in their application is inevitable; second-order rules are thus needed to resolve these conflicts without jeopardizing the basic concepts. To avoid the destructive intrusion of external review, sensitive internal oversight and some kind of accountability is both necessary and inevitable. Without internal restraint and effective self-governance, external intervention is more likely.

The Supreme Court increasingly has given constitutional protection to academic freedom principles by subsuming them under the rights guaranteed under the First, Fifth, and Fourteenth Amendments.[6] But as with all "rights," they carry with them correlative obligations.[7] Thus, the freedom of inquiry, and the freedom to teach, must be exercised in the context of professional responsibility and expertise. Tolerance and respect are due those of contrary views. The distinction must be drawn between attacking those who espouse ideas and denying them voice, which is unacceptable, and debating and possibly refuting the ideas themselves, which lies at the heart of the mission of the academy.

At the same time it is especially important that teaching does not become indoctrination, which creates a pall of orthodoxy that undermines the sifting and winnowing principle. There are other obvious limits as well: there is, for example, also no right to plagiarize, no right to falsify research results, and certainly no professorial immunity for incompetent performance or neglect of duties.[8] Violations of these conditions and responsibilities are not entitled to protection. To extend no protection to them is indeed to vindicate and strengthen academic freedom.[9]

Historically, the fight for academic freedom centered on external interference and censorship of unpopular ideas—by university administrators, boards of regents, legislative bodies, public officials, and powerful private interests. Such threats have by no means vanished, although we have moved (I hope) safely beyond the long night of loyalty oaths and anticommunist inquisitions.[10] Each generation, however, defines for itself a new orthodoxy of correctness, and it is inevitable that scholars and universities will feel pressures to conform to a society's evolving norms and beliefs. Chiseled into the stone facade of the central building of the University of Uppsala in Sweden are the words (in Latin): "To think is good, to think *right* is better." While that motto reflects the ecclesiastical origins of a great university and not its present eminence in the scholarly world, the words themselves have a haunting contemporary echo that challenges our commitment to free inquiry.

A vital scholarly community welcomes—indeed thrives on—the challenge of new ideas, however controversial or even sometimes distasteful. At the same time, it must reject the conformist imperative that often accompanies them. It matters little that today those imperatives may come not from demagogues but from well-intentioned lawmakers and bureaucrats, or even faculty colleagues; or that they may be camouflaged in a seemingly inscrutable funding process.[11] Whatever the source, they often appear in the form of benevolent or remedial principles of fairness and justice, or from misguided attempts to make people "think right," such as hate speech laws, prohibitions on speech in the classroom that might create a "hostile environment" or promote gender inequality, or attempts to censor or obstruct campus speakers who espouse distasteful ideas. But we cannot fight intolerance with more intolerance. Even as we emphatically agree that hateful and demeaning speech, like discrimination, is reprehensible and contrary both to American values and to the maintenance of an open and friendly university learning environment, we must reject both hate speech laws and the sanctioning of "incorrect" expression as inappropriate modes of redress.[12] The proper response, as Gerald Gunther has suggested, is "more speech, better speech."[13] This solution does not curtail speech, but rather embodies the famous "marketplace of ideas" metaphor.[14] Our trust in the wisdom of the general public, the cornerstone of democracy, requires us to allow others to hear and decide for themselves. Platonic guardians, protecting those more sensitive from offensive or disconcerting ideas, have no place in the university.

In addition to creating and maintaining a climate of tolerance, we must also seek an environment of equality. The principle of equal treatment is also indispensable to an open, tolerant, and congenial learning environment. There is no necessary conflict between the principle of equality and traditional academic freedom, but in practice there are frictions that must be addressed. We can and must support the goal of welcoming, protecting, and even empowering those who have been disadvantaged or unfairly treated—because of race, ethnicity, gender, religion, age, sexual orientation, or disability. Universities gain strength and legitimacy through diversity among the faculty, staff, and students. Efforts to achieve this goal through preferential student recruiting or staff or faculty hiring, or through programs designed to diversify the traditional curriculum (especially in times of scarce resources) are often challenged as undermining the meritocratic principle that is also central to a high-standard academic institution, thus impinging on academic decisions otherwise protected by academic freedom. In my judgment this contention is unpersuasive. It fails to recognize that academic freedom must protect not only individual scholarly activities and prerogatives but also the institutional mission.

Universities, above all institutions in our society, have a special interest in maximizing the congruence of equal treatment, an open learning environment, and academic freedom. How well they do so is an important measure of their distinction. Such congruence will have the further positive—and practical—consequence of reducing a university's exposure to adverse litigation consequences. In this age of litigiousness, American courts have generally been reluctant to interfere with *academic* decisions supported by appropriate redress procedures.[15] But the tide may be shifting. Academic freedom may be best protected—and adverse legal and political intervention avoided—not by a Maginot Line drawn around traditional principles, but by our own flexibility and responsible willingness to recognize and enforce appropriate *equality-producing* imperatives.

Threats to academic freedom do not come solely from outside the walls of the university. Increasingly, as universities have become larger and more complex governance structures, collective decisions must be made that potentially test academic freedom every bit as much as external pressures for doctrinal conformity. Former Yale University President Kingman Brewster, for example, has argued that "internal pressures for intellectual conformity" in the peer-review process are now the major threat to academic freedom.[16]

This interpretation is too doctrinaire and overinclusive; it sweeps with too broad a brush. But there can be little doubt that the faculty's collective governance responsibilities for curriculum and teaching, and for individual tenure, promotion, and salary decisions, can exert substantial conformist pressures, particularly on younger colleagues' research choices and teaching preferences and styles. As David Rabban has observed, "Intellectual rigidity, reluctance to admit professional error, careerist jealousy, political differences, and simple personal animosity may lead committees of faculty peers to misjudge the professional work of individual colleagues."[17] Personal ambition and competition for scarce resources are likely to exacerbate these temptations. The rise of faculty professionalism further complicates the matter.

Such biases, while inherent in the human condition from which faculty are not immune, cannot be sheltered under academic freedom. A fair and effective governance structure and remedial oversight process is thus necessary to identify and reject illegitimate academic freedom claims. The risk that individual academic freedom may be improperly compromised in the process does not gainsay the need for internal collective judgments or effective oversight procedures. The best protection against that risk is to ensure that decisions on academic freedom matters are made by those who share the basic principles and have a stake in their continuance. At the UW–Madison, for example, the Faculty Senate, pursuant to state law, has recently devised a special procedure to reconsider the merits of negative retention and tenure decisions at the departmental level alleged to be the product of discrimination or other impermissible factors.[18] This was a necessary compromise with the traditional and valid principle that positive tenure decisions require affirmative departmental assent. It was structured, however, so as to both maximize the likelihood of fair decisions and uphold the principle that tenure should be awarded only for superior academic performance.

In the modern university, academic freedom cannot be (and perhaps never has been) a completely laissez-faire concept. Both individual faculty members, and the faculty collectively, must have the freedom guaranteed by our sifting and winnowing declaration. Clashes are inevitable in individual cases, but ultimately, a collective responsibility to fulfill the university's mission and maintain the highest academic standards must be acknowledged.

Faculty must have maximum freedom to teach, to choose appropriate instructional methods, and to establish and maintain suitable standards and measurements of academic performance. A faculty member's course preferences, however, may have to yield to a department's judgment about courses required to meet student needs or professional certification standards. Likewise, an instructor's grading methods and standards, normally and properly a matter left to his or her discretion, may have to yield to a department's (or college's) minimum standards. There is, for example, no "right" of a faculty member to indiscriminately assign A's to all students, to eliminate all grading exercises or assign grades on an extraneous basis, or to treat students in an unfair or abusive manner.[19] Courses, and the instructional program, ultimately "belong to the department" and not the faculty member. Peer review of the appropriateness of course content and teaching quality and effectiveness is also entirely proper. But that collective responsibility must respect individual faculty autonomy and the principles of academic freedom. There is no litmus test, of course, to determine the legitimacy of a student's or faculty member's claims, or a department's contrary assertions. A responsible understanding of academic freedom and a working checks-and-balances system offers the best assurance that when such conflicts emerge, all rights and legitimate interests will be respected.

Thus, what President Brewster described as the major threat to academic freedom is better described as the tensions present in a continuing effort to protect individual faculty autonomy and initiative, to create and maintain an environment in which academic freedom can flourish, *and* to recognize the need for the university as an institution to govern itself in a responsible manner.

To fail to recognize this interdependence is to invite the worst-case scenario: that important educational decisions will be made by others, often those least qualified to make them, and those most likely to be threatened by nonconformity and new thinking.[20] Unlimited and unjustified claims of individual academic freedom, if carried to their logical conclusion, would result in academic disarray, the possible compromise of high standards of performance, and the impossibility of institutional coherence. Unlimited peer group or administrative control, on the other hand, would inevitably succumb to the temptations of repression, conformity, and intellectual suffocation in the guise of efficiency or the avoidance of political risk. Neither is acceptable.

A similar dilemma of balancing individual rights with institutional responsibilities occurs in the context of both state-funded and externally sponsored research.[21] The basic principles of academic freedom were developed in a very different and much simpler context. The explosion of sponsored research and the growth of the modern research university, however, have created a new arena in which those principles must be tested (and protected). Regardless of the funding source—university (state), federal, or private—certain governing principles have emerged both to ensure research independence and to protect the integrity of the overall enterprise. These include, at a minimum, two principles that are inextricably intertwined: the elimination of potential conflicts of interest, and the unacceptability of any external or self-interested limits on the dissemination of research.

At the level of principle, both are absolute. In practice, the latter is clear, widely accepted, and probably respected to a high degree; the former is murky and subject to varying interpretations in individual cases. Taken together, however, they underscore the need for administrative/faculty decisional and oversight procedures that are capable of uncovering and sanctioning abuses while at the same time respecting and protecting the fundamental right of individual faculty members to choose the subjects, and modes of research and dissemination, of their scholarly investigations.

Sponsors improperly abridge academic freedom by imposing limits on the investigation of controversial subjects, or on the dissemination of unfavorable results. Faculty who accept such conditions cannot claim protection. Private sponsors may, of course, limit their funding to subjects of importance to them, provided that the research that is funded is carried out openly by customary professional means. A faculty member does have the right, at least arguably, to contract for research or writing outside of the academic context without subjecting the process or the product to internal review or even to abide by professional standards—provided that it is accompanied by a clear statement of disassociation from the university.[22]

External prohibitions on the funding or carrying out of controversial research thought to have deleterious public consequences are, however, completely unacceptable. For example, recent efforts in the state legislature to restrict or prohibit rBGH research at the University of Wisconsin–Madison in order to protect the viability of the family farm, though ultimately futile, would have constituted a major abridgment of academic freedom.[23] So too would hypothetical restrictions or prohibitions on carrying out research that might have the effect of promoting smoking; on research testing theories that intelligence is largely inherited and thus casting doubt on the efficacy of compensatory learning programs for minority children; or research that might lead to the promulgation of unpopular political, social, or economic theories with alleged unfortunate consequences.

On the other hand, research *designed to reach* foreordained conclusions fails the test of objective inquiry and could properly be denied support and/or sanctioned in the peer-review process without infringing academic freedom. Likewise, researchers should not seek or accept funding for projects that are not scientifically important or not conducive to rigorous testing and peer evaluation. Negative peer judgments about such research strengthens rather than weakens the climate of academic freedom. Monitoring this complex, high-stakes, research enterprise with due regard for both academic freedom and the maintenance of appropriate institutional standards is exceedingly difficult but absolutely necessary.

Experience tells us that the impetus and opportunity for abuse may come not only from external funding sources, but from the internal processes of funding competition between and among faculty members, and from lamentable if understandable efforts to take self-aggrandizing research shortcuts. Animal and human-subjects clearance procedures, responding both to external legal requirements and to our own ethical judgments, are but one example of the ways in which the university, through appropriate procedures, acts to forestall endeavors that can only diminish academic freedom.

The bottom line is that academic freedom can be maximized, works best, and has the greatest claim to both internal and external legitimacy when it operates in a well-designed and open system of rules and remediation that clearly defines its boundaries as well as the designated channels and processes by which it may be tested. Both individual faculty and the faculty collectively, as well as university administrators, share responsibility for its nurture and protection. Illegitimate and unchallenged claims to protection weaken the structure of academic freedom and undermine public support for its principles. At the same time, every effort must be made to ensure that otherwise appropriate internal limits do not become the threats that President Brewster has identified as the major challenge to academic freedom today.

Notes

1. The Faculty Senate of the University of Wisconsin–Madison adopted the following statement on March 4, 1985:

    The University of Wisconsin–Madison has long been known as a center of free intellectual inquiry. The tradition of such freedom is expressed eloquently in the famous "sifting and winnowing" statement issued by the Board of Regents in 1894. The tradition was reaffirmed two years ago when the University was asked by government agencies to impose limits on the inquiries which could be undertaken here by scholars from certain other countries. Recent events have led some to question whether the University of Wisconsin–Madison remains committed to this tradition.

    The Faculty Senate reaffirms its insistence on freedom of intellectual inquiry and discussion. Free discussion requires not simply that speakers be free to speak but that those who wish to hear be free to hear what is said. We regard these freedoms as fundamental rights, and reaffirm the Madison faculty's commitment to their enforcement.

2. See, e.g., Walter P. Metzger, "Professional and Legal Limits to Academic Freedom," 20 *Journal of College and University Law*, 1, 5, (1993).

3. See, e.g., Daniel J. Alesch, "The University of Wisconsin System: An Agenda for the 21st Century" (Wisconsin Policy Research Institute, Inc. 1994).

4. This principle was reiterated and supported by the University of Wisconsin–Madison faculty in its 1970 "Statement Concerning Rights and Responsibilities of Faculty," Faculty Document 8-A, p. 4. (Adopted by the Faculty Senate on January 4, 1971.)

5. Cf. Metzger, "Professional and Legal Limits," 2.

6. See, e.g., William W. Van Alstyne, "Academic Freedom and the First Amendment in the Supreme Court of the United States: An Unhurried Historical Review," 53 *Law and Contemporary Problems*, 79, 81, (1990).

7. The 1915 Declaration of Principles, issued by the American Association of University Professors, noted that "there are no rights without corresponding duties." Reprinted in *Academic Freedom and Tenure*, edited by L. Joughin (1969), appendix A, 157–76. See also David M. Rabban, "Does Academic Freedom Limit Faculty Autonomy?" 66 *Texas Law Review*, 1405, 1409, (1988).

8. Rabban, "Does Academic Freedom Limit?", 1410.

9. Ibid., at 1409.

10. Obscenity, for example, is still very much under attack by university administrators. A University of Colorado English professor recently was denied a promotion as a result of writing a book on the "poetics of obscenity." Berny Morson, "Eroticism Tome Irks Regents: Officials Deny Promotion to CU English Professor Who Wrote Book on Erotic Poetry," *Rocky Mountain News*, September 15, 1994, p. 5A. Similarly, the University of Iowa has adopted a policy that requires professors to warn students if course presentations will include anything "unusual or unexpected." The policy was a response to student complaints of professors screening sexually explicit films in the classroom. William H. Honan, "An Unexpected Debate on 'Unexpected' Content in Classroom Materials," *New York Times*, October 5, 1994, p. B8. See also Robert M. O'Neil, "Artistic Freedom and Academic Freedom," 53 *Law and Contemporary Problems*, 177, 179–82, (1990).

11. See, e.g., Rebecca S. Eisenberg, "Academic Freedom and Academic Values in Sponsored Research," 66 *Texas Law Review*, 1363, 1369, (1988).

12. See, e.g. *UWM Post, Inc. v. Board of Regents of the Univ. of Wisconsin System*, 774 F. Supp. 1163 (E.D. Wis. 1991). In this case, the UW rule banning hate speech was found to be in violation of the First Amendment.

13. This concept has particular merit in the academic setting. In fact, the very notion of "sifting and winnowing" suggests that some ideas will be rejected in favor of others. The concept of "incorrect" expression or inquiry is incompatible with the search for truth, where no object is to be shielded from scrutiny.

14. See *Abrams v. United States*, 250 U.S. 616 (1919), where Justice Oliver Wendell Holmes wrote: "The best test of truth is the power of [a] thought to get itself accepted in the competition of the market...."

15. See, e.g., Van Alstyne, "Academic Freedom," 131–32.

16. Kingman Brewster, "On Tenure," *AAUP Bulletin* 58 (1972): 381, 382 (quoted in Rabban, 1411).

17. Rabban, 1411.

18. University of Wisconsin–Madison, *Faculty Policies and Procedures*, Sec. 7.10(C).

19. See, e.g., *Keen v. Penson*, 970 F. 2d 252 (7th Cir. 1992).

20. As the 1915 Declaration notes:
    If [the academic] profession should prove itself unwilling to purge its ranks of the incompetent and the unworthy, or to prevent the freedom which it claims in the name of science from being used as a shelter for inefficiency, for superficiality, or for uncritical and intemperate partisanship, it is certain that the task will be performed by others—by others who lack certain qualifications for performing it, and whose action is sure to breed suspicions and recurrent controversies deeply injurious to the internal order and the public standing of universities.
    American Association of University Professors, see note 7, at 173.

21. See, e.g., Eisenberg, "Academic Freedom and Values," 137–74.

22. This principle, however, sometimes causes difficulty, especially when it is his or her position in the university which grants the professor the standing, or the opportunity, to write or speak on public issues. As "public intellectuals" increasingly mix academics, politics, and government, and address controversial issues, the university inevitably will face some criticism and be forced to (and must) defend the right of faculty to free public expression.

See Janny Scott, "Journey From Ivory Tower, Public Intellectual Is Reborn," *New York Times*, August 9, 1994, p. A1.

23. "Feingold to UW: No rBGH," *Capital Times*, November 12, 1994, p. 6A. A decision not to fund such research, however, would not constitute such an abridgment.

Sifting and Winnowing:
Accountability/Assessment and Academic Freedom

JOSEPH J. CORRY

This 100th Anniversary celebration of the renowned proclamation by the University of Wisconsin Board of Regents regarding "that fearless sifting and winnowing by which alone the truth can be found"[1] is an opportune time to examine how the current level of high demand for institutional accountability has had an impact on academic freedom. This pressure for public accountability certainly carries with it a potential infringement on that freedom. However, I believe the outcome for academic freedom will be determined primarily by how universities choose to respond to the public's inherent right to ask us to be accountable. Will we wait and react defensively to each new set of challenges, or will we be opportunistic and redefine and restructure some university policies and procedures that may enhance our freedom in the long run?

The framework for this discussion requires a common understanding of the meaning of the terms "accountability" and "assessment." Accountability primarily refers to the capacity for responding to requests by producing appropriate records of events; its secondary definition refers to the quality of being explainable. Assessment is the act of estimating a value for some item or, in the case of education, a value for an outcome from various teaching objectives. Each term, particularly in its late twentieth-century application to higher education, suggests a desire to know about things objectively. The public wants to know more about what goes on within the hallowed halls of academe, particularly with regard to its publicly financed institutions.

Since at least the early 1980s, public requests for higher education to be more accountable have been on a rising demand curve. What has been happening during these last two decades to has prompt this focus on accountability? One background factor may stem from the general crisis in our national confidence that surfaced about twenty years ago when Japan and a resurging Europe began to eclipse the U.S. at its own game in the world of business supremacy. Analysts went scurrying to discover how it was possible that we

Joseph J. Corry is associate vice-chancellor at the University of Wisconsin–Madison.

could lose our vaunted superiority, which had been the hallmark of American capitalism since the end of World War II. An examination of our schooling efforts—the great emphasis on education that is central to this democracy—was an inevitable result of the loss of superiority. The system of education became a strong candidate for at least part of the blame when those studies began to show that, using reasonably comparable standards, American school children were falling behind in many crucial academic areas.

The publishing of *A Nation at Risk*[2] in 1983 acted as a major catalyst in raising a credible alarm about the weaknesses in American schooling, and it subsequently helped coalesce a wide range of interest groups to address the questions raised in that report. In the intervening years, other groups have continued the cry of concern, but by far the most politically visible effort and the one that ultimately became the most comprehensive was the initiative undertaken by the National Governors Association (NGA). The work of the NGA was seized upon by the Bush Administration, and the result was *America 2000*[3]. This document was intended to be a blueprint aimed at restoring our grandeur in education, not unlike the way in which the "Man on the Moon" project of the Kennedy presidency was intended to restore our national pride through spectacular triumphs in space.

Two active participants in the NGA during the development of those goals were Governor Clinton of Arkansas and Governor Riley of South Carolina. Given the current positions of those two men (Riley is Secretary of the Department of Education), it is little wonder that the Clinton Administration has adopted that blueprint, although bestowing on it a new name, *Goals 2000*. There are six major goals (see the Appendix for list), and among them is one that has as its major objective the measurement of student competency in English, math, science, history, and geography at the end of the 4th, 8th, and 12th years of schooling. It is this type of measurement that indicates our strong desire to improve K–12 schooling by achieving accountability through student outcomes assessment.

Any concern for improvement of K–12 schooling would naturally draw some attention because of higher education's role in the preparation of K–12 teachers. However, higher education has other major interests in K–12 success. For example, professors of mathematics and science have increasingly taken a direct interest in the teaching of those subjects in K–12 because of their long-term worry about the supply of well-prepared and scientifically interested college students in those disciplines.

It would be misleading to suggest that the intense pressure on the K–12 sector of education is repeated at anywhere near that intensity for higher education. However, nearly one-third of the county has established some mandated performance indicators for higher education, including Wisconsin; the federal government requires all institutions to disclose graduation rates; and we have just witnessed a major league struggle between the U.S. Department of Education and an alliance of the national associations for various groups of higher education institutions and the regional accrediting associations over proposed changes in accreditation requirements that are part of the Higher Education Act. As of June 30, 1995, every institution of higher education within the twenty- state area served by the North Central Association must submit a plan demonstrating that it is prepared to conduct assessments of general education and of every major, both undergraduate and graduate.

Intensity aside, the interest of the states and the federal government in gaining greater accountability, especially for public higher education, is strong and growing. These governments may even intensify their focus on higher education if the battles at the K–12 level become increasingly political. Reformers pursuing their interpretations of *Goals 2000* at the K–12 level are discovering that local school districts can be scenes of very heated arguments about some of the new national objectives. The larger, seemingly more distant, state-level institutions may be an easier target.

Finally, the financial factor may well be the most important force for public interest in accountability for higher education. Higher education increasingly plays a role as a major economic force in its own right within individual communities and states, and it functions as an important contributor to the economic success of the private sector and government through its provision of trained personnel. Since the end of World War II, higher education leaders have successfully argued that investments in higher education would pay off in manifold public benefits. State governments and the federal government, along with many foundations and individuals, have contributed huge sums to the development of the higher education enterprise. In the past, the value generated by these investments in higher education had been assumed to be realized by the recipients of the education, and then were transformed into important contributions to society and the economy. Under that model, the accountability indicators of student access to higher education and the number of graduates produced were suitable tests of success of the system.

With the challenge to our ranking among the economies of the world, however, the argument for increased investments in higher education shifted to emphasizing its importance as a strategic investment. In forcefully presenting that economic argument, higher education frequently described itself as a "bargain." Hence, it should come as no surprise that, ultimately, the customers of that "bargain" now wish to determine what they really have received for all those investments.

The political momentum for accountability in higher education appears to be on the increase. Recognizing that atmosphere, we first need to determine if the better strategy is to allow that momentum for accountability to take its natural course and react to each crisis situation, or to become proactive and to tackle the challenge of accountability directly. It is my contention that the proactive course is the best possible tactic to preserve academic freedom.

Accountability and assessment are not new forces within higher education. The United States has had a uniquely voluntary system of accountability for many years through the regional accrediting associations. These associations (such as the North Central Association to which the UW–Madison belongs) were purposefully developed, with major involvement of higher education, to be neutral and objective guarantors of the quality of the academic product. The analyses conducted by these accrediting associations as part of periodic reviews were based largely on input measures such as library holdings, numbers of faculty with Ph.D.'s, admission standards for students, etc., and on the innate academic good sense of the diversified visiting teams. Since these teams were composed of professors and administrators, the recommendations of the accreditation report could be readily understood by the institution.

This process worked quite well and was suited nicely to the growth era of the first three decades after World War II. By the mid–1980s, however, there were the stirrings of the winds of change described earlier. One of the first challenges directed at higher education was the degree to which universities engaged in professional management of their existing resources and in long-term planning. Proposals for higher education to engage in strategic planning came from many quarters and, in Wisconsin, from a report by a Board of Regents Study Group on the future of the UW System.[4] This new language reflected a new style, and was an early challenge along this path of accountability.

The UW–Madison prepared to undertake its decennial self-study for the North Central Association in the mid–1980s. The administration, in consultation with faculty governance leadership, concluded that it needed a Future Directions Committee to provide a set of ideas to guide the institution. Of special significance to the undertaking was the agreement with the North Central Association that the report of this committee would constitute the main contribution to the self-study requirement.

The Future Directions Committee engaged in an environmental scanning process as part of its strategic planning efforts; i.e., it sought to identify the major futuristic societal trends that could conceivably have an impact on the academic enterprise. Since the mood for accountability and the demands for measures of educational outcomes (i.e., assessment) were two of the trends identified, the committee gave attention to these concerns. A section on "Educational Outcomes" resulted. In introducing that section, the committee wrote:

> The ultimate test of any university's effectiveness is the difference it makes in the world it touches. The successful products are well-educated citizens, increased knowledge, and practical benefits to society. Unfortunately, too many products of higher education in the United States cannot be proclaimed successful. Although some people have questioned the value of research or the benefits of service, what concerns them most is the performance of students. Many attribute poor performance to inadequate or misguided educational objectives and poor instruction. Many others recognize that the causes of the problem are far more complex. To a greater or lesser extent, everyone agrees there is a problem, and many have attempted to find a solution.[5]

The key element in this statement, certainly with regard to this discussion about assessment, is the acknowledgment that ". . . too many products of higher education . . . cannot be proclaimed successful." Until these last two decades, the academy was left almost entirely on its own to define the terms of student success. Within this understanding, higher education proceeded to convince itself that whatever it defined in course instruction was *ipso facto* important and of the highest quality because of the inherent good sense of the profession. Consequently, when students had passed a certain number of these courses and were awarded a university baccalaureate, the public could and should rest assured that the basic ingredients for these graduates to succeed, sometimes at almost any imaginable career, had been provided to them by the academy.

Now the assumption that quality is defined as what is outlined in the institutional catalog and enhanced by input features, such as Ph.D.'s for the faculty and numbers of volumes in the library, is being challenged. As noted earlier, selling the merits of higher education at least in part on its economic contributions led buyers of those products to begin asking questions. Peter Ewell, a senior associate at the National Center for Higher Education Management Systems in Colorado, has become one of the chief interpreters of this evolution in public thought. As he noted recently in a keynote address to the North Central Association, "The time is long past when we [higher education] will be allowed to assess success only against goals that we ourselves establish."[6] Consequently, not only will higher education be held accountable for achieving its goals, but the setting of those goals and the design of the measurements to ascertain their success will be matters for public consultation and involvement as well.

There is a need for widespread faculty discussion of the essence of this new challenge. Braskamp and Ory have addressed this in their new work, *Assessing Faculty Work*,

> Faculty work under the principles of tenure and academic freedom, and thus they enjoy many individual rights. Society has given them its trust and considerable freedom to pursue their own work, needs, and interests. They have numerous opportunities to grow and develop. But society is also voicing more loudly the claim that faculty have a social responsibility to their institution and to the larger community. Being responsive, responsible, and accountable is part of the social contract that faculty make with society to justify its trust."[7]

A profession is granted status by the public through a grant of faith that the ethics of the profession are conducted as proclaimed. Medicine has been an accepted profession for years because of public faith that doctors are faithful to the Hippocratic Oath and will conduct themselves accordingly. It may well be that the academic profession needs to create its own version of that oath for the twenty-first century. Some calls for accountability have included a concern about the workload of faculty. We certainly do not want to open that item for discussion in this forum. However, it is helpful to recognize that if there is skepticism on this issue, albeit often because of lack of full knowledge about how faculty work, that skepticism may well increase as various forms of technology make it possible for faculty to be fully operational with their research and their students almost without ever setting foot in the classroom. The point is that timely consideration of an appropriate code of professional ethics to meet the challenge of the new century may be a worthwhile endeavor for the academic profession.

Throughout this paper, a recurring theme has been the increasing demand by the public to be heard regarding the quality of the products of higher education, primarily with a focus on undergraduate students. A related concept is that the push for clarification of academic freedom, which began in the 1890s and reached national fruition in the historic statement on academic freedom by the American Association of University Professors, coincided with the shift of the university from a civic enterprise in touch with its communities to its current emphasis on research conducted by highly specialized faculty members who probe ever deeper within the confines of their disciplines. According to this interpretation by historian Thomas Bender, that shift helped to create a bifold definition of truth, which Bender maintains is best described by Hannah Arendt in an article entitled "Truth and Politics," as a distinction between academic truth and political truth. In this perspective, the academy began to see itself as possessing a higher order of truth while the body politic operated at a distinctly lower order of truth.[8]

Bender believes that the academy's perception of this hierarchy of truth has been an unhealthy concept for the flourishing of knowledge and democracy in the age of the university. He suggests that John Dewey offered a more helpful theory because Dewey saw the need for a participatory community of truth makers searching for ever more secure but never completely secure truths. In such a search, there is no basis for a distinction between academic truth and political truth. "Politics and inquiry converge in the quest for better truths," states Bender. "Such a notion of truth may make us uneasy—both as academics and as citizens—but it may also make it easier for us to be at once academics and citizens in a democracy."[9]

Bender's analysis suggests a new approach to the question of the most suitable academic response to the cry for accountability. Precisely because higher education in this country has produced such a significant number of baccalaureates who are leaders in all fields, the academy has far less of a monopoly on the relentless search for truth, if indeed it was ever entitled to that self-perception. Talented people in many walks of life are also part of the learning enterprise and want to be acknowledged as such. The pace of technology in our lives, as an example of one force for change, is already so significant that every college graduate can now expect to need fairly frequent doses of continuing education to maintain a successful career.

Higher education is challenged to continuously improve its traditional forms of education while also creating quality in continuing education. Recognition of this challenge, often seen more clearly by those outside the academy than by those within it, is a major reason for the call for accountability. By developing student outcomes assessment measures, universities can provide a positive response to this call.

That call also includes a legitimate aspiration to develop new forms of partnership in the learning enterprise. Partnership is a concept under much discussion at this time. For example, several federal agencies award research grants only if the research is done in combination with enterprises in the private sector. This is just one manifestation of the use of funding power to force academics to consider changes in the way we conduct the business of the learning enterprise.

It is important to consider the part higher education plays in this learning enterprise. While the universities can debate about the percentage of that enterprise they represent, the focus should really be on the implications of the word "learning." Learning does suggest a two-way street, since wisdom tells us that we can learn in many different formats, not solely those within the comfort zones of our research disciplines. During this century, opportunities for higher education have been offered to a significant portion of our citizenry. Professors have an opportunity to learn from those who once occupied their classroom chairs as well as from colleagues within their disciplines. The return of many older adults to our undergraduate classrooms, as one demonstration of this effect, has been generally welcomed and well received by our faculty. But in the future, the vehicle of technology will also make it possible for many private enterprises to actively engage in teaching. We can either find ways to work with those new academic entrepreneurs, or we can meet them as competitors at various points in the academic marketplace.

The late Ernest Boyer, while president of the Carnegie Foundation for the Advancement of Teaching, challenged his colleagues in higher education to create a new focus to our basic mission by suggesting terms he found more descriptive than the traditional "teaching," "research," and "service." He proposed these terms: the scholarship of discovery, the scholarship of integration, the scholarship of application, and the scholarship of teaching.[10] The UW–Madison administration has taken the lead from Boyer and is proposing that we use a succinct working mission statement:[11] to create, integrate, apply, and teach.

At the University of Wisconsin–Madison, we celebrate the concept of "the Wisconsin Idea," which, along with the sifting and winnowing concept, also was developed at the turn of the last century. The Wisconsin Idea proclaims that there are no borders of access to knowledge at the physical edges of this campus, that we are committed to spreading knowledge to all corners of the state.

It is fitting that, as we prepare to enter a new century, the Wisconsin Idea should also be upgraded to describe the challenges of the future. It is fairly obvious that the original state boundaries are now more appropriately seen as global borders. It is equally important for a more broadly inclusive concept of the learning enterprise to be incorporated into the Wisconsin Idea. We have used terms such as "extension" and "outreach" to describe the flow of knowledge from the university to the public. We must recognize that there is also a flow of knowledge that can move from the public to the university if we open our doors to it. We need to acknowledge the significant pools of knowledge outside the university, as for example in public libraries and museums, federal research laboratories, and corporations of all shapes and sizes. We need to recognize that technology offers an opportunity to integrate these knowledge centers in a realigned learning enterprise for the twenty-first century. We have much to gain by listening and learning to interested citizens and leaders from all parts of the state and world.

We should consider a solution that both addresses an appropriate response to the calls for accountability and at the same time updates the Wisconsin Idea. We can do that by embracing the notion that **listening** is an equal part of a university's mission as it ventures into a new century.

A positive response to the demand for accountability and assessment, accomplished through a combination of creative initiative and good listening, will do much to help us restore public confidence in higher education. Engaging in a mutual discussion gives us the opportunity to demonstrate the value and necessity for academic freedom within the academy itself. We have no need to operate behind walls without an opportunity for public input. Completing the tasks of assessment and accountability publicly is the best way to preserve a future in which academic freedom is a recognized right of faculty, who carry out public responsibilities that can be ensured only with that protection.

Appendix:
The National Educational Goals

By the year 2000:

1. All children in America will start school ready to learn.

2. The high school graduation rate will increase to at least 90 percent.

3. American students will leave grades four, eight, and twelve having demonstrated competency in challenging subject matter including English, mathematics, science, history, and geography; and every school in America will ensure that all students learn to use their minds well, so they may be prepared for responsible citizenship, further learning, and productive employment in our modern economy.

4. U.S. students will be first in the world in science and mathematics achievement.

5. Every adult American will be literate and will possess the knowledge and skills necessary to compete in a global economy and exercise the rights and responsibilities of citizenship.

6. Every school in America will be free of drugs and violence and will offer a disciplined environment conducive to learning.

From: U.S. Department of Education. *America 2000*. Washington, D.C., 1991, p. 3.

Notes

1. Board of Regents, University of Wisconsin, 1894.

2. National Commission on Excellence in Education, *A Nation at Risk* (Washington D.C.: Government Printing Office, 1983).

3. Department of Education, *America 2000: An Education Strategy* (Washington D.C.: Department of Education, 1991).

4. Board of Regents of the University of Wisconsin System, "Planning the Future" (Madison: 1986).

5. Future Directions Committee of UW–Madison, *Self-Study for the North Central Association of Colleges and Schools, 1* (1988), p. 62.

6. Peter T. Ewell, "Regaining Our Balance: Accreditation and the Academy in an Uncertain World," (paper read as a keynote speech to the 99th Annual Meeting of the North Central Association, March 1994).

7. Larry A. Braskamp, and John C. Ory, *Assessing Faculty Work* (San Francisco: Jossey-Bass Publishers, 1994), p. xiii.

8. Thomas Bender, *Intellect and Public Life: Essays on the Social History of Academic Intellectuals in the United States* (Baltimore: Johns Hopkins University Press, 1993), p. 127.

9. Ibid., p. 139.

10. Ernest L. Boyer, *Scholarship Reconsidered: Priorities of the Professoriate* (Princeton: Carnegie Foundation for the Advancement of Teaching, 1990), pp. 17–25.

11. The comprehensive mission statement developed in 1988 and approved by the Board of Regents remains the official, complete version of the UW–Madison mission.

Challenges to Research Independence for Faculty

ROBERT AUERBACH

I wish to begin my remarks on freedom of inquiry among scientists at the University of Wisconsin by reading the following advertisements that appeared in a recent issue of *Science:*

> Assistant Professor, Molecular Biology . . . Applicants are expected to develop an independent research program with extramural funding.

> Faculty position—macrophyte ecology . . . Responsibilities include establishing a strong, externally funded research program.

> Faculty positions in biology . . .Two assistant professors . . . in plant sciences . . . [must have] evidence of potential to develop an independent, vigorous, externally funded research program.

These are typical of current advertisements for the recruitment of faculty in the physical and biological sciences. Such a requirement, the capability of raising grant money from outside sources, for new faculty in literature or political science or music is virtually unheard of.

The fact is that, unlike literature, history, political science, or music, scientists in the present era must have large sums of money to pursue their inquiries. To outfit a laboratory for an incoming faculty member in the biomedical sciences, even on a minimal level, will cost $150,000. To carry out even very simple experiments, one needs incubators, centrifuges, and microscopes. For modern research in molecular biology or immunology, the reagents cost tens of thousands of dollars a year, equipment runs into the hundreds of thousands, and ample technical assistance is essential. Without great sums of money, scientists cannot make even simple inquiries.

With this as background, the question I want to discuss is: Does the need for research funding exact a price in terms of academic freedom? I would answer "yes." The source of the funds, how it is awarded, and lately, the scarcity of those funds, all affect the freedom of academic scientists to follow their own ideas.

Robert Auerbach is Harold R. Wolfe Professor of Zoology at the University of Wisconsin–Madison.

In earlier eras, academic scientists were funded primarily by their universities. When I came to Madison, for example, the College of Letters and Sciences gave me an unlimited Fund 101 supply budget, and the Wisconsin Alumni Research Foundation was always ready to provide matching funds and backup insurance. But the sums needed were much more modest then. The university or donors to the university paid for the instruments, and, by and large, we were free to pursue our questions. Departments honored our freedom. We were beholden primarily to the university.

Gradually the nature of research changed. More and more, huge amounts of government funds were needed to accomplish national technological and scientific goals; the space program, the supercollider, and million-volt microscopes, such as the one built here in Madison, are examples. The government began to take an increasingly large role in the financing of university-based research through the National Institutes of Health, the National Science Foundation, and several government agencies. Scientists began competing for these monies. They were awarded funds depending, in large measure, on peer review, and the university had very little to do with it. Millions and millions of dollars poured into the universities so that now more money comes to us from grants than from tuition. The success of the academic scientist now depends on the opinions of outsiders and the funds of outside agencies.

Does the old maxim, "He who pays the piper calls the tune," not inevitably come to play here? We had a "War on Cancer," and funds were shifted and targeted for this subject. Immediately biomedical scientists tried to figure out how they could shape their research interests so that their questions involved cancer. The same calling of the tune is now in play with AIDS research and the Human Genome Project. Indeed, there are increasing numbers of so-called "Requests for Applications," where funding decisions in narrowly defined areas of research are now made by program officers of government agencies rather than through peer review.

Many scientists believe that such targeted research does not work well.

William Paul, newly appointed director of the AIDS research program of the National Institutes of Health, stated at last month's International AIDS Conference in Yokohama that he intends to steer more money in the direction of basic research.

Bernard Field, a noted Harvard molecular virologist, commenting in *Nature*, the most prestigious general journal in the biological sciences, makes the same point in discussing AIDS-targeted research: "We must not compromise research in other areas of basic science at the expense of these directed programs."

And, Baruch Blumberg, a Nobel laureate in the physiology of medicine, said: "We could not have planned the investigation at its beginning to find the cause of hepatitis B. This experience does not encourage the approach to research which is based exclusively on goal-oriented programs."

I believe most thoughtful scientists today feel that fundamental inquiries, where the individual investigators are allowed to follow their own ideas, are more likely to lead to progress. Thus, both the source of funds and how they are distributed affect freedom of inquiry.

Lately, the scarcity of funds affects freedom of inquiry in a most depressing way. A recently completed study by the National Research Council showed that the number of young scientists under the age of 36 applying for grants from the National Institutes of Health fell 54 percent in the last eight years—from more than 3,000 to fewer than 1,400. In addition, success rates were also greater in 1986: one third then but only one fifth by 1993. Thus, funding by the National Institutes of Health that was obtained by more than 1,000 young scientists in 1986 went to fewer than 300 in 1993.

Even grant programs designed specifically for junior scientists, such as FIRST awards, now have an extremely low funding rate and require extensive preliminary data that cannot be obtained without prior financial support. Young scientists are put in the position of soliciting industry sponsors—with their own business objectives—or joining an ongoing program in which a senior scientist has outlined the project and controls the funds. Success is measured in months, not years or decades; thus orthodoxy is promoted. The late UW–Madison Nobel laureate Howard Temin, when he came to Madison as a young, unknown scientist, would, in the present research climate, not have been funded. Were he to have held stubbornly to his idea of reverse transcription—the antithesis of the central dogma of molecular biology of the 1960s—he would quite likely not have received tenure.

Both individual academic scientists and the general public lose, I believe, by the fact that highly trained, intelligent, imaginative, eager scientists can no longer follow their questions in freedom. American scientists were envied throughout the world because of their freedom to pursue their ideas. The success of American science was attributed to the fact that junior scientists did not have to do the bidding of the conservative and tradition-bound Herr Professor on the German model, but could follow their inquiry freely, "untrammeled by limitations." That era now appears to be gone.

Challenges from Intellectual Property Rights

Janet L. Greger

S eeking knowledge and publishing important findings has always required wisdom and leadership. Because of the large successes and occasional mistakes made at academic institutions during the last twenty years, federal and state governments have implemented many procedural and policy reforms. Some of these, like the Bayh-Dole Act in 1984, have encouraged university-industry interactions by facilitating technology transfer. Some, like the current proposed regulations on research integrity, force academicians to forgo a certain degree of privacy to gain the funds they need in order to continue their sifting and winnowing activities in research and teaching.

The Panel on Scientific Responsibility and the Conduct of Research of the National Academy of Science stated in a 1992 report that "inflexible rules or requirements (on scientific ethics and university-industry relations) can increase the time and effort necessary to conduct research, can discourage creative individuals from pursuing research careers, decrease innovations, and can in some instances make the research process impossible" (p. 12). This statement emphasizes the importance of having a large and diverse group of academicians participate in discussions about intellectual property rights if balanced decisions are to be achieved.

Three important points need to be examined in particular. They will be covered in the sections that follow.

1. Do patents augment or hinder dissemination of knowledge to the public?

Recent congressional hearings demonstrated that at least some elected officials believe that inventions resulting from federally funded research should be dedicated to the public. At first glance you might think that publishing the details of the invention in literature makes it available to the public. In reality, taxpayers benefit most from academic research when inventions are patented. New drugs are a good example. If the invention was made known to the pub-

---

Janet L. Greger is professor of nutritional science, and associate dean of the Graduate School at the University of Wisconsin–Madison.

lic through publication, no commercial firm would devote extensive resources to developing the first commercial application, knowing that any of their competitors can step in and reap the profits of commercial exploitation once the invention has been proven. Patents and the seventeen-year exclusive position they provide to the inventor, or to the inventor's designee, are necessary for successful commercial development of inventions.

2. Do patents slow the publication process?

To obtain a patent, the inventor must fully disclose his or her invention. Thus, in some ways the act of patenting *ensures* publication. At the same time, publication of the details of an invention prior to filing a patent application can result in the loss of patent rights in most countries. However, in the U.S., an inventor can obtain a patent if a patent application is filed within one year of the date of the public disclosure (i.e., poster presentation or manuscript publication).

Because multiple patents are generally necessary to protect most work, scientists who think that their work is patentable should talk to staff at the University–Industry Relations (UIR) or Wisconsin Alumni Research Foundation (WARF) and make an invention disclosure report before they make a public presentation.

Some scientists are concerned that the desire to obtain protection may cause publication to be delayed for long periods, thus slowing scientific progress. While this may be true in industry, it generally does not appear to occur in academia. When delays occur, they are usually for less than three months.

3. Monitoring academic rights in university/industry collaborative projects

As states supply ever smaller percentages of funds to support research and teaching at universities, faculty increasingly turn to industry and industry consortia for funds. In many cases, faculty eager for funds view administrative procedures as problems, not protection, for their academic rights. Faculty and universities should be concerned about these three contractual principles:

a. Faculty and staff are expected to conduct research on a reasonable-effort basis. That means University of Wisconsin–Madison cannot accept contract provisions that impose penalties for failure to make progress or contracts that provide for withholding payment if the sponsor is not satisfied with results.

b. The UW does not knowingly enter into research agreements that involve commitments and conflicts with those accepted under other agreements. That means faculty and staff cannot relinquish all patent rights to an industry sponsor if their research is cosponsored by federal agencies that require all disclosures must be to WARF.

c. To fulfill its mission to disseminate research results, the UW–Madison cannot allow investigators to undertake studies that cannot be freely published. In recognition of industrial sponsors needing to protect proprietary information, and at the request of researchers, UW–Madison will enter contracts that allow sponsors to ask for a limited delay of publication, usually thirty days.

It is amazing how often faculty complain about the UW–Madison's adherence to these principles when contracts are being negotiated but how thankful they are later for these safeguards to their academic freedom.

One other area of university-industry relations that is becoming increasingly troublesome concerns the biological transfer of material agreements. These, in essence, were designed originally like patents, to protect ownership of material but allow for widespread dissemination of materials. The UW–Madison does not insist or strongly encourage, as many institutions do, the UW faculty and staff to utilize these documents to protect their rights. However, the agreements UW–Madison faculty and staff are being asked to sign are sometimes alarming. Some agreements not only protect the material in question and its direct derivatives but would prevent UW–Madison faculty and staff from licensing new substances developed while using the original material. In essence, faculty are being asked to sign away their academic rights and those of the federal agency that is sponsoring the research. Last year, one company demanded such extreme losses of rights in return for use of their materials that lawyers from Legal Services, the WARF patent attorney, and Graduate School deans met with faculty to advise them on their options before they proceeded.

A final area of concern in achieving balance between the right of faculty and staff to seek knowledge and the rights of the community at large involves conflicts of interest and data ownership. Of particular concern are occasions when faculty have reportable outside activities that involve ownership or control of more than 10 percent of a property that does business in the faculty members' area of research and teaching. These concerns will be explored at an ad hoc faculty committee this fall.

In summary, although discussions concerning intellectual property rights and research integrity have many controversial aspects, they really benefit us all by encouraging faculty and staff to continually evaluate and reaffirm the UW sifting and winnowing statement.

PART 5

A Reappraisal of
Sifting and Winnowing

Sifting and Winnowing: An Insider's View

PHILLIP R. CERTAIN

One of the greatest joys of being dean of the College of Letters and Science is the opportunity to bask in the reflected glory of so many others. E. A. Birge, our first dean, was in office when the Ely trial took place; I'm not sure at all what role he played. But for me to be dean on the 100th anniversary is both an honor and a humbling experience. And it is a challenge to reflect, along with my colleagues, on what "sifting and winnowing" means for us today.

My task is to react to the previous speakers and to reflect on whether "sifting and winnowing" is alive and well in today's university. Let me say that, in my opinion, it is as alive today as it ever has been. Students can explore widely our rich curriculum. Our faculty may be under scrutiny for the balance between teaching and research, but the content of teaching is usually not seriously threatened. As Dr. Corry has explained, even public demands for assessment and accountability can strengthen academic freedom, not destroy it.

But the struggle for academic freedom is never over. As Professor Szybalski discussed, powerful external forces do exist to impede free inquiry in some areas of research, particularly areas of scientific research with significant ethical implications. Professor Auerbach's and Dean Greger's contribution demonstrated the pernicious effects of extramural funding of academic freedom and research.

Nevertheless, in my opinion, the forces working against sifting and winnowing are not so much overt as covert, not so much without as within.

When I entered college in the heart of the Bible Belt in 1960, a faculty member told us during new-student orientation that we would have our religious beliefs challenged not directly, but rather because we would find that they were irrelevant to our college work. Likewise, I wonder if our feeling that academic freedom is relatively secure is because our academic discourses are often irrelevant to the larger world we live in.

Phillip R. Certain is professor of chemistry, and dean of the College of Letters and Science at the University of Wisconsin–Madison.

Dean Cronon assures me that the film we saw on the Ely trial was bad history, but nevertheless it did show that academic freedom protected Ely's ability to participate in and criticize the great social issue of his day. Now, unfortunately, very often we use academic freedom as a barrier that gives us permission to turn inward, away from the problems of society.

So in my remarks I want to focus both on some of the successes of academic freedom and on the barriers I see to a fuller enjoyment of our rich heritage.

But first, let us deconstruct the phrase: "fearless sifting and winnowing by which alone the truth can be found."

Fearless

This word brings to mind a person of integrity who searches out the truth regardless of criticism from peers or from persons in other positions of authority. This is the picture we have of Ely. Surely there are many scholars in the university who can be said to be fearless, some of whom have spoken at this conference. Another is Professor Don Kettl of the Political Science Department and the La Follette Institute, who has authored a critique of the Clinton administration's "Reinventing Government" program, and thereby gained national notoriety.

Students are often limited, however, in their search for the truth by their concern for future careers; the same can be said of some faculty. So long as the primary questions are: will this be on the final exam?; will this course help me get a good job?; will this project help me get tenure?; will this help me in this year's departmental merit exercise?—we cannot be said to be fearless in our search for truth. In fact, to the extent that these questions dominate our discourses, we can go no further in understanding this noble endorsement of academic freedom and we will have no freedom worth defending.

Sifting and Winnowing

This agricultural phrase means as much to most of today's students as a "governor on a steam engine." One hundred years ago, this was vivid imagery for the process of separating the valuable wheat from the worthless chaff. The point is: it takes a lot of chaff to obtain a little grain, and it takes a lot of false starts and dead-end searches to discover a bit of truth.

One small historical addendum, since it hasn't been mentioned by any of the previous speakers. In 1922, Liz Waters, who at that time was a person (actually a Fond du Lac high school teacher and a regent), not a dormitory, proposed in a report of the Committee on Student Life and Interests that the regents should agree that the sifting and winnowing statement applied both to teaching in the classroom and to the use of university lecture halls for public addresses. The regents adopted this statement. It was not an empty assertion, because later in the 1930s a group of students disrupted a public lecture in the Law School and threw the out-of-town speaker into Lake Mendota! This gave Dean Sellery the opportunity to express a stirring defense of academic freedom. You can read the details in the forthcoming history of the UW written by Dean Cronon and John Jenkins.

Truth Can Be Found

This is the hardest phrase in our famous statement. Our understanding of "truth" is much more complex and tentative than it was in 1894. Is truth something out there to be found, or is it an invention of the human intellect? If it is the latter, can we say that there is any "truth" at all?

Universities are places where intelligent people experiment with ideas and adopt very diverse stances and poses. There are indeed intellectual fashions, some of which open new paths, others of which fade away. This is part of the sifting and winnowing process. One of our privileges and responsibilities to explore "truth" within the relatively protected environment of the university is that we don't always have to make immediate "sense" in accord with the prevailing views of society at the moment. We can ask "what if" questions and seriously entertain and explore the intellectual and philosophical consequences of our tentative answers. Some of those questions and answers will become part of what we call knowledge; others will be set aside and not considered again. But the important point is that the outcome will be reached because we, as teachers and as students, have been able to think, experiment, write, and discuss our way through those questions.

In recent years, one extreme position has been to assert that there is no such thing as "truth," or at least that truth is relative at best. Adherents to this view argue that "truth" is a construct developed within specific historical, social, and cultural contexts; and this is true in fields ranging from literature (what is the true meaning of a Wordsworth poem?), through history (what really happened in the Ely case?), and even into the natural sciences (in the famous "two slit" experiment, does the electron travel through the left slit or the right?). In every field, the choice of research topics and the accepted norms of discourse are influenced by the race, culture, and gender of the scholar and this, it is claimed, makes it hopeless to determine the absolute truth or falsity of any statement. Some would argue that it is all a matter of who has the power to make certain "truths" stick.

It is of course a logical paradox to assert the truth that there is *no* truth. Even if one does not take this extreme position, it can be claimed that there are many kinds of truth: there is the deductive truth of mathematical reasoning, the inductive truth of scientific theories, and the relative truth of humanistic interpretations. The plurality of truths can lead, by this analysis, to a plurality of noncommunicating disciplines: C. P. Snow's *Two Cultures* run amok. One of our greatest challenges as scholars is to learn how to speak to each other through the disciplinary walls we have built.

Although perhaps out of intellectual fashion, I would still argue that the university is engaged in a search for truth: for what really is, for what really happened, for what something really means. This is a never-ending quest, and since the university is a very human enterprise, the questions that are asked and the methods that are used will change significantly over time. Yet being part of the university, I think, is to agree to be part of the search, to be a member of the community of scholars. It also means to agree to try to understand what all the other members of the community are looking for as well. The poetic understanding of a sunset can stand coequal to its scientific understanding; both have validity without co-opting each other's methodologies. We are all in the business of trying to understand, and while we often make mistakes, or fail to make proper distinctions, or overlook pieces of evidence, this does not deny that there is something out there that we are looking for.

Let us turn now to three barriers to the exercise of academic freedom. Surely there are more than three, but I would identify these as particularly relevant to UW–Madison: arrogance, apathy, and anonymity.

Arrogance

Simply put, this barrier is erected by scholars—students and faculty alike—who say: my way is right and is the only way. In the hands of a compelling personality, this sometimes works to stimulate students to think about subjects in new ways, perhaps in extreme opposition to the teacher. Unfortunately, intellectual arrogance on the part of the teacher more often just encourages the student to figure out what the teacher wants and give it to him or her in discussions, papers, and examinations.

Mr. Kotwicki's paper reinforces this point: "Regardless of university ideals, professors' evaluations of students' performances may reflect the degree to which the authority figures agree or disagree with the pupils' beliefs. To promote academic freedom in the classroom, professors must not use grades as weapons to polarize thoughts."

Sometimes, an entire discipline can be arrogant, claiming a special hold on the truth. In my own beloved field of quantum mechanics, which has been phenomenally successful in the twentieth century in explaining and relating many properties of molecules, the founder of the field, Erwin Schroedinger, stated "The new science arrogates the right to bully our entire philosophical outlook." Even though he discovered (invented?) quantum theory, he was profoundly disturbed by the doubt it cast upon his understanding of the truth.

Perhaps the success of scientific theory has bullied the philosophical outlook of many fields outside of the ancient sciences of mathematics, physics, and chemistry. To have respectability, practitioners in many fields seem to believe that their field must be theoretically based. As a theoretical chemist, I can only observe that the pretheoretical intellectual history of the sciences was quite long. As late as the eighteenth century some quite silly theories of chemistry were all the vogue, and even when I entered college, my own field of theoretical chemistry was not firmly established. This is not to say that people should not try to establish theories in any field, but the attempts should be modest, and the field should not be dominated by theory too soon.

Hear this warning from Einstein, given in 1922:

The theorist in the natural sciences is not to be envied, since Nature is a merciless judge of his work. She never says "yes" to a theory; at best "perhaps"; in most cases flatly "no." Every theory is bound to meet its "no" sooner or later, often very quickly after conception.

And what is the antidote to arrogance? Quite simply, it is humility. It is the ability to listen to others; it is the ability to be passionate about one's beliefs while receiving joy and stimulation from others whose ideas are completely different. The theoretician and the observer and the creator should all listen to one another. In all fields, they all have something valuable to say.

The notion that we are shaped by our cultural, historical, and even linguistic assumptions and contexts does not mean that truth is impossible, but is does put certain—and perhaps not always utterly knowable—parameters on that truth. It means that our ideas about truth are not necessarily transcendent, universal, true for all time, or able to describe what really happened. It means that our ideas about truth are inherently tentative.

Let me say that there is an institutional arrogance, too, that impedes the sifting and winnowing of ideas and issues in the 1990s, and that has to do with the lack of diversity among our faculty, staff, and students. It is important to emphasize that I am scolding the institution of which I am a part. So I am scolding myself. In his speech to us last March, President Carter said that the most threatening problem facing the world today is the growing separation between the rich and the poor. It is no criticism of the organizers of this conference to ask the question: how would the discourse have been different if the podium and the audience had not been mostly white, upper-middle class folk well-schooled in polite academic discourse.

It is very easy for us to be for diversity when the budget is flush; it will be much harder to be for it in the uncertain days ahead. But history is on the side of diversity. For those who may think that higher education was perfected sometime in the past, probably about the time of their sophomore year, let me remind us all that the students in Ely's time, as in our own, are students that were excluded by the private schools of the east. The Morrill Act opened up higher education to thousands of Wisconsin farm kids. I can imagine the "tut tuting" that went on in the halls of Harvard, Princeton, and Yale when this occurred. But today, the great public universities of the Midwest are at least co-equal to these former bastions of all learning. So just as the nation has gained from the participation of the farm kids of the Midwest, so will the nation benefit from the students presently excluded, no matter what the reason.

Apathy

If the previous barrier of arrogance is found mostly in some faculty, this barrier is raised mostly by some students. Is there fearless sifting and winnowing when the weekend runs from Thursday through Sunday nights? When the reason for all academic activity is the grade and not what is learned? When students sit passively through their classes?

Again, let me quote Mr. Kotwicki: "Few undergraduate students believe they are capable of challenging entrenched ideals, safe to speak out against the norm, or even smart enough to reach new, valid conclusions."

There are positive signs, however. Students of many backgrounds are getting involved in undergraduate research. The Honors Programs is growing even as the qualifications of the incoming classes increase. The challenge for the faculty is to make sure that these experiences are not just vita-building on the part of the students, but rather experiences where the student comes face to face with a bit of truth known at first only to the professor.

Anonymity

This is an institutional problem: the problem of a large university and the problem of large lectures. It is not an inevitable problem, nor is it one that cannot be overcome. But the lecture hall of four hundred anonymous students being lectured to by an anonymous teacher is not an environment for fearless sifting and winnowing.

Largeness does not necessarily mean anonymity; there are professors in our university who can hold the largest class in rapt attention. And smallness does not guarantee intimacy; it all has to do with the attitudes of the teacher and the learners.

Here again, there are positive developments at UW–Madison. There has been a growth in the number of small classes for freshmen taught by faculty. There has been a growth in the number of capstone seminars for seniors. And now after more than fifty years, there is in the works something of a revival of the Experimental College of Miekeljohn. Next year, in one of the Lakeshore Dorms, freshmen will have the opportunity to participate in a learning community with faculty, centered around the themes of liberal education.

As a final example, I point to the Wisconsin Emerging Scholars program in the department of mathematics. This is a calculus course aimed at high-ability women, minority students, and all students from rural Wisconsin high schools. Experience shows that even though these students have excellent high school records, they are likely to do poorly in the calculus sequence. The Emerging Scholars program treats these students as scholars, and encourages them to work *harder* than the ordinary student, and to work *harder* problems. The students attend the same lectures as all students and take the same exams, but they work cooperatively rather than competitively on their homework problems. What has the experience been? In its first year, by the end of the second semester, the two WES sections finished first and second among all calculus sections as measured by course grades. The chance of this happening randomly is one in a thousand.

Let me close by saying that I am a chemist, not a philosopher. My comments today are grounded in the practical workaday world, not in deep study and contemplation. You may have noticed a curious mixture of conservatism and liberalism in what I have had to say. I make no apologies. We should always be holding onto the past while groping for an uncertain future. I have benefitted from the comments of colleagues in South Hall and on the L&S Academic Planning Council. I would particularly like to thank Alex Nagel, Yvonne Ozzello, Peter Spear, Bernice Durand, and Mary Layoun for critiquing my remarks and providing insightful suggestions for improvements. My comments are my responsibility, of course, and my greatest hope is that some of you will disagree with what I've said. In that way, we will continue our wonderful tradition of sifting and winnowing.

Sifting and Winnowing: An Outsider's View

Mary Lou Munts

I t takes some temerity to speak at the end of this program as "the outsider." Actually I am something of a ringer because I am a University of Wisconsin Law School graduate, my husband received his Ph.D. in economics and taught here, and I was fortunate to represent many members of the university community in the Assembly.

My real discomfiture is that I am the only one without written remarks. When Lee Hansen asked me to speak, I made it clear that I had no time to prepare remarks as I was going off to Europe. That fortunately permits me to be like a butterfly that can flit around among the flowers. I have been fortunate to be able to be here for the remarkable trip of one hundred years, so I will be reacting to more than just the last speakers.

To begin at the beginning, just a few comments on the lessons and legacy of Richard Ely. It was well said that Ely would have had to be invented if he had not existed. Without him there would have been no sifting and winnowing statement by the regents for us to celebrate. Particularly fascinating was the speakers' examination of Ely's clay feet. He did not fit the televised portrayal in *Profile of Courage*; he was a rather arrogant man who did not encourage sifting and winnowing by his students.

Further, Ely was hardly a model defender of academic freedom, as he completely denied the charges against him, never forthrightly joining the issue of his Christian socialist beliefs. Nonetheless the great historical significance of the regents' statement is that it went far beyond his individual case. Even if in part prompted by partisan motivation to discredit the democratic superintendent of public instruction, sifting and winnowing went on to have a life of its own.

My next landing is on the interesting paper of Robert Lampman and David Johnson on the falling out between Ely and John R. Commons, and the paper by John Buenker on the period from 1893–1915. They contradict to some extent, as far as Wisconsin is concerned, Professor Rader's use of

Mary Lou Munts is a former Wisconsin state legislator, and former chair of the Public Service Commission, State of Wisconsin.

Ely's career to illustrate the turning point in American universities from one of "civic culture" to the "professional culture." As Rader put it, "the fast-growing universities and their faculties seized upon professionalization and specialization as a way of carving out a bounded and protected space within American society. Unlike civic culture, their professional culture turned inward, away from the community."

What is striking to me as a newcomer to these materials is that although the trial marked the turning of Ely from the tradition of civic humanism to a more professional career, it was Commons and his followers who took on the mantle of reform. They initiated the other great theme of the university, the "Wisconsin Idea"—that the boundaries of the campus are the boundaries of the state.

These two great themes of sifting and winnowing and the Wisconsin Idea of public service to the state have made the University of Wisconsin unique. Because of the Wisconsin Idea, UW–Madison has been less turned inward than Professor Rader's typology would suggest. His civic ideal has continued to have life, although at tenure or promotion time the professional ideal counts more heavily.

It is the Wisconsin Idea that has won the intense loyalty of people like myself in public life who have valued the university because it valued the state. To the extent that this commitment has weakened, it has hurt the university. However, this tradition seems to renew itself in each generation as one precious memory of mine illustrates. When the battle for marital property reform was finally won after thirty-five years, I ran into Helen Groves, who came running up to hug me saying, "Oh, Mary Lou, I wish Harold were alive. It's just like unemployment compensation."

Helen Groves, just from reading the newspaper, had realized that marital property reform was in its own way the same revolution as the first unemployment law in the country, which was pioneered in 1932 by her husband, Harold Groves, economics department member and Progressive legislator. For me it was Professor June Weisberger of the Law School who brought the Wisconsin Idea to the other end of State Street. What she gave me was not only years of dedicated work but extraordinary professional competence as she perfected some forty-seven successive drafts. Her credibility was critical to softening the opposition of the legal community.

UW–Madison has continued to evolve a melding of the professional and civic ideals—and the twin themes of sifting and winnowing and the Wisconsin Idea. Professionalism has narrowed the focus and polished the lens. Without the research efforts of June Weisberger and the students she supervised, marital property reform would not have occurred.

Next I would like to pursue two themes Robert Haveman noted yesterday that have been constant over the last one hundred years. One was the continuing tension between state officials and the university. He could not have been more prescient. Next we went to Bascom Hill to hear James Klauser announce for the governor that the university was to be spared the exercise of doing a budget with cuts of five and ten percent.

It was quite extraordinary to have Klauser's comments made in the setting of a distinguished university audience, gathered for the purpose of rededicating the sifting and winnowing plaque. But it is important to recognize that his was a response to a public dialogue that has been going on about the possible impact of cuts on the university system budget to meet the billion-dollar state deficit looming as a result of the state's commitment to pick up two-thirds of school costs.

All of us in the audience realized how important David Ward, leading this university, and Katharine Lyall, the university system, have been in carrying on a dispassionate public and private dialogue that resulted in an equally reasoned response. David Ward in his remarks appropriately tied his ability to be vocal to the tradition this occasion celebrates. The long underpinning in Wisconsin of academic freedom contributes to the ability of university leadership to participate in public life and to the climate of the solution. This is not to say that further controversies do not lie ahead in this budget and forever more. But when reasoned dialogue rather than high rhetoric prevails, it is always a moment to celebrate.

The other long-term theme mentioned by Haveman was the skepticism of the faculty of advocacy efforts as opposed to professional pursuits. How do advocacy and public service differ? Is what June Weisberger did advocacy? Of course she advocated marital property reform, but her real role was to provide the research help and expertise to make a workable law. Here "advocacy" is an extension of professionalism at the same time that it is participation in the civic culture. Perhaps it would be useful to take a more self-conscious look at how the Wisconsin Idea and public service fit into today's research university both nationally and worldwide.

Because a great research university is so dependent on federal and foundation funding, the serious issues discussed by Professors Auerbach and

Greger add new dimensions to academic freedom that deserve much greater attention. The public policy issues raised urgently need to be addressed within the university in coalitions with the broader academic community. It is worth noting models like Bob Lampman and others who successfully sought major funding for the Institute for Research on Poverty so that faculty and graduate students could pursue their research interests on topics of social importance.

The panel on hate codes was an interesting discussion for an outsider about the permissibility or desirability of limitations on hate speech. However, these issues were not sufficiently tied to broader issues of university policy related to race, gender, and ethnicity. Therefore I was pleased that this morning both Phillip Certain and Joel Grossman addressed the responsibility of the university to respond internally to these major questions in our society. Here we come back again to the issue that will not die: the moral responsibility of the university, Professor Rader's civic ideal.

The discussion raised by Joseph Corry about accountability struck a chord. In my career in state government I heard bitter comments from faculty about what they regarded as unnecessary infringement on faculty decision-making. Greater power has shifted to deans, campus administration, and system administration in response to demands from the legislative and executive branches for greater accountability.

The strong tradition of faculty governance at Madison is heavily indebted to the early protection of academic freedom, and, reciprocally, faculty governance is the bedrock on which academic freedom will continue to exist. Because faculty governance operates at the grass roots, demands from above, no matter how legitimate, do not sit well. Yet if there is not understanding of legitimate needs for accountability, the university does not fare well. That is why I admire the David Cronons and Phillip Certains within the system who work with such infinite patience to try to sort out the legitimate from the Mickey Mouse requirements imposed from above. However, the campus generally would profit from a more active dialogue about these accountability issues and how they can best be accommodated while preserving the strength of faculty governance.

Last, but not least, I would like to comment on what Raymond Kotwicki said from a student perspective. I loved his question about how to get students involved in sifting and winnowing. Kotwicki is on target in asking for your help to bring sifting and winnowing into the classroom, especially into the large lectures. More broadly, the question is how you help students understand why sifting and winnowing is important in theory and how it is done in practice. You're pretty darn good role models, but you could be better.

PART 6

Rededicating the Sifting and Winnowing Plaque

Introductory Comments

DAVID WARD

I would like to extend a warm welcome to everyone joining us this after-noon and to all of those taking part in our two-day academic freedom con-ference. It is clear from the list of our panelists and participants and the range of challenging topics, that we are commemorating a shining moment in the history of this university, and, I also think, in higher education in the United States. We are observing the centennial of the sifting and winnowing procla-mation made by the University of Wisconsin Board of Regents in 1894—a strong and eloquent defense of the principles of academic freedom. This mes-sage is emblazoned on a bronze plaque installed in 1915 at the entrance of Bascom Hall. It is a symbol in which we can take great pride. It serves as a constant reminder of a principle at the core of this university's mission. The statement is often referred to as our magna carta, because it also reminds us of the need for vigilance in protecting academic freedom and the continual chal-lenge that our campus has faced in preserving that freedom.

Let me set the stage for this afternoon's ceremony by giving you a brief summary of the events that led to the creation of this landmark statement. In 1894 one of UW's leading scholars, economics professor Richard T. Ely, came under sharp attack by an ex officio member of the Board of Regents. Professor Ely was accused of having encouraged strikes in two Madison print-ing shops, of practicing boycotts against nonunion firms, and of teaching socialism and other dangerous theories in his classes and writings. Shortly afterward, a committee of three regents reviewing the charges held a hearing on the matter. Those proceedings resulted in not only the exoneration of Professor Ely, but also a ringing endorsement of academic freedom for the university in general. The full board unanimously adopted that committee's conclusions. What is interesting, however, is that it took several years for the plaque to be placed there. And in a way there is a social history of Wisconsin in the declaration of that statement of freedom and its eventual mounting on this wall. For that process, our alumni and subsequent boards of regents must take great credit, perhaps as much credit as Ely himself.

David Ward is Andrew H. Clark Professor of Geography, and Chancellor of the University of Wisconsin–Madison.

One hundred years ago the Ely case prompted a public examination of the tenure rights of faculty. The contemporary version of this public dialogue deals not only with tenure rights, but the rights of free expression for students and visiting speakers. We must be conscious of both the origins of the sifting and winnowing statement, and of its present-day manifestation—a manifestation that is perhaps different but no less compelling and demanding of our great responsibility. Today we take this opportunity to reflect on the wisdom and vision of the statement we now commemorate. We are honored to be joined by several leaders of the state of Wisconsin, who from their own leadership perspectives will talk about how this benchmark of academic freedom continues to guide our present and future academic course.

Passing on the Tradition

James A. Klauser

Chancellor, and friends of the university. As a several-time graduate of the university, it is a particular privilege and honor for me to represent the governor, who is also a several-time graduate of the university, and the people of the state.

"Why are we here?" This is a fair question to ask. The chancellor gave us some of the history as we meet to rededicate a plaque of historic significance. But, we already have this freedom, this historic tradition of sifting and winnowing. I see from here the Law School Building from which I graduated. To me it represents the symbolic rule of law and the Bill of Rights. These ideas are the underpinnings of the tradition represented by the plaque. While I certainly concur in commemorating the plaque's historic significance, this event is more than a commemoration.

I think, more importantly, that the government of this state, the people of this state, and the university of this state, must all rededicate ourselves (in this generation) to preserve the tradition of sifting and winnowing by which alone the truth can be found. We must do this so that we may know the truth and it may set us free and continue to keep us free. Our responsibility is to these people and this human dynamic that occurred one hundred years ago. Our goal is to honor what they went through to develop and refine this concept. Our obligation is to pass this tradition down to the next generation, so that the rule of law, the Bill of Rights, and the capacity, freedom, and tradition to fearlessly sift and winnow are protected from both malevolent and benevolent encroachment. The university is and must remain a jewel in Wisconsin's crown.

I am now going to depart from this program. The governor and I talked several times today, and my message is about the process of sifting and winnowing we are about to begin on budget requests. This is an important process, one that I have been going through for eight years. Currently, we face some economic pressures, and we have some other challenges to meet.

As you know, my department issues instructions on how to prepare

---

James Klauser is Secretary of Administration, State of Wisconsin.

agency budgets. At the outset I indicated to President Lyall and Regent President Grebe that we could not see how the university, with increasing enrollment, could live with possible reductions of five to ten percent. Because of the complexity of this institution and what such reductions may require, the governor and I have reached a conclusion this afternoon that I communicate to you now.

I hope President Lyall and everyone else is listening because they are totally unaware of what I am about to say. Since we know at the outset that it is impossible to comply with a budget reduction and still maintain the quality and the integrity of this institution, it makes no sense to engage in an effort that would be futile in any event.

Even though the SAVE commission's report is not yet completed, we want to save the university, all the campuses, and all the people involved from having to engage in that activity. We will talk about other approaches as the budget may require and as we present the administration's budget to the legislature. We will work together to see that the budget remains intact. I apologize for my departure, but since I do not have opportunities to visit you as formally as this, I thought I might share this message with all of you.

The Freedom to Teach . . . And the Freedom to Learn

MICHAEL W. GREBE

It is a privilege, as a member of the Board of Regents of the University of Wisconsin System, to participate in today's tribute to and reaffirmation of the importance of academic freedom, and to provide brief comments from my perspective as a regent.

The now historic statement of this university's commitment to the principles of academic freedom was, after all, made by the Board of Regents in the aftermath of the Ely case. It was a committee of the Board of Regents that investigated the accusations against Professor Ely, exonerated him, and submitted its report containing the now famous "sifting and winnowing" statement. I believe that Professor Ely, who was a socialist and a member of the Christian Social Union, which sought to apply Christian principles and pressures to the solution of social problems, would be exonerated and defended by today's Board of Regents. That statement may not sound like a great revelation. In fact, the principles of academic freedom are so deeply ingrained in the fabric of the university and, perhaps, are too frequently taken for granted, both by the immediate university community and the greater public. Hence, the importance of this reaffirmation ceremony.

The Board of Regents now, as always, is a citizen board, not a group of professional educators, and we serve as a point of contact between the people of Wisconsin and their institutions of public higher education. It is our responsibility, as regents, to interpret and represent the interests and expectations of the people of Wisconsin with respect to their university. Under the *Wisconsin Statutes*, the board, in representing the public, has the primary responsibility for governance of the University of Wisconsin System. Those same statutes acknowledge that the "search for truth is basic to every purpose of the system." Accordingly, the Board of Regents is accountable for doing its part to promote the search for truth.

The search for truth, in turn, necessarily requires that we encourage intellectual balance and realism in campus debate on contemporary issues;

Michael W. Grebe, from the Milwaukee law firm of Foley and Lardner, is the president of the University of Wisconsin System Board of Regents.

but that balance and realism can be maintained only if we also preserve academic freedom and promote the free exchange of ideas on and off the campus. Academic freedom—the freedom to teach and the freedom to learn—is critical to the search for truth.

In 1894, the board's report on the Ely matter noted that its authors were "Regents of a university with over a hundred instructors supported by nearly two millions of people who hold a vast diversity of views regarding the great questions which at present agitate the human mind." Today's regents represent a university system with many more than a hundred "instructors" and twice as many citizens as one hundred years ago. However, those citizens continue to hold a vast diversity of views and are no less committed to individual freedom than they were in 1894. As a regent representing those citizens, I am grateful for the opportunity to participate in this ceremony and reaffirm the Board of Regents' support for these great principles.

"Continual and Fearless":
An Observance of Academic Freedom

KATHARINE LYALL

I t is a privilege, as president of the University of Wisconsin System, to take part in this afternoon's simple, yet meaningful, tribute to academic freedom.

Of necessity, the vision of a university president must be fixed on the future: on the next semester, the next legislative session, and, increasingly, the next century. Too rarely do we take the opportunity such as this to pause, to look back, and to reflect on a moment in a university's history whose outcome is still so very important to our future. On this occasion, we celebrate an event in the life of UW–Madison that has had immense value for higher education in general. Indeed, the protection of academic freedom makes American universities the envy of the world.

In observing the centennial of the Richard Ely case, I represent faculty colleagues throughout the UW System, as well as their students, all of whom are heirs to the legacy of academic freedom fostered by this decision.

Unfortunately, many faculty and students trundled off to class this morning wholly unaware of the Ely Case, its centennial, or its impact on higher education in the United States. We give more thought to the clothes we wear and the toothpaste we use than we do to the basic underpinnings of the modern university. Academic freedom is so much a part of our lives that it is easy to assume it is permanent and unassailable. A hundred years ago, Richard Ely and his colleagues made no such assumptions. His contemporaries included Edward Bemis at Chicago, Edward Ross at Stanford, and other professors who lost their jobs because their economic, political, and social views conflicted with those of overzealous trustees, benefactors, or government officials.

The Ely case was by no means the last such collision. Others arose in time and, in the words of historian Frederick Rudolph, "each case became a course of instruction (which governing boards found themselves taking

Katharine Lyall is professor of economics at the University of Wisconsin–Madison, and president of the University of Wisconsin System.

whether they wished to or not) on the right of the professor to the same freedom of expression enjoyed by businessmen, farmers, and workers."

"Sifting and winnowing" was a rallying cry in 1894. Later on, through thoughtful examination and reexamination, it became the bedrock value of free inquiry in free universities. By celebrating the outcome of the Ely case, and the principle of academic freedom that it came to represent, I believe we are reinvesting the words with their original power and meaning, and for that I am truly grateful. As I re-read the inscription on the Bascom Hall plaque, however, I must tell you that my own favorite words are these three: "continual and fearless." The real challenge to those of us who administer the affairs of the university is encompassed in those words. If you accept the challenge, you have taken an oath to be vigilant through the darkest night of McCarthyism. You have pledged to be watchful and brave-hearted in your devotion to honest and open-ended scholarship.

"Continual and fearless" is important, because the process of "sifting and winnowing" is not a temporary or an occasional matter, nor is it something you pursue only when conditions permit and conventional wisdom supports you. "Continual and fearless" means: *Every* class period. *Every* day. Even when it's inconvenient. Even when it's not popular.

There is a cost to that; we mustn't kid ourselves. The spiritual grandchildren of the people who challenged Richard Ely, and Galileo, are still among us. They vote, they withhold donations, and they clamor for professors to recant or even to resign. But whatever the cost that we and our institutions must bear, measured in dollars or in aspirins, the benefits of academic freedom are more than worth it.

Faculty and students who are bound only by their imagination and ability are people who create jobs, add value in the workplace, and invest in the dreams of others. They are the leaders whose tolerance, vision, and energy keep society moving, productive, and committed to "the search for truth."

During the past century, we have seen what can happen when faculty and students are instead bound by public prejudice, self-righteous committees, tyrannical juntas, and "star-chamber" tribunals. A university without academic freedom is no university, and is of no use to the people it serves.

The real outcome of the Richard Ely case is enshrined in our minds, not written on a plaque. It is carried invisibly and effortlessly, and perhaps thoughtlessly, in briefcases and backpacks, along with test papers, laptop computers, and peanut butter sandwiches.

It is marvelous that we live in a nation so free that we can take academic freedom for granted. But it is better to remember what that freedom cost, and who paid the price, and who reaps the benefits today.

If we remember the Ely case, and if we understand the full meaning of "sifting and winnowing," then we must also recommit ourselves, now and in the future, to the "continual and fearless" defense of academic freedom: as an honorable tradition, as an essential tool of our trade, and as the bedrock value of America's greatest universities.

Faculty Responsibilities to Sift and Winnow

WILLIAM S. REZNIKOFF

Secretary Klauser, Regent Grebe, President Lyall, Chancellor Ward, fellow faculty, staff, students, distinguished guests and friends. We are gathered here today to rededicate ourselves to the principles of academic freedom. The university is, at its core, a learning community. I believe that academic freedom is essential to an effective learning community, but academic freedom is also a privilege. To safeguard this special privilege of academic freedom, the faculty must fulfill several responsibilities.

The first responsibility for the faculty is to constantly practice, in our scholarship, the sifting and winnowing that academic freedom permits. We must constantly seek to discover the truths of our disciplines. In the experimental sciences the major constraint for achieving this goal is the growing limitation of external support. The major dangers are that we must spend ever-increasing amounts of time seeking the support we need instead of being scholars, and that we design our research to achieve that support and not to answer the core questions in our disciplines. Thus, we end in a vicious circle, and we lose sight of our real mission.

Our second obligation is to practice sifting and winnowing in our teaching. We see this as communicating the fruits of our research in the classroom, providing students with the tools so that they can ask critical questions in our fields, and challenging them to actually ask the questions. Armed with that education, we hope our students will leave here not with a fixed set of knowledge circa 1994 but rather with a process for continuing their learning throughout their lives.

We have another obligation to our students, and that is to make sure they are part of the scholarly adventure. Students should be part of our research enterprise. It is critical that university-based research is a direct and integral part of the learning process. Moreover, many of my colleagues feel as I do, that working with students in research is the most rewarding experience of our careers.

William S. Reznikoff is professor of biochemistry, and the Fall 1994 chair of the University Committee at the University of Wisconsin–Madison.

The fourth responsibility is to provide the public with the fruits of our endeavors. This public availability often seems like an invasion of our privacy and sometimes appears not to be wanted by the public itself. But if we do not stand up and debate the issues of BST or of O. J. Simpson's blood typing, the future public will ask why we did not.

Finally, we must be willing to speak out if we sense that academic freedom is under threat. I believe that most people in this state, in the media, and in state government wish to do more than pay homage to the principles of academic freedom; they wish to support it. However, we face a real if unintended threat to academic freedom in the issue of faculty workload. Faculty workload measures address one small but important portion of our careers, classroom teaching. This measure concentrates on the most obvious and simplest part of the learning process, to such an extent that it neglects the other important activities of the faculty that lead to a quality education. Equally important, it has the dangerous effect of usurping the time necessary for being a scholar.

I believe that academic freedom generates immense rewards for our society. However, to justify the public investment in higher education, we must not only fight for the privilege of academic freedom, we must use it and share it.

Reaffirming the University of Wisconsin's Commitment: A Statement to the Board of Regents, October 7, 1994

PHYLLIS KRUTSCH

The powerful and moving words written one hundred years ago in a Board of Regents' report exonerating Economics Professor Richard T. Ely are a landmark in the history of academic freedom. "Whatever may be the limitations which trammel inquiry elsewhere," the report reads, "we believe the great State University of Wisconsin should ever encourage that continual and fearless sifting and winnowing by which alone the truth can be found." Sixteen years later, the Class of 1910 donated a plaque immortalizing those words, and in 1915 it was affixed to the outside wall of Bascom Hall.

Last month, with the leadership of Chancellor David Ward and the University Committee, Economics Professor W. Lee Hansen organized a conference commemorating the centennial of the Ely affair and reaffirming the principle of academic freedom. At a rededication ceremony at the top of Bascom Hill, unequivocal support for free and open inquiry was expressed by Chancellor Ward, UW System President Lyall, Regent President Grebe, Department of Administration Secretary Klauser representing Governor Thompson, and UW–Madison's University Committee Chair Reznikoff. It was clear that the declarations of support for this core value of the university were heartfelt.

Prior to the rededication ceremony, a world-renowned genetics professor introduced himself and told me that the first time he read the words written on Bascom Hall, he cried. Waclaw Szybalski emigrated from Poland in 1949 and said he knew firsthand what happens when the principle of academic freedom is discarded. As a young scientist he was told by "officials" that he would be sent to Siberia if he continued his controversial research. Professor Szybalski was one of the conference presenters, and I read from his remarks:

Phyllis Krutsch of Washburn, Wisconsin, is a member of the University of Wisconsin Board of Regents.

When I joined the faculty of the University of Wisconsin in the winter of 1959, I was not aware of the existence of the "sifting and winnowing" resolution on the bronze plaque located on the outside wall of Bascom Hall. Its representation was not included with the university offer extended to me, and nobody took me for a stroll, to see it and to read its message during my visits here in 1959 or later, in 1960. It would have been such a touching and meaningful start for my transformation into a Wisconsinite.

Why is this "sifting and winnowing" statement so important? Because it so clearly and poetically states the principle of the freedom of teaching and research, because it is unique, because it stresses that the University of Wisconsin will not be swayed by temporary vogues or political trends, even if they should prevail at other institutions, and because this declaration is expressed in such beautiful and moving language. Maybe I am an incorrigible idealist and romantic, even at my age, but each time I read it, I feel a tingle go down my spine and I feel somewhat emotional, I am embarrassed to admit. I am certainly a devotee of this plaque, and I walk all my visitors and collaborators to Bascom Hill, to let them read it and be inspired.

Professor Szybalski believes, and I agree with him, that we in Wisconsin should make the sifting and winnowing statement more visible. He suggests, for example, putting it on our letterheads so that we will be reminded on a more regular basis of this first principle of the university.

In appreciation of the 1894 Board of Regents' courage, and to allow the current board to affirm the principle of academic freedom for the entire UW System, I asked noted Wisconsin historian and Professor Emeritus E. David Cronon to draft a resolution. I want to thank him publicly for his eloquence.

University of Wisconsin Board of Regents Resolution 6787:

Whereas, in September of 1894 the Board of Regents of the University of Wisconsin conducted an investigation of charges against Professor Richard T. Ely's teaching, scholarship, and his political, social, and economic views;

And whereas, after hearing and reviewing the charges and Professor Ely's defense, the regents voted overwhelmingly to reject the charges and exonerate Professor Ely;

And whereas, the conclusion of the regents' report constituted an eloquent endorsement of the principle of academic freedom in a free university, in particular the ringing sentence memorialized by the Class of 1910 on a bronze plaque mounted on the front of Bascom Hall: "Whatever may be the limitations which trammel inquiry elsewhere, we believe the great State University of Wisconsin should ever encourage that continual and fearless sifting and winnowing by which alone the truth can be found."

And whereas, for the past century the Ely case has been regarded nationally as one of the key events in establishing academic freedom not only in Wisconsin but across the country;

Now therefore, be it resolved that the Regents of the University of Wisconsin System, meeting one hundred years after our predecessors guaranteed Professor Ely's academic freedom, reaffirm our commitment to the untrammeled search for truth.

We call upon all members of our several academic communities—administrators, faculty, staff, and students alike—to guard this precious legacy, to consider differing points of view, and always to engage in "that continual and fearless sifting and winnowing by which alone the truth can be found."

Adopted by the Board of Regents of the University of Wisconsin System, October 7, 1994.

PART 7

The Photographic Story

This romanticized portrtait of Richard T. Ely is prominently displayed in the Chancellor's Office at the university. Professor Ely served in the Economics Department from 1892 to 1927. In 1886 he was a founding member of the American Economic Association.

Oliver E. Wells, Wisconsin superintendent of public instruction and ex-officio member of the Board of Regents, prepared the letter which appeared in The Nation *magazine on July 12, 1894, accusing Richard T. Ely of fomenting labor unrest and preaching "utopian, impractical, or pernicious doctrines" through his writings.*

Charles Kendall Adams served as president of the university from 1894 to 1903. He is generally credited with being the author of the "sifting and winnowing" language contained in the 1894 Regent resolution.

In an incident that evoked the Ely trial, sociology professor E. A. Ross came under attack in 1910 for supporting the right of the anarchist Emma Goldman to deliver a public lecture when she was invited to Madison by a group of students. A subsequent motion of censure was essentially neutralized when President Van Hise defended Ross's distinguished record of teaching and scholarship and his value to the university.

President Charles R. Van Hise addressed members of the Class of 1910 in June 1915 at the ceremonies held to mark the original installation of the plaque.

John R. Commons, a successor to Ely, was criticized in 1919 for his views on fair treatment for farmers. Under Commons, the University of Wisconsin became a leader in the study of labor history and legislation. He, too, became an early leader in the AAUP.

Alexander H. Hohfeld, professor of German from 1901 to 1937, was elected president of the Modern Language Association in 1913 and served as an early leader in the American Association of University Professors. The AAUP has consistently fought for the protection of academic freedom at colleges and universities across the country.

Mark Ingraham, professor of mathematics and dean of the College of Letters and Science from 1942 to 1961, is shown here with a portrait of his predecessor, George Clarke Sellery. Ingraham served as president of the American Association of University Professors in 1938–39 and consistently upheld the tradition of academic freedom at Wisconsin. When the School of Business vacated its original home in the Commerce Building in 1994, the building was subsequently renamed Ingraham Hall in his honor.

Helen C. White, professor of English from 1919 to 1967 and AAUP president during 1957–58, spoke at the rededication ceremony when the sifting and winnowing plaque was returned to its Bascom Hall location.

David Fellman, professor of political science from 1947 to 1979 and AAUP president in 1964–65, served as the primary drafter of the restatement of the principles of academic freedom adopted by the Board of Regents in 1964.

The photo below reveals that the plaque was not originally affixed in a permanent manner. This became painfully apparent in November 1956 when the plaque disappeared. Following its recovery, it was restored to its original location and anchored securely. Judge F. Ryan Duffy, president of the Class of 1910, and U.W. President E. B. Fred examine the newly secured plaque during the restoration ceremonies held on February 15, 1957.

Wisconsin Governor Vernon Thompson joined officials and dignitaries speaking at the rededication ceremonies held on February 15, 1957, in the Bascom Hall auditorium (room 272).

This photo was taken during the period of the late 1960s and early 1970s, when anti-war protests and demonstrations were a regular part of campus life. It shows that the defense of the plaque and its precepts was more than just a rhetorical exercise.

In December 1964, NBC-TV broadcast a dramatized version of the Ely hearing before the Regents as part of its "Profiles in Courage," a series based on a book by John F. Kennedy. Dan O'Herlihy, who played Ely, and Marsha Hunt, who appeared as his wife, are shown here in a scene from the production. The program also featured actors Edward Asner and Leonard Nimoy, who were to become major television stars in the 1960s and 1970s.

UW–Madison Chancellor David Ward is shown here (at left), assisted by Arthur Hove, on September 18, 1994, at the unveiling ceremony held in front of Bascom Hall, to rededicate the university's commitment to the sifting and winnowing statement.

Professor Waclaw Szybalski, Department of Oncology, views the plaque during the Academic Freedom Conference in September 1994, after his eloquent address on the meaning of the sifting and winnowing statement.

APPENDIX

100 Years of

SIFTING AND WINNOWING

at the University of Wisconsin–Madison

ACADEMIC FREEDOM CONFERENCE
FRIDAY AND SATURDAY,
SEPTEMBER 16 AND 17, 1994

Friday morning session: 8:45–11:45 a.m.
State Historical Society Auditorium

Theme: The Ely "Trial," the Economics Department, and the Emergence of Academic Freedom

Moderator: Robert H. Haveman (Economics), Chair, Department of Economics, UW–Madison

Video presentation of the Ely "Trial," from the televised series *Profiles in Courage*

"The Political-Economic-Social Environment Surrounding the Ely Trial" John Buenker (History), UW–Parkside, who is preparing a history of the Progressive Era (1893–1915) for the "History of Wisconsin" series

Open discussion

Coffee break

"Richard T. Ely: The University's First Economist, 1892–1925" Robert J. Lampman (Economics) UW–Madison, who is the author-editor of *Economists at Wisconsin: 1892–1992*, and David B. Johnson (Economics), UW–Madison

"'That Little Pill:' Richard T. Ely and the Parameters of Professional Propriety" Benjamin Rader (History), University of Nebraska-Lincoln, who is the author of the Ely biography, *The Academic Mind and Reform: The Influence of Richard T. Ely in American Life*

"Economists, Academic Freedom, and the Economics Profession" A. W. Coats (Economics), Duke University, who has written extensively on the history and development of the economics profession

Panel discussion by speakers

Audience questions

Friday afternoon session: 1:30–3:45 p.m.
State Historical Society Auditorium

Theme: Clarifying the Issues: Free Speech, Hate Speech Codes, and Academic Freedom

Moderator: James L. Baughman (Journalism), UW–Madison

"Free Speech and the Mission of the University"
Donald A. Downs, Jr. (Political Science), UW–Madison

"Hate Speech in Theory and Practice"
Ted Finman (Law), UW–Madison

"Hate in the Cloak of Liberty"
Linda S. Greene (Law), UW–Madison

Coffee break

Panel of reactors

"An Undergraduate Student's Perspective," Rebecca S. Schaefer (Undergraduate), UW–Madison

"A Faculty Perspective," Cyrena Pondrom (English), UW–Madison

"An Alum's Perspective," Mordecai Lee, Milwaukee Jewish Council for Community Relations

"An Outsider's Perspective," Thomas A. Still, *Wisconsin State Journal*

Questions and open discussion

Friday afternoon: 4:00–4:30 p.m.
Lincoln Terrace

Rededication Ceremony: 4:00–4:30 p.m. Lincoln Terrace

Reaffirming the University's Commitment to the Principles of Academic Freedom

Musical Prelude and Fanfare
    David Ward, UW–Madison Chancellor
    Tommy Thompson, Governor
    Katharine Lyall, UW System President
    Michael W. Grebe, UW System Board of Regents President
    William S. Reznikoff, UW–Madison
       University Committee Chair
Musical Finale

Friday evening session: 8:00 p.m.
Memorial Union Theater

Keynote presentation

    Moderator: W. Lee Hansen (Economics), UW–Madison,
       Conference Chair
    Introduction: Chancellor David Ward

    "Academic Freedom, Sifting and Winnowing, and Free Speech"
       Nat Hentoff, writer, columnist, and author of *Free Speech for Me—
       But Not for Thee*

Audience questions

Saturday morning session: 8:45–12:00 a.m.
State Historical Society Auditorium

Theme: Academic Freedom and Sifting and Winnowing at Wisconsin

Moderator: John Kaminski (History), UW–Madison

"Are There Limits to Academic Freedom?"
Joel B. Grossman (Political Science), UW–Madison

"Sifting and Winnowing Issues at the UW–Madison"
E. David Cronon (History), UW–Madison, coauthor of *The University of Wisconsin: A History, Vol. III, Politics, Depression, and War, 1925–45*

Audience questions

Coffee break

Theme: Reinterpreting the Sifting and Winnowing Statement

Moderator: Sharon L. Dunwoody (Journalism), UW–Madison
Commentaries

"Its Meaning and Significance to Faculty Members"
Waclaw T. Szybalski (Oncology), UW–Madison

"Its Meaning and Significance to Students"
Raymond J. Kotwicki (Undergraduate), UW–Madison

"Its Links to Accountability and Assessment
Joseph J. Corry (University Administration), UW–Madison

"Its Links to Research Independence for Faculty"
Robert Auerbach (Zoology), UW–Madison

"Its Links to Intellectual Property Rights"
Janet L. Greger (Nutritional Sciences), UW–Madison

Panel of reactors

"An Insider's View," Phillip R. Certain (Chemistry),
Dean, Letters and Science, UW–Madison

"An Outsider's View," Mary Lou Munts,
former State Representative and former chair,
Public Service Commission

Panel discussion among speakers and reactors

Audience questions

Concluding comments: W. Lee Hansen, Conference Chair

Adjournment: 12:00 noon

Academic Freedom Film Festival
Memorial Union (The Rathskeller)

Film Festival

As an adjunct to this week's program, the conference features a film festival focusing on the topics and questions raised in the examination of "Sifting and Winnowing."

Wednesday, September 14
    6:00 p.m.   Inherit the Wind

Wednesday, September 21
    6:00 p.m.   School Daze
    8:00 p.m.   Dead Poet's Society

Wednesday, October 5
    6:00 p.m.   The War at Home
    8:00 p.m.   Reception

Ongoing through February 1995
State Historical Society, 816 State Street (lobby)

Untrammeled Inquiry

An exhibit on the long-standing issue of academic freedom at the University of Wisconsin investigates the 1894 "trial" of Professor Richard Ely who was accused of using his university position to foment labor unrest. The ability of university faculty to study and teach controversial subjects is still questioned on today's campuses.

Academic Freedom
"Sifting and Winnowing"
Committee Members

Alexandra Atkins, *Undergraduate student*
E. David Cronon, *Humanities Institute*
Judith Croxdale, *Botany*
Sharon Dunwoody, *Journalism*
Joel Grossman, *Political Science*
W. Lee Hansen, *Economics, Conference Chair*
Robert H. Haveman, *Economics*
Art Hove, *Provost's Office*
John Kaminski, *Center for the Study of the*
    American Constitution
Robert J. Lampman, *Economics*
Ian Rosenberg, *Undergraduate student*
Michael Stevens, *State Historical Society of Wisconsin*

Acknowledgements

This conference and centennial celebration was organized under the auspices of Chancellor David Ward and the University Committee. The University gratefully acknowledges the support from the following: The Anonymous Fund, College of Letters and Science; the Evjue Foundation; and the University of Wisconsin Foundation.

INDEX